Desert

MONGOLIA

Bulunzir River
Anhsi •

KANSU

Kanchow

TSAIDAM MARSHES

Lake
Koko Nor

Sining

Kum Bum • > >

SHENSI

Lanchow

A M D O

Chumur River

Ho River

Labrang

CHINA

Huang River

AMNE MACHIN RANGE

Jyekundo •

Dre River

T

GOLOK

Dzogchen
Gompa

SZECHUAN

• Tachienlu

K H A M

• Chamdo

Chengtu

PO

KHA KARPO RANGE

Batang

Giamda
Showa •

Salween River

Yangtze River

Yalung River

YUNNA

Lohit River

Mekong River

• Likiang

ASSAM

BURMA

Irawadi River

Kunming •

93°   96°   99°   102°

FORBIDDEN JOURNEY

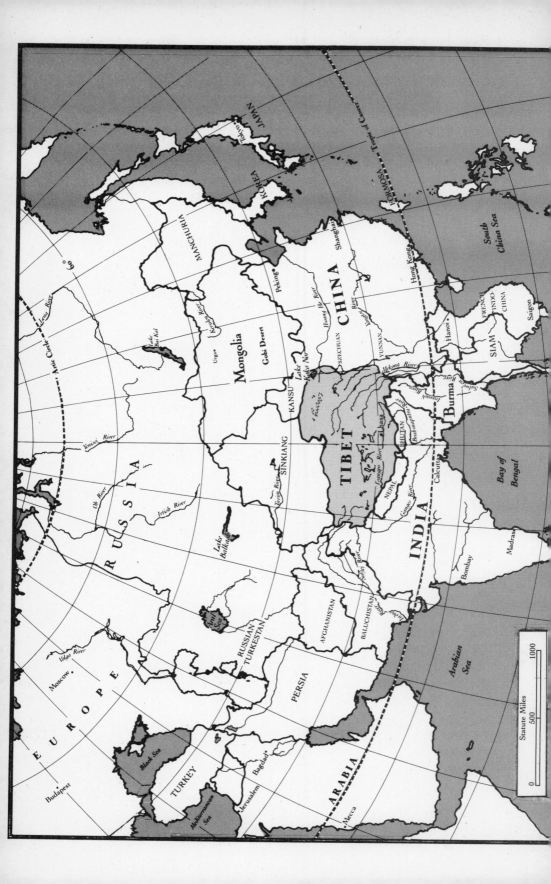

The Voyages of Alexandra David-Neel

1891–1893   India

1911–1912   Ceylon, India

1912–1916   Sikkim, Nepal, southern Tibet (expelled)

1916–1918   India, Burma, French Indochina, Japan, Korea, China

1918–1921   Eastern Tibet (Kum Bum)

1921–1924   Journey to Lhasa through eastern Tibet, Mongolia, western China and southern Tibet

1925   Return to France

1937–1945   Soviet Union, China, Sino-Tibetan border, India

1946   Final return to France

FORBIDDEN JOURNEY

THE LIFE OF
ALEXANDRA DAVID-NEEL

BARBARA M. FOSTER
AND MICHAEL FOSTER

1817

Harper & Row, Publishers, San Francisco

Cambridge, Hagerstown, New York, Philadelphia, Washington
London, Mexico City, São Paulo, Singapore, Sydney

Excerpts from *Forbidden Journey* have appeared in the *North Dakota Quarterly* Fall 1986.

The authors have made every effort to trace the ownership of all copyrighted material and secure permission from the appropriate copyright holders. Grateful acknowledgment is made to the following for permission to reprint excerpts from previously published material.

The Putnam Publishing Group for Marion Meade, *Madame Blavatsky: The Woman behind the Myth*, © 1980. Luree Miller, *On Top of the World: Five Women Explorers in Tibet*, Seattle: The Mountaineers, © 1984. The Bodley Head for the Estate of A. David-Neel, *Tibetan Journey*, © 1936. Collins Publishers for Charles Bell, *Portrait of the Dalai Lama*, © 1946. St. Martins Press, Inc., New York, for A. David-Neel, *Buddhism: Its Doctrines and Its Methods*, © 1977. Praeger Publishers for John MacGregor, *Tibet: A Chronicle of Exploration*, © 1970. International Creative Management for Hope Cooke, *Time Change*, Simon and Shuster, © 1980; reprinted by permission of International Creative Management. Harper & Row for excerpts from *My Journey to Lhasa* by Alexandra David-Neel, copyright © 1927 by Harper & Row, Publishers, Inc.; renewed 1955 by Alexandra David-Neel; reprinted by permission of Harper & Row, Publishers, Inc. Librarie Plon for permission to quote in translation from A. David-Neel: *L'Inde: hier aujourd'hui demain*, © 1951; *Sous des nuees d'orage*, © 1940; *Le Sortilege du mystere*, © 1972; *Journal de voyage: lettres a son mari*, vol. 1, © 1975, vol. 2, © 1976. M. M. Peyronnet, *Dix ans avec Alexandra David-Neel*, © 1973.

Endpaper map by Melanie Haage and Letha Hadadi.
Frontispiece map by Melanie Haage and Letha Hadadi.

Photographs: from A. David-Neel, *My Journey to Lhasa*—A. David-Neel between Two Tibetan Women, A. David-Neel's Hermitage, A. David-Neel between two Tibetan Nuns, The Marketplace at Lhasa, Yongden, Alexandra and Yongden in Front of the Potala—copyright © 1927 by Harper & Row, Publishers, Inc. Renewed 1955 by Alexandra David-Neel. Reprinted by permission of Harper & Row, Publishers, Inc. From Charles Bell, *The People of Tibet*—Men and Yaks, Coracles on the Tsangpo—Oxford University Press, © 1928. From Erich Teichman, *Travels of a Consular Officer in Eastern Tibet*—View of Tachienlu—Cambridge University Press, © 1922. From Archives A. David-Neel—Louis David, Alexandrine David, Alexandra at 20, Alexandra as Opera Singer, Philip Neel, Alexandra ca. 1910, Sidkeong Tulku, Lama Yongden, Alexandra at 87, Rope Bridge, Wayside Tibetans, Tibetan Ngagspa, Tibetan Nuns Wearing Wigs—by permission of Archives A. David-Neel, Digne, France. From Letha Hadadi, two photos at Samten Dzong.

FIRST EDITION

Library of Congress Cataloging-in-Publication Data

Foster, Barbara M., 1938–
    Forbidden Journey.

    Bibliography: p.
    Includes index.
    1. David-Neel, Alexandra, 1868–1969. 2. Scholars, Buddhist—France—Biography. I. Foster, Michael, 1937–   . II. Title.
BQ950.A937F67 1987   294.3′092′4 [B]   86-43007
ISBN 0-06-250345-6

88 89 90 91 92 HC 10 9 8 7 6 5 4 3 2

Contents

Foreword by Lawrence Durrell   ix

Chronology   3
Prelude: At the Border   5
Book One: The Parisienne   15
Book Two: The Learned Lama   77
Book Three: The Pilgrim   161
Book Four: The Master   237
Coda: The Legacy   315

Sources and Acknowledgments   325
Notes   329
Selected Bibliography   349
Index   357

Foreword

We are lucky to have this valuable addition to the ever-lengthening saga of studies and biographies of this gifted and versatile French traveler and student of comparative religion who actually went so far as to get herself ordained as a Tibetan lama in order to bring the requisite zeal to her adopted faith. Her books had already set a stamp upon her life, which had been taken up for half a century with travels in and around Tibet and the adjacent (and mostly forbidden) countries. The remoteness of the subject matter and the romantic veil that for so long shadowed everything to do with Tibet enabled David-Neel to project a highly colored portrait of herself and her doings, and her books were as eagerly read as novels. While nobody will accuse her of drawing the long bow, from time to time it is valuable to have an occasional corrective such as this volume in order to round out her somewhat enigmatic portrait.

In my own case I considered myself very lucky to have the chance of meeting her towards the end of her life, having admired her since I came upon her work during my adolescence. Needless to say, she conveyed the impression of complete authenticity, and everything she had to say about Tibet in general and Buddhism in particular was stamped with poetry and insight. She was a wonderful old lady, and thanks to her diligence in yoga had kept astonishingly young. Some of her facial expressions were those of a girl of eighteen, and the whole tempo of her discourse conveyed the vividness and warmth of extreme youth. Her physical beauty—she had small hands and feet of marked shapeliness—suggested that she had once been a loss to the theater, which was her first tentative profession. And if she was down to earth and at times even sardonic it was understandable, for she had lived to see Buddhism become something of a fad among the intellectuals of the left.

The anecdote that won me a weekend of her company and conversation is perhaps worth recounting, since it shows her in a characteristic light as the generous-hearted person she was. With the fall of Tibet the French government undertook certain measures designed to help refugees. Among other things, it settled about a hundred Tibetan children in the French Pyrenees at snowline, in climatic conditions not unlike those they had quitted. Here they had a great spiritual experience—they discovered skis and were completely captivated by this magical occidental invention. It became imperative to get them skis of their own, but there was no money available for such a purchase. Finally the welfare committee working on this project came up with an elaborate set of propositions by which the woman's magazine called *Elle* would commission me to undertake a portrait-interview of *Madame* David-Neel and thus provide a ski fund for the Tibetan children. My subject fell in with the suggestions and obligingly made herself available for a whole long weekend of talk. I think she may have found the final article a little fulsome, but at any rate it was quite sincere as was the title, "The Most Astonishing French Woman of Our Time."

It was perhaps inevitable that the Government of India should suspect her of espionage and try to keep track of her travels, but how lucky for us that they kept a methodical dossier on her, and that this documentation fell into the hands of her biographers, Barbara and Michael Foster, who have used it with insight and discretion to sketch a new portrait of this captivating woman—a portrait very much from the life. The new material makes the book not only original, indeed unique, but also indispensable for future biographers. With its help they have been able to check whole passages of the life that have hitherto depended purely on the veracity of Alexandra David-Neel's word.

It only remains to add that the old lady I interviewed was a person of exemplary modesty and by no means had set up shop as a sage or philosopher. She laid claim only to an unequaled scholarship and diligence in prosecuting her enquiry into the sources of Buddhism as it was practiced in the remote "roof of the world"—the Tibet of her day. She had taken everything in her stride, literally: danger, fatigue, disenchantment, failure. And it is good to feel that now, thanks to new scholarship like this book, her portrait is acquiring depth of focus.

—Lawrence Durrell

Adventure is my only reason for living.
                                    —*Alexandra David-Neel*

Chronology

October 24, 1868	Louise Eugénie Alexandrine Marie David is born in Paris.
1871	The Commune lives and dies.
1873	The Davids move to Belgium.
1888–90	Alexandra investigates the Society of the Supreme Gnosis, London. She discovers the Theosophical Society in Paris and Buddhism and other oriental philosophies.
1891	Departs for India
1895	Sings with the Opéra-Comique in Indochina
1898	Publishes *Pour la vie,* a libertarian essay
1904	Marries Philip Neel; her father dies
1911	Undertakes second Asian sojourn
1912	Meets Prince Sidkeong of Sikkim, glimpses Tibet, and has two interviews with the Dalai Lama.
November 1914 to August 1916	Lives as a hermit in the Himalayas
1917	Tours Japan and Korea
1918–20	Lives among the monks at Kum Bum monastery
October 1923	Sets out on a four-month journey afoot to Lhasa
February 1924	Reaches Lhasa, remains for two months
1925	Returns to France
1927	*My Journey to Lhasa* is published in New York, London, and Paris.
1928–36	Alexandra buys and inhabits Samten Dzong in Digne, France. Completes *Magic and Mystery; Buddhism; Initiations.*
1937–45	She lives in China during the Sino-Japanese war.

1941	Philip Neel dies.
1946	Alexandra returns to France to settle estate.
1955	Yongden, her adopted son, dies.
1959	Marie-Madeleine Peyronnet comes to Samten Dzong.
1968	Alexandra's 100th birthday is celebrated at Digne.
September 8, 1969	Alexandra, much honored, dies at Digne. Several projects are left incomplete.

Prelude: At the Border

David Macdonald was napping after tea. Spring afternoons were pleasant in southern Tibet, and since he was not expecting visitors, the British Trade Agent had retired to a bedroom in his house located within the mud brick fort overlooking Gyantse, Tibet's third largest town, and the surrounding fields still bare of grain. When an Indian servant awakened him, Macdonald was surprised to hear that a woman in a white native dress, wearing a hat with pointed flaps, and a young man in tattered lama's robes were demanding to see him. Despite his unassuming title, the half-Scottish, half-Asian official was the law in these parts, and his supporting detachment of Indian troops, officered by a few Britons, the sole military force.

His servant described the pair as looking like tramps, yet the woman spoke English tersely in the European manner. Macdonald had an ugly thought: the two might be another set of miscreants who had sneaked across the border, found the natives hostile, and were pleading for help. A few years ago an American daredevil, Schary, a strange little man, crossed over from Ladakh. His pony died and a servant ran off with his money; he had to beg and became an object of ridicule. By the time he crawled on hands and knees to the fort, he was covered with festering sores and was half-mad. He said he wanted to find the *Mahatmas*—the legendary wise men—and write a book about his adventures.

Coming fully awake, Macdonald realized he did indeed have a woman for a caller. Annie Taylor, the missionary lady who used to live at Yatung on the Sikkimese border where his own family stayed at this season, was in the habit of donning a disguise and slipping into Tibet to convert the lamas. But she had long since departed for England and, he guessed, heaven. No, it was probably his daughter Victoria and some friend. She was often up to tricks to fool him. She must have come by buggy—the sole wheeled vehicle in Tibet—to bring her dad preserved fruits and vegetables, for they grew there in the milder Chumbi Valley. Well, he would have the laugh on her.

Macdonald instructed his servant to show in the lady. He pretended to be asleep. He heard steps, a voice, "Mr. Mac-dó-nald?" Oh, Victoria was putting on a French accent.

"Go away! I've no time for a silly girl!"

"I am Alexandra David-Neel," replied the mature woman.

Macdonald popped up. Along with other border officials, he had been alerted to watch for this mysterious Frenchwoman. Aside from feeling like an ass, he knew she had no business being in Tibet.

However, the agent was a kindly man who, from his mustache down to his riding boots, resembled an oriental Teddy Roosevelt. He apologized and led his visitor into the sitting room. He noticed her eyes, filled with the light of the mountains, and that she was short, pale, and, save for an odd bulge round her waist, much slimmer than he expected. He wouldn't have dreamed that in the belt strapped beneath her clothes she carried exquisite gold jewelry—the gift of a maharaja—which she always kept on her person. Where she had stashed another appendage, an automatic pistol, isn't clear.

Madame David-Neel sipped tea, disappointed it was English style rather than the salty, buttered Tibetan tea that was almost a broth. She did not wait long to state her errand: she was bound from Peking to Calcutta through the heart of Central Asia, a journey that so far had taken several years. She and her adopted son Lama Yongden had gone the last several months on foot from Yunnan, China, across the unexplored Po country to Lhasa, Tibet's forbidden capital. She had circumvented Chinese, Tibetan, and British authorities by traveling through rugged terrain, often by night, and by disguising herself as a beggar. Fluent in Tibetan, a Buddhist, she was able to assume the role of a mendicant without qualm. They had slept outdoors or in the huts of the natives—known for their poverty—and had eaten what scraps they were fed. They had spent two months in Lhasa undetected. Now, sick and weary, she wished permission to lodge in the guest bungalow for a few days before crossing the Himalayas into India.

Macdonald was amazed and a little dubious. Assuming she was telling the truth, she had performed a wonderful feat for a woman of her evident age and slight physique. He knew Tibet and took a keen interest in its people and customs. David-Neel would have had to travel through jungles and over snow-covered mountain ranges, cross wide chasms on flimsy rope bridges with icy water rushing below, stumble down miles of crumbly rocks to find roads no wider than tracks in the mud. She must have fended off the wolves and bears that sometimes attacked peasants or woodcutters, and worse, the giant mastiffs that defended every village and mauled strangers on sight. Not to mention she needed to outwit legions of hungry bandits. Most incredibly, she had slogged through that wild, inaccessible country in the dead of winter! Macdonald politely asked for details.

Madame at first refused. She intended to write a book in which he and everyone who liked could read about her journey. Moreover, she was thinking of going to America where she was certain to lecture before packed houses. The official reluctantly reminded his visitor that the Government of India had denied her permission to travel in Tibet, indeed had expelled her from Sikkim. She wasn't flustered but shot back that it was none of their affair; Tibet was an independent nation. Besides, she happened to be a French citizen.

Macdonald kept his counsel. But he could recall that not many years past a high lama had been flogged and then drowned for unwittingly aiding an Indian spy to reach Lhasa. Others who were implicated had their arms and legs chopped off and eyes gouged out. Although Tibetans were by nature kindhearted and eager to gain merit through good deeds, no word in the language was more hated than *philing*, foreigner.

Removing her cap to reveal a wave of brunette hair, Alexandra reluctantly offered proof of her exploits. Gazing inward, she spoke of nights among the snowy wastes, of villagers who had opened their doors to her and Yongden, hoping that if the lama blessed their yaks they would proliferate like stars in the vast Central Asian sky. Thoughtful householders had invited the mendicants to sleep on their floors and, if they had any to spare, to share a stuffed sheep's belly. Because the pair were on pilgrimage, the hopeful peasants didn't neglect to fill their begging bowls with *tsampa* (barley flour) in order to assure a better lot in some future life. The Buddhist did not emphasize how close she and her son had come to making a meal for the vultures in the midst of nowhere.

Once at Lhasa, the interlopers had mingled with thousands of pilgrims flocking in from the countryside, and twenty thousand monks from the three large monasteries ringing the capital, to joyously celebrate the Tibetan New Year. They had witnessed the so-called devil dances of the masked lamas, the riderless horse races and archery contests among big fur-hatted nomads who resembled Genghis Khan's Golden Horde, as well as the ritual hounding out of town of the poor fellow chosen as scapegoat, who took on the community's sins. Packed in the motley crowd, they watched colorful pageants of giant figures made from butter, in no danger of melting at twelve thousand feet. Alexandra and Yongden had toured the Dalai Lama's awesome Potala Palace with its riches of gold, silver, and bejeweled statues of deities, its countless rooms filled with priceless porcelains and jades donated by pious Chinese emperors, and from its roof topped with gilt pagodas, they took in a view over the plains and distant mountains that repaid all their efforts.

Macdonald, one of the handful of outsiders who had visited Lhasa, doubted his guest no longer. When the woman who was beginning to seem much taller than her diminutive five feet, two inches requested a signed statement to verify her journey, the Trade Agent amiably complied, though the next day, May 7, 1924, he would also alert his superiors.

"*Madame,*" he said, "you have undergone incredible hardships. Your courage and vitality have succeeded where others failed. Unfortunately, by reason of the disguise you adopted, you saw Tibet only from the viewpoint of a poor pilgrim."

Alexandra could afford to smile. By humbling herself to beg she had won sweet revenge for earlier humiliations and triumphed over the mighty British Empire. She had shown what the will of a woman could do, now it was time to tell the world. Neither she nor the astute Scot could gauge the extent of her victory: the fame and honors due her in a life spanning more than a century. She would lecture to rapt audiences, achieving the success that earlier had eluded her on another sort of stage. Famous authors, explorers, presidents, and dictators would pay their respects before this Lamp of Wisdom, a name given her in Tibet. But as Alexandra grew older those few dear to her passed away, and at the core she turned hard and morose. In her heart, this Amazon of a woman would know disappointment and sorrow.

Most significant to us, Alexandra David-Neel had in her over a score of books that, translated into many languages, would sell into the millions of copies. Tellingly, her life and work continue to shape the lives of other people. Some of her readers yearn after exotic tales of the East or are fascinated by the seemingly weird rituals of Tibetan Buddhism. Women especially seek a heroic figure, well ahead of her time, on which to model their own actions. Many of her fans wish only to escape for a time into a good adventure story. At any rate, Alexandra's books are her legacy to us all, and it was through one in particular that we made the acquaintance of this remarkable woman.

The setting was perfect: a spacious whitewashed room with slowly turning ceiling fan, decorated with tropical flowers and opening onto a lush garden that mitigated the heat of south India. Pondicherry, a former French colony, retained its Mediterranean air, and at dusk with the chirps of crickets and hums of insects wafting through the opened doors, we felt immeasurably far from the roar of New York. Time: the midseventies; place: the library of the ashram founded by Sri Aurobindo Ghose, the patriot and philosopher who on the Subcontinent rivals Gandhi in the esteem accorded his memory. A portrait of Aurobindo, the rational mystic, hung on the wall, flanked by a luminescent photo of the Frenchwoman, known as the Mother, who had become the master's consort and successor. Partly, it was this lack of sexual prejudice, found too often among the allegedly enlightened, that had drawn us to this idyllic spot.

As well, we had heard of the small, private gatherings of seekers under the guidance of the learned librarian, Mehtananda, to discuss those subjects deemed by David-Neel herself to be "everything that relates, whether closely or more distantly, to psychic phenomena and to the action of psychic forces." Around us this evening sat a dozen others, ranging from fair-haired Swedes to a British couple burned red as lobsters from staying too long on the beach to a variety of Asians. Imagine our surprise when the tall, graying, dignified Indian announced that his topic was tantric sexual rites. In soft, well-bred English the librarian spoke of the higher purpose of sexual initiation, how arduous practices were undergone to achieve an evolved consciousness rather than erotic gratification, which after all could be come by in the usual ways.

The speaker told of male initiates trained to reserve their seminal fluid, even to retract after expending it. These adepts chose not to sacrifice the seed of life but to reabsorb it along with a complement of female energy. Their consorts, whom they worshiped, gained powers to rival the *dakinis;* these, in Tibetan lore, were considered as mother-goddesses who taught mystic doctrines and magical sciences. Others took Alexandra to be one, and she didn't entirely disagree.

A member of our group was a Tibetan, Burmese in features rather than Mongol. He verified the speaker's assertions, pointing to the example of the Sixth Dalai Lama. This rebel potentate, to the despair of his advisors, became the scandal of eighteenth-century Tibet. Recognized as the incarnation of the revered Great Fifth, this Dalai Lama had an eye for loose women. Come nightfall, he made the rounds of taverns and brothels in his capital, Lhasa. He wrote songs about his exploits until, at the instigation of the Chinese emperor, he was deposed and murdered. Some scholars, Western as well as Eastern, despite describing him as "the only erotic poet of the country," claim he was not a playboy but an initiate of secret knowledge. This is borne out by a pair of his verses:

> Never have I slept without a sweetheart
> Nor have I spent a single drop of sperm.

While were were playing the skeptical roles natural to an occidental education, our leader abruptly switched to the apparently morbid: rites practiced with the aid of the dead. We were invited to close our eyes and mentally transport ourselves over the Himalayan range to a rock-strewn plateau sixteen thousand feet high in Tibet, the roof of the world. *Rolang*—"the corpse who jumps up"—was one of the occult practices of the necromancers of Tibet. Even today a body is not cut up and fed to the vultures until a Buddhist lama has extracted what we would call its "soul" in the required fashion. The lama chants the service, which contains directions for the "soul" to find its way to the paradise of Maitreya, the Buddha-to-come. Otherwise, the spirit will turn into a hungry ghost that wanders about causing harm.

However, a sorcerer might obtain a corpse. Here is Alexandra's description of what he would do:

To animate the body, he lies on it, mouth to mouth, and while holding it in his arms, he must continually repeat mentally the same magic formula . . .

After a certain time the corpse begins to move. It stands up and tries to escape; the sorcerer, firmly clinging to it, prevents it from freeing itself. . . . It leaps and bounds to extraordinary heights, dragging with it the man who must hold on, keeping his lips upon the mouth of the monster, and continue mentally repeating the magic words.

Then comes the vital moment when the tongue of the corpse protrudes. The adept has to seize it in his teeth and bite it off, when the corpse collapses. If any part of the operation should backfire, the cadaver may escape to kill indiscriminately. The tongue, properly dried, will become a magic weapon dreaded by all but the most enlightened Tibetans.

At narrative's end the room in sweltering Pondicherry felt chilly. Without discussing our doubts, we asked how such closely held secrets had become known. In reply, the librarian produced a copy of *Magic and Mystery in Tibet,* which he informed us was *Madame* David-Neel's best-known work. We said that we had not heard of the author, and shortly thereafter the group, no doubt appalled by our ignorance, broke up. In the midst of a squall, palms clashing as the rain fell in sheets, the borrowed volume tucked in to stay dry, we hurried to our nearby hotel. Thus began our acquaintance with the woman who had elucidated these and many more mysteries. A search for the truth about her life would consume our next decade.

We left for Adyar, near Madras, and the ample library at the headquarters of the Theosophical Society. Here, at the turn of the century, Alexandra had sat under the spreading banyan tree to discuss arcane lore. Here we discovered *My Journey to Lhasa,* her breakthrough work, and many of the twenty-five books she had published during her long life, as well as some of the important articles. We located several short pieces about her, but they were confused and repetitious, a sure sign of error. Then there was *Alexandra David-Neel au Tibet.*

This book, by Jeanne Denys, had caused something of a sensation by claiming that Alexandra had never even gone to Tibet. Denys called her subject an actress, and alleged that she was an imposter who invented the stories of her travels and studies. This ill-tempered anti-Semitic tract was obviously pernicious, and its rancorous motives were made obvious by the author's insistence that Alexandra's parents had been modest shopkeepers, and that they were Jews who spoke only Yiddish at home. Still, it could not be simply dismissed. Denys, a dedicated enemy, had spent years digging for dirt, and she found some. We booked a flight for London, to seek for truth among the treasures of the library of the British Museum.

No doubt it would be gratifying to the schools we attended to state that, pursuing our researches in a sober fashion, we calmly uncovered the facts. But the hard truths about this extraordinary woman, like gold, lay buried in the depths of a treacherous mine of endeavor. The French intellectual René Grousset once quipped, "There exist two Madames David-Neel: the one who writes and the one who knows." Our breakthroughs came when least expected and surprised no one more than ourselves.

Over lunch in a small Greek restaurant hidden among the oriental bookstores of London, we queried Peter Hopkirk, author, correspondent, and collector of rare books on Central Asia: was he *certain* Alexandra made that forbidden journey to Lhasa, on foot, disguised, begging? "David Macdonald would have been hard to fool," he replied. But why not consult the Secret Files of the India Office for additional clues?

The subbasement of these splendid archives offered up rare nuggets of spying and duplicity typical of the British raj during the years of political rivalry known as the Great Game, and Alexandra unknowingly had been caught in the web of intrigue. Code name: the French Nun. She was entertained, watched, and her studies nearly foiled. Fortunately, we were able to obtain the other side of this unflattering story from Hugh Richardson, very likely the Westerner who best knows Tibet, and who in himself sums up all that is excellent in Britain's vanished empire.

Crossing the English Channel, we were initially disappointed. The Paris museums seemed to be lacking in Alexandriana. We decided this was one book that could not be written from a Left Bank café. However, at sixty, Alexandra bought a home outside of Digne in the Basses Alpes of southern France. Collecting her manuscripts and curios about her, she inhabited Samten Dzong, a "Fortress of Meditation." Here we discovered—under the protective custody of her last secretary, *Mademoiselle* Marie-Madeleine Peyronnet—a mother lode of approximately three thousand typescript pages of the traveler's letters to her stay-at-home husband, Philip Neel. What husband? None of her books had mentioned such a person. David-Neel carefully guarded her private life in order to cultivate her rarified public image. On separate occasions she had ordered both husband and secretary to destroy portions of her letters. Philip, who usually acquiesced, this once refused, but Marie-Madeleine was obliged to burn a packet of unidentified documents.

The remaining letters revealed that behind the impenetrable mask of an Amazon beat the heart of a real woman, alternately troubled or elated, happy or desperate. Often the letters were at odds with the published accounts. Yet the correspondence had its own slant, since frequently the turn-of-the-century wife, traveling far from home, didn't care to tell all to her husband, who was paying the bills. The image of *rolang* came to mind: writing the biography of this woman of power was a bit like bringing her corpse back to life. At any moment it could jump up, shatter our preconceptions and make off on its own.

"She was born an explorer," said Marie-Madeleine, as we took tea in the garden, a habit borrowed from the English that Alexandra had accustomed her to. But why Tibet? "It was bigger than life, just as was her character. It exhilarated her."

Why had she made that crazy trek to Lhasa in dead of winter, we inquired. Marie-Madeleine thought a moment, "She was turned back twice in the south"—literally, "put out the door"—"and twice in the north. It hurt her monumental pride."

By now Marie-Madeleine has been instrumental in the publication of a half-dozen posthumous works of her mentor, including her edition of the letters to Philip. In France biographies have appeared, but they have only succeeded in further submerging the actual thinking and feeling woman. She was not, as she has been dubbed, "Our Lady of Tibet." We may question if she were a lady at all. She was not Superwoman with a French accent, nor any kind of freak. Alexandra's destiny was not written in the stars; she made it happen in the face of the mightiest empire on earth.

What a various life she led! She was progressively a debutante, a liberty-seeking bohemian in Belle Epoque Paris, a failed opera singer, and the frustrated wife of a colonial bureaucrat in Tunis. However, once she turned East she found her course. So it was that, in her footsteps, we returned to the Orient. At holy Benares on the Ganges Alexandra learned to accept the impersonality of death. In Nepal she pilgrimaged to the ruin of the fragrant gardens of Lumbini, birthplace of Siddhartha Gautama, the historical Buddha. She paused at the border of Tibet, "on the edge of a mystery."

We found the Sacred Realm far less hospitable than had Alexandra. Echoes of the Cultural Revolution, long since repudiated in China proper, still persist among the obliterated ruins of the great monastic cities. The Dalai Lama has fled, Buddhism has gone underground, and even Tibetan medicine is outlawed. Therefore we journeyed to Dharamsala, northern India, that thriving Tibet in exile, to find a folk more cheerful about their misfortunes than we could imagine ourselves to feel. We hoped their patience would become ours.

In the Himalayas Alexandra had camped and stalked wolves and leopards to photograph. The paintings of another lover of these giant mountains, the Russian Nicholas Roerich, had only slightly prepared us for the fire opalescent sunrises, or as they are called, "the flowering of the snows," over mighty five-peaked Kinchinjunga on clear dawns. So we trekked and ruminated, but were we any closer to our goal? At last, in tiny Kalimpong, terminus of the old mule trains from across the mountains, we found a clue to our mystery—the character of Alexandra David-Neel—in the person of a lady of four score years: Victoria Williams, daughter of David Macdonald.

She told us about the encounter between Alexandra and her father at Gyantse, and how the Macdonald family had befriended her. The Trade Agent put up the weary traveler and loaned her money. Then he sent her to Victoria, a young woman of twenty, who gave her respectable clothes to wear down into India. The fifty-five-year-old explorer, terribly thin from dysentery, retained a magnetism. Victoria thought her the handsomest woman she'd ever seen. And Alexandra displayed a delightful sense of humor.

Why had she made that nearly suicidal journey to Lhasa? Why, quipped the Frenchwoman, because it was there and the bureaucrats had said not to. She showed them a sample of Parisian wit. In fact, Alexandra was not about to give away the deeper reasons for her pilgrimage.

Book One

THE PARISIENNE

Oh, how many trips I have made in divers worlds. And . . . since I am Parisienne, I have smiled . . . a broken-hearted smile sadder than a sob.
—*Alexandra David-Neel*

CHAPTER 1

Father and Daughter

Paris—divided and burning—May 28, 1871. Under a sky leaking rain, a well-dressed man with a neat gray beard toted a young girl in his arms along the Boulevard Voltaire. Deserted, this was one of the splendid new avenues driven through the city with the ruthlessness of a railroad train by Baron Haussmann, architect of Napoleon III's imperial capital. The girl in her pretty starched dress, hair braided and beribboned as though she were going to a party, slightly resembled *monsieur,* but indeed she was his daughter Louise Eugénie Alexandrine Marie David. To the despair of her mother, also Alexandrine, her father preferred "Alexandra."

Ragged gunfire could be heard ahead. *Monsieur* had difficulty peering through the haze compounded of a gray day and smoke from the charred remains of the palaces of the Right Bank. Out of view, the romantics known as the Paris Commune were making a last quixotic stand behind a barricade of cobblestones at the corner of rue de Faubourg du Temple and rue de la Fontaine, 11th arrondissement. The roar of army cannon answered their scattered musket shots.

Fearful, *monsieur* pushed on, keeping clear of the fighting. Despite his bourgeois appearance, Louis David had a reputation as a liberal journalist, a dedicated Republican. He was close to Victor Hugo, France's foremost man of letters and the scourge of the dethroned emperor. The connection was enough to hang a man during this week of reactionary terror. Under orders from the government in exile at Versailles, the army had systematically uprooted the rebels of Paris and would proceed to execute thousands, perhaps twenty-five thousand in all. Thus the popular rising about which Karl Marx was so ambivalent—because it was French, patriotic, and premature—dwindled toward its dismal end. If Louis David had to brace himself to keep from trembling, his little daughter's round face remained placid, her philosopher's gaze unmoved.

The two eventually reached their goal: the destroyed gate of Père

Lachaise cemetery. No one stopped them from entering, but they found the going rough. The muddy ground was littered with toppled tombstones, and from open graves protruded fresh corpses still clutching their enemies. Numbers of casualties from both sides had fallen round the bust of Honoré Balzac. Louis David trudged on, cradling his only child.

Ahead stood a stone wall. It was quiet now, but a few minutes earlier nearly uniformed soldiers had formed into ranks, shouldered arms, and on command fired. Figures, hands tied behind, collapsed like puppets with their strings cut. Those not quite dead moaned while another group was lined up against the wall. This well without bottom—defiant men and women, pregnant girls, weeping boys with fuzz on their cheeks—would be plumbed to its depth by the *haute bourgeoise* regime installed in the palace of the Sun King. The devils of the Commune must be exorcized.

The regulars, peasant lads who believed what they were told, used to good effect their *chassepots,* excellent rifles with which Emperor Napoleon had thought to stop the Prussian military machine. At Sedan, Bismarck's new cannon had blown away the French, and Napoleon had fallen from his white horse into the Iron Chancellor's hands. But if the imperial army had broken and run before the Germans, they could still murder their fellow citizens who wished to continue the war. Bismarck, besieging Paris, permitted the French to do his dirty work. He could not forsee that the blood-drenched stones of the eastern wall of Père Lachaise were to become the object of a yearly pilgrimage—the Lourdes of the Left—down to our day. The soldiers worked quickly, leaving a heap of bodies as they marched off.

For the fancily dressed child of two and a half, Alexandra David, the pile of fresh corpses formed her earliest conscious memory, festering in the depths of her psyche. We know of but one mention, appropriately from Benares on the Ganges in 1913, when she wrote to her husband:

Yesterday I suddenly realized it was March 18th, the anniversary of the Commune ... I never told you I was there, at the wall of the Federals, after the firing squad [and] while the corpses were being hurriedly piled in trenches dug [by them] for the purpose. ... A phantom memory of that stays with me. Since you are first learning of the fact, you will ask who brought me. It was my father, who wished me to keep [always] an impressive reminder of human ferocity.

Born on October 24, 1868, at St. Mandé, a comfortable suburb of Paris wedged between the Bois de Vincennes and the defensive wall surrounding the city, Alexandra later recalled her father and mother as "two statues who remained more than fifty years facing each other as strangers ... always closed to each other, without any tie of spirit or heart." As a student of deep mysteries, meditating in a hermit's hut in the Himalayas, she was still galled by the bitter memory of serving as a pawn in their tireless chess match.

"Why must one have parents?" she wondered in her provocative way. "How happy one would be not to have them."

Though the mature woman grew to realize that her parents were honorable, respectable people, she cherished a grudge for what she considered crimes inflicted upon her personality. With time, she shifted the blame to society at large, condemning the family of rigid, Victorian Europe as a devastating spectacle. She was to go through life resisting the natural currents of her emotions and, above all, any confining relationship. Instead, at an age when other girls began thinking of romance, she turned toward austerities, claiming as "my masters, Jesus, Epictetus and the Stoic philosophers."

Alexandra's father, Louis Pierre David, was born at Tours on July 6, 1815, to industrious Huguenot (Protestant) parents, Pierre and Anne. He came to manhood under the reign of Louis-Philippe, the bourgeois monarch brought to power by the Revolution of 1830, who could be seen strolling the promenades of Paris in everyday clothes. It was a period of mundane economic liberalism, material improvements, and spiritual malaise that perversely spawned the heroic poetry of young Victor Hugo and the titanic canvases of Delacroix. At first, Louis chose his father's occupation, the prosaic one of provincial schoolmaster.

But Louis David's politics were inherited and he, too, would pass them on to his daughter. Alexandra claimed descent "from a family which, for many centuries, suffered hard and continual religious persecution." Originally from the south, the Davids were reputed to have been Albigenses, "and other things yet, always on the path of ardent and difficult heresies." Alexandra remained mysterious about these "other things," but at any rate she thrilled to her father's stories of family travails.

As a young man, Louis was slim, earnest, with handsome features finely hewn. Eyes alight, he considered himself an activist. And the French genius for controversy was merely slumbering. In the 1840s, with the relaxation of censorship, Louis founded a Republican journal, *Courier d'Indre et Loire*. This was a local weekly containing very little of what we would recognize as news. Rather, it combined official notices, advertisements for land sales, humorous remarks, and veiled editorial comment. *Monsieur* David became a prominent citizen of Tours.

In 1848 revolution, harking back to 1789, swept through Europe and in France ushered in the ill-fated Second Republic. It was the heyday of the liberal democrats, the last opportunity to create a political order on the Continent resembling that of the United States. Vicomte Victor Hugo, already famous and a friend of the fled monarch, this once failed to grasp the trend of events and called for a regency. The great Romantic was preoccupied by his socially ambitious wife and by keeping two official mistresses. In contrast, Louis David wavered neither from bachelorhood nor his Republican principles, and he was elected from Tours to the Constituent Assembly. Truly "a man of '48," as Alexandra referred to him, he was radical only in the specific nineteenth-century French context.

In May 1849, a majority of males of the nation elected an Assembly dominatedby royalists and reactionaries. The liberals, including Louis David, were voted out. To this the workers of the twisty, medieval *quartiers* of Paris responded by prying up cobbles and rebelling. The army blasted away their barricades and terrible reprisals followed. Victor Hugo, by now a deputy, quipped that civilization had defended itself with the methods of barbarism.

Another new deputy, also named Louis and a friend of the great novelist, was to have an effect on Alexandra's youth almost as profound as would her father. Louis Napoleon Bonaparte, known as "the man of destiny," was the son of the first Napoleon's brother and Josephine's daughter Hortense. When the Republic was proclaimed, this middle-aged adventurer, who had failed in two previous attempted coups, returned from London to run for the presidency of France. Hugo supported him, although not the journalist Louis David, who had taken up his neglected affairs at Tours. Napoleon triggered a landslide in the provinces, especially among the peasants who supposed they were voting for the *first* emperor come back from the beyond.

The new president was mild-mannered, with short legs and a long mustache, a cynical man of "well-known sexual excesses," who liked to call himself a socialist. His managers, principally the politician Adolphe Thiers, considered him "an imbecile." Still, at the Elysée Palace Bonaparte's intimates began to address him as "Your Highness." Hugo, quickly disillusioned, took up his pen against the would-be monarch. "The principles of the democratic form of government have become dear to me," he wrote. "I am prepared to die for them."

At Tours, a liberal pocket, David continued to express his opposition to the regime. His Huguenot heritage underpinned his belief in individual liberty. The government sent gangs of thugs to smash the costly presses of such nay-sayers. Finally, during the early hours of December 2, 1851—the anniversary of Napoleon I's victory at Austerlitz—the president ordered the army to occupy strategic points in Paris, especially newspaper offices. Posters were run off and plastered over the city proclaiming the suspension of civil liberties and Bonaparte as savior of the nation. His *coup d'etat* was complete.

Juliette Drouet, Hugo's favorite mistress, arranged for Victor to flee on the night train to Brussels. He was dressed as a laborer in soiled clothes, passport forged. Juliette followed, as did many exiles from the growing tyranny. But what of Louis David? From Lhasa in February 1924, at her moment of triumph, Alexandra wrote her husband, "I am the daughter of a Freemason, banished by the Empire, publisher of the *Courier d'Indre et Loire* until 1852." Not important enough to arrest, alone, he too left for Brussels. It could have been about her father that Alexandra is said to have remarked, "How many are powerless because they think they are!"

Now at the center of resistance to the dictator, Louis entered the orbit of the inimitable, magnetic Hugo. When the novelist wrote in a few weeks *Napoleon le Petit*—exposing the ruler of France as a common criminal—he turned to his fellow emigres to disseminate it. Louis David helped smuggle hundreds of copies of the inflammatory tract into his native region, hidden in plaster busts of Bonaparte. The emperor never could shake the nickname of "little Napoleon."

How intense was the collaboration between the provincial journalist and the promethean writer and lover? Documentation is scanty, but we may venture that it consisted largely of Louis's admiration for the great one. When in 1853 Hugo was obliged by the authorities to leave Brussels for the isle of Jersey, Louis indignantly departed, but for Louvain. Hugo took both his wife and Juliette and various family members devoted to him. Louis had only himself to drag about the picturesque town of red-tiled roofs and winding streets reminiscent of the Spanish overlordship. If not entirely indigent he was getting close to it, although his personal failure rankled less than the shattering of his icon of reason.

The mature bachelor, who prided himself on his appearance, kept his head high and his graying beard trim—the badge of a Republican—and he continued to dress in a tight double-breasted frock coat as befitted a notable of Tours. The Flemish mayor of this thriving industrial town took pity on such a well-educated man down on his luck, and he engaged Louis to teach his two younger daughters French. Mayor Borghmans, certainly Protestant, may have been a fellow Mason. There also lived at his house his adopted daughter Alexandrine. Born January 30, 1832, she was now twenty-two and had been marriageable for some years. The practical mayor made no objection when, in 1854, Louis asked for Alexandrine's hand. The couple was married with a minimum of ceremony. Poor Louis! Unwittingly, he had hammered the last nail into the coffin of his hopes.

According to Alexandra, who is our only authority, her parents were bitterly unhappy from the start. The new *Madame* David was a practical soul who cared little for politics or ideas. Not formally religious, she had a mystical streak and had converted to Catholicism. A stocky woman who looked older than her years, she liked to wear her thick hair in a bun atop a round, complacent face. Big bosomed, she favored ruffles and lace when being photographed. Why had the intense Louis wed this *terre à terre* woman?

An exile, he faced bleak economic prospects, while in contrast Alexandrine, although an orphan, had been left a tidy sum by her natural father. The money, loaned to merchants in the textile trade, brought in a secure income. During Alexandra's youth, her family didn't lack for possessions, servants, and social standing. As summed up by Peyronnet, "The family ate well and richly. . . . They drank [fine] red wines with meat, and white wines with fish." Until Louis suffered severe losses on the Bourse in the Panic of 1893, he was able to indulge his only daughter in governesses, music and English lessons, and in pocket money.

The new husband and wife, like Jack and Mrs. Sprat, were oddly matched physically and temperamentally. They were of different faiths and clashed on that score. Alexandra, who would suffer, laid the blame on her mother. She never cared to admit that from the maternal line she inherited stamina, longevity, and good looks. For Alexandrine was solidly handsome, a complement to Louis's slender sensitivity. In this man and woman, we have a meeting of earth and water, which, while it smothers fire, may produce cement.

It remains a mystery how the Davids, after fifteen years of steadily souring marriage, finally conceived a child. Alexandra reported an amusing detail to Philip Neel:

During the pregnancy of which I am the issue, my mother passed her leisure time reading [the novels of James] Fenimore Cooper. This placid person, shaped by her Dutch heredity, a large matron, loved adventures in book form so long as she didn't have to live them. But she read them passionately all the while I formed myself in her, running, in thought, through grasslands and forests.

What effect this had on the unborn child, we may only guess. A more immediate result of Alexandrine's pregnancy was that Louis seized the opportunity to demand his offspring be born on French soil, so she would be a citizen. In 1868 the couple moved to Paris. The earnest "man of '48" found a drastically altered city. Baron Haussmann had rammed through wide boulevards, destroying the tortuous alleys of the medieval burgh. Everywhere rose gleaming new buildings with cafés spread out under rows of trees. Fashion and laughter ruled the day and more the night. At any hour Paris amused itself under the glow of gaslights. Jacques Offenbach wrote the gay tunes to which dancers kicked and showed their red satin *derrières*.

About the Second Empire Bismarck quipped, "From a distance it's stunning. When you get closer, however, there's nothing there at all."

The gorgeous facades along the boulevards obscured wretched slums behind them, and laborers and artisans faced an increasingly difficult task to feed and house their families.

Louis set up his wife in the suburb of St. Mandé, and on October 24, 1868, she gave birth to Alexandra. The infant girl was baptized three days later at the parish church. Once Alexandra became old enough to reflect on it, she hated being a child. Stoic practices such as sleeping on boards came naturally to her, and the Christian church fathers were her very early reading. Only much later did she complain of a want of love. Probably, the insidious friction between her parents was aggravated by the difficult political times.

France declared war on Prussia over an affront more imagined than real. The emperor, fulfilling his supposed destiny, rode off to battle at the head of his troops, though due to kidney stones he had trouble sitting his horse. At Sedan he lost an army, himself to prison, and the throne. The Second Empire folded its sets and in comic opera style rang down the curtain. France was rid of Bonaparte, but the Prussians were not so easily dispatched: they ringed Paris with troops and artillery.

The siege began on September 25, 1870. Bismarck, by cutting off the capital, meant to starve it into submission and bring France to its knees. On January 5 the Prussians added the terror of full-scale bombardment during the nights. Out went the lights, gone was the gaiety, but home from exile came the nation's idol, Victor Hugo. Thousands greeted his arrival at the Gare du Nord, and Judith Gautier, daughter of the critic Théophile Gautier, presented the renowned author with a huge bouquet of flowers. The promethean seventy-year-old responded by taking the pretty woman as an auxiliary mistress.

Within the beleagured city food grew short. The shopkeepers had no trade, and, as winter deepened, the poor had no fuel. Trees along the Champs Elysées were cut down, while the zoo provided elephant meat for the restaurants. Hugo wrote a small cookbook in which he promoted the virtues of boiled horsemeat, weed soup, and diced rat pie. "The soul of Paris is indestructible," he thundered. "Neither cannon nor famine can destroy her!"

Louis David opened his home to his old friends. Victor visited occasionally—a massive patriarch with a trim white beard—not least for the pleasure of bouncing a chubby two-year-old girl on his knee while he and the other men discussed affairs. Victor adored children and was not afraid to express it; his own were ill-fated, especially his favorite daughter who drowned. Alexandra the woman liked to recall him, although not as a literary or political influence. Rather, the physical, expansive Hugo made a belittling contrast to her sensitive, introverted father. "He scooped me in his arms!" the ninety-year old reminisced.

Hugo acted toward women as a man of his day was expected to, and although Alexandra would grow opposed to such machismo in theory, it exerted a certain attraction for her.

Two brothers of the noted family Reclus, active in Leftist politics, Elisée and Elie, were even closer to Louis and would significantly influence his daughter. The two brothers were going to be leading Communards, Elisée on the front lines. Their mother, *Madame* Reclus, took a prominent role as Commissioner for Girls' Education. Stewart Edwards, historian of the Commune, has written, "In pressing for women's education the Communards were going against the practice of the time . . . the prejudice for 'elevating' women above social and public life." In fact, a young woman lacking skills usually could choose only between the options of becoming a wife or a whore. Here we find the roots of Alexandra's dedication to the practical schooling of girls, its necessity if they were to achieve independence as women.

Despite the optimism of the Republicans, a monarchist-dominated Assembly met at Versailles and authorized the opportunist Adolphe Thiers to conclude a backdoor peace with Bismarck. Paris, reacting with an explosion of anger, prepared to fight the provinces as well as the Prussians.

During their brief period of governance, limited in area by the military lines, the Communards acted with a Puritan earnestness: They held meetings and made speeches, banned prostitution, arrested drunkards, and adopted orphans. However, when the Central Committee needed money to pay the National Guard, they applied to Baron Rothschild, who supplied credit at the Bank of France. Private property was never confiscated. The Commune dealt in the realm of ideas, and it featured, according to Louise Michel, its best-known female combatant, "the profound comprehension of human dignity . . . as comprehensive for women as for men." Even its utter failure, claimed Elisée Reclus, "raised up an ideal for the future."

When Victor Hugo again abandoned Paris, Louis David refused to follow. On Palm Sunday, April 2, 1871, the Versailles government commenced the second siege of Paris. The excited *citoyens* who sallied forth to do battle were a poor match for professional officers and heavy weapons. The regular soldiers, told they were fighting against immoral fiends, offered no quarter. Still, the Communards gave a good account of themselves. Elisée Reclus, throwing primitive hand grenades, was captured but merely banished to a prison camp. He was already a respected geographer and would live to become Alexandra's political mentor.

On May 21, a section of the defensive wall was discovered unguarded, and by nightfall soldiers were pouring into the city. The Communards fought desperately in their home *quartiers* behind their accustomed barricades. Men died willingly, women struggled against bayonets, and children threw away their lives. Incendiary shells set off fires, but other buildings were torched on purpose by the *petroleuses,* fighting women who impeded the army. Napoleon's monumental Paris became a huge bonfire watched in awe by peasants on nearby farms. It seemed like the end of the world.

Street by street the resistance was demolished. The Versailles troops lined up their prisoners and shot them as quickly as their new rifles would fire. Others were secured in cages until they went mad or were shipped off to Devil's Island. By week's end the Commune had expired against the wall at Père Lachaise.

Why was the respectable *Monsieur* David out wandering the streets with his little daughter? Thousands were arrested, hundreds shot on mere suspicion. Once interred it was nearly impossible to get free. The prefect of police declared, "The simple fact of having stayed in Paris under the Commune is a crime. Everyone there is to blame." He was outdone by the newspapers crying for blood. "What is a republican?" demanded an editorial in *Le Figaro.* "A savage beast."

Miraculously, Louis David escaped harm and returned home. Torn between loyalty and fear, he had taken no part in the Commune. Indeed, the former teacher, journalist, and deputy—an aging man with weary eyes—was no danger to the state. Muddled by despair, he communed with the wreck of his ideals. But what of the infant in his arms, the wide-eyed cherub in her fluffy crinolines; what effect had these sights on her?

Approaching womanhood, Alexandra scribbled sometimes in a black notebook, often bitterly. Typical is the following: "To believe in justice, in truth, in virtue among men, is to ask them for what they cannot give."

Or again, "It is better to die than to watch one's own defeat."

CHAPTER 2

Mother and Daughter

The offspring of elderly parents, Alexandra did not easily make, or perhaps crave, friends of her own age. At home, the domain of her mother, she felt confined. In her first major work she would recall:

Ever since I was five years old, a tiny precocious child of Paris, I wished to move out of the narrow limits in which . . . I was then kept. I craved to go beyond the garden gate, to follow the road that passed it by, and to set out for the Unknown. But, strangely enough, this "Unknown" fancied by my baby mind always turned out to be a solitary spot where I could sit alone, with no one near . . . I sought solitude behind any bush, any mound of sand, that I could find in the garden, or wherever else my nurse took me.

As soon as she was old enough, Alexandra tagged along with her father and his dogs on walks round their placid, leafy neighborhood. Undeterred by brisk winter days, they chatted together like grownups. Often their longer excursions ended at the Gare de Vincennes or the Gare de Lyons to watch the trains come and go. A great network of tracks had been built out from Paris to every corner of the country, and the Impressionists were soon to discover the lure of painting outdoors in the provinces. However, the dreams of this precocious child—fussily dressed with tiny drop earrings and necklace to match—refused to stop at the French border. "What a thirst to depart possessed me," she wrote, "when on the station platforms I yearned for Germany, Poland, Russia—a snowy immensity, infinity!"

Although Louis David may have sensed his daughter's uniqueness, he was bound by a mundane reality. Initially the Third Republic was so in name only, and a man of his stamp was out of favor. When Hugo returned once more, he was defeated in a race for the Chamber of Deputies. The patriarch of writers plunged into the life of the theater, took Sarah Bernhardt for a mistress, and abruptly in the spring of 1872, complete with ménage, he departed for Guernsey to write a successor to *Les Misérables*. Louis also would leave Paris, but for more practical reasons. In abject surrender to his wife, he agreed to a final retreat to Brussels.

First, Louis did something he kept secret from Alexandrine. Taking his daughter, he had her baptized over: made a Protestant. Alexandra never revealed her feelings about when, standing in a strange bare church, the minister in black touched her forehead and left a chill spot. In later years she spoke well of the Huguenots and, in dire straits, tried to find comfort in their services. It was in vain, but she did identify with their independent spirit.

Belgium was the land of *Madame* David. As a girl Alexandra fought against her mother, and as a woman she never entirely forgave her. She blamed her mother for everything, even for bearing a child. In adulthood she denounced birthdays as "a commemoration of the sinister farce our parents played on us by bringing us into this world." Alexandra was to grow fond of biting remarks, possibly for their shock effect, but hers was ultimately a lively rather than morose character.

Alexandrine Borghmans's descent is significant. Her natural father was Dutch but at least partly of Norwegian ancestry. His wife, Alexandrine's mother, was of mixed Flemish and Siberian stock. Later, Alexandra would make much of a hint of Mongol in her blood lines, without specifying it came down through her mother. Nor did she offer the information that her mother's inheritance formed the basis of the Davids' prosperity.

From photos, Alexandrine's presence appears intimidating in the way of those who are securely anchored and care little for speculation. In Flemish lace and pleated blouses, she ordered about her family and the servants, and in the marketplace she tried the patience of the traders with her demands. At home everything had to be kept spotless. "Where are the beautiful damask napkins that filled the armoires?" Alexandra would groan from far-off Tibet. "Where are the bedspreads from Holland and the fine porcelain dishes that were never used?" The parlor furniture was regularly polished, then covered up. No wonder, when at last the traveler had a home of her own, she filled it with a haphazard collection of strange oriental artifacts.

The young girl instinctively rebelled against a mother she would think of as a sheep unable to stray far from the flock. *Madame* David disliked being alone, while Alexandra reveled in the lyricism of windswept plains high above the ordinary world. She refused to credit her longevity to the maternal line, although she was aware of several centenarians on that side, including "a great-grandfather who ate and drank plenty and died at 104." Her lifelong, and perhaps immoderate, resentment toward her mother is summed up by her outburst, "I am the daughter of the man she did not love. I am his daughter alone, in spite of the blood from which she made me and the milk from which she nourished me."

Ironically, in her hundred years the pioneering feminist would grow close to a handful of men but only one woman. There is no truth to the recent assertion of Jean Chalon that "Alexandra hated men intensely," and that she had a pathological aversion to all things masculine. She described her father as the only person she really loved; she evolved an ultimately fruitful relationship with her husband; she adopted an Asian son and, for a time, she even fell in love with the youthful maharaja of Sikkim. We cannot find any evidence for this so-called aversion. However, the misunderstanding may stem from a remark that young Alexandra made about her short-lived brother Louis Jules.

When on January 26, 1873, after nineteen years of a hostile marriage, Alexandrine gave birth to a boy, the elder Louis was more embarrassed than delighted. His four-year-old daughter was also less than pleased. While watching her baby brother in the bath, she is said to have commented about his tiny penis, "Well, that I do not have."

Even if this story is apocryphal, the demanding little girl likely did feel jealous about the inevitable shift of attention to her sibling. Child or woman, Alexandra knew the way to center stage. When Louis Jules died at the age of six months, Alexandra acted openly content, but the episode must have planted within her a certain guilt. This is classical Freudian theory—penis envy and all—but Alexandra was after all a contemporary of the great Viennese physician and from the social class of women whom he specialized in treating. Her attitudes toward men and sex—which she could and did enjoy—were shaped by the century in which she was born.

An uproar followed in the David household, Alexandrine demanding to return to live near her adoptive mother. Louis, under the threat of a Bourbon restoration, without significant friends or hopes, couldn't resist for long. Thus in 1773 the curious five-year-old found herself transplanted from glittering Paris to dowdy Brussels. Since Belgium belonged to her mother, Alexandra took it as her own Devil's Island. Tearfully, she bade adieu to the "*guignols* [puppet shows] of the Champs Elysées" and its "carriages drawn by white horses." Brussels was not merely smaller, "its people drank a bitter liquid called beer, and they said *septante* and *nonante* instead of *soixante-dix* and *quatre-vingt-dix*." What savages!

Alexandra always boasted of Parisian birth and wit, but eventually she would look more kindly on her adopted land. To her readers she confided in a mature work, "Brussels smiled at my revolt. It guarded me for fifteen years, bound me in subtle ties . . . and conquered me." In late middle age, Alexandra prided herself on "having remained faithful despite so many years gone by." On occasion she felt drawn to Belgium for "stirring pilgrimages." But this was after the explorer had learned to breathe freely the chill air of the roof of the world. The child, hemmed in by her mother's bulk and immured in a stuffy Victorian interior, responded by flight.

Her first adventure occurred when, on the eve of the departure for Brussels, she managed to give an inattentive nurse the slip in the Bois de Vincennes. The horrified domestic alerted a gendarme, and after a widespread search the precocious girl was captured and brought to the station. For his trouble, she scratched the policeman. When Alexandra's chagrined father came to collect her, she showed no remorse, lending some credence to her insistence that "I was born a savage."

In Belgium Alexandra fled into the imaginary realm of books. Her favorites were the fantasies of Jules Verne and the equally fantastic American woods of James Fenimore Cooper. Dolls and dresses bored her, and for her birthdays she demanded volumes on faraway places, or better yet the whole world—a globe! She dreamed not of growing up to be a coquette, of fancy dress balls, but of "wild hills, immense deserted steppes and impassable landscapes of glaciers." At least, her parents might take her traveling on school holidays.

They failed to, and so Alexandra tried vainly to escape. It was the dependency of childhood that she hated, just as she would loathe the dependent status forced upon women. At first she went to a Protestant school, although her mother insisted on a strict Catholic governess. This woman brought her moody charge along on visits to a Carmelite convent. Their plain, whitewashed chapel was open for visitors to pray in, but Alexandra was fascinated instead by an inner sanctum barely visible behind high grilled doors covered by a black curtain. The piety of chanting caught her ear, the sense of adoration.

The governess took the veil, and the inquisitive seven-year-old demanded to be brought to see her, so that the nuns began to expect a youthful conversion. One day the mother superior, impressed by the child's spiritual intensity, invited her into their private sanctuary. This had been Alexandra's object from the start. When the curtains were drawn back, illusion yielded to reality: "On the reverse side of this border of shadows . . . there was nothing hallucinatory . . . [only] very large vulgar drapes of cotton, identical to those hanging in vestries."

The girl had naively envisioned the sisters as "virgins in hieratic attitudes among beds of lilies on the stained glass windows . . ." In fact, there was nothing medieval about them or their cloister; they were rough Flemish women who grew cabbages. Alexandra's eventual alienation from the Christianity of her day stemmed from its loss of emphasis on the mysteries. Conversely, at age ten she was struck by reading a tale about Buddha—an earlier incarnation than Gautama—who, on meeting a tiger in the jungle, gave his own flesh to feed her starving cubs. The sacrificial quality of the story thrilled her imagination.

At about this age, Alexandra, a robust child, turned sickly. When a doctor diagnosed anemia, *Madame* David seized the chance to remove her daughter from what she considered bad influences. She was packed off to Bois Fleuri, a convent school where rows of rosy-cheeked little Flamandes were stuffed like geese, fed seven times a day. Here, among girls her age, she fattened.

Bois Fleuri, which the student later rated as old-fashioned, enrolled four foreign students—"heretics"—with whom Alexandra practiced English. Already she had begun to read authors pithy enough to intimidate an adult: Augustine, Proudhon, Kierkegaard. Imitating the ancient Stoics, she subjected her body to rigorous trials, including sleeping on boards for a bed. That habit stuck, and even in old age she permitted herself only the luxury of dozing in an armchair. However, agreeing with Gautama Buddha, she eventually discarded physical austerities as wrong-headed.

The student loved to convene her friends in the garden to deliberate on abstruse subjects such as the make-up of the Trinity—no doubt to the consternation of their teachers. The twelve-year-old conversed with her English and American *amies* in these terms:

Alexandra: How do you understand the Trinity, the three who make one?
Friend: They say it is a mystery . . .
Alexandra: Not such a mystery, since they have discovered these three persons . . .
Alexandra: "In the beginning was the Word." Sister Marie-Helene recites this when she shakes a small bell from the top of the house on stormy days. She says it stops the lightning from falling. Do you believe this?
Friend: No.
Alexandra: When God speaks, it is the Word.
Friend: And the Holy Spirit?
Alexandra: It is when God thinks.

Indeed, thought was her god, and metaphysical ideas presented themselves to her in the midst of childhood games, surrounded by trees and flowers. Alexandra later joked, "One who believed in reincarnation of the same spirit might imagine that the soul of an old theologian had come to life in my little person." As a schoolgirl, she could wallow in pessimism worthy of a medieval scholastic. Then social radicalism, and later more significantly Buddhism—both concerned with putting an end to suffering—became the solace of an increasingly desperate young woman who felt betrayed by the crassness of the world. It took a nomad's life on the steppes of Central Asia to rid Alexandra of what her doctors termed "neurasthenia," or depression, which translated into suicidal impulses. Once she had glimpsed Tibet, her eyes "gleamed with the clarity of the Himalayas" and her step achieved a new elasticity. She was able to indulge "her two great passions—exploration and study—which in her youth made her an *enfant terrible*." Where the pretty young woman saw only darkness, the weathered elder reflected a light radiant as sunrise over the snowy peaks.

At fifteen an odd thing happened to break the student's routine: Alexandra got hold of an English journal put out by the Society of the Supreme Gnosis. It had been sent to her, at her request, by a certain Mrs. Elisabeth Morgan who, although she remains a shadowy figure, was to become Alexandra's first patron. She appears to have been a mature woman, an occultist, who befriended French students visiting England. As Alexandra sat alone in the convent garden, she stared at the pale blue cover with its enigmatic oriental symbols. The contents were still more perplexing: unfamiliar language, twists of thought, snatches of Sanskrit. The inquisitive one reacted out of character, declaring, "These people are crazy!"

Still, the somewhat crackbrained occultism represented by the Gnosis was to play a role in Alexandra's life when she was ready. In the meantime she suffered through the attainment of young womanhood. By age sixteen Alexandra was out of school and studying music privately at home. In her sixteenth year—all corseted into a bustled, ruffly gown buttoned up to her Adam's apple, and demurely holding a fan in her white-gloved hand—the young lady was presented to the emperor and empress of the Belgians, who also ruled over millions of subjects in the Congo.

An extant photo shows an unhappy debutante. Alexandra puts on a proper face and she is quite pretty. But at only five-foot-two—not much under average—she looks swallowed up in her gown. Still, her brown hair piled high, dark luminous eyes, a regular nose, and almost sensuous mouth, as well as a note of melancholy, render her mysteriously attractive. How did the dashing Leopold II react, or his dissolute wife Henrietta Maria? We can only guess. But already Alexandra can sense that men will want her, and not knowing how to respond makes her miserable.

Fresh attempts at flight provided a temporary escape. One summer while her family vacationed at Ostend, as did the royal family, Alexandra walked to Holland and then crossed the channel to England. She didn't accomplish much beyond sightseeing and she returned when her money ran low. A more remarkable venture occurred in 1885, in her seventeenth year, when Alexandra hiked alone over the St.-Gotthard Pass through the Alps to the Italian lake country. She was furnished with little more than an umbrella and the *Maxims* of Epictetus, a stoic whom she termed "the revered master of my youth." However, she allowed her mother to recover her at Milan. These early attempts at solo travel were not terribly serious, but they afforded the young woman glimpses of the great world and served to intimidate her parents.

By this time *Madame* David had grown weary of her daughter's eccentricities. She hadn't bargained on raising either a wastrel or a philosopher, especially one who was secretly taking notes for a book—

never in fact written—to be called "Modern Saints, Hermits and Miracle Workers." She hoped instead to find a proper suitor for the girl. In the meantime she would go to work in a shop selling *tissues* (fabric for women's clothing). Louis David was not in accord, but as usual his wishes counted for little.

Alexandra tried to assume the obliging air of a merchant but utterly failed. From outside the shop came an air played on a North African hand organ. It set her to dreaming in total oblivion of the customers. Commerce and she soon parted company, never to reunite. At eighteen a romantic streak lay beneath Alexandra's reserved exterior. This was to find an initial outlet in the continued study of music, begun at boarding school.

The girl was undeniably gifted, and such pursuits, while encouraged by her father, were also acceptable to *Madame* David. They might even enhance her daughter's marriageability. In preparation for the entrance exam of the Royal Conservatory of Brussels, Alexandra practiced piano and reviewed music theory. She entered the conservatory in April 1886, but it was for her soprano voice that she won a minor prize three years later. Louis David, who had faith in his daughter's talents, vigorously promoted her singing. What a contrast her sweet lyric voice, capable of hitting very high notes, made to the continual bickering of the David household, which could not agree on the young woman's future.

In 1888 an opportunity to escape offered and Alexandra pounced on it: Mrs. Morgan sent for her. She could study in London and board cheaply at the Supreme Gnosis. If her mundanely reasonable parents objected, she prevailed. She was under respectable sponsorship, and besides, in her heart she had already chosen a career in the Orient. Serious of purpose, she intended to become a medical missionary. However, when she talked of studying medicine, her mother doomed the plan: "You want to be a doctor? But the men themselves don't know anything. Just think . . . a woman!"

Momentarily, her dreams were turned into impossible mirages. Alexandra at this point in her development wished to "adopt modern ideas while keeping the timeless precepts of Jesus." She hoped to do good, and an interest in the East was not out of the question. But her being a woman posed a significant problem. In the 1880s, although France had built the Suez Canal and gained a preeminent position in Indochina, women, other than nuns, did not become missionaries and still less orientalists. Whatever the student's intentions, and they were necessarily vague, she would need to perfect English, the common language of educated Asians.

Traveling toward London, Alexandra was determined to make the most of her brief voyage across the channel. In order to prolong it, she set out for the Dutch port of Flushing. Here the passenger was guaranteed more hours aboard ship than at Calais. To the very end of her hundred years, she would love the momentum of travel for its own sake.

Alexandra described the incident:

The boat left in the morning . . . and since I was not yet sleepy, I strolled along the quay. It was not quite dark [and] shapes were still visible in the progressively thickening fog. Only rare passers-by, hastening toward their homes, emerged occasionally from the obscurity to instantly vanish. An ineffable peace spread through me, I felt myself marvelously alone. Of all the people who knew me, I thought, none know I am here . . . and if I died at this moment, no one would know who I am. This solitude, which I imagined to be absolute, diffused in me waves of happiness. The most exalted transports of the mystics, could they equal this state of infinite calm in which all physical or mental agitation has disappeared, and where life flows smoothly without jolts, without fragmenting itself into sensations or ideas, without any other taste except that of life?

The nascent philosopher, on the threshold of her first serious challenge, had experienced an insight, a breakthrough of the quality termed by Zen Buddhists *satori*. According to Christmas Humphreys, "It is the beginning and not the end" of the direct experience of reality. Next must follow "a period of maturing."

CHAPTER 3

The Supreme Gnosis

One evening in 1888 Alexandra descended on Victoria Station, a trifle unsure of herself. Confused by the swirl, she summoned nerve to ask directions in halting English. Fortunately, James Ward, a member of the Supreme Gnosis, picked the young Frenchwoman out of the crowd and conducted her to the home of the society. Although Alexandra had eagerly awaited this moment, once deposited in her dimly lit room she succumbed to an inner dread. Likely she burst into tears, a habit in these vulnerable years.

The chamber was vast yet sparsely furnished. On the wall hung a strange painting depicting the sea from which emerged lotus flowers, angels, and shells. Most odd were French doors covered by a shade pulled down so smoothly the effect was of a lacquered panel. In a rerun of the mystery of the Carmelites, the young woman sensed some presence behind the barrier. Alone in a foreign capital, she felt homesick.

When she lay down to sleep, vibrations from the painting disturbed her. "I had read," she later wrote, "that in the Middle Ages secret societies subjected candidates for admission to gruesome ordeals during which they tried to terrify them by bizarre means." Did the strange people of the Gnosis intend to scare her away? Drifting off, she was startled awake by a ghostly procession marching through the doors and around in arcane circles.

Certain she imagined it, she was determined to get hold of herself. Hadn't she always derided her mother for her baseless superstitious fears? Alexandra crept out of bed to examine the doors. Attempts to move aside the stiff canvas paneling failed; she saw no way to budge it. Finally, she managed to pry up a corner of the material and peek beyond: darkness. But the effort helped to regain her composure, since Alexandra rarely lost heart for long. There was an electric lamp in the room, and in this talisman of the new arcanum—Science—Alexandra put her faith. She kept the unaccustomed object lit by her bed, ready if the phantoms invaded to point it at them and scare them away.

At seven the next morning a maid bearing tea and biscuits awoke the soundly sleeping young woman. Without a thought, she pressed a tiny latch and parted the doors to disclose a pleasant garden, common enough behind a London townhouse. Alexandra hurried through her *toilette* to arrive at breakfast, but she was disappointed. Her tablemates looked emaciated, and when she complained about the sparse diet, they reprimanded her with a story about their president: he subsisted on a dozen almonds a day and an occasional orange.

Alexandra grew used to life among the gnostics, all older than she, whom she particularly complimented on their "perfect urbanity . . . and utmost discretion." They enforced no rules or dogma. Normally, they congregated in the large, comfortable library, rich in works on alchemy, metaphysics, and astrology, and they read whatever treatise struck their fancy. Smoldering incense sticks lent an oriental aroma to the book-lined room. Some were inclined to puff incessantly on Turkish cigarettes, while others in trailing white robes glided soundlessly through the thick blue smoke.

The novice enjoyed the scene to the hilt. But even at twenty her critical faculty kept her aloof from believers or a mushy mysticism. In old age, Alexandra, mind clear as a temple bell, wrote a reminiscence of her youthful search, which she then declined to publish. Since she was always eager for the attention and money a book would bring in, this is unusual. However, this veiled memoir might prove embarrassing, especially if one know how to read between its lines. Finally issued posthumously, *Le sortilège du mystère* (*The Spell of Mystery*) chronicles the seeker's adventures into the world of metaphysics, cults, and drugs. In banding with the gnostics, whom she long afterward dubbed "extravagants," her purpose was "to discover the motives behind their singular conduct." No doubt, she was genuinely curious and hoped to learn about the world beyond the confines of the normal.

Besides, where else could a young lady put up cheaply and safely in Victorian London? The gnostics, asking a minimum of questions, left her free "to learn to speak English perfectly," and she would grow sufficiently fluent to sometimes write her works first in her adopted language and then translate them into French. More immediately, Alexandra was able to delve into the wealth of knowledge stored at the British Museum. Her carrel at that famous library began to be piled high with commentaries on Hindu philosophy, Buddhism, and Chinese Taoism. Down the sidestreets were bookshops specializing in such matters, into which might stroll a real turbaned Indian!

Elisabeth Morgan lived in a suburb and Alexandra saw her from time to time. She referred to this shadowy figure as her "godmother," although *marraine* may also mean "sponsor." Perhaps Mrs. Morgan did exercise supervision over the still naive, attractive maiden. Alexandra's morals were akin to those of any young lady of the period. She pretended modesty and generally kept her distance from men. She was scandalized that James Ward, who came from a good family, had abandoned Oxford to do occult researches, and she was truly horrified that he eventually succumbed to drugs.

London at this time presented a regular smorgasbord of occult societies and personalities. The Kabbala and the Rosy Cross had their devotees, as did cenacles of Egyptian magical rites. Spiritualism was a craze among high and low alike. Victor Hugo had adopted it while living on Guernsey, and he spent days on end tipping tables to contact the spirit of his drowned daughter. Distinguished intellectuals such as Sir Arthur Conan Doyle investigated the phenomena, and Queen Victoria was known to have dabbled. But the popular field belonged to the great performing mediums such as Douglas Home, who could lift up individuals; Florence Cook, who materialized a being known as "Katie King"; and the master of the trance, William Stainton Moses.

In spite of her excellent recall, Alexandra never mentioned seeing any of these famous mediums. Can it be that for once she wasn't curious? She paid the Spiritualists less attention than later she would give to a common Indian fakir lying on his bed of nails. Alexandra instinctively regarded the occultism of London, and later Paris, as a fine show but essentially wrongheaded. But it was more amusing than humdrum Brussels.

The preeminent figure of late nineteenth-century metaphysical investigation was, of course, *Madame* Helena P. Blavatsky, founder of the Theosophical Society, who in 1888 was resident in a little villa on Lansdowne Road, South London. On Saturdays, starting in the afternoon and often lasting till the wee hours, *Madame* would hold forth on the elements of the Secret Doctrine, imparted telepathically to her by the spiritual masters of Tibet. *Madame* orated in a stentorian voice—audible for blocks in that quiet neighborhood—to rapt audiences of her followers, her soon-to-be-enemies, and those who attended to the latest fashion. Alexandra, in an undated entry in her notebook probably made a few years later, recalled, "One day while writing [to me], Elisabeth let drop the word Theosophy with the name of Blavatsky." She admitted this had opened "a new phase of my life." It is tempting to suppose that Elisabeth Morgan brought Alexandra to the Society's Saturday meetings, but there is no direct evidence of it.

However, the influence of theosophical thought on David-Neel was greater than she cared to admit. In her time, Blavatsky the person and her concepts were not to be evaded. Next to Queen Victoria, no other woman commanded the allegiance of so many respectable men. Her philosophy—the "wisdom religion"—contained strong feminist elements. Blavatsky, born of the Russian nobility, was nearly the first modern European to disregard class, caste (in India), race, and sex.

Anyone was welcome to adhere to the principles of Theosophy, which were addressed to humanity at large.

Most important, this blowsy Russian woman with her unkempt mop of hair and deep, brooding, blue eyes—"a sort of female Dr. Johnson," as William Butler Yeats called her—if she didn't originate the notion that the ultimate secret teachings were geographically located in the trans-Himalayas, from whence they were "broadcast" to a chosen few, did identify this concept with herself. She created the image of Tibet as Shangri-La, the mother lode of ancient lore. Here the weary traveler would be rewarded with incredible answers to man's perpetual questions about life, happiness, and death. This heavy woman, whose swollen legs barely permitted her to move, inspired what became a craze to crash the gates of the last forbidden land on earth. Alexandra, younger and more agile, would reap the harvest sown by the theosophical planter of ideas.

The time was not ripe. Alexandra at twenty was both impressionable and skeptical, more in tune with the strict scientific approach of *Madame* Blavatsky's nemesis, the Society for Psychical Research, which had been founded in 1885 to dispassionately investigate psychic phenomena. Still, for months she spent her evenings reading in the library of the Gnosis, amidst the decidedly occult haze exhaled by its members. She might glance at the door to an inner sanctum ruled off limits to the profane. There the initiates conversed with Instructors, higher beings from the astral plane who were otherwise invisible. One evening a newcomer named Learner entered, chose a book and sat down on the sofa. Suddenly Miss Holmwood, a seasoned member, pointed to him and uttered a horrified cry. All eyes fell on the poor startled man.

"Learner, get up!" Miss Holmwood ordered. "You are sitting on an Instructor."

It may have been that the astral being, confused by the smoke, had wandered into the library by mistake. Even the gnostics couldn't see him, except for the agitated Miss Holmwood. She flung herself down in front of the sofa, quickly deserted, and wrung her hands in pitiful abnegation. Now two others "saw" the Instructor, while the rest peered hopefully through the customary volutes of blue.

A curiously parallel incident was reported by Yeats in a letter to his fellow Irish poet Katharine Tynan:

A sad accident happened at Madame Blavatsky's lately, I hear. A big materialist sat on the astral double of a poor young Indian. He was sitting on the sofa and he was too material to be able to see it. Certainy a sad accident!

This is certainly an odd coincidence! Or was Yeats mistaken about the locale of the "sad accident"? Had Alexandra, writing about the incident some seventy years later, forgotten where she witnessed it—

at Madame Blavatsky's salon? She was always anxious to avoid comparison and not about to credit Blavatsky with any influence on her quest. We cannot solve this minor mystery, but we must treat Alexandra on Alexandra with some care, not swallow her tales whole as her earlier biographers have done.

More immediate to the young woman was her relationship with *Monsieur* Jacques Villemain, *artiste parisien*. She was attracted to the slim, elegant esthete, with his delicate features and pale complexion, as she would be to others who held some knowledge she wanted. Too, he gave the impression of being a "gentleman," which reassured and pleased Alexandra. She remarked with satisfaction, "One could scarcely imagine him indulging in the foolishness of the Beaux Arts Ball."

Villemain painted in a peculiar metaphysical style: landscapes alive with menacing anthropomorphic forms, as though each rock or tree held a secret inner self peering at the viewer. In the artist's room, where she visited him, Alexandra regarded one such landscape of a snow-capped peak dominating a deserted salt lake, the whole vast and empty yet peopled with indistinct figures. Thoroughly absorbed, she moved to touch the painting, when the artist whisked it away.

"Careful," he warned. "You are going to enter the landscape; it is dangerous."

Alexandra begged Villemain to explain himself, but, refusing to elaborate, he put her off with tea and toast. Shortly after, he went into seclusion to practice an ascetic discipline. Miss Holmwood confided that he was a probationer who desired admittance to the secret cenacle. The young man turned up in time, gaunt and withdrawn, his health damaged by the routine of privation. To cheer him, as well as to corner him into answering her question, Alexandra suggested that they visit the Crystal Palace remaining from the Great Exposition of 1851. Incidentally, the structure had been moved to the same neighborhood in which *Madame* Blavatsky held her Saturdays.

The pair boarded a train in the midst of a London fog. Villemain was silent, sunk in thought, and Alexandra promptly fell asleep. She awoke at a siding and, calling out, discovered they had boarded the express to Scotland—in the opposite direction. The trainmen hustled them off, but they would have to wait until evening when a local came through to return to London. There was nowhere to go; it began to drizzle, and they sat under a little shelter. Alexandra, seizing her chance, demanded: What *had* he meant by "entering into a painting"?

Alexandra knew that boredom, if not her wiles, would win out. Soon the youthful occultist launched into strange tales of fate and our astral doubles in the other world. The hours sped by, and although the notions elaborated by Villemain to his young friend were scarcely original, harking back to Plato, they would curiously correspond to deeply held beliefs of Tibetan Buddhism. Alexandra was especially struck by one story that, taken symbolically, was filled with portent:

An artist had painted a picture of an oasis in Africa. A woman initiate went to view it. She became lightheaded, as though she were falling right among the palms. She walked about in the desert and, feeling warm, she wiped her face with a handkerchief. A sudden convulsion attacked her, and the woman, after dropping the kerchief, found herself back in the artist's atelier, in an armchair where evidently she had fainted. Searching for her kerchief, she saw it painted into the landscape at the foot of a palm! The artist swore he hadn't committed such an incongruity, and others affirmed they had seen the painting without the offending kerchief. The woman must have dropped it while she was strolling in the landscape.

Villemain believed in astral doubles, in a parallel nonmaterial reality, but Alexandra sought a more tangible explanation. Perhaps it was all a communicable delusion. On their return to town, she demanded they eat a good Italian dinner. Next day she decided to leave London. Still, Alexandra couldn't rid her mind of the barren, hostile landscape painting shown her by Villemain. It was strange yet so inviting. Decades afterward, as soon as she glimpsed Tibet, the traveler found herself entering into a landscape as dramatically fantastic as a Nicholas Roerich canvas:

In the intense silence of these wild majestic solitudes, icy, crystalline purling brooks chatted gently. From the shore of a melancholy lake, a golden-crowned bird solemnly watched my caravan as it passed. . . . As we issued from the mists the Tibetan tableland appeared before us, immense, void, and resplendent under the luminous sky of Central Asia.

Financially dependent, Alexandra returned to Brussels in 1889 to resume the study of music and voice. She was included in a circle of young intellectuals revolving around the old radical Elisée Reclus. But she remained discontent. While her parents quarreled over her future, she took it in her own hands. Elisabeth Morgan gave her the opportunity to again leave home, arranging for her to board cheaply with a branch of the Theosophical Society in the Latin Quarter of Paris.

The society's address was on the rather racy Boulevard St.-Michel— the "Boul Mich" of student fame—and Alexandra, primed for adventure, walked along the avenue searching for the number. Unfortunately, it was occupied by a greengrocer. But nearby she spotted a door the width of a narrow closet. Could *this* be it? She did not suspect that the French Theosophical Society had split into several antagonistic factions, and she had found her way to the humblest.

Reaching the third floor, she rang the bell. A tiny woman appeared, who cried, "Edmund, it is Miss David!"

She retreated into the dark hallway, so slender that Alexandra had to press against the wall to fit through. Edmund Jourdan, the small woman's husband, hurried to welcome his guest. But there was no disguising the shabbiness of the dim flat. Let down, Alexandra needed all her stoicism to keep from breaking into tears.

Mrs. Jourdan showed her to a dingy room. A bare mattress and a chair stood in the center of the room. Behind a screen were a table and basin and various pitchers, which were supposed to make up for the lack of a proper bathroom. Alexandra, fastidious by nature, grew more depressed. Worse was to come when dinner was served. The hungry young woman joined the Jourdans and their three-year-old son at table. Her stomach rebelled at the sight of hunks of rock-like potatoes and a bloated piece of bread swimming in boiled dishwater. A few spoonfuls of this soup and Alexandra determined to fast. The cook noted her guest's displeasure, and twitching her meager face, she described the meal as "strictly vegetarian." Alexandra politely replied that she was used to dining meatlessly at the London Gnosis.

This made Edmund Jourdan peevish. He ridiculed the Gnosis for being "out of the direct line." Patronizingly, he explained that his "spiritual ancestors were old, very old, dating from the time when the entities who peopled the earth were still connected to the moon." Certain gifted colleagues, he went on, were able to communicate with the moon beings and gain a rarefied knowledge. Perhaps Alexandra was more impressed than she wanted later readers to think. She commented, "While young, one is able to amuse oneself with [such] foolishness."

The group adjourned to the salon, which filled rapidly with regulars who scrutinized the new arrival. Alexandra feared she would be ignored or that her ignorance of the East might be discovered. She hoped these critical Theosophists would accept a sincere neophyte. But when she let slip her stay at the Supreme Gnosis to a mature gentleman, he backed away as though she were contaminated. The gnostics, he spumed, were "vulgar and profane, possibly vile imposters."

Madame Dejean, a senior member, approached to second her colleague. "Skin and bone," she resembled a bird of prey about to capture a fish in its beak. Everyone grew silent as she broadcast her erudition, claiming *en passant* to be familiar with all the Indian holy books in the original. Alexandra demurely inquired if the orator had studied at the Sorbonne or the Collège de France. The self-styled orientalist retorted, "Those official professors . . . They know nothing of Sanskrit! In lecturing they emit a noise like the rattle of dry bones. Their courses are cemeteries."

A dejected young woman retreated to her room to gaze out the window. Where were the broad-minded searchers after higher truths promised by Elisabeth Morgan? The pedestrian traffic below caught her eye. Alexandra stood at the center of that gaudy merry-go-round—

intensely bohemian for rich and poor alike—dubbed *La Belle Epoque*. The *habitués* of the Latin Quarter streamed along the boulevard, gay, lively, or rude, flaunting their costumes or wares. "A strange crowd," she would term the flow, "which comes, goes and presses toward ends I cannot understand." She was disturbed by the gestures of a fancy harlot to hoped-for customers seated at the café: perhaps a penniless poet next to a duke incognito, both drowned in absinthe. Had human ancestors descended from the moon to arrive at *this*?

Alexandra came to value Mrs. Jourdan as "the most delicious idiot," who captured her sympathy. Upon her fragile form devolved the society's clerical work and every domestic chore. How she strained to be mother, businesswoman, and cook simultaneously. She broke down at intervals, and when the odor of burned food wafted under Alexandra's door, she would leave to eat at a cheap restaurant. Mrs. Jourdan's sole consolation was to talk of her husband's powers, of his ability to sit motionless until his fingers turned green, or of the spiritual aura that emanated from his cranium. Edmund Jourdan, a former Communard, had once written political tracts and even successful novels, but his talents were now devoted entirely to occult researches.

Several devotees made up an inner circle which read the Bhagavad Gita in French, comparing it to the Sanskrit on a facing page. Usually they jumbled the two languages as do immigrants on first arriving in a strange country. *Madame* Dejean was both textual authority and high priestess. The gutteral sounds that issued from her "rapacious beak" made Alexandra squirm. When the rest joined in, a monotonous din filled the apartment. Meditation sometimes took precedence over scholarship, and the group sat stiffly on hard chairs until well past midnight. When the sitters were nearly crippled, Edmund Jourdan would clap hands and cry, "Return!"

The word was a signal to the spirits floating in the ether, which had to be recalled correctly. The members were warned to remain absolutely still while Jourdan realigned their astral and corporeal bodies. Alexandra feared that one day the master might mistake his spirits and envelopes and cause souls to inhabit bodies they had never known. However, the devotees always looked blissful as they lit their lamps to descend into the subdued Parisian night.

Now and then the Jourdans took Alexandra on walks around the sleeping city. They began after midnight when the air was presumed pure enough to elevate the *prana,* the power behind the breath. The trio strolled through picturesque quarters to see, in Baudelaire's phrase, "street lamps tormented by the wind." Returning at four in the morning, Mrs. Jourdan brewed coffee while they chatted until dawn. Such hours wore on Alexandra, who had enrolled in Sanskrit under the venerable Professor Philippe-Edward Foucaux at the Collège de France. Interestingly, her teacher had translated Sanskrit works into

Tibetan and written a grammar of that lanugage. Typically, he had never visited the Land of Snows—forbidden to Western eyes—but he spoke often about it, never dreaming his pupil would reach its mysterious capital.

Alexandra repeated the pattern set in London, replacing the British Museum with the Musée Guimet. Here she read on Eastern themes, regarded the paintings and statuary, and met people of like mind. Comfortable in Paris, she sampled from the broad menu of esoteric societies. Perhaps the most intriguing was the salon held by the Duchess de Pomar (Lady Caithness) at her mansion on rue de l'Université.

Alexandra recalled how she had climbed rose marble stairs to the ornate bedroom where the duchess received visitors. The ceiling was painted with angels circling a huge gold star. The duchess, a Spanish beauty, had married first an aged nobleman who obligingly died, then the Scottish Lord Caithness. Since she considered herself to be the reincarnation of Mary Queen of Scots, a tiny chapel in her boudoir contained a portrait of that unfortunate. Habitually, twelve votaries led by a female medium sat around a table, fingertips touching. They silently awaited a presence, while the sensitive mumbled and drifted into a trance. Flashing lights, gray smoke, and a delicious rose perfume heralded the arrival of Mary's ghost—head intact—who when she kissed someone was supposed to leave a visible mark.

Alexandra, after she had experienced similar phenomena in Tibet, gave this possible explanation:

The "spirits" that manifest themselves at the seances are elementals, disembodied spirits but conscious. They are more or less intelligent but stupified by their incongruous state of being, lacking a material envelope and the . . . sensory organs with which to participate in the world to which they had [once] belonged. These elementals desperately wish to reincarnate, to become "tied up" with living people . . . [T]hese entities tend to occupy temporarily those persons incapable of opposing them, or those who submit voluntarily. From this we have instances of possession and mediumship.

Whether Alexandra fully subscribed to this theory she failed to make clear. Certainly she presented Pomar as a light society figure, almost a quack, devoted with her "beautiful dames" to "the religion of the boudoir." However, the duchess was the author of some weighty tomes, notably *Serious Letters to Serious Friends*. Due to their heretical views, her books had shocked the clergy of Europe. Pomar was an associate of *Madame* Blavatsky and Annie Besant, and became cofounder of the Paris Lodge of the Theosophists. This ambitious woman was a radical thinker who advocated the "reign of the feminine brain." Her models harked back to neolithic days when female divinities possessed the traits that once again would be valued in future society. Woman—fecund, sensual, intuitive, and nonviolent—should lead the way to a new race and an era of peace. The old warlike male rulers, such as those lords who had usurped the power of Mary of Scotland, would become obsolete and vanish.

Today similar ideas, if not entirely accepted, are current, and we may wonder why Alexandra, ahead of her time in many ways, showed minimal interest in them. She personally suffered from the rabid antifeminism found in French intellectual circles. "The destiny of woman and her sole glory are to make beat the hearts of men. . . . She is a chattel . . . only a subsidiary to man." So wrote Honoré de Balzac in what was typical of most French, English, or American men. The founders of Theosophy—Blavatsky, Pomar, Annie Besant—scandalized the establishment because they were independent-thinking (and loving) women. But Alexandra David's commitment to the feminist movement stemmed from different political sources and an inherently freethinking personality.

Already she was not afraid to act on her beliefs. At the Jourdans, Edmund would sometimes hold secret sessions from which his wife, considered too flighty, and Alexandra, too bold, were excluded. The votaries would file into the inner chamber—the only one heated—looking neither right nor left. The hush was dreadful but soon broken by ghostly cries coming from the other side of the locked door. Bored, Alexandra would leave.

One winter evening she returned early to find a bluish Mrs. Jourdan sobbing in her icy kitchen. Crouched on a stool, her whines were echoed by her small, shivering son. Through chattering teeth the mother explained that out of respect for the higher beings she was relegated to this Siberia. She wouldn't complain but she feared for the child.

Alexandra strode to the door and pounded, calling, "Jourdan, your wife and child are going to get sick," till a bewildered Edmund opened it. His young boarder dressed him down for abandoning his family to influenza or worse, while the spiritualists stared daggers at her. The man's only response was to try vainly to appease his followers. "What a regrettable interruption!" declared one woman. "I think the meeting is over!" The moon beings flounced out of the flat wihtout a nod in the direction of poor Mrs. Jourdan.

Scenes such as these contributed to Alexandra's awareness. Discrimination against women was common in occult circles as well as elsewhere. Women were decidedly not welcome to J. K. Huysmans, author of *Lá-Bas,* a study of the satanic lust of Gilles de Rais, "Bluebeard." In dismissing the literary salons of his day, his final complaint was that the women were always intruding. Still, Huysmans is the most intriguing of the devotees of sorcery who, though not many, were influential in *fin-de-siècle* Paris where decadence constituted both a style and an atmosphere.

Alexandra was aware that cells of satanic worship existed, but they did not tempt her. "It was reported to me," she wrote, "[that] there would be midnight meetings [in the woods], celebrations of psalmodies and burning of incense and the cult of the woman." These gatherings were attended by "delivery boys, bank clerks and their spouses," and indeed she had heard of them from a cleaning lady. The satanic mass was inevitably followed by a sexual free-for-all, or as the Victorian delicately put it, "a promiscuity of embarrassments."

In her mature years in Tibet, Alexandra did experiment with practices that in the West might be termed "black magic." She was on friendly terms and learned much from the most feared *naljorpas* (wizards). Much of what the pathetic Parisian magicians destroyed themselves in trying to accomplish, Tibetan sorcerers performed with ease, and they could, if they were of a mind, explain how. Unlike the faddish occultists, Alexandra had both a driving curiosity and a healthy self-protective streak. Why should she settle for fool's gold when she had begun to mine the real thing?

In her early twenties, Alexandra was pursuing her studies at the Sorbonne under scholars who "knew the roots of words and historical dates." She was not a full-time student in the American sense but kept up her musical studies as well. This was typical of her and of the European system: T. E. Lawrence, although he earned a bachelor's degree from Oxford, scarcely attended a single lecture; rather, "he spent most of his time wandering about England on foot, or reading medieval literature." Alexandra did not stray so far afield but spent day after day reading intensively in the excellent library of the Guimet, not only in Eastern thought and religions but history, folklore, geography. Her mind needed to comprehend the whole of a subject to deeply understand it. She wrote, "The Musée Guimet housed within its walls more mystery, esoterism and high secrets than all the sects dispensing imaginary and childish initiations that attracted and duped so many *naïfs.*"

The museum was a temple of learning to the avid seeker, its cozy reading room a sanctuary from the frenetic world. To reach it she ascended a grand staircase past glorious frescoes: of a Brahmin tending a ritual fire, Buddhist monks in saffron togas carrying begging bowls, a vermilion Japanese temple amid snowy cherry blossoms with icy mountains in the background, and other similar scenes. Each depicted an aspect of the theme of a pilgrim proceeding toward the unraveling of the supreme mystery. All the fascinating places in the world beyond Suez beckoned to Alexandra.

At the head of the stairs stood a large gilt statue of the Buddha enthroned, a smile hinting up his moon-shaped face. Alexandra would habitually salute it on her way into or out of the library. This enigmatic graven image spoke to the young scholar, although not in French or English. An object of prayer for ages, the statue had stored some of the energy, the devotion, poured into it, much as the earth holds the heat of the sun. As the sand of the desert can in the middle of the night give off warmth, so the stone Buddha returned the radiance of his vanished devotees. At least, this is the explanation preferred by Alexandra. But here she gives the rationalization, not the feeling.

Another instance of such communication comes from the noted British Buddhist John Blofeld. He writes of hearing an image of Kuan Yin, Chinese goddess of compassion and granter of favors large and small, reply to his doubts with the following words: "Look not for my reality in the realm of appearances . . . Seek it in your own mind." Blofeld, a most respected authority on Buddhism, kept this experience secret from Westerners for decades out of fear of ridicule.

Finally, Blofeld has accepted the belief that the being Kuan Yin can, at least in the realm of thought, communicate with him. Alexandra clung to the explanation that she had heard her inner self bounced off an outer, material form. Whether her feeling of oneness with the Buddha stemmed from a subjective or objective basis—a tenuous distinction in the East—it was in front of this statue in the midst of *Belle Epoque* Paris, while paying homage in the traditional Indian manner with palms pressed together in front of the heart, head bowed, that Alexandra received an instance of what her Huguenot forebears would have called "God's grace." Between her and the Buddha image passed an intimation of things to come.

It is mistaken, though, to suppose the basically unhappy and frustrated young woman had suddenly converted to Buddhism. Later in life she liked to give that impression, but really she was still oscillating from pole to pole. About this time she scribbled in her notebook:

Catholic by birth, Protestant by name, I have read the Koran and Plato. I have dreamed with India the myths of the Ramayana, and the sweet prayers of the Rig Vedas sometimes rise to my lips [as I kneel] in front of the hearth or the lamp. . . . Zoroaster almost enrolled me under his banner . . . How many voyages I have made in divers worlds!

Alexandra at twenty-one or two was still struggling to find her own way out of the common path. Still, whatever might intervene, the young woman had determined on a direction to her life. "Vocations are born," wrote the older woman, of her time at the Guimet. "Mine was born there."

CHAPTER 4

The Handgun

In 1889 the government of the Third Republic determined to hold another universal exposition, or world's fair, to commemorate the centenary of the French Revolution. President Sadi Carnot, the bearer of a great Republican name, inaugurated the proceedings, which were intended to display France's worldly and artistic wealth and to attract a horde of tourists to Paris. This city of two-and-a-half million had outstripped every rival as the capital of pleasure. Thanks to the appearance of what Parisians termed "the electric fairy," it was becoming a true city of light.

The exhibitions ranged from an enormous gallery of machines to the reconstruction of a street in Cairo complete with belly dancers. Many countries displayed their productions, but scientific discoveries such as Edison's phonograph and the Curies' radium were of the greatest interest to the throngs of visitors. In the center of the grounds stood the idol consecrated to the dawning age of engineering, that summation of French genius in soaring iron and glass: the Eiffel Tower.

Although this fretwork sculpture of giant proportion has come to symbolize Paris, the *citoyens* hated it at first. While it was being built, many were certain it would tumble down on their heads. Gustave Eiffel had to guarantee indemnity in case of an accident. A committee of artists dashed off a manifesto denouncing the edifice "dominating Paris like a black, gigantic factory chimney." Work proceeded, and although we don't have Alexandra David's reaction to the "vertiginously ridiculous tower," she probably favored it. The tower was a great symbol of scientific progress, in which she then believed, and of power—masculine—which she sorely lacked. 1889 marks the first of Alexandra's neurasthenic crises, not unrelated to events in the world about her.

"I have a terrible judge in me that won't let me rest," sighed the ambitious young woman that spring. She was studying English, Sanskrit, music, and voice. While she kept certain goals in sight, she could prepare for no definite career—those open to women were too limited.

Nor could she free herself from financial dependence on her parents, and she was obliged to bounce back and forth between Paris and Brussels. Not surprisingly, Alexandra internalized her objective situation and attempted to emancipate herself from what she deemed unworthy passions and habits. "I have seen the nothingness of human pleasures," she recorded in her diary. "I know of the highest but my strength is lacking to climb [there]."

Alexandra's morbid streak was winning out, and her diet of exclusively philosophical reading didn't help. At an age when other women thought of lovers or marriage, pretty and petite, she was tormented by understandable desires and fears. To her little book she confided her doubts: "To believe in love, to love, is to offer one's heart up to betrayal, infidelity that would wound it, to mistrust that would scorn it, to grossness that would make its delicacy fade." She had little better to write about friendship or men.

Death rather than life was on Alexandra's mind. "Under the golden tunic of the idols [I] find only emptiness or a dreadful corpse being devoured by worms." She predicted, wrongly, that she would die young. Alternating between numbing despair and stoic resolution, she nearly made the prophecy self-fulfilling by contemplating, and perhaps attempting, suicide. "How can I conquer a conviction that slowly seeps into me? There is an idea that, chased from my thoughts, always returns," she wrote. "If it triumphed I would kill myself." Then she would chide herself, remembering that she belonged to "a new cult made up of only a small number." She was where she had to be: "Don't bother yourself except to accomplish well the mission assigned to you, without worrying about the missions of others."

The above is suggestive language, especially for a former debutante who kept a pistol in her room. Hyperbole is always suspect, especially coming from a young woman trying to suppress her instincts, wishing admiration from men yet fearful of "choosing an hour of madness rather than sweet peace." But Alexandra's handgun was real, and at some point on the border of 1890–91, she loaded it and thought of pulling the trigger. She decided not to kill herself on two grounds, one Buddhist: "[O]ne of these bullets that is in the chamber will disperse the atoms of which my body is formed," but it could not "annihilate the spirit." She already believed she would be reincarnated to suffer the consequences.

The second reason was momentarily perhaps more weighty. Suicide amounted to "quitting [my] post like a deserter." True, the twenty-two-year-old, writing to herself, was capable of romantic posing, especially when she compared herself to Goethe's Werther. Still, her "lifestyle" in the early nineties suggests a pattern. She had comrades that she distrusted and lied to, and furthermore she possessed an undue amount of money, for which she chided herself. Alexandra also had access to drugs. There are hints that she was leading an underground life as a political radical. Nothing is certain except her mood, alternating between despair and rebellion: "I feel my blood boil and my skin creep in supreme revolt."

Alexandra, unlike the vast majority of women of her day, not only owned a pistol but later on when she had to use it, in Tibet, knew how. Her father, who kept hunting dogs, may have taken his daughter along and taught her to shoot. She certainly hated the sport, terming it the mere murder of animals. In the 1960s, Jeanne Denys insisted concerning Alexandra David, "She must have had a run-in with the law." The Belgian authorities informed Denys, "There exists [on Alexandra] dossier number 508–533 at the Foreign Police of the Ministry of Justice." Denys requested the folder but was denied. The authors have determined that such files are open only for governmental purpose or to relatives.

Denys's motives are suspect, but from the viewpoint of the Belgian police Alexandra was involved in shady doings. Over two decades later, the British Government of India, concerned about her activities there, investigated her past. They concluded that, at the least, she had radical associates in Paris as well as Brussels. Was the youthful thinker's bent toward anarchism more than theoretical; did it involve her in what today we would call a terrorist cell? In a much later work, Alexandra stated, "I profoundly despise everything connected with politics and I avoid mixing in such matters." Disillusion or cover-up?

The young woman survived her personal crisis, or really crises, and so did the French president Carnot. At the beginning of his term the Republic, threatened from left and right, appeared as unstable as Eiffel's folly. When an International Socialist Congress dared to meet in public, the bourgeoisie quaked in their parlors. They felt no more trust in the monarchist alternative, General Boulanger, the "man on horseback." However, at the opportune moment this would-be Napoleon got cold feet and refused to spur his mount; the reactionary coup fizzled.

By 1890, save for the indestructable Eiffel Tower, the exposition had faded into memory, and the good citizens could breathe a sigh of relief. *Tout Paris*—high and low—fell to entertaining itself. That summer was a lark to young Havelock Ellis. In *From Rousseau to Proust* he recalled the heady feelings he had then. He was welcomed with the budding esthetes who frequented the poet Mallarmé's Tuesday evenings, and with the rest of the Latin Quarter, he observed Paul Verlaine (whose love for young Arthur Rimbaud had wrecked his marriage) contentedly drinking himself to death at a café on the boulevard des Italiens. It exhilarated the aspiring bohemian—explorer of the forbidden realm of sex—to stroll along the wide, chestnut tree-lined boulevards. His admiring glances were returned by expensively garbed, if suspect, ladies who were accustomed to midnight suppers at sumptuous Maxim's.

They expected their entrance on whoever's arm to make every head turn.

Even the high life was financially comfortable for an Englishman. "Nowhere is existence cheaper than at Paris," insisted the travel writer Augustus Hare. Charming apartments were available for a pound per week, fresh food flowed in from the market gardens, and women acted like nowhere else. Not without reason, the Parisienne had become the universal sex symbol, whether in the silly farces of the period, the superb posters, or the absurd dreams of men far and wide. *Poules* were everywhere, plumed and bejeweled in their carriages or ragged and pitiful as they clawed at drunken workingmen in back alleys. At the Moulin Rouge, Toulouse-Lautrec drank absinthe and sketched the already painted girls as they kicked precariously in the air. To the *Belle Epoque* we accord the invention of the striptease.

Continental life had a more earnest and darker side, and it was within this somber margin that Alexandra presently moved. Here she came to feel the influence of the old Communard Elisée Reclus. After some years of wandering he had settled in the 1870s at Ixelles, a suburb of Brussels, and embarked on the composition of his grand *Géographie universelle*. This was one of the first truly scientific works in the field. A monumental task, Reclus didn't let it absorb him entirely; he was always at the service of his comrades. One of these was Louis David, who was more often than not his neighbor at Ixelles. The Davids were steadily refused permission to reside in the capital, and they moved about from house to house in the suburbs.

Reclus was no armchair theoretician, but an uncompromising radical. He continued to edit the far-left review *La Rive Gauche,* and to write such provocative, if absurdly titled, manifestos as *Worker Take the Machine! Farmer Take the Earth!* He officiated at the marriage, dispensing with clergy or magistrate, of his two daughters to like-minded young men. Most important, he threw open his pleasant home with its lush garden to young people whom he encouraged to gather and air controversial notions. It was under the roof of this apostle of free love that Alexandra met political exiles, bearded freethinkers, emaciated poets, and other merchants of dreams.

Here men and women, genteel or working class, were welcomed equally. These hopeful ones would sit around a table on which perched a couple bottles of cheap wine and argue philosophy or politics late into the night, each ecstatic face lit by an interior flame. Alexandra, the mature author, wondered what had become of those early comrades. Older, wiser, she knew at least some, in their search for justice, had "won the crown of martyrdom, dying young after bitter lessons, despairing of humanity." In a sense, these rebels would be reincarnated on the streets of the Left Bank during the 1968 student uprising, to which Alexandra lent her blessing in her hundredth year.

Elisée Reclus was a father figure to the young woman, or rather a counter to her own weak-willed father. Like Louis David, he was her teacher—the next in a line of exclusively male mentors. A photo of Alexandra from those years, taken in Reclus's garden, shows her dressed soberly in a high-collared blouse buttoned to the neck, a man's tie folding into a skirt that falls to her boots. She appears to be a perfect bluestocking. Her hair is curly, short, and unadorned; not a frill relieves the austerity of the ensemble. Clearly, she doesn't frequent the *maisons* of Worth or Doucet, where socialites flock to spend lavishly on the latest fashions. This pretty young woman won't break the heart of any petty prince or rotund banker. She stands at attention, right foot forward as though to be off to some distant place.

For the moment, Alexandra got no farther than Paris, which she termed "fatal . . . weighing upon [my] soul." There black still more than red was the color of rebellion, as though in mourning for the crushed Commune. Its leading figure had been Auguste Blanqui, the "Old One," a perpetual plotter and jailbird. Famous for his black hat, suit, and gloves, Blanqui bequeathed to the French Left an aesthetic of conspiracy for its own sake. After a general pardon the exiles had returned, to mix with nihilists from Moscow, Marxists from Berlin, and especially anarchists from every industrial slum in Europe. A heady aroma of revolution wafted in the air.

The artistic situation, too, was in ferment. Paul Gauguin and his followers began to make a change in static, academic perceptions with their *Salon des indépendants*. These neoimpressionists felt they were at war with the very eyesight of the bourgeoisie, not to mention the investments in Cupid sporting with nudes that the rich had hung on the walls of their mansions. The painters, along with symbolist poets and other riffraff, called themselves anarchists and freely contributed their work to *Le revolt* and other provocative far-left reviews. Gauguin made the ultimate break when, despairing of Europe, he left for Tahiti to rediscover the splendor of barbarism. In effect, he declared the chasm between individual creativity and the constraints of Western society to be unbridgeable. He and writers such as Pierre Loti launched the vogue of Orientalism, which was to find its way into the parlors of the middle class and into the heart of a sufficiently susceptible young Parisienne.

Alexandra's dreams of the East might have remained mere fantasy had not a trick of fate intervened. By 1891, in her early twenties, her alternatives were narrowing. She might teach or become governess to a rich brat, or, as her parents hoped, marry well. If she were more of a coquette she could find a wealthy old protector and scheme to get included in his will. The properly brought up *Mademoiselle* David wasn't bohemian in her tastes: she hesitated at a singing career with its in-evitable demands of the flesh.

In any event, Alexandra did inherit—out of the blue—a considerable sum on the death of her "godmother." This may mean her mother's adopted mother, or perhaps Elisabeth Morgan. Had the latter ear-marked the money for her *protégée* to visit India? This is what Alex-andra immediately considered doing. *Madame* David was appalled and insisted she invest the entire sum in a nice little tobacconist shop. Louis, aged 76, semiretired and living off stocks and rents, weakly seconded his wife's eminently practical plan. He understandably wished his only child to remain close to him.

Alexandra was thrown into more of a quandary than she later cared to admit. In Paris she was entering doubtful company, or as she puts it, "certain refined nihilist and anarchist salons." Then there were the groups *"mystique-gnostique-occultiste,"* usually following some guru, with which she was acquainted and away from which her parents wished to pry her in order to reintroduce her into "the *haute bourgeoise* social milieu pertaining to [my] family." To one of these cults, led by Sri Ananda Saraswati, the young woman resorted sometime in 1891 to resolve her dilemma.

The followers of this popular guru heavily used drugs, particularly North African hashish (concentrated pollen of the marijuana plant, often laced with opium) for the purpose of obtaining visions in astral travel. Here Alexandra, hoping for a revelation, smoked a hash ciga-rette. She wrote about it in *Sortilége,* although she disguised herself as "a curious young man" and wrote in the third person. This indirection is typical of one who would eventually become a master of masks.

A few puffs on the butt induced a dreamlike reverie. The young man saw himself—or rather his astral double—"in the vestibule of his parent's home at twilight, the vestibule and stairs enveloped in a gloomy light. . . . The phantom voyager was seized by a frightfully oppressive sensation, weakness, an agony both physical and mental." He feared that once having entered he would be made a prisoner, a robot, and a "violent horror" of this fate awoke him from the dream. His—or her—decision could be postponed no longer. "[That] same evening the young man reached a port from where, some days later, he left for the Orient."

Although Alexandra felt her use of hash on this occasion to be ben-eficial, a recent biographer claims she never again smoked it. There exists no evidence on the matter, but the claim is typical of her later years when she denied that drugs were ever useful in occult or mystical investigations. In assessing this shrewd woman, we must constantly be wary of playing the dupe. In spite of never formally writing an auto-biography, Alexandra was able to structure the view of her held by succeeding generations. She took pains to distance herself from occultists, yet she certainly practiced a version of astral or etheric travel, and in *Sortilége* she described its mechanics and sensations in some detail, the while admitting its visions might be the product of autosuggestion.

At any rate, the young woman instinctively understood the message of her subconscious, and she quickly fled her parents' designs on her money and freedom. For over a year she traveled through Ceylon and India to the foot of Mount Kinchenjunga on the Nepali-Sikkimese border, its five snowy crowns overwhelmingly visible on a clear morning from Darjeeling, beckoning the voyager on to the mysterious beyond.

Not a great deal is known about Alexandra's first voyage to the Subcontinent at twenty-three. On her second, far more significant journey, which began in 1911 and lasted some fourteen years, she would at first recapitulate her earlier itinerary before plunging into the forbidden land of Tibet. She brought with her on this initial trip certain preconceptions: she clubbed with the Theosophists while in India and may have formally joined the society there. She had an interview with Annie Besant, *Madame* Blavatsky's successor, at the society's headquarters at Adyar. In the spring of 1893, back in Brussels, she wrote to Besant to ask her advice on meditation. Passages such as the following from an article penned in 1904 by Alexandra David, "The Religious Power of Tibet," show a clear and lingering theosophical influence: "It seems that living so close to heaven, these inhabitants [the Lamas] are naturally brought close to the superhuman beings they are thought to be. . . . They have reversed the fable of the gods descending from Olympus to mingle with men."

Reflecting an inner, and continuing, contradiction, the earnest seeker had declared herself in the same article to be "a rational Buddhist," a reformer, one who wished to return to the stark Socratic simplicity of the actual man, Gautama, who had become Buddha. In Benares, holy if impoverished city on the banks of the Ganges River, Alexandra studied yoga with a naked eminence, Bashkarananda, who lived year round in a rose garden. "Perhaps the Swami wasn't very erudite," she wrote, "even though he composed several treatises on Vedantic philosophy. But he had a deep understanding of Indian thought, and with him I was to have been initiated in my twenty-fifth year."

However, Alexandra's studies were destined to be interrupted. She retained a fond memory of her nut brown guru, and when she returned to Benares nearly twenty years later, she rushed to the garden. Bashkarananda had passed away with her youth, and the roses were strangled by weeds.

During the fateful winter of 1892–93, Alexandra, having spent her own funds, and worn down by the heat, famine, and poverty of India, returned to the familiar overcast grayness of Europe. To a degree she had succeeded in her goals of finding the contemplative life and sitting at the feet of wise men. In Brussels, once again dependent on her parents, she responded by a sharp turn to the Left. Encouraged by Elisée Reclus, she set to work on an anarchist "hymn to life," the lengthy essay *Pour la vie*. "This is a proud book," Reclus would state in its preface, "written by a woman prouder still." He could speak with authority, since eventually he was going to bear the risk of publishing this immoderate tract.

The ideas set forth in *La vie* originated in part with two Chinese philosophers who flourished in the fourth century B.C.: Mo-Ti and Yang Chu, who had challenged the accepted bases of social order. Alexandra freely acknowledged her sources, for they shared the modern perception that humans should forget about the gods and live well on earth. According to Mo-Ti, people should be kind to one another out of self-interest. He suggested that, in order to avoid unpleasantness and unrest, people act toward their neighbors as though they loved them. But it was best to ignore abstract ideals, since human beings hadn't the capacity to carry them out. Alexandra admired this early philosopher's absence of heroic rhetoric, and she supported his contention that an equality of wealth would discourage warfare and the struggle between classes.

Yang Chu was a real fire-breather. He blasted all laws, particularly those that confined human instinct. People must be free to attain happiness in the world, and institutions or custom only trammeled them. All one had to do was live in accord with universal order (nature) and disregard social directives. Yang castigated those cowards who went toward death like "chained animals never having lived." Sounding contemporary, he urged everyone to "be yourself."

Another major influence on Alexandra's thought was Max Stirner, the German individualist who reacted against Hegel in the mid-nineteenth century. His life was mediocre, but his book *The Ego and His Own* converted Alexandra from a libertarian in spirit to one in doctrine. Stirner, scorning the common person as "a dog dragging his chain," celebrated the egotist brave enough to heed natural instincts, which he assumed were in accord with "the laws of the universe." In the German romantic tradition, he glorified the self. "Every moment," he wrote, "the fetters of reality cut the sharpest welts in my flesh. But *my own* I remain."

Stirner anticipated Nietzsche's assertion that "God is dead." He implored humans to give the ego free reign, even if it meant committing crimes. At his most bellicose, he announced, "I prefer one free *grisette* [whore] over a thousand virgins grown gray in virtue." Of course all this has the ring of *La Bohème*, not to mention the sort of nasty romanticism that would help to provide the underpinning for a fascist aesthetic. However, Alexandra, who personally couldn't stand to take orders—but who would grow very good at issuing them—echoed the frustrated German with: "Every moment a man submits to an outside will is an instant taken away from his life."

From a distance, the well-bred young woman sympathized with French workers, among the worst paid in Europe. These descendants of the revolution lived hopeless lives in squalid warrens, while the rich spent more ostentatiously than ever. The explosive situation indeed led to the *Manual for the Perfect Dynamiter*, an anonymous best-seller in radical circles of the 1890s. But Alexandra, like Stirner, held that one must emancipate oneself, learn rebellion rather than revolution. She was not cut out to become a heroine of the Left, another Louise Michel. Unlike that fighter (literally) for women's rights, heroic speaker, and France's "Red Virgin," Alexandra was both too thoughtful and too self-absorbed to accept a role, even a leading one, in a mass movement.

The most intriguing aspects of *La vie* are those that stem from Alexandra's heartfelt experience. She damned the artificial faith of her mother and a "cruel god who makes one pay in advance for celestial happiness by pain and tears." Early experiments in mortifying the flesh, in her desire to become saintly, had resulted in "an overly sensitive soul" unfit to meet the demands of the world. The society of her day she viewed as the "enforcer of constraint and death." She condemned the amassing of property and particularly by inheritance. This was bound to lead to "covetous children who had no interest beyond inheriting from their parents."

What was the relationship between this extended literary outburst and the events of 1893? Panic gripped the stock markets of the capitals of the world, and, compounded by the collapse of French efforts to build a Panama Canal, it was especially acute on the Paris Bourse. Louis David's treasured investments turned into worthless pieces of paper. He could no longer afford to underwrite his daughter's fancies, and her inheritance was much diminished. Her shock at the loss, and the necessity of choosing a means of livelihood, turned to anger at a society where her own position was threatened. Hopelessly lost in the crowd of *Belle Epoque* pleasure seekers, Alexandra found herself equally out of step with the tempo of politics as desperation led to an uncompromising terrorism.

While the youthful *philosophe* scribbled, groups named "The Handgun" or the "Terribles" counterfeited, robbed, and assassinated in the name of Anarchy. Never very many, these terrorists—with methods that seem quaint today—succeeded in thoroughly frightening the bourgeoisie. A certain Ravachole, a former grave robber, managed to blow up a few houses and maim people. Condemned to death, he refused a priest and marched to the guillotine singing the Marseillaise.

Showing scorn was *de rigueur* for convicted anarchists, who soon became the heroes of popular ballads. Their bombs were usually cast-iron soup pots with the lids fastened firmly over sticks of dynamite and iron scraps. Imagine sneaking such a contraption into a public place! Still, in 1893 a bomb was thrown from the gallery into the Chamber of Deputies, wounding several lawmakers. An unbalanced young man, Auguste Vaillant, immediately confessed to the crime, and he too was sentenced to death. "Long live Anarchy!" he cried at the end.

Executions of anarchists began to draw large, enthusiastic crowds, especially the guillotining of Emile Henry in 1894. He had hurled a bomb into the café of a railway station filled with people sipping aperitifs. When asked in court whether he intended to wound innocent people, he replied, "There are no innocent *bourgeoises*." Georges Clemenceau, the World War I leader, sympathetically witnessed the last moments of the brave, if deranged, youth's twenty-second year.

The wave of terror crested with the murder of the popular president of the Republic, Sadi Carnot, on June 24. An Italian stabbed him to death. France had been pushed too far, and the police raided leftist dens and homes, rounding up the usual suspects. Thirty anarchist writers and journalists were put on trial, but their witty replies turned the proceedings into a fiasco. Nonetheless, some radicals fled into exile and others went underground. Elisée Reclus, who had argued that even robbery by a poor man was justifiable, accepted the safe position of professor of geography at the New University of Brussels. Anarchy, as a political movement, was decapitated.

Although Alexandra David hadn't yet published her subversive "hymn"—and wouldn't until five years had passed—she was known to the police in Brussels and Paris. They retained dossiers on her, which they passed on to the British nearly twenty years later. Evidently she was guilty of nothing really incriminating. More immediate was her problem of contributing to her own living. Alexandra was obliged to fall back on strictly feminine assets: brunette good looks and an excellent soprano voice. In pursuing her new career, she found it prudent to lose herself in the obscurity of Paris, to forget most of her old comrades, and to assume an alias.

CHAPTER 5

Manon

From 1894 to the end of the decade, *Mademoiselle* David lived and worked as an aspiring *chanteuse*, performing under the name of *Mademoiselle* Myrial (from a character out of Hugo). Was she ashamed of her new profession? Sopranos were the stars, the sex symbols, of turn-of-the-century Europe. If successful, they were public figures, obliged to make grand entrances on the arm of a duke or count at select restaurants. They were expected to dress naughtily and spend freely and to sleep with the influential older men of their milieu, composers and impresarios. Otherwise they failed to land the coveted roles.

Information about Alexandra's stage career is scanty to the point where the librarian at l'Opéra de Paris could find no trace of her under any name. But from the actual evidence we may conclude she had a lyric, coloratura voice, delicate enough to attempt the fragile ornamentation of Leo Delibes's popular "Bell Song." She sang roles composed by Bizet, Gounod, Puccini, and especially Jules Massenet. Her great success was as Manon, the coquette with a soft heart and an ominous fate. Toward the end of this artistic period of her development Alexandra wrote a more or less autobiographical novel; never published, it reveals an aspect of her inner self.

"High Art" (subtitled "Memoirs of an Actress") includes a rare tender scene in which Alexandra's mother plays a part. She is writing of her youth in Belgium:

With my passion for adventure is linked the extreme love of music. In the summertime I sometimes accompanied my mother to Ranelagh where they gave symphonic concerts. This was my holiday which allowed me to live a special, totally different life, awakening in my soul a thousand different feelings—joyful or painful—desires, confused regrets . . . With the end of the concert I would return next to my mother, silent, trembling.

Whatever her other preoccupations, Alexandra had clung to the love of music. Now, however, she studied with an almost feverish diligence. When she had exhausted the resources at the Brussels Conservatory, she moved on to Paris. She composed music and, as usual, her goal was high: to win the coveted Prix de Rome. Massenet had done it, so why shouldn't she? In this she did not succeed.

Living as a poor student in Paris was difficult now that she had to search for her daily bread, alone in the immense city. Alexandra later reminisced about her "herring days" when a grocery store would give her potatoes and a dozen herrings on credit. Boiled together, this was all she had to eat as she practiced scales. Still, the glamorous world of opera promised a way out. "Magic art, divine art, I only saw by it. I devoured scores, impassioned by them as though they were novels come alive where I heard heroes speak in harmonious phrases . . ."

There was another side to the operatic life, and Alexandra commented grimly on how she watched backstage mothers turn their daughters into whores. She, however, had a backstage father: Louis David, always full of helpful advice or nostrums, fully approved of his daughter's direction. The opera was a conventional course, if fraught with certain dangers. He was delighted when, solely on her talent, she was selected in autumn 1895 to tour Indochina with the road company of l'Opéra-Comique. She was to be billed as their *première chanteuse* in Hanoi and Haiphong.

"I had nostalgia for Asia before I ever went there," Alexandra once quipped. On board the steamer bound for the Gulf of Tonkin, the singer's cabinmate criticized her for bathing daily, claiming it would ruin her skin. Alexandra didn't care for "the jovial and libertine society" in which she found herself. Nor did she have any compliments for France's "devil colony" where the young men and women of the company gave themselves up to "intrigues."

Her first triumph was as Violetta in *La Traviata*. She immediately sent a clipping from the local paper to Louis David with instructions to bring it to the notice of the Belgian papers. This was a pattern she was going to repeat in different circumstances with the man we may term her backstage husband. The *première chanteuse* was already creating a certain image. She studied her roles with care and even oversaw the making of her costumes. She sang Thais in a "coat of silk entirely covered with pearls and gold," which she had copied from a description given by a courtesan of that epoch. She portrayed Delibes's Lakmé—a role of great delicacy—with success, fed herself well (for a change), and obeyed her father's injunction to take quinine regularly and avoid the "miasmas of the terrain."

Then Alexandra made a grave, if understandable, mistake. The director of the opera house at Hanoi, impressed by her ability to fill the house, offered her two hundred francs per night to sing Carmen several nights running. Recalling her "herring days," the singer, in her prime at twenty-eight, accepted. Carmen is a part for a husky contralto, the lowest female voice. The great Maria Callas burned out her voice by abusing it, attempting this very role, and so, alas, did the youthful Alexandra, although the trouble was not immediately manifest.

The would-be prima donna returned to Paris for the season of 1897. She had already initiated a correspondence with Jules Massenet, cleverly asking his advice concerning the character of Manon. He had taken unusual pains with the psychology of his opera. Alexandra perfectly understood that lost but striving woman, unwilling to accept a mediocre lot; and France's leading composer in a letter of that spring praised her "voice and [her] talent." We don't know, however, that he ever heard her sing. A projected rendezvous seems never to have happened. However, Massenet, an obliging man, recommended her to Leon Carvalho, director of the Opéra-Comique, before he fled the Paris winter for the south.

Alexandra was left to face Carvalho by herself. The director, despite his fame as the composer of sentimental operas, was a hardheaded businessman. He recognized the singer's potential and offered her a bit part at three hundred francs per month. This was little more than she had earned each night at Hanoi. Louis David flew to the rescue, writing to his old friends, including one senator. But political lobbying proved useless in artistic circles: Alexandra could starve in Paris or sing for better pay in the provinces. In the spring of 1897 she departed for a tour of the Midi.

In the Midi, Alexandra experienced her first sexual encounter. Previous biographical opinion has suggested that she had a strange aversion to men. The idea is patently absurd of a woman who loved her father, had a long marriage, adopted a son, and who dreamed of her own sort of romance. In reality she was neither unnatural nor a prude. True, she could pretend scorn: "Love seemed to me a pretty invention of the novelists." But she had a great need for, and responded to, fatherly affection. Victor Hugo, a bear of a man, was the first to unabashedly hug and fondle the little girl. This physical authority was an essential quality that Alexandra would look for in a husband. Eventually she was able to transmute the father role into that of mentor or guru, although those men too would be physical types. Finally they became her companion explorers, respected equals.

Alexandra was attracted also to another type of man, the younger brother or friend. Possibly this made up for the early loss of her own brother. A certain sexual aura, although muted, pervaded these relationships. Eventually this need was filled by her adopted son Yongden. Of course, Alexandra's ideal man would have to play both roles simultaneously, to be at once authoritative and sensitive. Alexandra summed up her stance in a letter of 1904 to her husband: "I don't offer little sentimentalities, a lot of sob-stuff. But I would grandly love [the man] who showed himself worthy, who loved me as an equal."

Did her ideal man ever come into view? We believe so, but only after it was, in a strict sense, too late. In the meantime, the grown woman of nearly thirty had tired of her chastity. She was slipping from the status of maiden to that of old maid. Conventional marriage she still considered out of the question, since it would deprive her of most legal rights. What she needed, especially if she wished to live in Paris, was a roommate rather than a husband.

Alexandra found the right young man: Jean Haustont, composer and fellow orientalist. A photo shows a tall, slender, earnest fellow without much force of character. He is attractive, appropriately bearded, and he was probably fair-haired. Jean had been born in Brussels in 1867, and he was introduced to Alexandra by a painter at a meeting of the Theosophical Society. Clearly they had a lot in common.

In the unpublished novel "High Art" Jean is depicted as the pianist Pierre: melancholy, with troubled blue eyes. He falls in love with Cécile (Alexandra), the glamorous singer, while she feels "tender pity for this lone boy . . . whom no one cared about or loved." While they flirt weakly at rehearsals—the touring opera company is at Bayonne—a certain Greek stagehand is eying Cécile. He has a more vivid idea of what she would look like with her clothes off than does poor Pierre.

The events described in "High Art" cannot be taken literally, especially when they contravene the psychology of our real-life characters. In the novel the Greek brutally rapes Cécile, who swoons and falls into a brain fever that lasts for weeks. Her life hangs by a thread as loyal Pierre nurses her, soiled woman that she is. This sort of melodrama was popular in its day, but it doesn't ring true: Alexandra was never so passive. The stagehand was probably her first lover, but only because she had wearied of her virginity and decided to make use of him. Jean Haustont, whom she desired, was not the type to initiate an affair, still less to deflower a virgin.

Alexandra was at her pitch of beauty at this time. A photo of her dressed in an elaborate opera costume shows a fully rounded but still petite figure, a symmetrical face whose most striking feature is a pair of brooding almond eyes set in high cheekbones. The nose is her father's straight but delicate one, and her mouth is set in a sensual pout, lower lip turned out. The ensemble is capped by a frizzed coiffure from which trails a long fake braid. Later, when her looks turned matronly, she continued to carry herself with the air of a beauty.

Alexandra and Jean moved in together in a flat in suburban Passy, and here they lived and worked for most of the next three years. Significantly, they went under the name of *Monsieur* and *Madame* Myrial, which Alexandra would adopt as a *nom de plume*. They wrote a lyrical drama in one act—"Lidia"—Jean the music and she the words. No one seemed interested in staging it. Quiet bohemians, they visited Elisée Reclus, who gave them his blessing, as did Louis David. The old gentleman liked Jean and corresponded with him when his daughter was away on an operatic junket. He envied what he supposed was their true love.

In 1898 Reclus published *Pour la vie* in Brussels and no one took any notice. Alexandra still couldn't obtain an engagement in Paris or any of the other major opera houses of Europe. She began to frequent the salon of Joséphin Péladin: Rosicrucian, author, and playwright, self-styled reformer of the Catholic Church and of the canons of art, and a middle-aged man who, due to his rich, titled followers, had real influence in artistic circles. Of course, she hoped for a part in one of his plays.

Alexandra wrote that Péladin was no charlatan but learned in the Western occult tradition. He genuinely wished a return to "the noble, esoteric and magical tradition" of the church of the Middle Ages. Failing to impress the pope, he founded his own order along mystical lines. He revived the ancient Syrian rite and proclaimed himself "Sar." His style was elegant, and he and his followers dressed in elaborate robes while performing endless ceremonies of which he was the grand master. The movement, profoundly reactionary, was antithetical to democracy and the French Revolution; it professed loathing for Masons, Protestants, and Jews. Moreover, Péladin showed an extraordinary distrust of women. Their place was as servants or virgins to be deflowered; alternately, they might through instruction become fairies. They must learn to make their bodies light in order to float, to grasp objects almost without touching them. As she watched a fat Flemish woman go through these exercises, Alexandra wondered, "How many porcelain cups would be the price of this lesson?"

Despite describing them as "a coterie of snobs," Alexandra was well known to Péladin's intimates. Once, she wrote, "I found myself on the stage where they were rehearsing one of his plays." The Count de Larmandie, directing, complained to her that the star, "an artiste of distinction," wouldn't play the part as the Sar demanded: naked throughout. Naturally, because the play demanded nudity, the Sar felt "desolated." Alexandra claims to have been shocked, but it is possible that she herself was the "artiste" who refused to undress. In writing of her bohemian days, she often chose to hide behind the third person.

If Alexandra refused to strip for the Sar, she soon afterward saw him figuratively disrobed. Péladin's mother, a simple woman from the Midi, brought her to his home, in his absence, to discuss the matter of the rebellious star. "Isn't it natural for an actress to be nude?" the mother insinuated. Very few persons had been invited to this sanctuary, and the reason instantly became obvious: it was a mess. In the poor, ill-lit, shabby apartment, Alexandra contemplated a carpet soiled by innumerable cigarette butts, cheap furniture, and a writing table in total disarray. Meanwhile, Péladin's mother chattered of the Indian maharajas who sent gold and would give up everything for her son. Alexandra exited in haste, aware that it could be dangerous to know the Sar's sordid secrets.

The singer's career was going nowhere, and as novelist and essayist she was rejected and unnoticed. But she hadn't entirely tired of Jean or *la vie bohème*. "Art is all of earthly beauty," she wrote, "all the magic of the material world . . . In it is [found] all voluptuousness, all sensuality of the flesh and the soul." When, in the autumn of 1899, the opportunity arose to perform with the Opera of Athens, a second-rate house, she didn't hesitate to go. However, her voice was no longer so reliable. Louis David sent a remedy for her bad throat: a decoction of dried figs and raisins with honey added. To herself the singer admitted, "Work has become insipid."

In the summer of 1900—while Paris indulged in another universal exposition—Alexandra, still under the guise of *Mademoiselle* Myrial, sent her parents a curt note from Marseilles stating that she had accepted an engagement with the municipal opera in Tunis. Her career was on a predictable downward spiral: from the second company to the provinces to the colonies. For a time Louis David received no more news from her, and he inquired anxiously of Jean, "I can't imagine she would be in Passy without writing to us." The earnest young musician knew no more about it than her old father. Alexandra had dropped him for another man.

Of Pierre, the character who represents Jean, Alexandra had written, "He was like a friend that one would marry for sweet and tranquil affection, having nothing about him of the stranger that one falls for out of infatuation or passion." Did Alexandra underestimate Jean Haustont? An introspective man, he invented a novel musical notation scheme based on vibrations. He eventually went to China where he taught music and lived out his days. Alexandra, who would ask him to visit her in North Africa, for whatever reasons, and who would correspond with him in the Orient, made no effort to find him there. Once she had met the stranger she was going to marry, she never accorded Jean much weight.

Philip Neel, a bachelor at the age of thirty-nine, was a man who appeared to have everything except a wife. Born at Alès in the south of France, his family of ancient Norman stock came from Jersey, and his father, of the same name, had been a Methodist missionary. His mother was the daughter of a Protestant minister. Philip, in contrast to Alexandra, was one of ten children; however, his parents saw to it that he got the best education—in engineering—then available. Choosing North Africa as the setting for his career, Philip was instrumental in constructing the railroad line from Bône, Algeria, to Guelma, Tunisia, of which he was made chief engineering officer.

With his air of an English gentleman, Philip favored frock coats, high collars with cravat and stickpin, or else while on duty a cutaway jacket worn with contrasting knickers and high socks, as well as a jaunty cap. His features were finely, though not artistically, cut, eyes cold blue, mustache alert. Alexandra later wrote to him, "You are an elegant monsieur, and I recall that my aesthetic sentiments . . . have more than once brought me to look upon you from a distance with pleasure, like gazing at an objet d'art." Perhaps the key word here is "distance."

Alexandra's most recent biographer has described Philip Neel as "the Don Juan of 1900 in all his splendor," and he alleges that, overwhelmed by the engineer's masculine attractions, she fell madly in love with him. As we shall see, Philip was actually a bumbling country Casanova, crude in his advances and riddled with guilt. Meanwhile, the Parisienne, at the height of her beauty at thirty-two and worldly wise, must have caused a stir among the lonely Frenchmen at Tunis.

It isn't known precisely when Alexandra met Philip, but the location was likely the casino. This was the center of social life for colonial society, at least for the men, and here they gathered to gamble, gossip, and listen to light entertainment. Once in a while a *chanteuse* from Paris would sing the latest café ballads. Thus the military officers and petty bureaucrats forgot, for the moment, they were far from home in an Arab land.

By early fall of 1900 the entertainer at the casino was none other than Alexandra Myrial, formerly of l'Opéra-Comique. She played piano and sang light arias for her polite, if not deeply attentive, audience, one of whom was the chief engineer. Philip had a yacht of sorts, *l'Hirondelle* (the *Swallow*), to which he invited the glamorous Parisienne. Not only did she accept on September 15, but she may have gone to bed with him then and there. In her diary is scribbled, "Hirondella prima volta." For the first time in *his* life Philip Neel had seduced a woman of his own social class.

The yacht was the usual scene of Philip's trysts, but these had nearly always involved cheap whores, or as Alexandra would put it, "gorgons from Marseilles who stank of garlic." When one of the girls, feeling she was worth it, asked for more than the going price, Philip sent her away rather than pay up. This missionary's son liked to sin, but cheaply. He had a postcard made up with a photo of the *Swallow* on one side, and he mailed it with identical gallantries to all the girls. Naturally, at first, he assured Alexandra she was the only woman in his life. If there had been others, he couldn't recall their names.

Philip, a gentleman with a compulsion to do the right thing, demanded from the start, "When are we getting married?" Alexandra put him off, replying, "Never in our lives." But both were of a suitable age and compatible background, and they were inclining toward marriage. Yet Philip had a kinky side: he took and kept intimate photos of his conquests, which he carefully filed with their letters. This bureaucrat's mentality, even in regard to sex, was going to cost him.

In 1902 Alexandra accepted the more attractive post of artistic director of the casino, possibly obtained through Philip's influence. In contrast, she temporarily joined an expedition of German botanists into the southern desert, where she indulged her interest in ethnology and studied the Bedouins. She also continued to write occasionally for radical reviews. In "The Origin of Myths and Their Influence on Social Justice" (*Free Thought* [Brussels, 1901]) she attacked the Judeo-Christian tradition and its priests as the descendents of witch doctors. Buddhism, on the other hand, she declared to be rational and liberal. She didn't wish to abandon revolution to the uneducated masses, but she rather hoped for a revolution of thought and sentiment to free the individual.

Alexandra traveled sometimes to Paris where she stayed with Jean Haustont at their old flat in Passy. He came to visit her in Tunis during the summer of 1902. Perhaps she aimed to make Philip jealous, playing on an attraction that, for both, was winning out over their "malice, caution and mutual prudence." In September 1904, Alexandra taunted the man now her husband, "I told you from the beginning, I'm not pretty, I'm not fun . . . Why did you persist? Did you become infatuated?"

At any rate, the budding author needed to maintain a link with her Paris editors, and that same year she published two articles in the influential *Mercure de France*, required reading for Left Bank bohemians. One was on "Korean Religions and Superstitions," the other on "The Tibetan Clergy and Its Doctrines." It was as though she could see into her own future.

By the winter of 1904, Alexandra, Philip's avowed mistress, had moved into his lovely native-style home, La Goulette (Waterwheel). On account of his curly hair, she chose the pet name "alouche," which she supposed meant "sheep" in Arabic. It doesn't, but no matter, the nickname "Mouchy" stuck to him. For a while, though, it appeared that Alexandra and her Mouchy were going to part bitter enemies. Either by accident, or more likely design, Philip left his old love letters where his mistress might well discover them. She did, and far worse, she found her own letters mixed in with the rest.

Philip's reaction to her barely suppressed rage was nonchalance. While she "experienced a strong temptation to rub his nose into his lies," he amiably exhibited his "gallery of little women." There were four years of correspondence with "a poor whore of a Renée," cards from "fat Marthe," and various photos of lovelies such as Blanche ("a girl from Bordeaux with a comb in her hair") and Paula ("the one he found too costly"). None of the women was pretty, and Philip and Alexandra "laughed like comrades" over their crudeness.

To herself Alexandra rationalized, "What can it matter to me that the man was a skirt chaser? He isn't my brother or my husband." Still, she was so furious she couldn't bear to write Philip's name in her diary, substituting an X. She comforted herself with a faint bit of philosophy, "What annoys me is his mania to play at being a big deal. Eh! Aren't we all beasts and imbeciles at times? It's ridiculous to act disagreeably and wish to be set on a pedestal."

But it rankled that Philip had deceived her, swearing he kept no mementos of previous affairs, that she was his all in all. What infuriated her most was his sending his photo to the girls, so he became "a figure in a whore's collection." Nor did he act ashamed; the discovery of his cache caused him to strut like a peacock. It proved his virility, a desirable attribute in a husband.

Once she cooled down, Alexandra realized she was dealing with a coxcomb. It was about this time she considered writing a piece on "The Woman in Love and Marriage," subtitled "The Battlefield of the Sexes." She didn't write the essay, but more importantly Mouchy had delivered to her his past as hostage. Alexandra divined the Methodist guilt that lurked beneath his pose as man of the world. Philip at forty, patron of prostitutes, had to redeem himself through marriage. She, thirty-six, had trouble keeping her weight in check. Her feminist principles were strong, but the reality of a poor, lonely middle age was too bleak.

On August 4, 1904, Alexandra recorded, "I have married this terrible Alouch at the French consulate in Tunis." Thus the curtain rang down on Act One of "the heart-rending comedy."

CHAPTER 6

The Woman in Marriage

Alexandra did not marry for emotional reasons but out of calculation. Her choice of husband proved brilliantly correct and her timing downright lucky. Philip was put through the formality of writing to Louis David to request his consent. The elderly gentleman, approaching ninety, expressed his astonishment: "Until today my daughter had shown her firm will to never surrender her liberty, and she protested continually against the inferior state that the law imposed on a woman in every regard after marriage."

Louis, rather than take Philip's word that he earned ten thousand francs per annum, checked with the president of the railroad, who praised the engineer's character and his pension. A contract was duly drawn up stipulating the separation of goods between the partners. At this time, Alexandra owned some jewels of no account, a private library worth three thousand francs, and coins and bibelots worth seven thousand francs. She was to be responsible for one-quarter of the domestic charges. Although this arrangement seems modern, it was made necessary by the wife's lack of legal standing; otherwise, her husband owned everything.

For their honeymoon, the newlyweds sailed to France, then went by train to the spa town of Plombiers, where they took the waters. After a week they parted—Philip back to Tunis, Alexandra to Paris to make the rounds of publishers. She was still trying to sell her novel and libretto, but there were no takers. She met Jean Haustont and his new mistress, but, clearly, she encountered a certain coolness. On her thirty-sixth birthday in October she was lonely. "Naturally my delicious parents showed no sign of life," she wrote to Philip. "They have forgotten this morbid date, [and] they have for a long time forgotten they have a daughter."

Alexandra had written more correctly than she realized. In early December, after receiving word that Louis David was dying, she hurried to Brussels. Alexandra's dread of marriage was based on witnessing that of her parents, and what she found at the family home confirmed her worst fears. She informed her husband, "The [very] walls are witness to my miserable youth, and a future that I see as too similar to the past . . . breaks my heart just as much."

Her old hatred for *Madame* David revived when she discovered that she had denied the dying man proper linen and handkerchiefs. She herself was lodged in a freezing attic, while her mother conveniently fell ill. In the face of such stolid, uncaring cheapness she felt helpless. "I am demoralized," she confided to Philip. "My brain is filled with infantile, inept reveries . . . I sincerely regret not having some religious belief in which to absorb myself."

Alexandra's love for her father and need for his approval were deeply buried. Having these old ashes stirred up caused so much pain she felt she couldn't go on. Still, she discouraged Philip from joining her, and she held out until December 21, when Louis passed away. She felt relieved. "*Et voilà!*" she wrote to Philip, "tomorrow we clear the deck—the funeral and mourning. My mother, who belongs to the cult of the dead, has just given me a program that . . . I can't accept. I can better order things."

Even as Alexandra took charge she was aware of a new worry. "I know—don't I, Mouchy," she anxiously inquired, "that I can count on you? Because I can't get my hands on anything due to the succession [in the will]. . . . My mother will take advantage of her illness to present me with bills I shouldn't have to pay."

Louis David was interred without fuss on Christmas Eve 1904. Alexandra went to stay with Elisée Reclus while she saw to affairs. She was careful to secure the modest sum of twenty thousand francs that was coming to her immediately. Then she fled home to Tunis, "like a little girl," as she joked with Philip, "to rest my head on your shoulder." For the time being she had found a substitute father. But lurking in the background was an older, more profound paternity: the shadow of Genghis Khan.

La Goulette, the Neels' villa by the sea, was a lovely Moorish home with whitewashed walls, arcades, and arches, a cool patio, and playing fountains. Over the next several years it would provide a healing refuge for Alexandra's frequently bruised ego. In August 1905, while redecorating her home, she learned that her early mentor Elisée Reclus had died. Although she left for Belgium to pay her last respects, she was preoccupied by a problem of the opposite sort: Philip wanted a child.

More depressing to Alexandra than the death of the man who had been a second father to her was returning to the David household at Brussels, as cold as a mausoleum. She stayed just long enough to oversee affairs. From here she penned a heartfelt letter to Mouchy explaining why she feared parenthood:

The child for me would be a god to whom would go all my adoration. He would be my unique hope and I would only exist to see him live the life I hadn't . . . to realize the ideal I failed to attain. . . . But it could happen that I would become a person in whom lodged a spirit different from my present one . . . It would be the story of my mother [over again] . . . that wretched woman in whom disappointments only changed into rancor and spitefulness against her unsuspecting child.

Parent and child, because each placed so much hope in the other, were doomed to alternating love and antagonism. Disillusion awaited "those imprudent women who look to motherhood for consolation from an ill-matched union." Alexandra admitted that Philip had an instinct for simple happiness, to be a normal husband and father. In denying him these basic pleasures, she felt obliged to attack the institution of the family as it was then constituted. She bombarded him with arguments, intimations of his past sins and an occasional appeal to his higher nature: "One must not allow the preoccupations below the belt to mount to the brain." Her husband responded, much to the point, "I have a very bourgeois soul, incapable of all the subtleties you ceaselessly stir up."

The first two years of this marriage were stormy and uncertain. Although Alexandra liked to refer to Philip as "my dear friend," it was more from hope than reality. Each needed the other, but each hated to admit it. Sometimes, as in a letter from London in September 1906, Alexandra would tantalize her mate, "If I had you here, I would squeeze you tight." More often their correspondence featured mutual accusations. Each insisted that the other tried to keep "a light scornful smile fixed on your lips during the grossest bestial rapture," which suggests that their physical lovemaking was intense and convoluted, done out of an unwilling attraction.

Shortly after Alexandra left Tunis, a former mistress of Philip turned up to reassert her rights. He let his wife know, at least in part to make her jealous. She didn't rise to the bait but welcomed the intruder. From Paris she wrote, "I can't hide my real desire to avoid hurting your poor friend, which is mixed with an even stronger desire to continue having a person who knows you so well care for you. She, better than any other, will be able to assist me in the serious battle I expect in freeing you from your errors."

Alexandra reminded Philip that he had created this painful situation and he must act discreetly in order not to trample on the discarded mistress's feelings. She had been a fool to give up her trade to depend on a man who, in the nature of things, would grow tired of her. However, she presumed his conduct had been dictated by "our charming mores." But charity could go only so far: Philip had better be on his guard, since his old lover might plot revenge.

Alexandra's offer to have the woman come live near them is reminiscent of Victor Hugo's arrangement whereby Juliet Drouet always lived in a little house close by his ménage, and even his wife came to depend on her. Philip was no Hugo, and by autumn 1906 he was threatening divorce. He had given in and resumed relations with this former mistress, for which he characteristically blamed Alexandra. "You let me go on a path that is disloyal to you," he complained. "Too late I wanted to confess and tell you I regretted it. Useless. You gave me as bad a time as you could, and we are still stumbling down the same muddy path."

At times Philip could be more reasonable than his errant wife. He reminded her:

We've known each other for some time already . . . [and] we're getting older, especially me who, unlike you, can't be considered robust. Are we going to have to carry this heavy load till the very end? Do you really know me? . . . A middle-class life suits me. You're the antithesis of that. Others say it and I think they're right. So what shall we do about this marriage of ours, in which you play a part though you blame only me?

Alexandra, who had lost her father and to a degree her bearings, wasn't about to let Philip go. She returned to Tunis that winter of 1906–7 for a trial reunion. "Let's not consider what we used to be," she admonished Mouchy, "what we have done or what we are to each other. Let's just see that we are alone and can help each other."

Philip, although he had "made relics of [his] low-class mistresses's letters and photos," provided Alexandra's sole refuge at this date. She adored the comfortable Arab house with her hoarded mementos, and the calming waves of the Mediterranean Sea. Even more satisfying was the sweep of the desert with its oases of majestic palms silhouetted against an orange sky, the timeless tonalities of the desert as, at twilight, Bedouins led their camels to the sweet water given by the grace of Allah. A trip to the south provided balm to her nervous soul and material for a short story, "Before the Face of Allah," published first in a small French review, then in Italy.

Try as she might, Alexandra couldn't tolerate for long the role of bureaucrat's wife. A photo snapped in the patio of the Neels' home shows her reclining on a chaise lounge, a prosperous, slightly overweight matron in an oriental dressing gown: the colonial lady about to summon a servant to refill her cup of tea. Her hair is tidy, upswept, and parted in the middle. Around the patio are plants that give an illusion of the tropics, but nothing is wild except the eyes of the caged wife.

Alexandra's deepening feminism posed yet another conflict. The legal status of women in France and its colonies remained abysmal. Adultery was an offense only if committed by the wife. A woman had no right to vote and once married practically no rights at all. The social reality was still worse. Alexandra recalled that at the Sorbonne she had been taunted by male students, and she had seen young women pressed between doors and kicked down stairs, all because they had "the imprudent audacity to wish to earn their living by means other than their sex."

Bearing children hammered the final nails into the coffin of a woman's hopes. The drudgery of those days was bound to overwhelm her. Alexandra herself claimed to be inept at homemaking, and one way or another she usually found servants to do the chores. However, she clearly understood that for most women marriage would be their profession, and that once married they could never escape despite "disgust, [or] a heart wounded by their husband's infidelity." Far worse was the situation of unwed mothers, "trapped by the consequences of a gesture of love." For them there remained nothing but grudging charity or walking the streets.

These were not the issues addressed by the 1906 Congress of Rome hosted by Italian women. At least as reported by Alexandra in the *Tunisian Dispatch,*

This Congress was a party. The organizers . . . belong to the Roman aristocracy. There is a certain taint on those who are called vulgarly and simply Madam.

The former anarchist led a small cabal that demanded the Congress protest against "the atrocities endured by women in the Russian prisons." After the failure of the 1905 revolution, young women were being indiscriminately raped, tortured, and hanged by the czarist police. The Congress found the suggestion called up "visions too brutal, too shocking," for them to accept. They refused to adopt it.

One outgrowth of this Italian junket and a later one in 1908 was that Alexandra met a young socialist journalist named Benito Mussolini who became interested in her work, and who remained so despite his later notorious career. Indeed, she had little difficulty publishing several feminist articles in these years, the most interesting of which was "Liberation of Women from the Costs of Maternity" (*Le Monde,* 1908). The author took a position so modern that, although many of her suggested reforms have been adopted, some remain mere proposals. Reacting against the view, typically expressed by Balzac, that a wife was "a slave whom one must set on a throne," she wished marriage to be thoroughly rationalized. Because it was humiliating to be dependent for money, wives should be paid a salary by their husbands for housework and childrearing. They had the right to support if divorced, and the courts ought to enforce it. The notion of illegitimacy should be banished and schooling made free and universal. Children were the responsibility of society as a whole, and there could be no abandoned orphans or unwed mothers in distress: the state must act as parent of last resort.

The essentials of this program—radical for its day—had been pioneered during the Paris Commune and propounded from one soapbox or another for decades afterward by Louise Michel. However, Alexandra was not the one to make speeches in working-class districts, still less go to jail, to bring her vision to fruition. Yet Alexandra never lost interest in the feminist cause. In 1919 she wrote an emotional letter to Philip from a Tibetan monastery, where she had learned that the Chamber of Deputies was considering granting women the vote. She wondered if France would continue to behave barbarously, and she pointed out the disadvantages to a nation of disenfranchising half its population. The legendary Gallic politeness toward women she dismissed as mere hypocrisy.

If France has no place for a woman such as she, Britain and its empire were more liberal. In 1906 Alexandra went to London where she worked on an edition of her favorite Chinese philosopher. This was published the next year as *The Philosophy of Meh-ti and the Idea of Solidarity*. She became friendly with Dr. T. W. Rhys Davids and his wife, Caroline, with whom she shared a common outlook. Rhys Davids had founded the Pali Text Society in 1888 and was just then instrumental in establishing the Buddhist Society in Great Britain. Both husband and wife were indefatigable translators from the original Buddhist writings in Pali, the sacred language of Ceylon and Southeast Asia, home of the Theravadic school, quite different from the northern school Alexandra was to encounter in China and Tibet. Caroline, in particular, was an avid searcher after the actual unadulterated teachings of the historical Buddha, as witnessed by her later biography *Gotama the Man*. Alexandra was delighted to know such a woman, and they kept up a correspondence, now lost.

In London Alexandra found herself part of a worldwide Buddhist revival sparked by the teachings of *Madame* Blavatsky, who had declared herself a Buddhist in Ceylon in 1880. The revival's main propagandist was the Singhalese who called himself the Angarika Dharmapala (roughly the "Homeless Preacher"), and one of its initial goals was the recovery into Buddhist hands of historical sites in India sacred to them. The movement was reformist, akin to Protestantism in its mistrust of the priesthood and rites and ceremony. It included the prolific Japanese writer on Zen, D. T. Suzuki, who helped instigate the Zen flowering in California in the 1950s and 1960s, and various other figures and publications. Alexandra came to know Suzuki in London and would visit him in Japan. Her insistence that Buddhism was relevant to the modern world and compatible with radical social thought shared common ground with these active seekers. She was not as isolated as she evidently felt.

In 1907 Alexandra faced her deepest emotional trial, crying out to Philip, "I am sick, I have lost my mind." She came close to a total nervous breakdown. From Paris on May 24, she hastily wrote her husband:

Old age is overtaking me quickly. Until marriage my eyes were wide open before me, I overflowed with plans. Suddenly all hope is dead and strangled in a kind of torpor which impedes rebellion. I feel that I am going to die, and I live in agony now with occasional sharp horrible shocks . . . [It is] terrifying. My gaze only looks back. My life is over and I feed on what I was.

When Philip complained that he too had sad memories—of his absent wife—she responded by calling the past "a basket of rags." Apprehensive about remaining in Paris, Alexandra feared returning to Tunis. "I'm tormented by a perpetual and sick anxiety," she wrote. "If I take a walk, I regret I didn't go another way. Sitting in one place, I want to be somewhere else . . ." She fled to London where she consulted doctors to no avail; one predicted the worst: "Neurasthenia is taking over." She tried Switzerland for a rest cure, and by autumn she was back in Paris, rather worse.

Alexandra then did some uncharacteristic things. She attended services at a Calvinist church, which merely deepened her pessimism. She couldn't sleep because of "a soul rubbed raw." She went to the opera to hear *Madame Butterfly*—she had helped with advice on the set—but she grew "nervous to the point of having to leave." She couldn't bear Puccini's music and resented being in the audience rather than on stage. Ears ringing, stabbed by sounds, Alexandra fled the house.

What was wrong with this woman who would one day bestride the Himalayas? "Today I am ugly, old and poor," she wrote to Philip on October 30. "[I am] finished with hope, and yet I have not resigned myself . . . to descend to the depths which lead to the black hole." Rising from her writing desk, Alexandra looked in the mirror to see a displeasing image with wrinkles and patches of gray hair. Worse was the resemblance, real or fancied, to "those features I hate"—her mother's. The former *artiste*, approaching forty, had grown corpy, petulant and neurotic. We know little about the state of her physical health, but she was clearly sinking into depression.

At this time, Dr. Sigmund Freud was treating women with such symptoms at his clinic in Vienna. *Madame* David-Neel presented a classic picture of Freud's definition of hysteria. She had turned her unresolved, and thus unacceptable, emotions inward to make herself sick. What she conceived of as failures frustrated her, while her marriage of convenience ran counter to her principles and inclination. Yet she could not afford to surrender the security it offered. Too, she felt guilty for wounding Philip, for not making the home that would have suited him. Naturally she struck out at her husband for giving rise to this guilt, then in the next breath extolled him: "You are civilized, you have enormous qualities of a practical man, of economy, of work." These are the qualities she thought she lacked.

In fact, Alexandra didn't engage in the new vogue of psychoanalysis. Instead she turned to what was truly hers. "Be your own light," the Buddha had said, "and you will be composed and need search for nothing." Alexandra resumed her neglected oriental studies at the Collège de France under Professor Sylvain Levi. Here was a mentor precisely right for her stage of evolvement. Levi not only taught Sanskrit but wrote on Hinduism set in its broad social and cultural context. He was the author of a book on the Indian theater and another on the Brahmanic doctrine of sacrifice. He was very influential in scholarly circles, and his tutelage of Alexandra would last until his death, although by then he had learned much from his pupil.

Buddhist, orientalist, feminist, Alexandra kept on the move. During the next few years she made a circuit of Paris, Brussels, London, and Rome, taking out time now and again to visit Philip in Tunis. She attended various conferences, took tea along the boulevard St. Germain, where this meant champagne, and countless times in London where she and her friends drank plain tea. She stalked editors in their dens, particularly Rachilde at the *Mercure*. She was rewarded by his publishing her "Contemporary Buddhist Thinkers" in December 1909. Although these intellectuals were men and women with whom Alexandra stayed in touch, the correspondence is largely lost. "I believe in the superiority of the philosophical teachings of Buddha," declared the author. "Buddhism has mastered my mind and I only see through it."

In 1910 Alexandra lectured to good crowds at the Theosophical Societies of both Paris and London. She was delighted to address a group of Indian medical students at Edinburgh. She was working on and published at Paris in 1911 *Modern Buddhism and the Buddhism of Buddha*, a title that reads no less awkwardly in French. The work has some importance for what it led to, but it is based solely on book learning rather than the hard-won knowledge gained from experience.

"I took the right road," the author informed her husband. "I have no more time for neurasthenia." He replied that she was publishing under the name of "Alexandra David"; did that imply she no longer considered herself his wife? Not at all, she shot back, he was better than anyone else she saw around.

Yet Alexandra felt something essential to be missing. She wrote from London that she wasn't having much fun. She was fed up with *poseurs* who took a facile interest in the East. Supposing they were informed, they asked the most absurd questions. One eccentric insisted on writing a life of Buddha in Miltonic blank verse. Others possessed only second-hand opinions and could only quote the critics. True, a more sophisticated sort attended the salons of Sylvain Levi. At one of these, when she spoke animatedly of "the living Hindu philosophy that is not limited to the past or its place of birth," she found that the guests deserted Professor Levi to gather around her. She was gaining a reputation, she assured Philip, and *their* name—David-Neel—was well-known in these circles. But she felt a bit of a *poseur* herself.

In 1911 Philip responded by proposing that Alexandra visit India to perfect her oriental languages. He would pay for a voyage of about one year. To a degree, he had surrendered to his wife's notion of marriage, and perhaps he had found a new mistress. Alexandra jumped at the chance, and by August she was aboard a steamer bound east of Suez. She wondered, "Am I truly en route? I can't believe it!"

Once again Philip became "my little dearest Alouch," her delicate and devoted friend. From India, Alexandra's letters at times verged on the romantic. One day she informed her husband that she'd felt "the sensation of [his] embrace, an affectionate kiss, a memory of things long ago . . ." Left to his supposed bachelorhood, Philip wasn't entirely abandoned, for his wife liked to send him advice. He must wear his galoshes in the rain, eat properly, and sleep in a warm room. On a deeper level, he should stop depending on others. "It is only in dreams that human beings are sweet and so good to have near us . . . In reality they are the sharp stones in the corners that we hit against and are wounded by." Meditate, counseled the seeker, cultivate an inner calm independent of the "feverish agonizing drama" that is the world.

Alexandra kept in mind who was subsidizing her search. One day that year, when she received a photo of her husband, she teased him about how British he looked. He ought to be called "Sir Neel." She was good at appealing to his vanity, and Philip couldn't help imploring her to come back. She played an elaborate game with him—stalling, cajoling, sternly lecturing. Ultimately, Philip was a man of honor, for in spite of occasional threats he never cut off her funds. When others in colonial North Africa dropped spiteful hints, he spoke blandly about "my wife who likes to travel."

On one occasion, Alexandra, in her witty style, assured her husband he hadn't been cheated in marriage. "Evidently you might have preferred another sort of partner. . . . But considering overall among the flirts, fools, and . . . busybodies who form the lot of wives, you haven't gotten such a bad share."

Replied the down-to-earth Mouchy: "All these words ring hollow and empty, and two arms, a shoulder to rest [my] head on, would be much better."

Instead, over a period of fourteen years, the engineer received more letters—amounting eventually to three thousand typed pages—and handwritten articles to type and forward to journals, as well as books, furniture, and bibelots all bearing an Eastern postmark. Philip became the wanderer's lifeline to the West, and without him her work scarcely would have been possible. In 1914 Philip moved without sending his home address, suggesting caustically that he could be reached at his office. Alexandra, demanding to know her "legal domicile," exploded: "Haven't you dreamed I must be able to give this information to my acquaintances [and] the editors of reviews where I write? . . . Haven't you dreamed either that it is a little outside the normal, the habits of the herd, for a wife not to know where her husband lives?"

Perhaps this marriage was an illusion on both their parts, a fiction. If so, it must rank as a brilliant work of art that ended in giving mutual satisfaction. It ennobled Philip Neel and permitted him a major share in his wife's adventures. As Alexandra meditated in a sky-high cave with a magical Tibetan lama, roamed the Central Asian steppes with the caravans of hairy yaks, or supped with gentlemen brigands at peril of her life, the cautious engineer partook of her pain, joys, and knowledge. He, too, explored the world.

Book Two

THE LEARNED LAMA

He who would harm another is no seeker after truth,
He who would act wrongly toward another is no
  monk.

—*from Dhammapada*

CHAPTER 7

India Absurd and Marvelous

On a baking mid-August evening in 1911, the steamer *City of Naples* sounded its horn and pushed off from the quay at Bizerte. The Arab women hanging on the rail sent up a cacaphony of shrill howls to match. Third class was above rather than below, and the poorer travelers, headed first for Marseilles, then Suez and beyond, kept their belongings bundled on deck. Down in the hold stirred a tribe of rats, intent on good meals to come. The passenger *Madame* Alexandra David-Neel was pressed among the natives, while her husband Philip stood on the dock in the fullness of his dignity. Tumult about her, she watched in silence as his silhouette grew smaller, dimmer, erased by the night.

Although traveling first class, Alexandra hated the voyage. The Arabs "crawling around" eating with their hands from grimy baskets, the odors from poor sanitation and a scorching sun, the rats that got into her cabin, made her feverish. She felt that odd microbes had infected her, and she thought wistfully of an early return. But the dice were cast: Alexandra wouldn't see her "dear Mouchy" for fourteen years. By then she would have graduated from a student of the East to a learned lama.

Despite her discomfort, Alexandra wrote lucidly about what she proposed to accomplish. At present she had exhausted her stock of knowledge. Yet there remained for her "an honorable place to take in French Orientalism"; not that of a specialist confined to "dry and dead erudition," but to convey the essence of living Eastern philosophy. Audaciously, she hoped to go beyond even the great historical figures, to follow their ideas further than they had done.

Eventually, Alexandra would produce a work, published in Paris in 1951 following Indian independence, the title of which translates as *India Yesterday, Today, Tomorrow.* The book is a fond memoir or travel narrative culled from her several voyages to India, and is unabashed about the sights she witnessed. Such a ramble, while intriguing, did not make David-Neel's unequaled reputation. It does show her small regard for the integrity of genre—she liked to tell a good story—as well as her positive loathing for chronology. Though facts interested her, dates did not. So, taking the cue, we shall proceed on a geographic plan, relating the encounter of the Parisienne with the enormity of the Subcontinent while moving, as she did, from south to north, but for now omitting one foray into the Himalayas.

Alexandra complained bitterly about the food on board ship, giving the example of lentils boiled with onions for dinner. If she had guessed what slops she would one day beg for—and relish! Colombo, Ceylon, pleased her no better than had the voyage. Merchants swarmed around like flies, buzzing about their silks and sapphires. She was infuriated by the sight of a canary yellow statue of Buddha into whose open hands a devotee had placed a pack of toothpicks, while another left a jar of peas. She spoke at the Theosophical Society and gave a conference at the Royal College before heading into the countryside.

Dressed in white, wearing a huge hat with a white veil, and being pulled about in a rickshaw, Alexandra enjoyed playing the *mem sahib*. For two months she visited the holy sites, including the bo tree grown from a cutting of the original one under which Gautama had received his enlightenment. But modern Buddhists were scarcer than in Paris, and it was all too sweet and simple. "I am not able to get out of my head," she declared, "that I am in Switzerland." She was happy to sail away across the Gulf of Mannar on a tub without electric lights.

At Madurai Alexandra passed an enchanting evening under the stars, inhaling the "first intoxication of the perfume of India." She had arrived in the south, land of the fine-boned, dark-skinned, emotive Dravidians. This ancient people, who had resisted the conquering armies of Aryans (bearers of Sanskrit) and Moghuls alike, were ardent worshipers of the Hindu trinity: Brahma the creator (to whom there are no temples, no images); Vishnu the preserver (who sometimes is pictured as a boar—digging to the roots—but whose best-known incarnation is as Krishna the blue cowherd); and Shiva the great destroyer (whose many arms flail a whirlwind of blades, who is the fire of purification and of generation, and who is adored by the most proper matrons and chaste maidens in the shape of a giant stone *lingam*—a phallic symbol—over which they pour pots of melted butter or suffuse with garlands of flowers, "sweet and suffocating like amorous flesh.")

Alexandra, who grew more at ease where allegedly she didn't approve of the customs, frequented the huge, gaily painted Menakshi temple dominating the town. This enormous rectangular structure dating from 1560, then as now was a beehive of activity, as though it sucked energy from its steaming, listless surroundings. Chocolate brown figures in bright silks flitted about or hovered over stalls in the outer courtyard. Beggars begged, peddlers hawked glass bracelets, while folk gossiped and bargained for flowers and fruits with which to propitiate the deity who reigned within: Shiva, fearsome savior. At intervals gourds sounded to summon the faithful to prayer amid billows of incense, marigold petals, and a rosewater mist.

Best were the processions on the frequent feast days. First the enclosure rang with a racket of conchs and gongs: "The notes brief, violent and imperious, the echoes resounding as an affirmation of . . . dare I say magic?" Then the Brahmin priests issued from the temple precincts with the enthusiasm of a charge, while the devotees dragged an enormous wooden-wheeled chariot through the streets, atop which Shiva danced death and salvation. This was a sort of juggernaut. Men naked save for loincloths, smeared with ash or painted with symbols, held up torches like weapons. The devout crouched along the way of the cortege or flung themselves down to kiss the paving stones after the god had passed. The pandemonium sent chills to the marrow of the observer's bones.

Alexandra admitted that the scene appeared scary, and, if not satanic, at least in the domain of "the Other, as one said in the Middle Ages." Yet how preferable it was to the insipid parades held in what remained of Christian Europe. Here, "You penetrate[d] to the core of the sacred terror of which the Greeks spoke but knew nothing." Within, the grand sight was the hall of a thousand exquisitely carved pillars, each illustrating in stone an aspect of Hindu mythology. Various inner sanctums were closed to the public. There priests with naked torsos performed ancient ceremonies, and there took place the notorious tantric rites, sexual practices of which most Westerners have heard. Alexandra, hiding in a secluded spot, witnessed the rites one evening.

This was the temple of the fish-eyed goddess Menakshi, one version of Shiva's consort. The wife of such a well-endowed god must be beautifully shaped, with ample hips and large breasts, and thus her statues depict her. Upon her were modeled the *Devadasis,* sacred prostitutes. These dancers were slaves wedded to Shiva at birth. Occasionally, a woman's freedom was bought by a wealthy votary who paid the temple treasury a sufficient sum. Then he took her away to become his own concubine. The dancers performed only for the highest caste Hindus, and sons of the best houses avidly attended the rites.

Alexandra watched perhaps forty women whirl in dim light to the accompaniment of flute, guitar, and drums. The musicians followed the steps of the performers, to mimic in sound the lascivious sway of dark, willowy torsos. A steady rhythm built and was accentuated by gauzy revelations of bare bosoms, which entranced the male congregants. Although the dancers, trained from childhood, supposedly were skilled in the erotic arts, Alexandra found nothing refined or graceful in the display. She considered it an Asian burlesque. No Puritan, she had read the *Kamasutra*—the ancient Indian manual of erotic techniques—with appreciation, but these women who were soft from a lazy life violated her standards of beauty.

The Madurai males went nearly wild. Stimulated by spiraling hips and breasts, their lust rose to a crescendo. One, eyes dilated, began to writhe and gulp in ecstatic parody of *samadhi,* the state of unthinking bliss. Suddenly, the dancers jumped from the platform and the devotees tore after them toward the innermost chamber where dwelled the couple Shiva and Menakshi. The usually curious Alexandra did not follow to witness the final divine fulfillment. Instead, she wrote, "I flattened myself between the prancing legs of a giant stone horse protruding from the wall to let the infernal wave pass. Then I gained the exit. I had discovered a new, intimate aspect to the dwelling of the gods."

Shiva is never without a consort, yet he is the chosen deity of the most ascetic yogis who seek from him the destruction of desire. *Shaktas,* however, worship Shiva through the several images of his wife, for it is *shakti,* power, they seek, which they find in the principle of the female, even cows. Among this cult are those we would call magicians, "distillers of love-potions, amulet-makers, spell-casters, healers and miracle-makers. . . . Their holy books are the Tantra."

Tantrism, though despised by proper Brahmins, may be older than yoga or Hinduism itself. More methodology than philosophy, the Tantra has roots in the ancient transpolar matrix of beliefs termed shamanism and perhaps in the neolithic worship of feminine deities. It always involves the oral transmission of secrets from master, or guru, to disciple, and it aims to acquire magical powers in order to immediately affect both the world within and without. Until a few decades ago, this occult science was practiced most purely and devoutly in Tibet, the land where time had stood nearly still.

The importance of this mysterious system to the life of Alexandra, the French rational Buddhist, was crucial. Although she grew learned in several branches of oriental thought, she became famous due to what she knew and wrote of Tibetan Buddhist Tantrism. Only the difficult techniques she had studied made her arduous journey to Lhasa a success. In fact, Alexandra was identified as a tantric adept even before she became one.

The seeker traveled northward by train through forests of teak and past clearings in which drowsed age-old villages, a kind of psychic hum emanating from the click-clack of the train's wheels. Along the east coast the beaches were dotted by palmyra palms, and Alexandra expressed her approval of a people whose domestic economy was based on the coconut rather than the cow. At the major stations comfortable bungalows awaited Europeans where the native chambermaid could skillfully massage weary legs. Her companions proved interesting, and the Brahmins respectful, to the lone woman traveler.

But in writing to Philip, Alexandra complained bitterly of the heavy monsoon rains:

Where is my India of bygone days, ardent, singed, with . . . its roads where the dust swirls in a golden powder in the brief pink dawns[?] . . . The low clouds [are] uniformly gray, the green trees, the green fields [are] too green! The muddy roads where the [cart] wheels dig in and squirt red-brick water and the showers that pierce you, the nights where you shiver huddled in your covers . . .

At such times Alexandra can sound like her contemporary, the poet Mallarmé; or even echoing Baudelaire, "The Orient without sun is nothing but a heap of filth."

She had worse to say from Madras, where she denounced the entire Brahmanic system based on the Vedanta (the sacred Vedas, or scriptures) and caste. She found the Vedantists "deplorable, anti-human, anti-social . . . They have brought India to the miserable state in which she finds herself." And that was "a population of slaves that squirms and crawls around in the smoke." She dismissed native hospitality as impossible for a European. Her squeamishness showing, she found the homes of the Brahmins, as well as the habits of their domestics, too filthy for her to consider eating in. So she betook herself to the very comfortable headquarters of the Theosophical Society at nearby Adyar.

Here Alexandra voiced complaints of a different sort. She luxuriated in a vast room in a house that resembled the Trianon of Louis XIV. The grounds by the sea were extensive, and in the evenings a collection of what she termed lunatics wandered over them, lanterns in hand. There was a European count, a beautiful circus performer turned missionary, a contingent of mature ladies. A certain Herr Grunewald peered through gold-rimmed glasses at old texts in the library to ascertain how medieval rabbis had manufactured *golems,* robots who did their will. A Swedish girl vowed to starve herself to death for the experience. No one disturbed the near skeleton until Annie Besant cabled from England, "One must live!" The Swede broke her fast, returned to table, and hardly anyone noticed.

The meditating Theosophists were equally indifferent to the venomous snakes on the grounds. Alexandra wrote her husband how one might likely encounter a king cobra, marked with the sign of Shiva. When he rose upon his coil, neck swelling, eyes like fire, the victim could only pray. The cobra, though charmed by the squeal of a pipe, knew no fear, and its bite meant a quick, agonizing end. But she assured Philip that "Adyar was a peaceful oasis."

Nights enthralled the seeker, who sat in the dark listening to nature's tropic symphony. Many of the Westerners, determined to concentrate on some *mantra,* or formula, couldn't bear the uncanny racket. Alexandra cleverly made this "surge of creation" her meditation. In the darkness humans shrank to their proper insignificance, while "thousands of animal creatures frolicked . . . with joyful hearts, in search of nourishment or their loves; or [were] moved along by the pleasure of flying, creeping, running, singing, whistling, buzzing and feeling alive." She had no difficulty attuning to "these thousand voices which cry about the Truth."

Alexandra maintained that the practitioners of yoga—either in its physical or more spiritual branches—could tell one another by the light in their eyes. This way or some other, several Vishnuites found her at Adyar and begged her to come join them. First they quizzed her on the Hindu scriptures, giving her answers the rapt attention accorded to the Cybele pronouncing on the outcome of the Persian War. Adorned with togas and smeared with ash, they appeared to reverence Alexandra. She wrote Philip, "India of twenty centuries ago rose up before me with all its ardent and ferocious mysticism."

On further inquiry, Alexandra learned that the yogis' guru was an elderly woman who sat naked in an arbor in a public park. She had been meditating there for decades and was growing worn out. Her disciples were seeking a likely replacement. "Sweetly," teased the Frenchwoman, "I insinuated that, somewhere on another continent, lived a *monsieur* who was my husband and who possibly might show scant enthusiasm for such an *avatar* [goddess incarnate] of a wife."

Alexandra was more interested in an invitation to represent France at the International Congress of Moral Education to be held at The Hague in August 1912. That she accepted shows her expectation of returning by the next summer. She assured Philip she was gathering valuable documents and hoped to write a book on living Hindu philosophy "quite different from [those] written by our pedants of the bookstacks." Her works would be pleasant to gaze on in their old age together. For the moment, she was enveloped by "India's magical coat," rocked in a "beautiful infinity."

Alexandra's first Christmas far from her home made her morbid. It rained, and as though to emphasize her loneliness, the Europeans were merrily celebrating the birth of Jesus. Those who preached of Christ, she wrote bitterly, were among the ones who would have stoned him. Crucifixion was the reward for those who tried to save humanity. She missed Mouchy and wished he were close so she could hug him. Of course, India would bore him; he would only be interested in the beautiful railroad bridges built by the British.

Alexandra, once attracted to the missionary life, could be at her most acerbic when preaching. It is not entirely surprising that she failed to respond positively to a man whose philosophy resembled that of Jesus: Gandhi. Not yet revered as a *Mahatma* (great master), he was entangled in the thick of the struggle for independence. Although his influence was already considerable, Alexandra recoiled from what she regarded as his reactionary tendencies, especially his denial of the benefits of industrialization. In part the contrast is between a man's and woman's point of view. Women, having done so much drudgery, seldom delude themselves about its joys. Nor did the Parisienne care for Gandhi's emphasis on village values and homely tasks. As Luree Miller has wrily pointed out, "A liberating achievement many women of means as modest as David-Neel might envy was that she never learned to cook but always managed to be served."

Alexandra was deeply impressed by another figure in the independence movement, Sri Aurobindo Ghose. When she met him in November 1911, this Oxford-educated patriot and poet, approaching forty, had already shifted his direction from revolution to founding his International Institute of Spiritual Culture and Research. He was to become one of the great mystical philosophers of our time. However, the British Government of India still feared him more than Gandhi. Ironically, he was to call on Indians to support the Allies in World War II, while Gandhi's unfortunate position advocating nonresistance to the Nazis is well known.

Aurobindo believed that humanity could perfect itself through a form of yoga. He advocated what he termed the "super-mind," the mind transcendent in both life and death. Looking forward to a new age of spiritual brotherhood, he spoke out against discrimination on the basis of caste or sex. Alexandra paid several calls on Aurobindo at his home in Pondicherry. In a letter dated November 27, she bestowed high praise on him:

I spent two beautiful hours discussing the ancient philosophy of India with an interlocutor of rare intelligence belonging to that uncommon breed of rational mystics with which I am in sympathy. He thinks with such clarity . . . such a glow in his eyes, that he leaves you with the impression of having contemplated the genius of India . . .

Alexandra realized that Aurobindo and his guests were being watched by the all-too-conspicuous police. She lightheartedly ignored a warning from the Madras chief of police about visiting "the home of monsieur suspect." This bravado was going to cause her grave difficulties over the next decade or so. True, not long afrerward she dined sumptuously at the right hand of the governor of Madras, after he was allegedly completely reassured she had no leanings toward independence. So Alexandra supposed, and she has been echoed by her previous biographers who like to stress her respectability and prominence, as though she were a society matron on a charity jaunt. In fact, a secret report made two years later to Sir Arthur Hertzel of the India Office, London, referred to:

Mme. David-Neel's visit to . . . Pondicherry to visit the leading extremist there. You will see from [a previous] telegram of 19, Dec. 1911 that the [governor] in Madras was advised to inform the Viceroy at Calcutta of her proceedings.

In the circumstances we may perhaps assume that the G of I [Government of India] knows all there is to be known about her?

This overly optimistic assumption was based on "secret enquiries in Paris" begun immediately after Alexandra's interview with Aurobindo, and which had turned up elements of her radical past. The British were worried by her former associates and by her use of various names, and they suspected she might be an agent of the French or some other government. The governor had been alerted promptly: "It might be well therefore not to lose sight of her, and to inform the . . . criminal investigation department of Calcutta."

The Government of India performed its surveillance with diplomatic finesse; its agents kept a wary eye on the Frenchwoman's travels and contacts. Several officials who proved most helpful also reported her movements to the viceroy. When they supposed it necessary, they thwarted her efforts. This ambiguity on the part of British officialdom continued throughout Alexandra's stay in the Orient. For her part, it took painful experience to learn that the British government was a collective opponent worth outwitting. Fortunately, their spying has left for us an objective record of the traveler's moves across the chessboard of Central Asia, and of how a lone middle-aged woman won through to Lhasa.

By the New Year, Alexandra had moved north to Calcutta. At first this Bengali capital of all British India—home to intellectuals such as Rabindranath Tagore, yet largely a commercial creation of the nineteenth century—failed to impress her. She dismissed the city as "a collection of tattered rags," stressing its unhealthfulness. Each year when the Ganges receded a plague broke out. In a reforming mood, she damned the pervasive ritual and caste. Instead of making obeisances to renowned swamis, she shook their hands. "How empty of passion is their philosophy," she declared, "and how scornful of the sufferings of the community of mankind, devoid of charity and compassion."

However, more to Alexandra's liking, she was known here from reprints in the *Indian Mirror* and the *Statesman* of articles published in Europe. She boarded comfortably with a Mrs. Walters where "everything is very English." She admitted that parts of town resembled London's St. James's or Kensington Park, and that evening's gray mist on the Ganges "put the Thames to shame." Prominent persons in the British community welcomed her, and off she went to "*luncher*"—Gallicizing English words was a regrettable habit—with a Justice of the High Court, Sir John Woodroffe. Soon she was dressing for "dinner among bejeweled ladies and gentlemen in their finery."

Woodroffe, a serious student of the Tantra, began to publish in 1918, under the pen name Arthur Avalon. He wrote and edited several authoritative volumes on this still misunderstood system, and indeed he is regarded as one of the founders of oriental studies. Alexandra, who was not given to praising her rivals, instead wrote disdainfully that the judge swore to her he expected "material benefits" from his worship of *shakti* (female power). She did respect him, but more as "an aristocrat and gentleman of high culture." Woodroffe was able to provide her introductions to both Europeans and Hindus. He and his wife gladly took Alexandra to Indian receptions and *kirtans* (devotions, usually with music).

The judge was an initiated devotee of Kali, Shiva's consort in her most ferocious guise. In the style of the ancient Semitic gods, she demanded the sacrifice of animals, and until the British forbade the practice, of humans too. Kali's temple on the Ganges ran with gore from beheaded goats, sheep, and water buffalo. Alexandra, when she visited, had to lift up her skirt to the calves while wading in seas of sacrificial blood. "What a foul charnel house!" she exclaimed.

The rational Buddhist tried to sound equally critical of the elaborate religious processions where, in spite of the grinding poverty of the masses, elephants were decked out in cloth of gold, huge emeralds and rubies, and camels in a thin network of beaten silver and gold. Yet the spectacle thrilled her to the core. The reformer grew genuinely angry over the custom of infant brides. Often these girls were wed to old men, a marriage that couldn't be consumated until menstruation. If their intended died, they found themselves widows at twelve or thirteen—still virgin. Not for long; barred from remarrying, they usually became prostitutes and were displayed in cagelike rooms. She felt it was praiseworthy that an American school was educating some of the unfortunates.

Alexandra tended at times to fall into a carping attitude she herself termed "Huguenot." Besides making for dull prose, it is untrustworthy, because she too could be callous in the midst of misery. While in a boat on the river, her rower pointed to an object washed up on the bank. It looked like a chubby leather doll, but closer up proved to be a dead man. A ravenous dog was gnawing his face, leaving a gaping hole and exposed teeth. Alexandra watched as the dog eventually tired of its tough meal. Then she ordered the rower to pull nearer so she could get a proper photo. She hoped her shots would come out. "Don't tell anyone I stop to take pictures of such objects," she cautioned Philip. "Westerners have peculiar ideas about death."

Little by little the spell of the East won over the activist. Overlooking the Ganges, she wrote, "The evening came rose and pale lilac on the pearl-gray stream." Her criticisms became muted or refreshingly clever. When a Brahmin priest haughtily refused an offering of chocolate, she tossed him rupees, which he avidly scooped up. Alexandra was reminded of a saying of the Roman Emperor Vespasian, "Money has no odor." Once, annoyed by the antics of the fakirs, she lay down on a vacant bed of nails. Reclining, she greeted a British tourist, "How do you like India?" She explained that she needed a nap and was lucky to find a handy couch.

Alexandra couldn't help sensing change within herself. "A bit of the lassitude that comes through the disdainful smile of Buddha has taken me over." Her ambition remained, because she continued to see "beautiful fat books dancing in front of my eyes." But first, she would have to come to terms with Mother Ganges which, indifferent to worship, flowed serenely over life and death alike.

In March 1913, Alexandra returned to the Ganges Valley, to holy Benares, after extensive travels in Sikkim and Nepal. She was crestfallen. She had pried open the door to forbidden Tibet, only to have it shut in her face. She was racked by a fierce desire "to learn what no explorers have even approached, to do what no European has yet done." Trying to forget what might have been, she sighed, "How beautiful the dream was, what a pretty end to life for the little old lady in glasses!" At forty-four, she turned once more to the study of Sanskrit and Vedanta.

Benares, which means, "resplendent with light," has been the religious capital of India since the dawn of history. When Gautama Buddha came there around 500 B.C., he saw ancient temples contemporary with Babylon, Nineveh, and Thebes. All devout Hindus yearn to worship at its holy places and to expire on the banks of its sacred Ganges. Thus they further their wish for no additional rebirths on earth but rather immersion in the Oversoul, Brahmin. Ultimate liberation from the wheel of life is assured those who repeat, as does Shiva himself, "Rama!"—a name of God—directly before they die in Benares.

The town is a maze of small streets and ways containing innumerable temples and shrines. Most striking are the *ghats*—stone steps stretching for miles to lead down from the steep bank to the river—and the crowds on them. The best hour to view the melee is at dawn. Devotees young and old execute yoga poses; zealots, eyes riveted on the rising sun, stare into its already blazing rays; a votary of Vishnu, hair matted in filthy pads, holds his arm high and immobile: it has shriveled up thin as a pipe cleaner. Phantom forms emerge from the low-lying mist to take ritual baths, while saucy cows amble along the terraces. *Saddhus* (holy men) intone drawnout mantras to the cosmic One. Mother Ganges is stage and play—bathed in by maids and matrons who decorously change wet saris for dry ones with lightning quickness. Worshipers rinse their mouths with the holy water—into which corpses are tossed—and the widows, segregated in special houses along the banks, call plaintively for their own deaths.

Alexandra easily fell into sympathy with this atmosphere of charged piety. She had tendencies toward the ascetic, and now she adopted the saffron robe of the *sannyasin,* or renunciate. When Philip, who understandably felt threatened, accused her of "egotistical isolation," of having married God as would a Christian nun, she assured him the situation was different. The robe of dawn color itself constituted "a fortress and a refuge" that did away with the need for stone walls and iron grilles of a convent. Although she didn't desire the life of a monk—meditation and fasting—she warned Philip that, if he pressed her to return prematurely, she could retire to a cave in the Himalayas or a hut in the jungles of Ceylon.

A boast, perhaps, but one that made clear to Mouchy that the woman he loved was fast slipping from him. Alexandra confessed to missing "the smiling quietude" of their marriage, the big house, the delicate dinners, but only a little. It was a life "half-asleep," and underneath she'd felt "an infinity of despair" at never being herself. Now she was learning the illusory quality of this self. When a naked beggar asked her for alms, she replied, "I am a *saddhu.* I possess nothing."

In almost the same breath, Alexandra reassured her husband that he was still married and to a person of note, that he could be proud of their name. The College of Sanskrit had called a conference to honor her with the title of "*savant en philosohpie,*" sort of an honorary doctorate. Imagine, here in the citadel of Hindu orthodoxy, a European, a woman, a Buddhist, to be so exalted! All the Brahmin priests attended, squatting on their haunches and listening raptly to her discourse on Vedantism. It was an event without parallel.

Alexandra had made rapid progress in Sanskrit, the notoriously difficult language of the Vedas, due to the tutoring of an elderly pundit who came to her once in the morning and again in the evening. The Brahmin possessed amazing knowledge of the ancient texts but scant common sense. When a cholera epidemic broke out, he declared that it was the invention of evil strangers. He scoffed at the European for having her room at the Theosophical Society scrubbed daily with a disinfectant. He declared that microbes didn't exist and it was useless to keep clean.

Funeral processions went by at any and all hours, but Alexandra stuck to her studies though the temperature soared to 104 degrees Fahrenheit. At night, beneath a protective net, she cursed the mosquitoes that kept her awake with their buzzing. She stayed away from the worst infected zones, for the poor, dying like crushed ants, couldn't afford to burn their dead relatives' linen and by reusing it spread the disease rapidly.

There is no trace of the plague in Alexandra's letters to Philip, who would have become frantic. Later on she recalled this vignette:

Ram! Ram! In the dark some people pass on the road, chanting the divine name. The torches they carry cast a gleam over the leaves and trees of the garden. . . . The voices fade, but others are already heard faintly [as] they approach. Ram! Ram! . . . These are the dead who are being carried to the cremation field on the banks of the Ganges.

Partly to gauge the epidemic's progress, more from interest, Alexandra went down to the burning *ghats*. She squatted among the relatives and the yogis to watch dead bodies being incinerated on wooden beds, their ashes afterward fed to the Ganges. Day and night the spectacle continued, people carrying on their religion by setting others aflame, knowing that at last their turn would come to be consumed. The Frenchwoman was fascinated by the solid fellows who did the work, torsos naked, a brief garment barely covering their muscled thighs. The operation reminded her of a ghastly sort of cooking. The workers, armed with long poles, flipped pieces of disjointed bodies into the heart of the fire, turning them like meat on a spit. The pelvic bones, seat of procreation, resisted longest. Clients, dead or only near it, awaited their fiery transport to eternity. "Miserable people probe the river for jewelry still clinging to the arms of the rich. And the[se] pariahs who dig . . . at the foot of the cremation *ghat* don't appear to get any richer."

The pundit also had money worries. He spoke to her transparently of a friend who was losing all his disciples. They no longer believed in God and wished to emigrate to England. But if this friend could learn to work miracles, disciples would flock round. Alexandra knew the Tantra, so she must teach him, she must take him to magical ceremonies. The friend was willing to do anything, even eat the brains of a dead person.

Where had the old fool got this notion? No use to explain she didn't believe in the sort of magic he wanted. Hadn't she been to the Himalayas, to Tibet? Every Indian knew that sorcerors lived there and even the English said so. The pundit demanded to meet practitioners of the black arts.

Alexandra might laugh him off, but not the illness that afflicted her in late summer. She felt feverish, dizzy, down in the dumps: the first symptoms of the plague? Practically delirious, she saw visions of the Himalayas, of "lakes that reflect snowy peaks, cascades in the forest." The delusion eerily resembled the painting showed to her long ago by Jacques Villemain, the young artist at the Gnosis, when he warned her about falling into the landscape.

Her malady proved to be, rather than cholera, an ailment of the soul. Alexandra longed for the chill of the mountains, the vistas and pure sparkling air of the high steppes. A brief glimpse of Tibet had captivated her, made her prisoner of a dream. Writing to prosaic Mouchy, she demanded, though more of herself, "[What] if no one in the world had lived their life and followed their star, where would we be?"

Word came that an apartment in the royal monastery of Sikkim awaited her. Instantly recovered, Alexandra packed her bags, tent, folding cot, and a galvanized tub she claimed to be portable. From her stays in Britain, the Parisienne had acquired two unlikely habits: she drank great quantities of tea, and wherever she might find herself—meditating in an aerie among the peaks, slogging through the jungle or under siege by bandits—she insisted on a hot bath daily.

CHAPTER 8

The Edge of a Mystery

Is it a man who is speaking to me? This short yellow-skinned being clad in a robe of orange brocade, a diamond star sparkling on his hat, is he not, rather, a genie come down from the neighboring mountains?

They say he is an "incarnated Lama" and heir prince of a Himalayan throne, but I doubt his reality. Probably he will vanish like a mirage, with his caparisoned little steed and his party of followers, dressed in all the colours of the rainbow. He is a part of the enchantment in which I have lived these last fifteen days. This new episode is of the stuff that dreams are made of. In a few minutes, I shall wake up in a real bed, in some country not haunted by genii nor by "incarnated Lamas" wrapped in shimmering silk. A country where men wear ugly dark coats and the horses do not carry silver inlaid saddles on golden-yellow cloths.

This scene begins *Magic and Mystery in Tibet,* David-Neel's most sensational work and, with its translation into at least nine languages since its appearance in French in 1929, probably her most popular. Her interlocutor was the Maharaj Kumar (Crown Prince) of Sikkim, Sidkeong Tulku. A *tulku* is roughly speaking a "phantom body." In the popular mind it is a living Buddha, or to be more precise, the successive incarnation of a great and holy spirit. The Dalai Lama is the best-known example of a *tulku.* Sidkeong had received this emanation from his granduncle, who died shortly before he was born.

The prince at thirty-three was the eldest son of the maharaja of Sikkim and *pro forma* abbot of the royal monastery. He was more handsome than Alexandra revealed, with deeply thoughtful almond eyes, even features, a strong nose and sensuous mouth, hair caught up in a thick braid clasped in silver, and carrying himself with a fitting air of command. She wrote of their meeting some fifteen years afterward and from the considerable distance of southern France, yet her language was underlaid by emotion.

She had first ventured toward the Himalayas on a lark. In March 1912, while still in Calcutta, Alexandra received an offer from the venerable Sanskrit college at the holy city of Hardwar: room and vegetar-

ian board, servants, a private tutor, and access to the faculty for ex-
plications. This would enable her to become a scholar the equal of any
in the West. She accepted and informed Philip, "While waiting, this
week I am going to Sikkim." Before leaving she attended a dinner
where Sanskrit speeches, literary allusions, and plays on words went on
interminably. The whole was presided over by a fat maharaja in gold
brocade and a rose turban—"ugly as several chimps"—whom the
speakers constantly compared to a god.

The usual clatter of the Indian railway proved a welcome diversion,
and once among the foothills, Alexandra took to horse. Mounted on
a "charger"—a small mare—and preceded by her porters, she compared herself to Don Quixote. The land was very different from that
of Spain, for she traversed "forests with enormous trees rotting with
age." She found the high jungle placid yet mysterious: in a favorite
image, "a perpetual curtain behind which go on things you are never
allowed to see."

In the mountains above Darjeeling—that salient of India on Nepal's
eastern flank—while crossing huge tea plantations at over seven thousand feet, Alexandra's mood also heightened. She encountered horsemen in Tibetan garb wearing gigantic curved cutlasses. Recalling that
she claimed descent from Genghis Khan (on her mother's side), she
exulted, "This is Mongol Asia, Yellow Asia." Although she rode astride
as even proper Englishwomen assured her she must, she complained
of "the murder of the natural cushions."

Alexandra was going to visit "a pope of thirty-seven years, a sovereign in exile," that is, the Thirteenth Dalai Lama. On the way she stayed
at the *dak* bungalow at Kalimpong, terminus of the mule trains carrying
wool from across the Himalayas. Built by the British to house traveling
officials, these simple, comfortable, out-of-the-way bungalows were also
frequented by European wayfarers or better-class Indians. Of course
each was not always up to par, and the Parisienne complained pee-
vishly, "What a strange country where it takes so many servants to be
so poorly served." She perked up with the arrival of the dashing prince
straight out of a fairy tale.

Alexandra was introduced to "a very amiable young man who seems
very intelligent." With his crowd of retainers, each carrying a long dagger stuck in his belt, the prince appeared the model of an oriental
despot. In fact he had been given a European education, first by tutors,
then at Oxford. Afterward he was sent on a grand tour of Asia to
acquaint him with the reigning monarchs. Left to himself, Sidkeong
preferred the tweeds and manners of a country gentleman.

His father, the old, ailing maharaja, was a well-intentioned but superstitious man, traditional though not religious. His great joy in life
was to go gaming for bird or beast, and if he neglected to hunt for
more than a week, the demon that he worshiped was likely to drive

him mad. The maharaja had lost his first wife, Sidkeong's mother, then married a noblewoman from Lhasa by whom he had a second son. This queen, Yeshe Drolma, although named for the Tibetan goddess of mercy, had an iron will that she attempted to impose on her lackadaisical husband. She wanted her son and not Sidkeong to inherit the throne.

In ancient times the women of Tibet had ruled forts and whole provinces. In Alexandra's day their legal and social position was superior not only to other Asian women but to women in Europe, according to W. W. Rockhill, the American ambassador to China. Still, Yeshe Drolma was special: she wrote a history of Sikkim (under her husband's name), and she appears to have been "a practitioner of the Black Art." She kept the state seal, and insofar as a Sikkimese might, she ruled.

The British had made plans for this tiny principality wedged between Nepal, Tibet, Bhutan, and India. Not yet part of British India, the Government of India through its resident political officer was regularizing it preparatory to absorption. The maharaja's retainers were cut from three hundred to fifty, and commercial development was set afoot. Prince Sidkeong was the chosen instrument for whom a dynastic alliance had been arranged with a Burmese princess, against the tradition of the maharani being Tibetan. Thus the handsome young man was reinstated as heir apparent for imperial purposes.

Alexandra was instantly attracted to Sidkeong because of his charm and a pixyish quality and also out of respect for his stance as a Buddhist. A *tulku*, he was reverenced by his people. He usually treated folk beliefs lightly and was a reformer whose model was Milarepa, the great twelfth-century Tibetan poet-sage and anchorite. The prince, thrilled to find a Western woman who thought as he did, immediately invited Alexandra to his capital. Since he had to travel ahead with his men, he provided an escort: Dawasandup, headmaster of the Tibetan boarding school at Gangtok. She described their journey of three days thus:

Shrouded in the moving fogs, a fantastic army of trees draped in livid green moss seems to keep watch along the narrow tracks, warning or threatening the traveler with enigmatic gestures. From the low valleys buried under the exuberant jungle to the mountain summits covered with eternal snow, the whole country is bathed in occult influences.

Dawasandup proved a companion to match the landscape where "it [was] fitting that sorcery should hold sway." Born of hillmen forebears of the Kazi or landlord class, he had inherited their penchant for the mysterious. He had studied with a tantric guru and courted secret intercourse with the *dakinis* (feminine deities) in order to gain magical powers. But the rather dapper man was the slave of two passions: he drank and read to excess. His drunken bouts were only occasional, while he carried on his reading at any time or place, and he was known to fall into a long, ecstatic trance over a text that especially pleased him.

His pedagogic method was equally peculiar. He couldn't bear to spend time in the classroom and assigned his duties to a lower master who felt much the same. The pupils would run wild until one day without warning the headmaster appeared to quiz them as sternly as a judge of the dead. He ordered one boy at a time to answer questions, and if the lad failed, the next in line had to slap his face. So it went down the line, for all the boys knew nothing. When the students failed to hit hard enough, Dawasandup beat every one. Waving a heavy stick, he jumped around hollering "Han!" as he whacked the boys' arms. They howled a chorus of laments but never studied any harder.

However, Dawasandup was an interpreter frequently employed by the British. The Earl of Rònaldshay, governor of Bengal, thought highly of him as a man of learning. W. Y. Evans-Wentz, the American-born Oxford scholar who compiled *The Tibetan Book of the Dead,* adopted Dawasandup as his mentor and collaborator. He faithfully edited the former's life of Milarepa, which he rendered into English from traditional sources. The headmaster ended his days in 1922 as a respected professor at the University of Calcutta, prematurely dying of the heat before he could quite complete a Tibetan-English dictionary. Now, as he and Alexandra approached Gangtok, the capital of Sikkim that was not much larger than a village, they were greeted by a sudden, severe hailstorm. Remarkably, this descended from a clear blue sky as though by magic.

Gangtok, nestled among terraced rice fields at six thousand feet, still remains an important trade depot, "a kaleidoscope of races and costumes" where "many tongues are spoken by the Tibetans, Sikkimese, Lepchas, Indians, Sherpas and Bhutanese who load and unload their pack trains." In Alexandra's day, there was a small British colony made up mainly of missionaries, while the British Resident oversaw His Majesty's affairs in both Sikkim and southern Tibet. Once a year he trekked over the mountains to visit the trade agency at Gyantse, some 130 miles into the Land of Snows.

Dawasandup, horrified by the freakish storm, rushed off to consult a *mopa* (oracle), and Alexandra went on to be welcomed by the prince at his private villa. The first floor, containing the sitting room, was furnished according to European taste, but on the floor above were snarling images, a Tibetan altar, and statues of Buddhas and saints. Scattered about were excellent works of art gathered by the prince in his travels. The modest villa, set in the lovely palace gardens, reflected both the sensitivity of the man and the split in his personality.

Wonderful conversations followed. First a Yellow Hat lama arrived from Tibet—this is the reformed branch, headed by the Dalai Lama and always celibate—and shortly thereafter a Red Hat lama—the older, less numerous branch whose members may marry. Sidkeong, in a brocaded robe, would preside from a low couch. Alexandra sat opposite him in an armchair, while the lamas, draped in their garnet-colored robes, sat to either side of the prince, and Dawasandup as interpreter squatted tailor fashion on the rug. A strange tea was served—"the color of faded roses and flavored with butter and salt." Rich Tibetans, of whom it was said, "Their lips are always moist," drank endless bowls of this tea, often with rancid butter. Most Westerners refused it.

Fortunately, Alexandra took to the brew at once, observing without comment the oriental etiquette that indicated a person's rank by the elaborateness of the tea service. The talk continued for hours, and the seeker plied the lamas with questions on the mysteries of initiation, magical powers, death, and the beyond. A lama is not an ordinary monk (or *trapa*), but usually more venerable and always better educated, and these two were the equivalents of doctors of philosophy. Alexandra delighted in bringing together two stalwarts of the sometimes feuding Red and Yellow Hat schools.

Although the prince was more concerned with reforming the small and decayed monastic establishments of his country (all Red Hat), he held an open mind toward esoteric lore. Alexandra was eager to gain information on anything she considered curious and original. Thus, although she loved the conversations, she jumped at the chance to go on tour with Sidkeong to inspect the outlying monasteries of Sikkim. The country varies in terrain from tropical jungles in the south to the snowy ramparts of the northern mountains, more closely packed than any comparable spot on earth and culminating in 28,150—foot Kinchinjunga, third highest of the Himalayas and more impressive in towering stature than Everest.

The night before the pair set out for Podang monastery, of which the prince was abbot, was May first, the anniversary of Gautama Buddha's enlightenment; it was full moon. Before retiring the two said their devotions, meaning they read and discussed Buddhist literature. The man and woman spoke in subdued tones, and lacking electric light, they saw by "the light from their intelligence." Sidkeong complained wistfully that he could not bring his ideas into practice because his authority was only nominal, far inferior to the Dalai Lama's. Indeed, he struck Alexandra as "a little bird kept on a string," and she decided to take him under her wing.

She went to bed but barely slept. Outside a small orchestra played through the night, consisting of two *gyalings* (oboes), two *ragdongs* (very long trumpets), and a pair of kettledrums. The Tibetan-style concert sounded sinister enough to raise the dead, and truly this unearthly music must be heard to be believed. An earlier traveler, Captain Knight, called it "the most diabolical uproar . . . since the first invention of music." Later Alexandra would describe the cacaphony to Philip as "the sonorities emitted by our own organism when . . . in complete silence [we] listen to the noise of our own machine functioning."

The former diva arose next morning delighted by the serenade but giddy from missed sleep. The prince's party was followed by an honor guard of musicians playing trumpets so long that small boys had to go ahead to hold them off the ground. Gradually, they wended their way upward, accompanied by a cortege of lamas who, in pointed bonnets, reminded Alexandra of medieval inquisitors. The monks' red hats and robes added extra splashes of color to a scene adorned with rainbow-tinted waterfalls and hundreds of varieties of orchids.

Sidkeong, like Alexandra, was an amateur botanist, and he showed his guest a few of the four thousand plants and ferns that made Sikkim an exquisitely varied garden. Farther up, the tropical vegetation gave way to hardier Alpine species, spruce, firs, and birch. Here and there a gigantic lily poked its graceful neck through the shade of the forest. Gaudy butterflies struck the visitor's fancy, and she observed at least seventeen different varieties: one with a jet-black body and huge wings resembling a bird's in flight. The explorer-to-be responded more naturally to the cooler heights than the hothouse closeness of the lowlands.

It rained, frustrating Alexandra's efforts at photography. She yearned to record the startling specimens of plants and people to send to Philip (with instructions to save for inclusion in future works). However, the prince diverted her with tales of his gaily dressed subjects, many of whom lined the road to pay homage, spinning prayer wheels that sighed in the wind. Actually, these implements omnipresent in the Buddhist world do not precisely offer up prayers but quotations from scripture meant as salutations to spirits in other realms to ensure their favorable regard for those on earth.

Sidkeong possessed an encyclopedic knowledge of the dwellers within his principality: the commercially minded Nepalis, creamy-skinned, shy Lepchas (the aboriginal inhabitants), and the sturdy Bhutanese who were herdsmen and traders. Alexandra's gaze kept roaming to the lordly, swaggering Tibetans. How splendid they looked with huge ear ornaments of turquoise, jade, and coral, worked charm boxes round their necks; they led horses draped with saddlebags in bright, clashing colors.

When the weather cleared, Alexandra took roll after roll of photos. She and the prince in beige raincoats offered an odd contrast to the multihued Asian throng. As they scurried back and forth to focus the cameras on their tripods, they resembled reporters come to interview the bewildered heathen. But Alexandra assured her husband she was no Cook's tourist. "You will be one of the most important spouses," she boasted.

Podang *gompa* (a monastery, although not cloistered) was relatively small, like other Sikkimese religious establishments, housing no more than one hundred monks. It was a bastion of unreformed conservatism. On a terrace dominating the valley, prayer flags waving from every space, it appeared to be a Chinese landscape painting sprung to life. The monks welcomed their abbot reverentially, although he lived like a Westerner most of the time. It annoyed Alexandra when a delegation of notables prostrated themselves on their stomachs three times. The prince, too, was embarrassed before his guest. Alexandra, to show respect to the holy place, did no more than fold her palms and give the Hindu salutation. Let the lamas judge her rude, she refused to bow to men or images.

Certainly there existed a vast gulf between Alexandra's rationalist beliefs and those of the inhabitants of Sikkim's sixty-seven monasteries. These monks of several older sects peopled an infernal spirit world with ferocious deities dressed in diadems of human skulls and necklaces of bone. Still, the frightful aspects of the tantric universe weren't as alien to the orientalist as they had been to more naive, if intrepid, travelers. One William Carey termed the monks "ignorant, idle and unscrupulous," and their thoughts "a nightmarish chaos of gods, devils and hobgoblins." Even the great travel-writer Isabella Bird—the first woman admitted to membership in the Royal Geographical Society— called Buddhist sacred literature, which she couldn't read, "fairy tales and stories of doubtful morality." To Alexandra, the apparently lewd paintings that she found on the monastery walls of beings copulating— or trying vainly to escape the many-tiered Tibetan hells—depicted humanity trapped in *maya*, the world of suffering erroneously thought to be real. Terrible-looking men and women, joined in agony, teeth clenched, naked with many serpentine arms, were warriors in the constant battle against lust and illusion; the corpses beneath their feet were slain passions.

More troublesome were the endless prostrations she and the prince had to endure before they could adjourn to the oratory for the usual tea and conversation. She joked to Philip that her relish for the salty beverage was a sure sign of "Tibetan naturalization," and she promised to bring home the recipe so they could brew it in Tunis. Even Giuseppe Tucci, the Italian archaeologist who wrote several tomes on Tibet, found the tea an inexpressible ordeal, which he underwent solely out of politeness.

That evening, seated on a low bench, Alexandra addressed the assembled monks. The reformer emphasized the virtues of early Buddhism and the need to banish the insidious fetishes that had distorted the great doctrine's message. Nor should the masses be permitted to wallow in superstition, since "the ivory tower of the thinker unworried by others is the castle of perdition." The congregation heard the foreign woman respectfully, although they distrusted her influence on their abbot. For Buddhists, decadent or not, tolerance was a pillar of their creed.

The dance of Yama—Lord of Death—concluded the festivities. Young boys danced with skeletons, rattling and clanging human bones. The actors wore masks featuring fanged mouths full of ulcers, and bloody, bulging eyes. Meanwhile the prince told Rabelaisian jokes to his cronies. He seemed unaware of the boys, who were pretending to eat the brains of the dead. Alexandra, stupefied by the show, was taken aback by the childish, irreverent attitude of the audience. She comforted herself with the thought that, in the Buddhist tradition, they regarded death as an incident in life, no sadder than other events.

The night had more to offer. Alexandra was allowed to sleep in the sanctuary, and the prince's divan was arranged on one side of the high altar, hers on the other. Although domestics hovered about to serve them, they couldn't impede the fleas that climbed up and down her legs. Mosquitoes, relentless as Tibetan demons, were also devouring her, and the patter of small feet meant rats scurrying around to nibble at the food offerings.

These annoyances couldn't dim the moment's hypnotic splendor. Soft moonlight intruded through the balcony and caressed the face of the pillars. A lamp cast dancing shadows on a golden statue of Buddha, while yellow zinnias emitted a subtle perfume. Alexandra recalled how in ancient Greece a novice who aspired to initiation had to sleep in the sanctuary at the foot of the altar. Would some strange magic befall her? She had a strong feeling that at last she was going to learn secrets never before revealed to a European.

Alexandra's euphoric mood deflated with her descent to Gangtok. Letters from Philip awaited her, wondering when she would return, complaining of her growing mysticism as once he had complained of her being too mental. She replied that intellect had its limits, that she was "savoring something else, opening another door." As far as she was concerned, the most corrupt Buddhist was preferable to "the overly zealous Christian missionaries" who occupied the diminutive capital. Her jaunts and late night tête-à-têtes with the bachelor prince had caused tongues to wag. The Europeans were certain that all Asians were immoral, and since she was sleeping at the royal palace, near Sidkeong's villa, they suspected the worst.

Ironically, the most serious accusation against Alexandra was that, by mixing with the prince and high lamas of the land, she "appeared to favor an idea that was too egalitarian." The inherent superiority of white skin was threatened! Amusingly, the former Belgian debutante in her turn damned the local British as mediocre *petite bourgeoisie*. "Here, the woman talks endlessly of making jam, [and] her husband plays the violin," she spat. On a far higher plane was "the strange [Tibetan] music that resembles nothing known . . . so grave, so slow, it gives you chills in the night.'

The sort of evangelical personality abhorred by Alexandra was beautifully depicted by James Hilton in his classic *Lost Horizon*, the novel published in 1933 that may have been influenced by Alexandra's work, and whose theme bears a curious resemblance to her life. Hilton gives us a rather sympathetic Miss Brinklow: courageous, narrowly sensible, and inquisitive. "Aren't you going to show us the lamas at work?" she demands at Shangri-La. This mature maiden lacks any genuine openness of mind but is eager to see "something picturesquely primitive that she could talk about when she got home. She had an extraordinary knack of never seeming very much surprised, yet of always seeming very slightly indignant . . ." For Miss Brinklow the heathen existed only to be converted, and so, stuck in Shangri-La, she dutifully learned Tibetan, in order to save the souls of those already in paradise.

The missionary Annie Taylor presents another real-life case. In 1892 this intrepid zealot entered Tibet from China, in a "naive and ill-prepared . . . attempt to reach Lhasa." Yet this small, middle-aged woman, a semi-invalid in childhood, was turned back only one week's march from the forbidden capital. She had an unfortunate propensity for handing out cards with biblical texts printed in Tibetan, and although most of the natives were illiterate, this may have impeded her. Of the lamas she remarked, "Poor things, they know no better; no one has ever told them of Jesus."

An Englishman of a different stamp resolved Alexandra's housing problem. The Resident, Charles A. Bell, invited her to lodge with him. Although Bell, later Sir Charles, did a number of favors for Alexandra and initially forwarded her research, the two were bound to clash. Bell was born at Calcutta into a British imperial family. He went home for schooling, first to Winchester on scholarship and then to Oxford. By 1891 he had joined the Indian civil service and was posted to Bengal. The fair-haired, bright-eyed, strong-willed young official was less rugged of physique, and the climate nearly killed him. He struggled with malaria, and a transfer in 1900 to the hills of Darjeeling came just in time. In order to prolong his stay in the heights, Bell plunged into the study of Tibetan. In 1905 he published a *Manual of Colloquial Tibetan*, an excellent guide to the spoken language that saved his life.

In 1908 Bell was appointed British political officer in Sikkim, and gradually he came to dominate the relations of the Government of India with this principality and to influence policy toward Bhutan and Tibet. When in 1910 the Thirteenth Dalai Lama fled across the Himalayas and went into exile at Darjeeling, he found in Bell a firm ally of an independent Tibet. The two continued a remarkable lifelong friendship, and the Great Thirteenth was pleased to say of the Ideal Civil Servant, "We are men of like mind."

By inclination Bell was a scholar. He was observant, free of racial prejudice, and able to mingle freely with Tibetan lay and Buddhist officials. Alexandra recognized at once that the Resident was the actual power in the principality, and she thought she divined his country's ambitions when she declared flatly, "England is in the process of very quietly taking over Tibet." Certainly this was in line with the Great Game of Central Asian rivalry as outlined by Lord George Curzon, the former viceroy to India and empire builder par excellence.

However, the Frenchwoman was overstating the case. The Anglo-Russian Agreement of 1907 had neutralized most of Tibet, although it recognized British dominance in the south. Bell himself, to his disgust, was not allowed farther north than Gyantse. Eventually, after his retirement, Bell would write several authoritative books on Tibet, its people and culture. No European man knew the country better, and perhaps Alexandra, with her sharp eye, detected a literary rival.

In contrast, Prince Sidkeong treated her in a manner almost worshipful. He shared her philosophical outlook and desire for a reformed Buddhism. What could endear a pupil more to his mentor than collecting her remarks in a scrapbook to keep by his bed? At other times the prince acted more of a playmate to the plump woman a dozen years his senior. He took to loading her with presents, and on one occasion, when she was at her desk writing letters, he cradled a baby yak (the hairy Tibetan buffalo) in his arms before the window, offering it to her. Bell had to be concerned with Alexandra's growing influence over the prince, and so he ushered her into the Residence where she would be comfortably lodged and he could watch her.

Alexandra was not slow to inform Philip just how cute she found the thirty-three-year-old prince, how young in spirit, and how he made everyone around him happy. Nonetheless, he was a hard worker, in charge of forests, agriculture and education. Pointedly, Alexandra remarked that he would "certainly make an excellent husband." Still more indiscreetly, she described their jaunts together into the mountains. Sidkeong, short but sturdy, was a first-rate mountaineer who, no matter how high or slippery the climb, never showed fatigue or ill humor. After one particularly steep ascent that caused Alexandra's head to swim, she glanced up to see her partner scurrying fearlessly ahead. All this outdoor activity made the matron appear younger, slimmer. "There are days when I don't recognize myself in the mirror," she wrote. "The years have been erased from my features . . . and in my eyes shines the light of the Himalayas."

Following a day's trek, night in an isolated bungalow was cozy. Outside, the demons might prowl and witches gather, but within there were no closed doors between the two soul mates. First they would dine together; then, "We will light the incense, we will read a page of philosophy . . . dream a little the dream [that was] Buddha's. Each time we travel together we have in the evening our little cult . . . until one in the morning." Then the Prince, a master of discreet elegance, would retire.

Learning of this proved too much for Philip, who literally couldn't stop dreaming of his lost wife. Neither overly suspicious nor a fool, he sensed something more going on than a merely platonic affair. There was no denying a strong romantic current between the mature woman, attractive and stylish when she chose to be, and the dashing young prince. That their feelings for one another were based on a shared, vital view of the world only fanned the slowly growing fire. Alexandra had never before found this quality of understanding, of spiritual dedication, in a man who physically pleased her. Sidkeong combined ease of companionship with the authority of a prince. He was everything that the mundane, hypochondriacal Mouchy could never be, and Alexandra didn't mind flinging it in her husband's face.

Naturally Philip felt betrayed. He had undertaken to support a scholar, not an oriental potentate's mistress. Worse, it was made clear that he had failed to come close to the one woman who mattered to him. According to his next letter, he went for a long melancholy Sunday walk along the margin of the sea, lonely and miserable. Was his desperation such that he contemplated suicide? This letter, like most of his others, is lost, but Alexandra responded to it with unusual urgency.

She offered to return immediately if the pain of her absence were truly so severe. She reassured "her very dearest Mouchy" of his wife's fidelity and that she always thought to return to Tunis: "I dream of the books I am going to write [there]." She felt she was through with fleshly pleasures; she willingly paid this price for abandoning home and husband even temporarily. Begging for patience, Alexandra deftly switched the subject, reminding Philip that Buddha had been an active man of affairs just like himself.

In fact, Alexandra was going through a process of abandoning the obvious for the refined, the *sexual* for the *sensual*. She devoured her exotic surroundings, including the tawny beauty of both men and women, through its sights and sounds, via her eyes, ears, every one of the five sense organs. This is not Puritanism but a quickening of perception that is a large step on the tantric path to power. However, her development was far from complete, and we are left with the question of whether she did or didn't have a sexual affair with the prince of Sikkim. Philip supposed so, likewise the missionaries, but there is no real evidence. Bell, who would have made it his business to find out, is silent on the matter, even in his unpublished notebooks.

Sidkeong gave Alexandra some remarkable gifts. We have seen these precious bracelets, earrings, and *objets,* and as is the custom in the East, they are nearly solid gold. The explorer, no matter how desperate her plight, how poor, hungry, and cold she grew, refused to sell even one piece. She carried the jewelry on her person during her marathon journey through unmapped Tibet, when if anyone had caught sight of the treasure, it could have cost her and her son their lives. The prince's baubles rest now at Digne, France, and if these beautiful objects could only speak, they might tell a lovely tale.

Alexandra's training as a singer stood her in good stead in her climbing excursions. Born with strong lungs, she had studied breath control. Yet she was nervous before her first serious camping expedition. She claimed that her daring was "a victory of spirit over matter, of will over flesh." She never quite lost the fear of hurting herself. The prince obtained for her mounts, yaks, tents, and bearers and waved her off on a trek to fifteen thousand feet—just below the line where the abominable snowman is rumored (mostly by Westerners) to prowl.

Thrilled at being her own woman and entranced by the eerie light where "shadows radiate mysteriously with a brightness which is neither sun nor moon, which seems not to descend from the sky but emanate from the objects themselves . . . from something in back of their material forms," Alexandra sped along in front of the party. She had to wait three hours in stinging snow for her servants to come up and boil tea. Her tent barely closed, and by next morning it was an inconspicuous dot on the snow-covered heights. Alexandra, too ill to budge, felt her chest bound by pain. She had to do something quickly or the snow would be her shroud. If it was pneumonia or heart trouble, the odds were against her.

Then she grew unreasonably calm. How noble to perish among these majestic mountains, alone with the gods! Her last wish was to get a picture of her death site for Mouchy. Bulky camera in hand, she crawled from the tent, pointed, and snapped. She felt better, inched back, and groaned for her people. Hot tea and a steaming footbath revitalized her blood, and the ache was dimming. Soon, in the saddle, she was heading for the next ridge.

This trek proved to Alexandra the joys of solitude, of sleeping in a tent in the high Himalayas, and of eating rations cooked outdoors over a yak dung fire—provided a servant did the cooking. She had seen "a country of dreams . . . orange peaks that slice the intense blue heavens. . . . The orange mountains [were] crowned with a coiffure of snow. And the valleys were drowsing with little lakes of frozen water . . ."

The Tibetan plateau lay before her, resembling nothing so much as the mystical painting shown to her years before at the London Gnosis. Should she descend to it? She knew such a step was strictly forbidden by both British and Tibetan authorities. The question was settled for her by the Sikkimese porters, who were freezing and demanded to turn back. They took to fighting one another for a place at the fire, and Alexandra had to separate them with a whip.

She wasn't faring much better. "I have no more skin on my face," she later wrote to Philip, that admirer of pretty women. "My eyes are completely burned with large red pads on my eyelids. My nose covers my whole face . . . My skin is hanging, my lips are a huge white blister." She cured the latter by slitting the skin with a sharp knife.

After her return, Alexandra had an irrepressible desire to make another expedition, to get stronger bearers—Tibetans—and climb back, this time to cross the forbidden line. All the Europeans in tiny Gangtok felt the same strange fascination, although none dared act. When Dawasandup revealed to her that the hailstorm had been a warning and that the oracle predicted she would face terrible difficulties if she attempted to live in the Land of the Religion, the rational Buddhist didn't deign to reply.

Outwardly, the Frenchwoman—who to some seemed a dilettante, to others worse—continued quietly about her studies. She said nothing of Tibet, certainly not to the British Resident or the missionaries. To Mouchy alone she confided, "I remain bewitched, I was on the edge of a mystery."

CHAPTER 9

The Living Buddha

"Forbidden Tibet! Westerners have called it that for centuries!" wrote Lowell Thomas, Jr. The most inaccessible land on earth, it has always lured explorers, missionaries, and searchers after both spiritual truth and the secrets of perpetual life. Shangri-La may be a fictional place, yet its equivalent has been sought for both above and below ground in this kingdom protected by the ramparts of the Himalayas. Despite its location on the roof of the world, with valleys at fourteen thousand feet, and until recently its official policy of remaining closed to outsiders, Tibet has drawn an array of adventurers who dared to penetrate the sacred, if haphazardly guarded, realm. For the rest of us, we know less than we suppose about this *ultima Thule*.

Tibet is a large country—about one-third of the continental United States—and its influence has been decisive over an area of Central Asia nearly three times its own size. Its immediate neighbors are difficult to reach: to the west, Ladakh (Kashmir) and a wild bit of Bengal; to the south, the mountainous states of Nepal, Sikkim (now incorporated into India), Bhutan, and half-charted portions of Assam and Burma; to the east, the Chinese marches, formerly inhabited by brigands and Tibetan-speaking nomads, or inhospitable portions of Szechuan and Kansu provinces; and to the north, the vast desert spaces of China's Sinkiang province. Mongolia lies beyond, and more westerly so do Afghanistan and an Asian corner of the Soviet Union. Population statistics are murky and politically entangled; there are some six million ethnic Tibetans, two-thirds of whom live in what is presently western China, and the remaining one-third in the so-called Tibet Autonomous Region of China, the old heartland, now an unwilling part of the People's Republic. Since 1959, when Chinese troops brutally crushed a popular uprising, a considerable émigré community has taken root in India, concentrated in the north.

If we were to ask an average American who rules Tibet, he would likely reply, "the Dalai Lama," a little uncertain as to just who, or what, that might be. But the Fourteenth in the line of Dalai Lamas, and perhaps the last, lives in exile in India. So did the Great Thirteenth from 1910 to 1912 after he, too, fled a Chinese invasion. During the latter's wanderings in the diaspora, Alexandra met and interviewed him. Initially skeptical, the lord of Mahayana Buddhism came to accept the foreign woman as an insider, a member of the faith. The Thirteenth went out of his way to further her mission, encouraging her studies and answering many abstruse questions.

In one of her books, some years later, Alexandra would claim: "The Dalai Lamas have every facility for receiving full instruction in the noblest philosophical and mystical doctrines of Lamaism. For my part, I am in a position to assert that the Dalai Lama whom I met was profoundly versed in these doctrines and was fully capable of expounding them." Privately, at the time, she informed her husband, "This man does not have my sympathy . . . I don't like the kind of hierarchical Buddhism over which he presides. Everything is affectation in him, he has neither cordiality nor good will."

Tibetans, at the end of an evening of light diversion, will sit cross-legged, and someone will say, "Let's talk about religion!" In order to understand the unique phenomenon that is the Dalai Lama, and more specifically Alexandra's reaction to the Thirteenth, it is necessary to understand more about the religion of Buddhism, especially its founder. Bear in mind that each Dalai Lama is regarded as a living Buddha.

The historical Buddha, Siddartha Gautama Sakyamuni—his given, family, and clan name—was born in the sixth century B.C. in what is now southern Nepal. Significantly, he was of the Kshatriya (warrior) caste, and according to Alexandra, his father was "a chieftan reigning over a small state lying at the feet of the Himalayas." Siddartha's immediate family, although noble and wealthy, was by no means fabulously wealthy or powerful. The boy's mother died soon after giving him birth, and he was raised by her sister, also the raja's wife.

The young nobleman received the best education of his day. In his country the Hindu Brahmins were not so influential, and he grew up unfettered by worldly cares. He married, had a son, and appeared content. Then at twenty-nine Siddhartha had his head shaved, donned the plain yellow robe of a *sannyasin,* or renunciate, and rejected the goods of this world "with satisfaction, as throwing off dirty and ragged clothing." Although the tradition of religious mendicants was well established, the young man's family were all horrified. There is a certain parallel to Alexandra's situation, and she remarked that one first has to be comfortable to become a Buddha; otherwise, the allure of material things would be too engrossing, too persuasive.

Alexandra continued:

Gotama thirsted for spiritual illumination, and ended by finding it; but not in the schools of the famous philosophers which he had at first entered as a pupil, nor yet in the ascetic practices so highly valued in India, despite his prolonged and cruel experience of them. It came to him when he sought it only in his own mind, when he was meditating in solitude, under a tree.

This surely appealed to a woman who, since youth, had sought to escape, sometimes desperately, from a cloying society.

Siddartha had become the Buddha, the Awakened One. He preached his first sermon at the Deer Park outside Benares. Though differing in content and emphasis, as a statement of belief it has made an impact on people's minds no less than Jesus' Sermon on the Mount. These separate moments appear to sum up the earthshaking messages of the two founders of universal faiths. Here in the citadel of the Brahmins— much as Jesus dared the high priests—Buddha denied the value of self-mortification and denigrated the uses of ritual and sacrifice. He declared that all things spring from a cause, and the cause of human suffering is nothing less than the craving for life. The human search for pleasurable sensation leads inevitably to pain. Following the Eightfold Path puts an end to *karma,* successive rebirths, and leads to *nirvana,* cessation, the blissful void.

Buddha did not suffer crucifixion, but rather, begging bowl in hand, went from city to city and with his disciples spread the message. He passed away in his eightieth year, it is said from eating spoiled boar's flesh. "A splendid example of energy," he lay down in a flowering grove and, with nearly his last breath, gave the teachings to an utter stranger. He informed his closest disciple Ananda that the rules of the order might be changed as the monks saw fit, that anyone qualified could lead them. He insisted he had held back nothing. As translated by Alexandra, his final advice to his disciples was: "Dissolution is inherent in all formations [living beings]. Work diligently for your deliverance!"

Buddhism, destined to die out in its native India, spread to other lands. The terms *Mahayana* (Greater Vehicle) and *Hinayana* (Lesser Vehicle) are used to differentiate between the Buddhism of northern and southern Asia. The split came about early as the Mahayana budded from the stem of the Hinayana in northern, Sanskrit-speaking India. According to Sir Charles Eliot, diplomat and scholar, the newer faith proved "warmer in charity, more personal in devotion, more ornate in art, literature, and ritual."

Especially in Tibet, the Mahayana stressed the supernatural spirit of the Buddha, of which innumerable Buddhas past, present, and future are but emanations. Along with this concept, at least as mystical as the theology questioned by the young Alexandra, came the worship of *bodhisattvas*—beings who reject *nirvana* until all humankind can join them. Cults are dedicated to these heroes, who must continually reincarnate to fulfill their beneficent purpose.

"Warriors, warriors we call ourselves," begins a favorite text of Alexandra's. "We fight for splendid virtue, for high endeavor, for sublime wisdom." When, in the seventh century, the barbarian Tibetans became interested in Buddhism, they appropriated the Mahayanism of nearby Nepal and Bengal, which featured a magical and daring approach dubbed "tantric" after its books, the Tantras. It was the warrior king Strongtsan Gampo who, at the insistence of his two wives, one Chinese and the other Nepali, first sent scholars into India to study and translate Buddhist texts. They had to fashion an alphabet, since Tibet had none, and physically carry the books on their backs over the sky-high barrier of the Himalayas. This tradition became central to Tibetan Buddhism, and Alexandra would become rightfully proud of her translations *from* Tibetan and the collection of texts she brought back over the mountains *to* India and the West. No other woman has performed such an astonishing task, and nearly at the cost of her life.

Not until the mid-eighth century did the tropical plant of Buddhism take root in the frigid soil of the Tibetan plateau. Tibet had become an important military power. The king sent for Padma Sambhava, "a renowned yogi-sage, skilled in magic and mysticism, who probably came from Swat." He was a harsh but clever man able to adapt his teachings to the demonology already in place. The preexistent shamanist religion, known as Bon, emphasized protection against a horde of malicious spirits. Considering their environment of biting winds, glaciers, sudden storms, forbidding mountains, chasms through which rush icy torrents, and a light that presents distant objects as near and near ones as receding, the Tibetans' bone-deep belief in sorcery is scarcely surprising. Padma Sambhava presented himself as the great exorcist empowered to subdue the most ferocious demons. His act consisted of "demon-quelling rituals, bragging self-praise, and displays of magical powers and self-transformations." This is the sort of fellow a barbarian king, or well-to-do merchant or herdsman, is pleased to hire, and Guru Rimpoche, as he is referred to by Tibetans, was able to build the country's first monastery, Samye, and to become the fountainhead of the several Red Hat sects. Though his name is associated with the *Tibetan Book of the Dead,* he apparently drank, consorted with women, and practiced tantric sexual rites.

At first, Alexandra regarded the Buddhism descended from Padma Sambhava as decadent and superstitious. She leaned toward the reforms of Tsong Khapa, born in 1357 near Lake Koko Nor in Amdo. This founder of the Yellow Hat discipline, the established church of most Tibetans and Mongols, turned monk at seven and absorbed instruction from a variety of teachers, including Roman Catholic missionaries. In early manhood he went to Lhasa and, under the secular rulers, began to implement his reforms. He instituted a true monastic discipline complete with hierarchy, celibacy, and communal prayer, while discouraging magical practices. Tsong Khapa was behind the founding of the three great monasteries of Ganden (Joyous Mountain), Sera (Rose Fence), and Drepung (Rice Heap), thereby surrounding the capital with yellow-hatted monks and insuring a clerical veto over the acts of government. He also established Tashilhunpo at Shigatse, unwittingly giving rise to the Panchen Lama, rival to the Dalai in prestige and in bestowing favors on Alexandra, the foreign female Buddhist.

"Thirteen Dalai Lamas succeeded to the [throne] before the coming of the present monk-king," wrote Alexandra. "Only two of them—for very different reasons—became famous." The Great Fifth, with the aid of Mongol troops, seized secular power in the seventeenth century. Indeed, *Dalai* is Mongol for the sea, vast and profound. The Fifth built Lhasa's enormously impressive Potala Palace, and he determined the powers of the Dalai Lamaship as definitively as had Innocent III those of the Roman papacy. When the Manchus succeeded to the Celestial Throne of China in 1644, the Fifth journeyed to Peking where the emperor bestowed upon him the title "Universal Ruler of the Buddhist Faith."

The Great Fifth ruled as an autocrat in Lhasa. His death was concealed for over a decade while his chief adviser, said to be his natural son, continued to preside in his name. There can be no dynasty of Dalais; the successor is not his son but his reincarnation in a newborn male child. Each is an emanation of the Bodhisattva Chenresi, patron deity of the land. Thus Tibet's ruler was often an infant of rude peasant parentage raised in the halls of state. However, due to the conniving at court, the Sixth Dalai Lama was not announced until 1697 when he was in his teens. He had been found but left to live normally with his parents.

Alas, the remarkably winning lad was a merry one: he drank, wore jewelry, and chased women all night long. Melodious Purity—so he was named—wrote beautiful love songs that are still sung by Tibetans, for the people adored him. Indeed, Alexandra insisted, from her own experience, "A sort of half-secret cult is [still] paid to him by the good folk of Lhasa." She attempted some free translations of his poems, which are very condensed and allusive. Here is one:

> Peace you prattling parrots [those who blamed him],
> In the willow wood the *djolmo* [a tuneful bird] wishes to sing
> Whether terrible or not
> The gods and demons in wait behind me,
> I would make mine the sweet apple
> Which is here before me.

Melodious Purity understood the sort of double or symbolic language requried both of a poet and an initiate in tantric sexual practices. As David Snellgrove put it, "[E]ven the literal is concealed beneath the jargon of their secret language." The motive has been twofold: fear of exposure and fear of the obvious misunderstandings. Concerning the Sixth, Alexandra wrote that he led a life of "what appears to us [as] debauchery, and would indeed be so in the case of any other than an 'initiate' into that singular training of which it is difficult to speak outside a medical treatise."

Alexandra's view of the Sixth, and the basis of her attraction to tantric rituals—where, as she admitted, "The wine which has to be drunk . . . is real wine and the women with whom one must be united is any woman, *except* one's legitimate wife"—is nicely echoed by the scholar Agehananda Bharati:

The paradoxical situation is that the tantric appears to the orthodox Hindu and Buddhist as a libertine, whereas in reality he preserves a state of complete celibacy. The famous, or infamous, Sixth Dalai Lama had his problems vis-à-vis the orthodox reformed clergy, but I feel reasonably sure that they did not recognize the tantric disciplinary element in his case.

Certainly the Manchu emperor failed to be amused. But the actual deposing of the living Buddha from his throne was accomplished by a Mongol army in Tibet. Then the emperor invited Melodious Purity to Peking in a mockery of the usual honorifics. On the way he had him poisoned, much to the outrage of the Tibetan people. Nonetheless, this initiated the habit of murdering young Dalai Lamas when they approached manhood. The Ninth, Tenth, Eleventh, and Twelfth conveniently shed their earthly guise at about the same age. The Tibetan noblemen acting as regents preferred it, and so did the two Chinese Ambans (ambassadors) residing in Lhasa. However, the Thirteenth proved more canny than had his predecessors, and he lived to grant an audience to a stocky, middle-aged Frenchwoman, very determined looking, who claimed to be a Buddhist and who barraged him with such a multitude of exacting questions about the faith that he had to consider his answers carefully.

Kalimpong, India—twenty miles from Darjeeling—April 15, 1912. The inhabitants of this bustling trade mart, whether Nepali mule drivers, broad-faced Bhutanese, mustachioed Tibetans, or swarthy Hindus, or even the handful of British functionaries, were in a state of excitement bordering on the feverish. Flags flew, banners waved, and a bust of the late Queen Victoria presided benignly over this outpost of empire. In a chalet belonging to the raja of Bhutan on the outskirts of town, Tibetan servants bustled about preparing for the day. Despite a drizzle, some were planting bamboo poles to form an avenue in front of the modest building. Others hovered near their master, the living Buddha, who was seated cross-legged on an elevated bench draped in yellow in a corner of the topmost room. None of the retainers was too busy to chatter and gossip.

From the marketplace with its crowds lining shuttered shops, indifferent to the wet mist shrouding the stage set of Himalayan peaks, came a chorus of approval: a European woman was being carried past in a dandy, her four bearers doing their best not to jiggle her. The crowd caught a mere glimpse of her, swathed in a raincoat, face covered by a light salmon veil. If the populace had been told, "She is Alexandra David-Neel," they wouldn't have cared. By sticking out their tongues—a sign of respect—and pointing to the bust of Victoria, they showed they regarded the lady as an emanation of the queen, who in turn really was Palden Lhamo, patron goddess of Tibet. In the East, truth can be as manifold as a "thousand-layered" Burmese pancake!

Within the dandy, Alexandra's mind was afloat in a dream. The weather reminded her of Belgium, of walks under rainy skies with her father. "If I am somebody," she thought, "it is due to the long chats with him." How he would have loved to hear of her adventures. Sadly, Alexandra wished her dead father would appear magically on the road so she could stop everything to hug and kiss him. But she knew that, a man who had suppressed his feelings, Louis David would be embarrassed. "He didn't love me any more than my mother," she sighed.

Once inside the chalet, Alexandra had to pass the royal chamberlain, whom she felt was brusque. Although the protocol for her visit had been decided in advance, lapses occurred. Ushered into the presence of the Dalai Lama, she found that he had abandoned his throne to sit in a simple chair by the window. This was extraordinary, since he always sat higher than anyone else. Had he divined her dislike of pomp?

Alexandra recognized him from his portrait: a slightly stooped figure with wide open, riveting eyes, slightly evasive, a waxed mustache, and enormous ears (a sign of wisdom), wearing a peaked yellow cap and maroon robes. She pressed her palms together before the heart in salutation. Someone slipped a white silk scarf into her hands and she presented it but forgot the proper words. He wasn't very tall and, a trifle unwillingly, the rebel bowed her head, whereupon the Dalai Lama reached out to bless her.

As the two conversed, the Thirteenth wondered aloud how the Frenchwoman, alone in her faith in a foreign land, could have become a Buddhist without a master. To himself he must have questioned whether she were a Buddhist at all. The missionaries, fond of disguises, would go to any lengths to convert his people. Alexandra's knowledge ran deep, and she soon satisfied him on that score, even made him smile. She tried to ignore the officious chamberlain who continued to interrupt. However, she had to admit that those Europeans interested in Buddhism were of the older, Hinayana school.

"It is precisely because I suspect that certain religious doctrines of Tibet have been misunderstood that I have come to you to be enlightened," said Alexandra. This greatly pleased the Dalai Lama, who decided she must be an emanation of Dorje Phagmo, the "Thunderbolt Sow," Tibet's only female incarnation.

In turn, Alexandra interrogated her host. "What is the path of salvation, the path of clairvoyant wisdom?" He calmly replied, "You know it. It is perservering reflection, untiring meditation." She hadn't been impolite, merely employing the traditional method of discourse. Lamas must commit hundreds of sacred texts to memory, and when they are called on, repeat the appropriate passage. But the eager visitor fired off so many queries that she and the Dalai Lama agreed she should submit them in writing. He promised to answer fully, and she would have unique documents, of great value to an orientalist.

The interview over, the visitor received another silk scarf and backed out. Luckily there was no furniture to bump into, and besides she had practiced this maneuver at the court of Belgium. The crowd outside was awestruck when she emerged, since the Compassionate One had allowed this European woman a full hour of his precious time. Alexandra was thinking, "What a marvelous article this will make for the *Mercure!*" To Philip she wrote candidly that the Thirteenth, while "not an imbecile," was far from "an intellectual in our sense." The scarf smelled so musty she shoved it into a corner of her bathroom.

The crowd would not have to wait much longer. The Dalai Lama was due to appear, and with legs permanently bowed from meditating for hours each day since early childhood, he would mount his makeshift throne. The pilgrims would pass before him: rich or poor, traders and cowherds, Buddhists, Hindus, and animists. On the highest born he must place both hands, on landowners one hand, on merchants just a finger or two. Even the lowliest beggar could expect to be touched with a tassle to complement the blessing from the incarnation of Chenresi that was bound to bestow good fortune.

After all, hadn't this god on earth through the power of his spells overthrown his enemy, the emperor of China? Was he not about to return triumphant to Lhasa, the universal ruler of the Buddhist faith?

CHAPTER 10

An Invisible Barrier

Since there has been only one Dalai Lama in fourteen different bodies, the task has been to find him after each death and rebirth as an infant. Tibetans acknowledge dozens of similar incarnations, called *tulkus* or "phantom bodies," of which this Grand Lama has been considered the most estimable. The method of locating him was essentially fixed. Within a year or two of the previous sovereign's passing away, a council of lamas would consult the state oracle for general directions. Then a high lama was sent to a particular lake under the waters of which resided the Dalai's imperishable soul. While staring into the icy blue water, the lama would have a vision, and perhaps that night a helpful dream. He should picture the looks and whereabouts of the child-sovereign too clearly to be mistaken.

Once located, the candidate was put to the test. Appropriate bodily marks were considered, but the main thing was that the tiny boy recall everyday articles used in his past life, for example, a much-fingered rosary. He had to choose from among lookalikes with unfailing accuracy. Later, memories of previous incarnations would come to him, and he would feel instantly at home with unknown places and people. And now that the old order is overthrown and the Chinese occupy Tibet, how will the next Dalai Lama be chosen, or will there be a next? The Fourteenth incarnation, who will decide, has not said.

Even traditionally, the Manchu emperor had the right to confirm the choice of a new Dalai Lama. This was done in a manner subject to manipulation: the names of several likely candidates were dropped into a golden urn, and the Chinese Amban picked out one with the aid of chopsticks. We suspect he had tucked the successful slip up his enormously long sleeve. In the case of the Thirteenth, the indications were so clear that the suspicious Tibetans refused to employ the urn. The emperor grudgingly acquiesced, and so before he was aware of it, the Thirteenth had begun to defy China.

The lad was reborn in 1876 of ordinary peasant ancestry. He was taken from his mother and father at two, enthroned at three before a horde of grave lamas prostrating themselves, and then educated by learned professors in Buddhist ritual and metaphysics. Surrounded by serious-minded adults, he had to study night and day, was denied play-mates, and hardly ever saw a female. He learned little of the workaday world either personally or from books, and not much about lands out-side Tibet. Naturally, he became dependent on his advisers.

Traditionally, when he reached eighteen, the Dalai Lama was ex-pected to assume his temporal authority. First he had to make a journey to "The Heaven Lake of the Goddess" 150 miles southeast of Lhasa to commune with Palden Lhamo, guardian of the Tibetan state. Her chapel was "furnished with stuffed carcasses of wild animals and other fearsome objects . . . She is powerful and easily angered." On the way back to Lhasa, the living Buddha was given a holy pill, "to renew his vitality and make his countenance shine." Face aglow he passed into his next incarnation. A lavish funeral would be held where it was an-nounced that the Compassionate One had departed the world due to despair at the wickedness of his people.

The Thirteenth, who had a natural aptitude for politics, was clever enough to avoid swallowing the poison pill. According to Charles Bell, a Chinese official remarked that "affairs had been managed very badly." Neither Peking nor the Government of India was accustomed to dealing with an adult sovereign of Tibet.

During the nineteenth century the British, in fits and starts, had been moving northward, taking over the Darjeeling district and, dating from a treaty in 1861, establishing a protectorate over Sikkim. In 1910 a similar arrangement, although more at arm's length, was negotiated by Bell with Bhutan. The British political strategy termed by Lord Cur-zon the Great Game required that Russian expansion eastward be stopped short of Buddhist Central Asia. A Russian Mongol, Dorjieff, had studied with the lamas in Tibet. This alleged student of Buddhism became a close adviser to the young Thirteenth. Lord Curzon, the vice-roy, fearing that Dorjieff was an agent, sent several letters to Lhasa, ostensibly to open discussions on trade. Always he received the same reply: "We have no dealings with foreigners."

In 1904 Colonel Francis Younghusband, backed by a small army of *sepoys* (Indian troops), was dispatched to pay a diplomatic call on the Dalai Lama. Younghusband was one of the most intrepid and knowl-edgeable officers on the Indian frontier. Interestingly, he would evolve into something of a mystic and an admirer, with reservations, of David-Neel. Other officers on the expedition were Captain L. A. Waddell, who would write the comprehensive but biased *Tibetan Buddhism,* and young David Macdonald, just beginning his stint of twenty years in Tibet.

To the surprise of the British, the Tibetans fought bravely and held up their advance in the Chumbi Valley. Here Macdonald met Annie Taylor, who had penetrated farther into the country than any other missionary, male or female. Once the army had dragged its cannon over the mountains, the defenders, who had only antique muzzle-loading rifles and no sense of modern warfare, could offer no serious resistance. Still, at every stage, Younghusband tried fruitlessly to negotiate, while the general in actual charge of the troops had to overcome the reluctance of his men to machine-gun the foolhardy Tibetans. The British pushed on, complaining of roads so poor they had never felt the weight of any wheeled vehicle. Soon everyone became entranced by the wild, magnificent scenery. As the army approached Lhasa and caught sight of the golden roofs of the Potala Palace, a race developed to be, in Macdonald's words, "the first living European to set eyes on the Forbidden City of the Lamas." On August 4 the British entered, "tearing aside the veil of centuries."

The Dalai Lama had fled north to Mongolia, so Younghusband opened negotiations with the regent, the abbot of Ganden monastery. While the Dalai Lama camped in the remote grasslands of the steppes and his devout Mongol subjects flocked to pay him homage, an Anglo-Tibetan Convention was agree upon and ratified by the Tibetan Assembly. The document laid the basis for Tibet's foreign policy in the twentieth century and strongly supports its claim to independence from China. Neither the Manchu emperor nor his Ambans were consulted. The convention forbade foreign occupation of any portion of Tibet or intervention in its affairs. Of most importance to Alexandra David-Neel, the convention stated: "No representatives or agents of any foreign power shall be admitted to Tibet." It did permit the British to open "trade marts" at Yatung (Chumbi Valley) and Gyantse. Alexandra realized that, in fact, the British empire had leaped the Himalayas to include part of southern Tibet. This bit of arm-twisting diplomacy occurred the same year she married Philip, and it was to have an impact on her doings nearly as extensive.

Mongolia could not long support the Thirteenth and his entourage, and although he made overtures to Russia, the Buddhist spiritual sovereign was obliged to betake himself to Peking to bend his knee at the Celestial Throne. The Empress Dowager Yehonala and her nephew the emperor received him, after which at Yehonala's instigation his title was amended to include the phrase "Sincerely Obedient." The dowager, who claimed to be a good Buddhist, was above all an unscrupulous politician, and the 1908 subordination of the Dalai Lama to the last Manchus is an argument advanced by the People's Republic of China in asserting sovereignty over Tibet today. By flying from the British, the Dalai Lama leaped from the frying pan into the fire.

He would soon have his revenge. The Chinese emperor, addicted to drugs, was fading fast, and most likely a final dose of poison finished him. Yehonala selected an infant for the throne, and in her seventy-third year, she boasted she would surpass the years of Queen Victoria. She failed to outlast her nephew by two full days and died cursing the rule of women and eunuchs. The Dalai Lama conducted a joint funeral service, and after inspecting the monasteries of eastern Tibet he made his way toward Lhasa. Before he arrived Chinese armies had invaded his country, looted, set fire to monasteries, melted sacred images for bullets, murdered hundreds of monks, and perhaps worst of all, torn up ancient books to sole the boots of the soldiers. It was a preview of 1959.

The Tibetans resisted as best they were able, while the prematurely aged Lama fled over the Himalayan passes in dead of winter into the arms of his former enemy, the Government of India. In exile in Darjeeling he met Charles Bell, who became a lifelong friend and ally. However, the British considered themselves bound by treaties with Russia and China, and so could do little for the Dalai Lama beyond treating him with respect. His request that Tibet become a protectorate under the British empire was, for better or worse, denied.

Yet the prayers of the lamas proved efficacious: the senile Manchu dynasty collapsed under the weight of its depravity. Sun Yat-sen's Young China, taking time to establish itself, forgot about the Chinese garrisons in distant Tibet. The troops pillaged, then mutinied. The Dalai Lama sent word to his people to rise and kill the invaders. For this he was criticized by Prince Sidkeong, who told Bell, "It is a sin for a Buddhist to take a share in destroying life, a great sin for a lama, and a terribly great sin for the highest of all the lamas." But the Thirteenth emanation of the Bodhisattva Lord of Mercy, thrust rudely onto the stage of world politics, had learned his lines. This was the All Knowing One who granted Alexandra an audience in 1912, and whom she would interview a second and final time in Ari, a tiny village just short of the Sikkim-Tibet border.

When writing to her husband, especially if she were asking for funds, Alexandra liked to stress the scholarly side of her journey. To one of his frequent complaints about her absence, she replied, "With what I gather today, I will build a refuge for my old age [out of] my books and my studies." In fact, she was looking years younger and feeling vivacious. The woman was sensitive to the glamor of her surroundings, aware that she was a privileged person at an opportune time: the largely beneficent years of the mature British Empire. The maharajas had lost their teeth and were quaint curios to play among, while the world war threatened evanescent as lightning on the far horizon.

On the June before he crossed into his own country—the moment had been fixed by court astrologers—the Dalai Lama was receiving only royalty. Nonetheless, folk streamed out of the hills to catch a last glimpse of this god on earth, and to the local nationalities were added Chinese soldiers expelled from Tibet, evidently bearing no grudge. A bargain had been struck: the Han could go in peace if they left their modern rifles behind. These would be useful to a new-model Tibetan army trained by the British.

While attendants beat back the overly curious mob with knotted whips, Alexandra sipped tea with the maharaja of Sikkim and Prince Sidkeong in a bungalow nearby. A tiny owl, a present from the two, looked on from its perch. Ceremony was followed, and the old maharaja's cup and saucer were of gold with turquoise inlay and a superb pearl, the prince's of silver with a button of coral. Alexandra was disappointed when tea was served her in a plain porcelain cup.

She accompanied Sidkeong, who would act as interpreter, to see the Thirteenth. "Everything was in confusion in the small house," she related, "with masters and servants rushing about." The Dalai Lama was cordial yet hurried: "One felt that his mind had already crossed the mountain pass that marks the frontier and was busy organizing the profits of his victory."

To Alexandra's surprise, the Lama handed her written answers to her abstruse questions. She might write to him for further explanations, their correspondence to be forwarded through the Resident. Alexandra understood that the Compassionate One had made a remarkable exception for her. Women were seldom minded in such matters. Of his own wife, Charles Bell wrote, "She was careful not to speak to His Holiness, for that would have offended Tibetan custom." Yet the Frenchwoman, in her next letter to her husband, remained critical of the Thirteenth. "He is better instructed and [more] clever in philosophy than is supposed in the West," she admitted. "This justice one must do him." Still, "The Dalai Lama doesn't appear to be of the same character as the one he calls Master [i.e. Buddha]."

Bell, who knew the Thirteenth better than any other Westerner, observing him in and out of state, held a different view. The Resident claimed he was "frank and open not only in conversation, but in his dealings generally." Neither did he neglect the spiritual side, being "strict in his devotions." Through an aide of the Dalai Lama, Bell found out, "He was fond of gardening and would plant seeds and seedlings with his own hands. And he would visit his [pet] animals, the Bengal tiger and the other animals."

However, Bell did admit that with the passing years the Thirteenth Dalai became increasingly an autocrat who could punish swiftly and arbitrarily. He was to gather into his hands more secular authority than even the Great Fifth. During perilous times, he necessarily acted as a true head of state. We are reminded of a Tibetan proverb: "In a powerful country religion goes down." Unfortunately, this may hold still more true for a sovereign.

Whenever possible, Alexandra verified her accomplishments with photos, and she persuaded the Thirteenth to sit as she snapped away. But when she developed the film, "The Dalai Lama appeared like a ghost; it is like the 'spirit photographs' one sees of vague forms." She assured Philip that the photos were not dark, "but confused as if I were near a whirlwind." She had no explanation, but she was reminded of a story told her by Caroline Rhys Davids. The photographers attached to the Younghusband expedition had taken many shots of the interiors of temples, of the gorgeous Buddhas and elaborate altars, brushing aside the objections of the lamas. When they tried to develop the pictures, "on their plates there was nothing." Alexandra wondered if she were "a victim of a phenomenon of the same occult sort?" But why?— she and the Dalai Lama were on excellent terms.

Alexandra was favorably inclined toward one command given by His Holiness: "Learn Tibetan!" Her desire already had been awakened by another curious incident. Shortly after their first interview, while she watched the Thirteenth bestowing his blessing on the mob of pilgrims, she noticed a man seated on the ground wearing dirty, torn monastic garments, hair wound around his head like a turban. He was sneering at the goings-on. Alexandra had Dawasandup make inquiries, and she learned that the man was a wandering *naljorpa* from Bhutan. This is a species of ascetic, often living in a cave, who possesses magical but not baneful powers. Soon afterward, the seeker forced the reluctant schoolmaster to accompany her on a visit to the *naljorpa* in his cell at a nearby *gompa* (monastery).

The strange man was stuffing his mouth with rice and answered their greeting with a grunt. Alexandra tried to speak to him, at which he chortled and muttered a few words. Dawasandup, when pressed, revealed that he'd said, "What is this idiot here for?" After a bit, the hermit proved more communicative, damning the Dalai Lama as a sham. "Would the Precious Protector need soldiers to fight the Chinese or other enemies if he possessed [real] power? Could he not . . . surround Tibet with an invisible barrier that none could pass?"

Alexandra was taken aback by this filthy fellow, although she admired his necklace of human bones and his wild air. She demanded to know who he thought he was. He laughed noisily, comparing himself to a pig rolling in the mud. "To fashion stars out of dog dung, that is the Great Work!"

The *naljorpa* addressed Alexandra in earnest. She must enter Tibet and be initiated there by a master. It was essential that she quickly learn Tibetan. For a foreigner to travel in the Sacred Realm was forbidden, but she could bypass the dangerous populated places, even Lhasa. She would find the wise ones in remote caves or in the forest. If the British obstructed her, why not go through China?

It was too bold for Alexandra to accept at once. On their way out, she gave Dawasandup a few rupees for the mendicant. When he insisted that the *naljorpa* take the money, Dawasandup suddenly staggered and fell back against the wall, clutching his stomach. The magician hadn't moved an eyebrow, but now, with a grin, he got up and left the room. Had this louse-ridden fellow peered into Alexandra's future, or merely her character? For that matter, had the "all-knowing" Dalai Lama sensed that the strange French Buddhist might accomplish great things, if only she knew Tibetan? And what of the "invisible barrier"—was there such a thing? In fact, it would take another fifty years—half of the twentieth century—before the Land of Snows fell under the soiling footsteps of an invading army.

For a time, Alexandra heeded neither beggar nor sovereign. She had determined to renew her Sanskrit studies. Leaving Sikkim in November 1912, on her way to Benares (to lodge with the Theosophists) she leisurely toured Nepal. She was wrongly convinced that her chief work in life would be to compile some monumental tome of comparative religion, perhaps on the differing forms Buddhism had taken in various countries. This was the sort of study to set the heads nodding in the refined salons of Paris. Not to seem unduly ambitious, she informed Philip, "I would easily renounce signing what I will write."

More immediately, the pilgrim wished to visit the birthplace of Gautama at Lumbini and then make a sortie into the Tilora jungle on the Indo-Nepalese border. She recalled the story she read when young, how the previous Buddha gave his body to a tiger to rend to pieces as a meal for her hungry cubs. Of course, in her forties, Alexandra the skeptic had embarked on "the pilgrimage of a non-believer." Courtesy of the maharaja of Nepal, she was transported over the mountains in a sedan chair. It was a lark, a chance to camp in the jungle, which she termed "a delightful abode for a sage."

Tropical nights, with "the perfume of orchids floating in the air, lightning bugs dancing in the shadows," simultaneously soothed and enlivened her. Unfortunately, the Tilora was populatd by man eaters large, small, and winged, and none of her retinue of twelve coolies, several personal servants, and, courtesy of the British Resident, four elephants cared to venture into its depths. Taking a single boy she pushed in one afternoon until she reached a pleasant, partly cleared spot. She sat down cross-legged, admiring a bright blue bird chirping on a bough. Her boy was "vagabonding" far behind.

Alexandra turned pensive. The eighth anniversary of her father's death, recently passed, had opened old wounds. She recalled her mother's mean triumph in watching Louis David die. But her father, too, had disapproved of her bohemian ways and studies. He couldn't bear the resemblance to what he might have been. Suddenly, she heard rustling among dead leaves to her left: "the cautious steps of a cat, but a heavy cat." Gingerly peering into the brush, she spotted about twenty yards off a long reddish body stripped with black. The creature was half-hidden by foliage, and so she thought, "a zebra!" Then, "There are no zebras in this country, and the fur is too red—a tiger!"

The Frenchwoman sat very still. To run would be stupid; in two bounds the huge cat would be at her throat. Quieting her thumping heart, the former devotee of Paris cafés shut her eyes and forced herself into deep meditation. She struggled with her fear, knowing that yogis could calm wild beasts by their detachment from fear. She didn't wish to dishonor her *sannyasin*'s robe. She forgot the imposing tiger— visualizing it as reddish leaves mixed with black leaves—and she hoped the tiger would do likewise. When, after some time, she looked up, the creature was gone. Not content with this victory, Alexandra attempted to recreate the big cat's image. To a philosophical Buddhist, the idea of a tiger is as real as its physical presence. But in the spot where the beast had stood, she saw only a corner of blue sky. Interrupted by the arrival of her boy with an elephant, Alexandra returned to camp.

Philosophy aside, in how much actual danger was she? The naturalist George Schaller has pointed out that the notion of the tiger as inherently ferocious is largely a fiction perpetuated by trophy hunters, and that "tigers are even-tempered, gentle beasts which assiduously avoid any confrontation with a person on foot, an exception, of course, being the rare maneater." Clearly, the European traveler didn't know this, nor could she interview the animal on its gustatory preferences. She reacted with courage, not so much instinctive as directed by will and reinforced by discipline. Like most of us, Alexandra had to fight to be brave.

That night the distant but startling roar of a tiger made the boys around the campfire jump. The big cat was getting a good meal, but was it the same one? Alexandra regretted she hadn't committed "a Western deed: to take my camera and photograph the beast," so that she might send the snapshot for her Mouchy to admire.

During this period Alexandra the woman, still youthful and attractive, if overweight, was wrestling with a tiger—her libido—more difficult to subdue than the one in the jungle. There are several instances of her investigating the mysteries of tantric sex. We have learned that in general she became involved, but we may never know how deeply. For descriptions of her activities, we have mainly her accounts written much later for publication. Philip was told nothing of his wife's midnight viewings of, or indulgences in, these secret seances. But whether in Nepal or India, the Frenchwoman knew where to find the hidden soirees that culminated in *maithuna,* sexual union, of which she publicly insisted she was merely a reporter.

Typical was that given in December by a peasant sorcerer not far from Katmandu. Alexandra observed the goings-on "disguised as a young Tibetan boy and lying prone on her stomach in a hayloft under which the *shaktas* [devotees, male and female] were united." The preliminary ceremony lasted an interminable while and featured the consumption of the five forbidden substances—wine, meat, fish, a grain supposedly an aphrodisiac, and finally sex—by young Nepali couples of the Hindu upper class. Alexandra watched with repugnance as a goat was sacrificed and the participants smeared its blood on their faces. They continued to drink heavily. "Suddenly the lamp went out," she wrote. She heard "the sounds of stools overturned, steps, drunken hiccups, gasps, bestial groans [that] rose up in the darkness. The abject orgy had begun." Alexandra admitted she might have stayed on, but she was troubled by the presence next to her of her serving boy, Passang, actually a sturdy young man, who perhaps was getting too engrossed. So the pair "descended silently from the hayloft and disappeared into the night."

Whether on this occasion matters happened just as Alexandra claimed is unimportant. Later she would attend midnight soirees more to her liking. Surely, these sorts of debased practices were not for her. John Blofeld, writing on tantric method, points out, "[T]he techniques for hastening Liberation by transmuting the force generated by the passions could, if misapplied, easily lead to debauchery." Alexandra, like the misguided seekers at the orgy, sought the power stemming from the divine female (*shakti*), but on a level more refined and efficacious. She did not cease to follow the tantric path, the hallmark of which is experimenting with one's own mind as well as body.

First, the forces of cause and effect—which we in the West often prefer to call fate—with a sudden chill, slammed shut one door in order to open the way.

CHAPTER 11

Of Life and Death

In December 1913 Alexandra, fleeing the fevered heat and plagues of India, returned to the tiny capital of Sikkim to an amazing welcome orchestrated by the crown prince. Some miles from town schoolchildren lined the road, teachers at their head. The principal offered her the traditional white scarf as a mark of honor. Farther on a deputation of lamas greeted her, followed by an assemblage of nobles and land-owners, loading her down with scarves. Finally Prince Sidkeong appeared, and he and Alexandra "entered Gangtok in the midst of the most picturesque procession imaginable."

She only half-jested that she felt like Poincaré, the president of France. However, staying at the British Residence to avoid gossip, she became quickly disillusioned. Here, on a hill overlooking both the town and another, significantly lower hill with the royal palace and Sid-keong's villa on it, she had to take English tea constantly and dress for dinner. Everyone was kind, doubly so at Christmas when they gave an amateur concert followed by a sumptuous dinner. It made the adventurer feel as though she were "a mean old crone in a nursery of frolicking brats."

Alexandra was hanging about waiting for an end to the Anglo-Chinese-Tibetan conference at Simla. Chinese stalling drew this out for six months. The Frenchwoman hoped to visit Bhutan—seldom allowed—but its maharaja claimed to be involved in the treaty-making. She wrongly supposed that Charles Bell, preoccupied by his role at the conference and by concern over expanding Russian influence in Mongolia and Tibet, had said nothing to the maharaja about her proposed trip. Worst of all, Sidkeong was hurried off to Simla to no purpose save to pose for an occasional photo in unflattering tails and top hat. She was displeased by his dance to the Resident's tune.

Alexandra found compensations. She had begun to study Tibetan, which she discovered to be much easier than Sanskrit. She didn't expect to become fluent, only learn to read, and she hoped to travel a little in Tibet if permitted. Hearing Tibetan music again, the deep, pensive strains produced a pleasant distress, as if "all the beings wandering from world to world since the beginning of time were calling out." The concert took place at the local burning ground for corpses, which underscored the effect.

For the New Year 1914, the Sikkimese monks presented Alexandra with "a superb robe of a lamina." The garment had been duly consecrated, and now the orientalist was transformed—to the extent a robe could do it—into an ordained Buddhist clergywoman. Most importantly, the garment identified her with the long tradition of coreligionists who had studied and copied manuscripts, pilgrimaged, deprived themselves, and even died for their beliefs. Caressing its folds lovingly, she wrote to Philip, "What a pity photography cannot reproduce the colors."

The robe of dark red felt had a blue silk kimono-style collar and a yellow fringed waistband. High Lhasa boots of leather and felt embroidered in auspicious patterns accompanied the outfit, topped off by a bonnet of golden Chinese silk. The monks, besides bestowing a rare compliment on a foreign woman, had provided a warm garment to insulate her in the Himalayan heights.

Given time on her hands, Alexandra began to fret about her health. "I am tired," she sighed. "I feel old, people seem to me demented and foolish." Wisely, she got out on a round of the monasteries, explaining Buddhist *sutras* (discourses) to the young monks. She set up a new tent that astounded everyone. It was comfortable for living even in the winter. She assured Mouchy she would send it home to him in one more year, when they could play explorer together. But for now she felt "the resistance of invisible forces" that kept her from advancing in her studies, and she demanded to return "a person of note among orientalists."

"My dearest," she informed her husband, "questions of money trouble me greatly. I know you are making sacrifices for me in order to further a course you disapprove of." Nonetheless Alexandra needed more money, as she would frequently, and she could not name an exact and final sum, as Philip had requested. All she could truthfully reply was, "enough."

Tramping about in the heights, Alexandra perked up. "The air of the mountains is nourishing by itself," she observed. It didn't greatly bother her that, a former gourmet, she had to settle for coarse food and at times nettles and ferns. Still, she would dream of the peas and asparagus from the gardens around Paris. Another echo of her youth returned agreeably: then she had marched for hours across the Alps, never tiring. But at her age—forty-five—she hadn't supposed it was still possible.

Here it happened that one evening after a long trek, as darkness threatened to close in before she could reach a far-off village, she suddenly felt sure-footed, her body light as a feather, and that she could walk on swiftly forever. The Tibetans made this occasional, subjective experience known to many hikers into an esoteric science they called *lung-gom,* of which Alexandra had heard but wished to learn more. Inadvertently, because of the time of day and her previous fatigue, and due to her fixing her gaze on the distant goal, the hiker in the Himalayas had duplicated just the right conditions to become a trance walker. Night fell but did not impede her from reaching her goal.

Alexandra wished to master the technique, but further investigation would have to wait. Her movements at this period have been something of a mystery to her biographers until now. It is evident that, growing impatient, she tried the first of her end runs around British (and native) bureaucracy. In the secret files of the India Office we find a communiqué dated 22 January 1914, Assam (northeast India—to the south of Bhutan, where she was not looked for), from B. J. Gould, a political officer:

A French lady named Madame David Neel, who is a Buddhist and is deeply interested in Buddhist philosophy ... showed me a letter from the Viceroy which indicated that the Viceroy was interested in her projected journey, and [she] produced a letter of introduction from Mr. Bell to see the Marajah of Bhutan. . . . Mme. Neel has proposed that she should visit the Chumbi valley and Bhutan by herself.

So the highest British officials were still supportive of Alexandra's researches, although within bounds that would not offend native rulers or break treaty commitments. They were probably not entirely candid with her. The same official continues:

Privately the Marajah has informed me that he is afraid that complications may ensue if a lady without a European escort wanders about Bhutan, and especially if she displays a desire to visit monasteries. He is also apprehensive that if he grants a lady permission to enter Bhutan on account of her interest in Buddhism, he may find difficulties in keeping missionaries out ... As to the Chumbi valley, there can, I imagine, be no question of her being permitted to go there.

Alexandra, barred from Bhutan by the limiting mores of her day, turned her attention to southern Tibet. In India she had requested that the French ambassador pressure the Government of India to allow her to visit Tibet to study Tibetan religion and philosophy at Shigatse. In so doing she probably made a mistake. On February 2, 1914, an unnamed British officer responded unofficially to the ambassador's application, though not to the ambassador,

there was some reason to suspect that her objects were not quite so innocent as she would have them appear. . . . As regards Tibet we are pledged not to permit private travellers to enter the country without consultation with the Russian government. There seems no reason why we should allow a French traveller admittance which we refuse to our own officers.

Indeed, Charles Bell was not allowed to accept the Dalai Lama's repeated invitations to visit Lhasa, an issue over which Bell threatened to resign in 1918.

It is clear that Alexandra was plotting her course carefully. Frustrated in one direction, she approached her goal via another. She knew how to apply political influence, even though this might backfire. To present her weighty letters of introduction to a lesser functionary in Assam, while nearly everyone's attention was focused on Simla well across India, was a clever ploy. It was only when she was definitively blocked from Tibet that the determined orientalist dropped the niceties and went ahead anyway. She understood the likely consequences, did not act out of some mystical impulse, and there were no nasty surprises as she later claimed.

In the meantime, the death of the old maharaja on February 10 caused her to hasten to Gangtok. Despite his agonies, the maharja had persisted in trying to substitute his younger son as heir. Alexandra strongly backed Sidkeong's ascension to the throne. She found the funeral ceremonies impressive: processions, rites in the open air, lamas chanting gravely in the temples, a veritable orgy of sound and color. From early morning until late at night the long horns blew and bass drums rolled, giving her delicious chills. This was one grand opera in which the former singer, as she preached a sermon before a large, rapt audience of lamas, didn't mind playing a supporting role.

Alexandra was happy to be reunited with her gamin prince, who now donned the robes of state as maharaja of Sikkim. She was quick to scent danger in the air of the intriguing little court. One afternoon as they customarily took tea, she pleaded with Sidkeong to move with caution. A life-size statue of Padma Sambhava stood imperiously in the corner. Since all the monasteries in Sikkim were unreformed Red Hat, he was venerated as their patron saint. Although his brand of magical Tantrism was beyond the ability of most monks, it was greatly admired, Meanwhile the new ruler held ideas along the lines of Tsong Khapa, the Yellow Hat reformer of Tibetan Buddhism.

To make her point, Alexandra, indicating the image, teased that the local clergy had been worshiping an evil spirit for centuries. Her companion began to reply, but it was the statue, harsh features silhouetted by the flickering light of an altar lamp, who took the slur personally. His ghostly voice cut in, "Nothing you can do will succeed. The people of this country are mine. . . . *I* am more powerful than *you*."

Alexandra told herself that she hadn't really heard anything, she must be imagining this reprimand from the long-dead Padma Sambhava. Then why did the maharaja blanch and vigorously fall to defending himself? "Why should I not succeed?" he demanded. Had there been a message addressed to him, or was he able to pluck the thought from Alexandra's mind? We cannot know the answer, but the incident may be taken metphorically: a religious statue usually will have enclosed within it sacred texts to give it power. And Padma Sambhava is supposed to have hidden potent secret writings in various images. No doubt, the ancient magician still in some sense speaks to Tibetans.

The maharaja chose to disregard the warning. The earnest young ruler swore to purge the monasteries and to employ the rod where necessary. The use of liquor and tobacco must go, the monks should pray regularly, banish superstition, and educate themselves as true Buddhists.

Actually, Sidkeong had a more pressing problem. Once the mourning period was done, he was scheduled to marry Ma Lat, a Burmese princess whom he scarcely knew. It was an affair of state designed to cement relations between the two British dependencies. The princess was bound to cause trouble because allegedly she was hot-headed and modern in taste and dress. She even played the piano! Besides, the maharaja loved his Sikkimese mistress, a commoner by whom he'd fathered a son. Supposing Alexandra to be worldly-wise, he turned to her for advice. She insisted that he do his duty and marry the Burmese. Once the newlyweds had children, because Sidkeong was so young at heart, all would go well between them.

When we consider Alexandra's adamant refusal to bear children, her advice seems two-faced at best. No doubt her tender feelings toward the maharaja would be less disturbed by a dutiful rather than a love match. Not incidentally, she wished eventually to visit both Burma and Siam in company with Sidkeong. She went so far as to open a correspondence with the Burmese princess to encourage her. Then, too, perhaps Alexandra's attitude was softening, since she wrote to Philip, "Aren't we all kids at heart, each playing a game, and the most wise and acute know it is a game . . . and this knowledge is all of wisdom?"

However, the Oxford-educated maharaja grew so distressed by his marital dilemma that, on a jaunt with Alexandra to an outlying bungalow, he consulted with a high lama of exceptional powers. The lama's guru had been a seer, and he too could read the future. Without knowing the subject at hand, the seer fell into a trance, twitching painfully. He opened his eyes and seemed an entirely new man. "He moved his lips with difficulty and said in a [different] voice: 'Do not be disturbed. This question will never have to be considered by you.' " He staggered off, leaving his royal patron bewildered.

Alexandra's troubles with *her* spouse were coming to a head. Philip was threatening to look elsewhere for a tender, compassionate mate. In a more practical vein, he complained bitterly of having to rattle around in a big house by himself, and he warned his wife that if she didn't come back soon, she would no longer fit into his life. Alexandra employed a whole spectrum of ways to deal with her husband, whom she intended to keep at a distance, but nonetheless to keep. Philip Neel was her lifeline to Europe and America and their publishing houses, as well as a geographical, and thus emotional, anchor. Most important, he sent money. Had she been a poverty-stricken yogi, how warm a reception would the Frenchwoman have received at the petty courts and diplomatic residencies of Asia? Finally, the errant wife assured her husband, "I love you better and more profoundly than ever."

It is remarkable how this woman kept up a live relationship, entirely through the uncertain mails of those days, during nearly a decade and a half of meandering in outrageous places. Sometimes she coyly complimented her "big sheep," such as, "My dearest Mouchy, it is a great pleasure to gossip with you . . . to read your letters." At other moments, when Philip moaned about his lot, she subjected him to purgative doses of philosophy: "It's cold and sad when you ask other people to help you, to warm you, to ease the burden inherent in existence." Surely, he was no worse than others, but she hoped he would get over always needing somebody by his side. Tellingly, she observed, "You have lived among women [who appeared] like lambs, or angels; you never looked at what they felt at the bottom of their hearts."

If cajoling failed, Alexandra could direct threats to North Africa. In May 1914, Philip sold the house in Tunis and moved to the headquarters of the railway in Bone, Algeria. The detachment of his lamina wife turned to rage. How dare he take such a step without consulting her? She had loved their big Arab house, "with [its] iron grillwork, massive doors, little lamps in shadowy corners," which had "nurtured [her] dreams." Philip was the fickle one. She reminded him of past moral torture, of "calculated humiliations," of how he once "abused the difficult situation in which [she] found [her]self."

Alexandra knew how to pierce through Philip's armor to his vulnerable conscience. She sang well the café ballad of the elder roué seducing the tender young thing. Still, she was genuinely concerned with appearances, as befit her bourgeois upbringing. In secret she could watch a tantric sex rite with aplomb, but the Frenchwoman's announced morals were strictly Victorian. Indeed, the unforgiving mores of her time demanded that, by leaving hearth and husband, she must surrender hopes of security, intimacy, companionship, if not respectability itself. She had made a choice as difficult as Gautama's, which she reaffirmed to her husband by refusing to become "an old woman [who] pick[s] out hats that carefully hide a face each day more wrinkled . . . To give and go to teas and dinners, to listen to the empty chatter of men and women marching to the slaughter like a flock of silly sheep."

When she could no longer stall or reason with Philip, Alexandra threatened to become an anchorite. He would lose his last hold over her. During the early fall, Alexandra came upon the four nuns of Chorten Nyima, who lived reclusively amid wild scenery on the Tibetan side of the border. She was tramping with her servants in the mountains and the temperature was falling below freezing. Sick with the grippe and an abscess in her ear, she felt taken by a determination to plunge into the land of mystery. Here, surprisingly, she found the weather crisp but dry and the sunshine radiant.

The little monastery was set high among eagles' nests and air so clear that the rocks glittered like semiprecious stones. Cliffs carved by erosion, sprinkled with pastel-colored pebbles, "formed around the *gompa* an impassible, wholly mineral scenery from which emanated a serenity beyond expression." Chorten Nyima means "sun shrine," and an ancient legend held that a *chorten* (burial monument) containing precious relics had been transported on the sun's rays from India to here. Secret writings of Padma Sambhava were said to be hidden on the grounds. According to popular belief, 108 springs—the Tibetan magical number—watered the area. While only a few were visible to the vulgar, the pure of heart surveyed a well-watered scene indeed.

Once thriving but neglected over the years, the *gompa* had deteriorated into a crumbly heap occupied by a handful of nuns. Alexandra was moved by the quiet courage of these women whose daily lives were fraught with danger. Snowed in half the year, the nuns often came near to starvation or falling prey to wild beasts. More terrifying to them, they had to combat evil spirits who took on strange forms. A certain plant was most demonic, for it grew on the edge of dizzying precipices in order to lure victims down into the abyss.

Alexandra would discover that Tibetan women had—and have—a singular character. They didn't flinch from living or traveling alone over their untamed, bandit-ridden country. They willingly braved a hostile climate and terrain to make pilgrimages and practice their religion. In *Born in Tibet,* Chögyam Trungpa Rimpoche, the founder of meditation centers throughout the West, paid tribute to the fearless nuns who sheltered him on his flight into exile from pursuing Communist Chinese troops. The well-known independence of Tibetan women greatly helped Alexandra on her own pilgrimage to Lhasa.

The nuns at Chorten Nyima, despite dirty faces and tattered robes, proved as generous as they were able. They begged Alexandra to share what they had, including their rude enclosure. After inspecting the ruined city, she chose to pitch her tent outdoors in sight of snowy, inviolate peaks jutting into an azure sky. But once the brilliant sun sank behind the mountains, and the gloom of night spread, everything froze. The warmth of her lama's robe and boots kept the outlander alive. She didn't dare budge out of the covers to save her dried foods from turning to ice. The brutal weather confirmed an old Tibetan proverb, "The coldness of this land will stop tea from pouring."

Woolen gloves didn't prevent the wind from cracking her fingers, nor did constant oil applications keep her face from blistering. Still, she found herself meditating in air that showed her breath as condensed vapor, and the hermit's way impressed her as a natural path toward self-realization. "Solitude, solitude," chanted Alexandra, as gusts threatened to blow away her tent. "Does one become a visionary, or rather isn't it that one has been blind till now?"

"I don't believe in free will," Alexandra responded to Philip when he accused her of egotism, of playing at being a saint. She was merely following the path that had opened before her. Besides, Buddhists admitted of no saints, only "those who know and are awake." The individual ego that most people doted on had been created by various causes and in turn was a cause; this so-called self was not unique nor imperishable but constantly in flux. Events in spring of the year 1914 illustrated Alexandra's view on a grand scale. In Europe the major powers, ever more deeply entangled in moves and countermoves, yet hostage to quirks of fate, seemed bent on proving their incapacity to either learn or act. "Imbecility is the great god of this world," sighed the philosopher.

Through the summer Alexandra waited at the palace guest house in Gangtok for funds from Philip. He hadn't written in months. Her boredom was relieved when the young maharaja brought tidings from Simla: the British, Chinese, and Tibetans had signed a convention, which Peking almost immediately disowned. Chinese troops were invading eastern Tibet. Worse, the conference reinforced the notion of a Tibet divided into Inner (closer to China) and Outer, with China claiming ultimate suzerainty over the whole. After six months of talk and Chinese stalling, British diplomacy had failed to budge them, leaving the Tibetans dissatisfied but still more dependent on British military advice and recognition. The ensuing Sino-Tibetan border conflict would run parallel, in minor key, to the overwhelming theme of violence known, at the time, as *The* World War.

Alexandra heard the news from Philip, at last, and she responded on August 10 rather surprisingly. War with Germany was inevitable and, since France had reliable allies, a good thing. France had avoided fighting only through concessions and humiliations that must come to an end. In a demonstration of "Realpolitik" that would have been the envy of the Iron Chancellor, Alexandra asserted that Russia would suffer but hold up for a considerable period, Britain would be immensely valuable for its navy and its colonies, and Germany was bound to starve to death. That she proved correct is less surprising when we recall that her political godmother was the Paris Commune. The French Left wanted to fight to the last against the Prussians; it was the Right that bought off Bismarck with huge chunks of French soil.

Alexandra's reaction soon surpassed the reasonable. France, she declared, represented "civilization, ideas of progress, the emancipation of the human spirit," as opposed to German "barbarism" and "authoritarianism." France's brave soldiers were defending the Republic against the inhuman Prussian military machine. When she heard that the enemy had overrun Flanders and taken Brussels, Alexandra wailed, "Poor little Belgium!" She anguished over what would become of her mother who, old and senile, might die from the shock of seeing German troops. Such solicitude for her hated parent was no sham but the welling up of natural feelings long since suppressed.

During the next months, Alexandra wandered about in the mountains accompained by a fellow orientalist, the Scotsman McKechnie, a specialist in Pali, and their retinue of servants. Her state of mind was unsettled, and as soon as she returned to where she could receive or send mail, she demanded news of the war in Europe. When Philip reproached her that someday she would regret being so far from home during these tragic hours, she responded, "I have weighed the question . . . of abandoning forever my studies in Asia." If she were a man she would return at once to enlist in the army. But to serve as a nurse—the role assigned her as a woman—she regarded as too insignificant.

Still, Alexandra was delighted that France was pursuing "glory and honor . . . the heroism of our ancestors." One can almost hear the Marseillaise, that most militant of anthems, blaring in the background while she proclaims, "We are French! To cease being French would be to cease to exist!" Alexandra's sole fear was that "the Allies won't be able to annihilate Germany as she deserves." The menacing monster of Prussian militarism had to be crushed forever so the world could live in peace. The medals proclaimed this "The Great War for Civilization," and Alexandra apparently agreed.

Considering the hundreds of thousands of young men who were to die or be maimed in the trenches, and the wreck that would be made of European society; bearing in mind that, according to the Buddhist view of causality, a First World War must lead to a Second, how can we explain such blatant jingoism coming from the mouth of a truly clever woman? First, like the others, Alexandra was convinced the war would be won quickly. She understood nothing of combat waged with machine guns, tanks, airplanes, and poison gas. Napoleon III had led his glittering troops into battle mounted on a charger, while the Prussian army was thought very unstylish. Alexandra would learn the hard way what modern warfare had to teach, but not before she had beome, in a limited way, a resourceful captain of men.

In the meantime, the common cause reunited her in spirit with "dear darling little Mouchy" whom she longed to hug and kiss. Since the seas were too dangerous for her to sail home, talk of returning was put off indefinitely. Philip sent money, and when it was temporarily held up others came to her aid, including the maharaja of Nepal, who took an interest in her studies. Boasted Alexandra, in unfortunately apt language, "I am a phenomenon, and I explode in the civilized world."

It was no peaceful disposition, still less a mushy mysticism that would have her lapsing into bliss at the drop of a biographer's pen, that drew this warrior to the renunciate's life. Rather, she says, "I esteem unreservedly . . . those yogis who have broken with all nursery games and who live alone with their audacious thoughts." These extreme individuals she classed rightly with intellectual freethinkers such as Reclus or Stirner. But the yogis, Tibetan or Indian, went far beyond any European, for they possessed the secret oral teachings of tantric lore. This door to the mysteries had remained closed to her, but now she had won acceptance as a disciple by a renowned *gomchen* (great hermit). First, as though to erase any lingering doubts, Alexandra was going to suffer a terrible blow.

On December 14 at Lachen, a tiny monastery in the mountains just before the high passes of Tibet, Alexandra heard that, after a sudden, brief, unexplained illness, the young maharaja of Sikkim had died. It took six days for the news to arrive. At first she was simply shocked, muttering, "Poor boy, so attached to life, he stayed such a gamin at the age of thirty-seven." Then she recalled their last outing together when Sidkeong, dressed in an Alpine suit, had climbed so quickly ahead of her she thought his heart and lungs were made of brass. At the summit, savoring the stillness, they meditated on a rock like a pair of wild birds. Then he was obliged to descend toward the cares of the court, while she was going higher into the Tibetan Land of Snows.

Sidkeong, a mountain sprite, leaped from boulder to boulder, waving his Swiss hat, calling back, "Goodbye! Don't stay too long." Now it was finished, she would never see him again. "I loved him very sincerely," Alexandra was moved to confess, "this dear little boy-king whose motherless childhood was so sad and whose father was an enemy." The two of them shared an identity of views, of wounds, that Philip Neel the man of affairs could barely understand. On occasion, the woman hinted at her despair at not finding that special someone who makes all the anguish worthwhile. By her unassuageable sorrow at the maharaja's death, we may conclude she *had* found him in the person of an Asian monarch, just before he was lost to her with grim finality.

However, Sidkeong was a *tulku,* a "phantom body" who, according to Tibetan belief, should only die when he wished, perhaps to be reborn at a more auspicious time. Thus the lamas were talking about mystic reasons for their ruler's passing. When Charles Bell pumped an informant, he got the following:

Ku-sho says that he heard that the cause of the illness of the Maharaja Sidkeong tulku which was followed by [his] death was from his negligence of services to his ancestral Cho-kyong [demon defenders of the faith] and by his introduction of offering [them] candles instead of butter lamps. Secondly that he proposed to marry a princess of Burma, which angered the Cho-kyong, as she had been of an alien nationality, and that she does not follow the Cho-kyong. Moreover during his illness the late Maharaja failed to observe services properly toward his ancestral deities or gods on the usual lines. But Ku-sho does not know the cause of his death.

If Bell learned any more than this, he did not commit it even to his private notebooks.

No doubt Sidkeong had pushed his reforms with undue haste, thereby making not only demonic but material enemies. He relied considerably on foreign Buddhists, inviting to his country both Europeans and learned monks of the southern school. He appointed them as teachers over his own lamas and invited them to preach at the monasteries. Alexandra admitted she had initiated the practice of regular sermons before the assembled monks. What they thought of a foreign woman preaching to them is not recorded but may be imagined. Nobles at the court also opposed Sidkeong, as they would any reformer. But his most powerful enemy was his stepmother, the Dowager Queen Drolma.

Throughout the Himalayas there grows a sinister flower, the blue monkshood. In former days an essence distilled from this plant was used to tip arrowheads; a mere scratch killed. The skill in concocting this subtle poison has not yet been lost, and Queen Drolma, practitioner of subtle arts, likely possessed it. When her stepson grew ill, she called in a physician to attend him in his last agony. Finding nothing specific, the doctor administered brandy. He listed the cause of death as heart failure.

Half a century later an American, Hope Cooke, married the crown prince of Sikkim, nephew of Sidkeong. His father the maharaja, a guilt-ridden old man haunted by the imperious ghost of a woman, was the younger son put on the throne by Queen Drolma. He soon died, and the American became Queen Hopela and pregnant. Browsing about the rather gloomy royal palace—the same that Alexandra knew—she came upon an unused room with a glorious view of the mountains:

It's the room, I hear, in which my husband's uncle and previous incarnate, [Maharaja] Sidkeong, was killed—either by gross ineptitude or deliberately—by a Bengali physician employed by the British because Sidkeong had proved too wise and strong an obsbtacle to British paramountcy in Sikkim. Although the details of [Maharaja] Sidkeong's death are grisly . . . this room seems neutral, free of spirits, and is sun-filled, even though a sparrow-nested eave hangs over the window . . . I want this room for the baby.

It is not surprising that the Sikkimese court blamed the British for Sidkeong's death. What matters is that it rankled so many years later. Certainly the loss proved a nasty surprise to Charles Bell and was not at all to Britain's advantage. However, Queen Drolma ultimately would not have her way. Neither her line nor Queen Hopela's rules today in Sikkim. Newly independent India completed what the colonial power had begun; Sikkim is a state in the world's largest democracy.

Whatever effect Sidkeong's demise had on the pace of history, it shattered Alexandra's dreams of clubbing together with the nobility of Asia. Throughout the winter of 1914, living in her tent at the remote monastery, she felt a great ache in place of her heart. Wisely, she declined to attend the lengthy and elaborate funeral rites for the maharaja, culminating in cremation. She did go to a nearby ground to watch the burning of a peasant woman's body. She recalled mournfully how not long ago Sidkeong had spoken of their traveling together and how he would introduce her to his friend the king of Siam. It grew so cold she had to warm her feet by the crackling pyre. Suddenly, she couldn't help imagining Sidkeong aflame, his dark hair a torch, his crisp little hands sizzling, the abrupt explosion of the brain inside his skull. . . . In Sikkim it is believed that if a person dies violently his ghost may linger for some time, apearing to those dear to him.

Once, when the maharaja was still prince, Alexandra described him—skin showing tawny in golden silk, almond eyes bright—as "a genie from a fairy tale" who sat on a tiny throne in a make-believe court. Her adventures then seemed a fantasy better than the 1,001 nights. But she feared that the prince, a magician, would blow upon the assembly—he would turn into a mushroom, the courtiers into blades of grass. "It is impossible that this is real!"

The transience of friendship, of love, were brought home to Alexandra. How stupid to cling to other people, who were bound one day to crumble to dust. Life on earth was the realm of Shiva the destroyer; indeed, "It is Shiva himself." The Parisian Buddhist, though learned, hadn't worked sufficiently on herself. She was now to turn from the perishable to the imperishable, spirit soaring like an eagle over the craggy wilds.

CHAPTER 12

Cavern in the Clouds

1914: the year the world went to pieces and Alexandra David-Neel took up the life of a hermit. The death of the young maharaja put an end to her notions of parading from one oriental court to another. The Great War prevented her return to France, and instead, in the heart of the mountain fastness, she entered into an intimate relationship with another man, where he was the master and she the disciple. Often Alexandra had complained concerning the inner workings of Tibetan Buddhism, "Everything is so closed, so secret; the people and things themselves are so reticent." A "great miracle" occurred when a great hermit, a reputed sorcerer, accepted her as his pupil. She would study under him in his "cavern in the clouds."

Alexandra first met the Gomchen of Lachen in 1912 at Gangtok where he had descended reluctantly to conduct a ceremony at court. When Prince Sidkeong introduced the Parisienne, he couldn't have imagined she would become the disciple of this revered mystic. Or could he? At any rate, it was his legacy to his dear friend. She found the lama, about fifty at the time, beguilingly ugly. Garbed for his part in the tantric ritual, he wore a five-sided crown, a rosary necklace of 108 pieces of skulls, an apron of carved human bones and a *phurba* (magic dagger). His hair was plaited in a long thick braid that touched his heels, and from his ears dangled gold rings studded with turquoise. Alexandra had never seen such eyes like hot coals. No wonder common folk supposed he could fly through the air, kill people at a distance, or command demons.

During the next two years, Alexandra occasionally spoke with the Gomchen in his apartment at the monastery. This collection of a few humble structures, home to a handful of monks, was perched on a mountain slope overlooking the little Himalayan village of Lachen at eight thousand feet, inhabited by sturdy, superstitious hillfolk. Lachen means "the big pass," and the main occupation of the region in the northeast of Sikkim, aside from subsistence farming, was the raising of yaks employed to carry goods across the nearby high passes to Tibet. These good-humored, sure-footed, shaggy, horned beasts also provided the natives with meat, dung for fuel, and hair to weave into tents, and the female (a *dri*) gave milk to churn into the omnipresent butter.

The first few conversations with the lama were difficult. A beginner at Tibetan, Alexandra needed to use the Reverend Owen, from a nearby mission, as interpreter. The dedicated minister did his best, but seated stiffly in an armchair between the two Buddhists who assumed a lotus posture on the rug, legs tucked up, he felt out of place. Fortunately, the Gomchen was dressed in a more everyday vein: "a white skirt down to his feet, a garnet-colored waistcoat, Chinese in shape, and through the wide armholes, the voluminous sleeves of a yellow shirt . . ." These long sleeves, which in the old photographs hang nearly to the ground, were a mark of the mandarin class, indicating that the wearer had sufficient servants not to need to use his hands.

Questions and answers flew hot and heavy between master and would-be disciple. The two ranged over the history and doctrines of Buddhism; they discussed everything from abstruse points to the need for ritual. Owen tried to keep up, but his translations grew perfunctory. The Buddhists took this as a signal to settle quietly into deep meditation, continuing their dialogue by other means. The minister, not daring to leave, fretted over being late for his Bible class at the mission.

Despite the barrier of language, Alexandra and the Gomchen were instantly delighted with one another. She felt that here was a clear-thinking, bone-dry skeptic who had penetrated the trappings of religion to its inner core. "What he says is marvelous, audacious, frightening." For his part, he told her solemnly, "You have seen the ultimate and supreme light. It is not by one or two meditations that you have arrived at the conceptions you express. After this there is nothing more." Alexandra felt certain there was more and that the Gomchen could guide her to it. So in the early autumn of the first year of the world war's carnage, inspired by the nuns of Chorten Nyima, she determined to climb the dizzying heights to the hermit's hideaway, the Cave of Clear Light at De-chen, twelve thousand feet in the sky.

In *Magic and Mystery in Tibet*, Alexandra related how she was staying at a pleasant *dak* bungalow at Thangu, a short half-day's outing from the hermitage. However, she had no horse. The Sikkimese in charge, afraid his European guest might walk, offered his own horse, a small tame reddish beast. Alexandra mounted and the horse threw her into the air and down on a patch of grass. Knocked cold, she awoke in pain but not badly hurt. The bungalow keeper was mortified.

"This horse has never before acted like that," he assured her. "Watch me. I shall make it trot a little."

As soon as the man grasped its bridle, the puny animal ferociously kicked him onto some rocks where he landed on his head. Half de-

ranged, he was carried off ranting that the pony was perfectly tame.
The natives attributed this episode to the power of the Gomchen, who
they claimed had set up a psychic barrier to guard his hideaway. Alexandra's servants looked glum and warned her not to go. A lad of
fifteen, Aphur Yongden, recently entered into her service, cowered in
a corner crying. From her sickbed the seeker ridiculed their talk of
harmful demons, and when two days later the lama sent a mare for
her, she rode her up the steep, barren trail until she spotted the waving
prayer flags of a hermitage.

The Gomchen came out to greet her, and they shared a pot of buttered tea in a cave finished with a rough wall and gaping holes for
windows. After tea the Gomchen retired to his own cavern about a mile
further up the mountain. Darkness fell before Alexandra could accus-
tom herself to the surroundings. Her servants spread blankets on the
bare rock floor and disappeared. No moon, she could barely spy a
glacial mass of mountains above the gloomy valley. She peeped out her
head: shadows! The roar of a distant waterfall punctuated the otherwise still night. Alexandra, fearful of tumbling into the void below,
crept back inside.

The moment she lay down, the kerosene lamp went out. She had no
matches and couldn't move an inch for fear of breaking a limb. A biting
breeze blew, while a single star shone through the window onto the
visitor's hard couch. She supposed it mocked her, demanding, "What
do you think of a hermit's life?" Mustering her spunk, she replied
aloud, "Yes, I am all right . . . Thousands of times better . . . ravished,
and I feel that the hermit's life, free of what we call the goods and
pleasures of the world, is the most wonderful of all lives."

Next day Alexandra scrambled up to the Gomchen's Cave of Clear
Light. In 1895, without fanfare, the lama had established himself in
this cell. For five years he saw no one, subsisting on scraps of food left
before his door by herdsmen. When these superstitious folk solicited
him for a blessing, or more likely a curse on an enemy, he ignored
them. The hermit's conduct so impressed the several monks of nearby
Lachen that he gained an authority over them, and they improved both
his diet and surroundings. Indeed, by the time of Alexandra's arrival,
she found things rather too comfortable to suit her image of the master.

The Gomchen's cave was larger and better furnished than the one
below. A wooden step led to the entrance, which was hidden by a curtain; one entered into the kitchen, then back via a natural opening to
a small grotto, the living room. Here wooden chests formed a sort of
couch, large cushions were placed on the ground, and slabs of brightly
painted wood were set up on feet as low tables. Farther back were the
usual altar offerings: copper bowls filled with water, grain, and butter
lamps. Religious scrolls covered the uneven walls, and beneath one of
these stood an inconspicuous cabinet said to house the demons sub-

servient to the potent lama. Perched in the clouds, the aerie commanded a romantic and solitary site.

Terms of a discipleship were agreed on whereby Alexandra promised absolute obedience to the guru for an indefinite period. She especially must not take any journeys without his permission, a proviso her husband might have envied. In return the anchorite dropped his cherished plan to go into a traditional three-year, three-month retreat. Instead, Alexandra would teach him English while he improved her Tibetan. If she proved worthy, the Gomchen would reveal to her the secret oral teachings of tantric Buddhism. Alexandra was quick to grasp this "rare chance . . . to penetrate the doctrines no other Orientalist has understood."

Alexandra knew she wasn't the first Westerner to study Tibetan Buddhism. Since the arrival of Jesuit missionaries in the seventeenth century, a long line of priests, spies, adventurers, and lunatics had showed up at the mountain frontiers of the Land of Snows and, one way or another, plunged in. Some had fallen ill or been killed, others were expelled eventually. Quick to write books, their learning was usually superficial. One of the best of the early scholars, the Hungarian Csoma de Koros, in the nineteenth century walked all the way from his native Transylvania to sojourn at Lamaist monasteries in Ladakh and elsewhere. Although he failed to discover the origins of the Magyars, he did write and publish in English a pioneering dictionary and grammar of Tibetan. In the mid-nineteenth century Evarist Huc, a determined French abbé, besides making a few Mongol converts wrote an influential account, particularly of Kum Bum monastery, on which James Hilton based much of his *Lost Horizon*. However, these men could report nothing first-hand of the practices of a Tibetan hermit, and it was about such alleged wizards that wild tales were spread.

After joining her tent to the lower cave, Alexandra moved in, filled with the spirit of adventure. Yongden and the other servants were housed in a hut a few yards away. The Frenchwoman had no intention of performing herself the menial tasks necessary to keep alive in the rarified atmosphere, and Yongden, just out of school, wasn't much help either. She joked with Philip, after assuring him her arrangements would save him money, "One brings boxes of conserves when one is a Western hermit. It is a game if one wishes . . . [but] not to the taste of everyone."

Alexandra found that life reduced nearly to the essentials, despite the solitary nights passed in a cave, pleased her, and the Gomchen treated her like a younger sister. He supplied her with yak butter, milk, and fruits from his own limited store. Unfortunately, he fancied himself a cook and invited his pupil to dinner. His mutton soup was foul, and Alexandra, after she downed it with a smile, was forced to rush outside and disgorge it. She was sick all night. Next day the astounded lama made her feel better by descending to her cell to discuss abstruse Sanskrit works.

In mid-November their idyll was broken up. The Gomchen, obliged to return to his monastery on business, didn't dare leave the foreigner alone to face the snows of a Himalayan winter. The hermitage was inaccessible for four whole months when drifts blocked the trail. So Alexandra accompanied her teacher and set up the tent at Lachen. She found it comfortable enough, boasting that with a kerosene heater she could keep the temperature in the "rather nice range" of 45 degress Fahrenheit. Her lama's robe helped keep her warm, until one night in early January, weighted by snow, the tent fell in on top of her. She wasn't hurt but moved into a cell in the monastery. "I'm still too tied by the cord that binds me to the world and to civilization," she complained. "I'm not yet awake from the bad dream."

The folk of Lachen and their primitive communal notions proved a real nightmare. There were some eighty families in the neighborhood, growing barley and potatoes, pasturing yaks in the summer, and all year practicing "the most absurd caricature of a socialist government imaginable." When goods were bought, such as potatoes, they had to be bought equally from all growers, whether the spuds were large or small, sound or rotten. Anyone who sold privately was fined. Everyone had to plant and harvest on the same day, and the proceeds of all labor, beyond subsistence, and all fines went into a communal fund from which a feast would be given. Unfortunately, the elders and the monks got the good things to eat, the poor got scraps, and the women nothing. Of course, Alexandra rebelled against the system. She bought at market from individuals and threw a feast for the women. She became *persona non grata* to the officious elders.

Other distractions at Lachen included the nearby Protestant mission, also not to Alexandra's liking. The British ladies had converted a few Tibetans by giving them clothes and presents, as well as Bible lessons. These acts of charity confused them, since poor as they might be they were accustomed to make offerings to their holy men. It smacked of bribery to the French Buddhist, although outwardly she remained on chatty terms with the missionaries. The women who came to her cell for tea and biscuits—which she baked herself—couldn't help staring at the Gomchen. Probably they considered him "a dirty old man," for the lama was pretty robust for his age and his manners were those of "a clodhopper." No matter, it was politic for Alexandra to keep on their good side.

Tibetan women were another matter. She found them "picturesque and charming to look at." They braided their jet black hair in a variety of ways, always studded with turquoise and silver. She gave a sermon to some nuns but was distracted by their "perfect smiles and warm brown eyes."

Alexandra tried to put the young maharaja's death behind her, but her temper was frayed by unexpressed grief. When both the village and monastery celebrated the Tibetan New Year by a feast worthy of a Breughel painting—"interminable gluttony and drinking in the open air"—she could scarcely hide her disgust. She watched in glum silence as the normally hardworking peasants and frugal monks let loose. Shanks of meat sizzled and cooking pots bubbled, while the cooks stirred strange brews with their fingers. The valley teemed with racing and wrestling figures, and up above the handful of monks danced clumsily in a sort of chorus line. Everybody was getting tipsy on *chang*, the local barley beer.

Alexandra sought out the Gomchen to complain that the dissolute clergy were showing disrespect to their late sovereign, as well as violating Buddha's precepts. She demanded that he put a stop to the carousing within the monastery grounds. Mockingly, calling her "*Mem Sahib*," the lama suggested she go commiserate with the prudes at the mission: "They also believe that God wishes everybody to be the same."

She realized she had fallen back on outworn attitudes, but Alexandra wrote to Philip concerning the incident, "I still think there are people who behave badly and need to be converted and corrected." Once again she had been pierced to the Huguenot core. Still, as the revels grew more fevered, men and women staggering about, she felt absurd. *She* was the outsider here. The others were doing as they always had done. She headed for the mountains where the winter sun shone brilliantly on the snowy crests. A recent fall added to the silvery carpet. Alone, Alexandra planted herself on a rock and strapped herself upright in the Tibetan fashion. Master of miles of scenery, she let go of care, slipping into a deep, deep meditation beyond joy or sorrow.

Through the winter, Alexandra made amazing progress in Tibetan. She found herself conversing fluently with the Gomchen, who spoke with a proper Lhasa accent, and she began to wonder if he were a wizard. Her feelings toward this "truly ugly [man] dressed in filthy robes" swung between repulsion at his peasant ways—"We have nothing in common but the color of our robes"—to awe at the clarity of his thought. When he spoke on Buddhist metaphysics, eyes glowing with fervor, the bond of *chela* (disciple) to guru was being forged; indeed, she was being tied in to the long line of masters who had preceded him.

In Tibetan Buddhism, Alexandra understood, "the telepathic method is regarded as the highest," superior to both written and oral teachings. However, there were few masters left able to employ telepathy, and fewer disciples "sufficiently developed psychically to be capable of receiving instruction in this way." The seeker was fortunate beyond her immediate realization; this science, as it was regarded by initiates, speeded her progress immeasurably. She provided a matter-of-fact description of the process:

When the pupil has exercised alone for a time, he may sit in meditation with his master in a silent and darkened room, the thoughts of both being concentrated on the same object. At the end of a given period, the student tells his teacher the phases of his meditation and these are compared with those of the master; concordances and discrepancies are noted.

This unified state of mind developed, perhaps less formally, between Alexandra and her master. Later, camping in the wilds, she would record instances of the use of telepathy at great distances, or the getting and sending of messages "written on the wind."

In the summer of 1915, the Gomchen returned to his mountain hideaway and commenced preparations against the lengthy winter, and there Alexandra joined him. "Among these vast horizons one dreams differently . . . has strange sensations," she wrote to her engineer husband. "I was a nomad of Central Asia in one of my previous lives . . . The memory of this returns to me from deep within up here on the high steppes." In sight of the five peaks of mighty Kinchinjunga—called the storehouse of the treasure of the gods because its snows were first to reflect dawn's gold and last to don the sable of night—the Buddhist prepared for her personal exploration into the mysteries of being. But she could undertake this search only after performing more mundane tasks that would insure her survival.

Her cave, the lower, was improved considerably by adding on a wooden two-story structure. On the ground floor the outer room was divided in two by a curtain: one half served as combination kitchen and study (the best place to keep warm), the other half as a bedroom that communicated with the cavern. Upstairs was a guest room, and any currently unused space was taken up with stored goods. Alexandra had the convenience of an indoor toilet (though not plumbing) and a tiny outdoor balcony. Too bad the whole had been done by local peasants who were horrid carpenters.

From halfway around the world, Philip sent practical advice about the building of what he called his wife's "Huron hut," since she had compared herself to a heroine in a James Fenimore Cooper novel. After months of mistakes the dwelling was tolerably completed, carpets laid on the floor, and the walls painted, and Alexandra was able to exult, "I am a householder in the Himalayas!" She heaped praise on Mouchy for helping to make real her wildest childhood fantasy. Assistance came, too, from the new maharaja, Tashi Namgyal, Sidkeong's younger half-brother, who sent a quantity of expensive brick tea. This and the twelve kilograms of yak butter furnished by the Gomchen, plus a little salt, were the ingredients of that beverage drunk so constantly by the Tibetans. Alexandra thrived on this odd brew, proving her to be Central Asian by atavism. When the Gangtok porter who had carried the bricks unloaded them, he looked about and commented, "This is no place for ordinary men, it is only good for *saddhus* [yogis]."

September brought the "little winter"—a prelude—and snow as high as a man, although Alexandra continued to take her daily bath. Doubts began to nag her, but she plunged into Tibetan studies. The Gomchen spoke freely about the inner meaning of Buddhist doctrine, and he grew rhapsodical on the lives of famous mystics; but he turned reticent when she brought up hidden tantric rites. No doubt, he felt the force of the Frenchwoman's skepticism, and that someone as strong-willed as she would have to make her own discoveries. Her crisis of spirit deepened until Alexandra could scarcely bear to be alone. At night she had pains in her heart and terrible dreams about the war. Desperate for information, she sent Yongden into the snows to seek out the latest stale news on the fighting, so far away. Unknowingly, she was on the edge of a breakthrough in her practice.

To divert his pupil, the Gomchen took her climbing. If in thought he was wildly venturesome, in mountaineering he proved steady and taciturn. Alexandra, much slimmer from a sparse diet, felt chipper as a young girl. She pushed out of mind earlier climbs with the handsome maharaja. The behavior of the lama—"a barbarian philosopher"—bewildered her, since one moment he was genial, the next sardonic. His eyes first showed "glimmers of flames at their depths," then misted over with tears before he burst out laughing with the innocence of a child. He had a strange weakness for a pet cat.

The pampered kitty lived in the hermit's cave and was accustomed to eat from the Gomchen's hand. One day, annoyed at the comings and goings of porters, the pet ran away. That same night, telling no one, the lama left in search of her. Without warm clothes or provisions he walked all night, feeling his way with a stick. The path led across dangerous waterfalls, around steep cliffs, and over fallen boulders. Finally, the Gomchen reached a spot where he expected the truant to arrive, but in fact the cat had circled home. The great sage spent four nights in a dank cave, and when worried villagers searched him out, they received a scolding for their trouble. The exhausted lama trudged home, sneezing and coughing, to find his kitty yawning and stretched in her usual place by the fire.

By early autumn the Gomchen had retired into his cave, "an escargot in its shell." All about reigned confusion. In Tibet the warfare continued against the Chinese invaders, and in Sikkim the peasants were resisting conscription for the big war overseas. Nevertheless, many thousands of Gurkhas and other Himalayan dwellers volunteered to fight in Europe or the Middle East, willing to soldier wherever the pay was fair. The price of supplies shot sky high, and Alexandra was anxiously awaiting the last caravan of the year before the passes were closed by snow. It finally arrived with loads of butter, rice, corn, barley flour, potatoes, turnips, lentils, and beans: the whole of the former gourmet's diet for the next few months.

Christmas Eve 1915 probed the depth of Alexandra's despair. Tired of "dirty old yogis," she was dying to get home to Mouchy, "if he would reserve a corner where [she] could do her Orientalist work." Her rheumatism, troubling all long, had led to fever, nausea, and pain so severe she sometimes couldn't stand up. This night, asleep in the back of the cave where it was warmer, she was awakened by a servant. The roof of the upper level had caught fire. Out she trudged into the snow in her nightdress. Shivering, she watched the boys put out the blaze. At five in the morning, the mountains loomed like vast shadows, and an odd calm spread over her soul.

Soon a warm robe arrived from Philip as a present. Wearing it made Alexandra weep, and although she was looking forward to an early return once the sea lanes became safer, she wrote Mouchy that first she wanted to visit Japan, where she expected to be well received. The seeker didn't realize the profound changes already at work in her. Once the heavy snows fell and she was trapped, she began to make great strides.

All winter the Gomchen permitted his disciple to invade his solitude. Every other day, dressed in a heavy outer cloak and high felt boots, she set forth on the slippery path to the lama's cabin. There his wife— he was Red Hat and permitted one—removed Alexandra's wet things and hung them before the fire to dry. She served hot buttered tea to professor and pupil, who fell to work over the subtleties of Tibetan grammar, history, philosophy. The session done, Alexandra donned her cloak and boots and flung herself into the glittering light of late afternoon. Making her way down, she might sing an old chant:

> Alone on a mountain
> possessing nothing
> sleeping on the rocks of a cavern
> One feels free
> stripped of all beliefs
> greater than a raja
> greater than God.

Day in and day out the landscape, under the dominion of majestic snowcapped peaks, was "bathed in extraordinary silence, with all the little streams and cascades mute," and Alexandra was left to her imaginings. Her sole diversion was a bear who came by to be fed. Subsisting on a plain diet, nowhere to go, Alexandra had to come to grips with her own phantoms. Desires, hopes, and fears dissolved in the acid of self-knowledge. In meditation her life was played back:

I see myself a child at St. Mandé. A young girl at Brussels. I hear my father and mother speak. I see myself at Tonkin, in India, in Tunisia. I attend the Sorbonne, I am an artiste, journalist, writer. Pictures in the corridors of editorial offices, boats, trains, unwind like a roll of film. Within [me] there is joy, laughter, shivers of triumph, pain, tears and nameless torture.

Still the Buddhist sat, just as millennia ago Gautama sat, until what others thought of as her self was like one deceased. No clear-cut stages marked the path toward enlightenment, and no transport of joy (*samadhi*) enlivened it. She experienced only steadily growing, quiet courage.

Alexandra's strength increased sufficiently to attempt an experiment with *tumo* breathing, one of the Tibetan practices that seems, but is not, miraculous. She had stumbled on its good effects inadvertently, much as with *lung-gom* walking. One evening, huddled by the fire, she began to breathe rhythmically and felt her feet warm up. But she soon grew tired. From her reading she knew what was happening. *Tumo* was the most vital practice of the anchorites, enabling them to survive brutal weather without fuel, of which there is little in the mountains, naked or clad only in a light shift. The transcendental yogi Milarepa, its foremost exponent, praised *tumo* as the best clothing. About Milarepa's disciples, the Oxford scholar Evans-Wentz has written, "They were proof against extremes of cold . . . and so needed to wear no other garment [than cotton] even in the arctic winter of the high Himalayan altitudes of Tibet." Alexandra, although she had plenty of clothes, grew weary of going about like an ambulating package. "Ah, if it were only a little warmer," she would sigh. "I have never loved the cold."

In mid-March, as the weather moderated, the curious one moved alone into her yak-hair tent and dispensed with her bulky wrappings. The predictable result was a flare-up of her hereditary rheumatism, complete with pain and fever. The Gomchen grew sufficiently alarmed to instruct his overeager pupil. These methods, described in *Magic and Mystery*, were a first for Alexandra. Earlier she had enumerated the principles for Philip: autosuggestion and retention of breath. *Tumo* is a meditation on the fire within.

Like all Tibetan exercises, *tumo* is spiritual. The aspirant must have permission from his guru and a proven ability to concentrate. He must be isolated and avoid foul air and noise. Before sunrise he sits scantily clad in the lotus posture doing various drills to clear the nostrils. Then with the out-breath he expels pride, anger, covetousness, and sloth, and with the in-breath he draws into himself the Buddha spirit. Slow, deep inspirations act as a bellows to fan a smoldering fire at the pit of the stomach. If the practitioner is successful, warmth will rise to encompass his whole being.

The traditional test for graduates of this course was arduous. On a frosty night with a hard wind blowing, the aspirants were led to the bank of an ice-encrusted river or lake. They sat on the ground, cross-legged and naked. Sheets were dipped in the water and one was draped over each man's torso; using *tumo,* he was expected to dry it. Then the sheets were soaked again and the exercise repeated. By daybreak the successful practitioner might have dried as many as forty sheets.

Alexandra's final exam was less exacting, but we know of no other woman who has done *tumo.* On a moonlit night she proceeded to a lonely mountain stream and bathed. Afterward she sat naked and meditated until dawn. This occurred in the crisp air of spring, and although at first Alexandra felt no ill effects, she soon came down with a severe cold. Still, she had conquered a lifelong aversion to harsh weather, and now she could step out on her balcony before dawn, clad in thin muslin, to catch the first hint of gold on Kinchinjunga's five crowns.

Tumo has been witnessed by several Westerners, including mountain climbers and scholars. Giuseppi Tucci, the intrepid Italian archaeologist, interviewed its adepts during his various journeys in Tibet. Lama Govinda, a German who perhaps became more integrated into Tibetan spiritual life than David-Neel, practiced and wrote of it in terms similar to hers. A German of a different order, Adolf Hitler, was intrigued by the military potential of *tumo.* He couldn't comprehend that, rather than a trick, *tumo* is a physical means of cutting one's dependence on others preparatory to a spiritual emancipation. The great Milarepa owed his name to it, for "repa" means "cotton-clad one."

By summer 1916, Alexandra's isolation was drawing to a close. She couldn't relish the role of disciple for long. "I never let myself be taken in by the illusion that my anchorite's home might become my final harbor," she wrote later. It was an episode, although a crucial one, in her life as a traveler and investigator. Even from a practical point of view, Alexandra had been extremely fortunate to study with the Gomchen of Lachen:

He would often stop our reading to tell me about facts he had himself witnessed ... He would describe people he had known, repeating their conversations and telling me about their lives. Thus, while seated in his cabin or mine, I visited the palaces of rich lamas, entered the hermitages of many an ascetic. I travelled along the roads, meeting curious people. I became in that way, closely acquainted with Tibet, its inhabitants, their customs and their thoughts: a precious science which was later on to stand me in good stead.

The lama had made possible Alexandra's successful journeys, but he also piqued her to get out on the road. In this he may have acted deliberately. The Gomchen accepted his disciple only after he conducted a careful dialogue on her understanding of the Clear Light, a concept essential to Tibetan Buddhism. Briefly, this involves no light or luminescence at all, but, according to Evans-Wentz, "The Primal ... Clear Light symbolizes the visual condition of the mind in the primordial or true state . . . unruffled by the process of the [worldly] thought-process . . . inseparable from the realizing of the Voidness, the Thatness of all that is." Slippery as this concept may seem, and it has been badly mauled by Alexandra's previous biographers, it means that the Gomchen approved of his disciple's philosophical grounding but he wished her to put her ideas into practice.

Certainly, Alexandra sometimes looked sadly, almost with terror, at the path that wound down the mountain into the valleys, which one day would lead her back to the mundane world of sorrows. But that was the way to France, North Africa, home and husband. There existed another direction, and with the arrival of warmer weather the traveler turned her attention to the forbidden passes to the north. She indignantly pointed out that in the past, before the Anglo-Tibetan entente, the Land of Snows had been far simpler to enter. She found roadblocks set up along the Himalayan routes some fifty kilometers from the Tibetan border. Fortunately, she was well *within* those posts, and only a half-day's hike lay between her and a world of knowledge.

Alexandra's two difficult winters spent in cell and cave bore fruit many years later in a slim, deceptively titled volume, *The Secret Oral Teachings in Tibetan Buddhist Sects*. The book, written by Alexandra at eighty and first published in 1951, is not arcane but a reflection of the long rational conversations she had with her teacher while the buttered tea simmered and the wind howled outside. Alan Watts called it "the most direct, no-nonsense, and down-to-earth explanation of Mahayana Buddhism which has thus far been written."

Alexandra's thought is as cool and clear as a Tibetan lake. The spirit of Gautama Buddha pervades it, the pressing need to transcend the pain of isolation and to achieve the peace of knowing all is Nothing. By the latter term Buddhists do not mean literally nothing, or even illusion, but the Void from which matter springs and into which we— the many perishable egos—are constantly dissolving. "Ashes to ashes, dust to dust." Writing to Philip, Alexandra expressed the principle of impermanence in an immediate, personal vein:

If I hadn't left, if I hadn't opened my hand and let escape what I held there, if I hadn't renounced . . . the things would have left me. If one [of us] hadn't opened his hand, whatever was squeezed there, like fine sand in the dunes, would have escaped from between vainly clenched fingers.

Shortly before parting from the teacher to whom she owed so much, Alexandra suggested the outline of such a book. The master scoffed:

Waste of time. The great majority of readers and hearers are the same all over the world. . . . If you speak to them of profound Truths they yawn, and, if they dare, they leave you, but if you tell them absurd fables they are all eyes and ears.

We may assume he was playing the devil's advocate, since he, too, was a reformer, deeply distressed by the ramifications of Sidkeong's death.

Some twenty years later, another Western seeker, the young man of German descent who would become a Tibetan lama, visited the Gomchen at De-chen. The land of his forebears had gone mad, and the world was drifting toward a second great calamity. Inspired by the example of David-Neel, the saddened scholar turned East for enlightenment. The maharaja of Sikkim, by then middle-aged, extended help by equipping a little caravan to take him to the venerated hermit. The eager pilgrim was obliged to halt for the night at a bungalow not far below the hermitage.

Strangely, before falling asleep, the young man felt as though another had taken possession of his mind and he was losing his identity. He fought the growing magnetism, jolted into action by the terror of annihilation. Tensely, he drew a self-portrait to prove that he still existed. Then he was able to sleep. In the morning he climbed up to the Cave of Clear Light. The hermit greeted him with a smile and served tea. They spoke of Alexandra and looked over newspaper clippings about her that had somehow reached the Gomchen. He praised her "endurance and strength of character." Was the old lama aware of what had gone on the night before?

The Gomchen warned against what he termed the disease afflicting the world—morality without wisdom—and he offered the seeker a subject for meditation: The Eighteen Kinds of Voidness. Before he left, the future Lama Govinda became convinced that the innocent-seeming yogi had sent the force that invaded his inner self. Moreover, he was certain he had chosen Alexandra as the ideal person to broadcast the ancient, secret knowledge of which humanity stood in imminent need. Her works, translated into the major languages, were being read by millions. If they failed to alter the traumatic course of history, it was beyond the power of any sage or author.

Alexandrine David, mother of
Alexandra David-Neel

Louis David, father of Alexandra
David-Neel

Alexandra, "première chanteuse" of the
Opéra Comique

Alexandra at 20, a youthful feminist

Alexandra, the married woman, 1910

Philip Neel, her husband, 1910

Sidkeong Tulku, Maharaja of Sikkim

Representatives of Tibet, Great Britain, and China at the Simla Convention, 1914. Sidkeong Tulku is in the front row, second from left, Sir Henry Mc-Mahon is in front row center, and Charles Bell is in the second row behind McMahon to his left.

The Thirteenth Dalai Lama seated with David Macdonald.

Tibetan nuns

Wayside Tibetans extend a typical greeting.

Alexandra's hermitage, at 13,000 feet in the Himalayas. The author is seated at right.

Tibetan rope bridge of the type Alexandra crossed on the way to Lhasa

Men and yaks clearing the road to the Chumbi valley
under deep snow.

Men in coracles on the Tsangpo river

Alexandra and Yongden in front of the Potala, 1924

The marketplace at Lhasa

Alexandra between two nuns of the Red Hat order

Kampa Dzong, a fortress

Dorje Phagmo (Thunderbolt Sow),
Tibet's only female incarnation,
and her sister.

Tibetan Ngagspa (wizard)

Lama Yongden, Alexandra's adopted son

Yongden

At Samten Dzong: Alexandra's cameras, gold jewelry, necklace of bone, "rings of the initiate"

At Samten Dzong: Alexandra's travel kit—watch, compass, pistol, jewelry pouch, cooking pot, bonnet

Alexandra at Samten Dzong at 87

Asia Marvelous and Diverse

Charles Bell's job was to defend an established empire that, at least to its subject peoples, appeared unshakable. Not a dashing sort such as Lawrence of Arabia, liable to grab headlines and attract biographers, Bell perhaps accomplished more of permanent worth in the realm of mutual understanding and trust. Undramatic about his attachment to Tibet, he warmly supported its interests and set policies in motion that helped keep the country independent until the 1950s. In 1919 he would resign as Resident in Sikkim to work full-time on his studies, but in the next year he returned as special ambassador to Tibet. London had decided to grant him a stay in Lhasa.

Before the World War, Britain had agreements with both Russia and China that constituted a sort of Closed-Door policy to the Sacred Realm. By 1920 those other two empires had fallen into disarray, and Whitehall felt free to pursue its own policies, including strengthening the Tibetan army. Bell was sent to Lhasa, remained nearly a year, and gathered much material of interest. In 1921 he again resigned and retired to an estate in Berkshire. Amid a fine collection of oriental artworks, he wrote books on the people and religion of Tibet, as well as his *Portrait of the Dalai Lama,* about both the institution and his good friend the Thirteenth.

Bell was open-minded, accurate, astute, and sympathetic to Buddhism and its practitioners. However, his final loyalties were fixedly British. He was never in danger of becoming, in Lawrence's words, "the man who could see things through the veils at once of two customs, two educations, two environments." Such a man, insisted the author of *Seven Pillars of Wisdom,* was bound to go mad. But what about a *woman?*

In July 1916, when Alexandra David-Neel set out for Shigatse in southcentral Tibet, she was crossing more than a geographic border. Although she traveled at the invitation of the Panchen Lama, she knew she risked the wrath of the Resident in Sikkim. She was aware that the British policed the frontier, allowing past only their own representatives and a few merchants. In her own words, "They [the British] have run a telegraph line all the way to Gyantse, and they have stationed soldiers and military telegraphers there, and so-called 'commercial agents' who are political agents for the whole region."

Probably, at this time, Alexandra failed to realize how closing the country to foreigners was essentially a Tibetan policy promulgated by the Dalai Lama and the abbots of the great monasteries around Lhasa. The latter were afraid that foreign influence would weaken religion, more specifically, their own hold on affairs, and they vigorously opposed any modern ideas or visitors. It was good policy to hide behind the British. As Hugh Richardson, dean of Tibetanists, has written, "The Tibetans were far from simple and naive when their own affairs were concerned. They used us [the British] as a cat's-paw to keep people out." One authority with a more open mind was the Panchen Lama, the abbot of Tashilhunpo monastery, who held spiritual rank nearly equal to the Dalai Lama and exercized a local temporal power.

Alexandra, accompanied by Yongden, crossed the border on horseback, trailing a pack mule carrying two small tents and provisions. With a magic suddenness, masses of angry clouds dissolved and the sky turned into a deep blue setting for a sun whose light struck sparks against distant snow-shaded peaks. The houses were built of stone with flat roofs, and the cast of people's faces was Mongolian. At Tranglung, Alexandra visited a sorcerer who reputedly could make ritual cakes (*torma*) fly through the air to punish his enemies. He turned out to be mild-mannered and polite, unwilling to harm a fly. The pair wandered on, sleeping in the huts of peasants when they could. The European didn't try to disguise herself, finding the people friendly and police as rare as crime. After all, this mysterious land beyond the sentinel mountains, which had seen the flowering of Buddhism, was negligent home to the most outrageous of yogis and magicians.

Melting snows made the rivers tricky to ford. While the travelers were hoping to attain Kuma, a village of thermal springs, a freak storm stranded them shy of their destination. Out of the blue hail struck, then snow began to fall so quickly it soon reached to their knees. A nearby brook overflowed into their camp, and the discouraged pair had to spend the night huddled under one soggy tent. Alexandra felt that these trials were too fatiguing for the brand new Amazon that she had become. Yet, as she wrote later, "I travell[ed] very slowly so as not to miss anything of interest . . . that I might absorb in body and spirit as much as possible of Tibet whose heart I was at last about to penetrate, but probably might never see again."

Alexandra brightened when she reached Tashilhunpo, beyond the busy market town of Shigatse, and the large monastic city of red and white houses appeared even more splendid than she had imagined.

On impulse, Alexandra sent Yongden to request lodgings within the enclosure, knowing it was unheard of for a foreign woman to dwell among the Yellow Hat celibates. She was delighted when comfortable rooms were placed at her disposal. Inquisitive functionaries were soon quizzing the visitor on her origin and business. At first they confused Paris with Phari—pronounced alike—a village to the south. Then a debate ensued over whether the Frenchwoman was or wasn't a foreigner. She maintained that since *philing* ("stranger") literally meant someone from overseas, and you could reach her country by walking (Csoma, the Hungarian, had done this), she wasn't one. In the midst of the confusion, there appeared an unassuming gentleman in a simple habit.

Alexandra was won by the Panchen Lama's refinement. He knew where Paris was and pronounced it correctly. His conversation was that of an educated man and a sincere Buddhist. Alexandra had supposed that the country beyond the Himalayas would grow wilder, but she realized that, on the contrary, she was coming in touch with an old, truly civilized people. In 1906 the intrepid, not to say brash, Swedish explorer Sven Hedin had visited the Tashi Lama, as he referred to the Panchen. He was struck by the abbot's unfeigned charm, his warm smile and kind expression. Even Charles Bell, concerned that the Panchen was a potential rival to the Dalai, stated, "On account of his great sanctity his influence is very great." However, he sensed that the still young man didn't lack worldly ambition.

This incarnation of Amitabha, the Buddha of Infinite Light, treated Alexandra as a person of high rank. He took seriously the Tibetan name bestowed on her by the Gomchen: Lamp of Wisdom. The prelate and his mother conducted their guest to every nook and cranny of the monastic establishment. Alexandra was stunned by the "barbaric splendor [that] reigned in the temples, halls, and palaces of the dignitaries." Gold, silver, and turquoise decorated doors, altars, and tombs. Common household objects used by important lamas blazed with jewels. While there was no denying all this magnificence, the display finally struck the seeker as " unrefined and childish." She couldn't help yearning for the solitudes where bears and leopards prowled, and for the Gomchen "who spurned the vulgarities which are the insignia of grandeur in the eyes of many."

The orientalist did thrive on dialogues with the monks, some 3,800 strong, half of whom were scholars. "The special psychic atmosphere of the place enchanted me," she would write. "I have seldom enjoyed such blissful hours." Nothing in Sikkim had approached this. As ever, Alexandra was demanding of herself, adding, "My journey to Shigatse has also revealed to me the scholastic Tibet, its monastic universities, its immense libraries. How many things are left for me to learn!"

When the Panchen, impressed by the European's sincerity and knowledge of scripture, invited her to remain in Tibet under his patronage, she was tempted. But Alexandra's keen nose for political winds warned her that the number two lama lacked the authority to make his word stick. Quarrels between the courts at Shigatse and Lhasa were almost inevitable, and, in 1923, the Panchen did decide to flee to Peking. He would never again see his homeland.

Alexandra wasn't ready to live out her days as a yogi on the roof of the world. Her luggage, books, notes, and photo negatives were stored at Calcutta. Paris and London were asking her to give conferences on Hinduism and Buddhism; why, even the Americans were interested! First she was headed to northern Asia, ready to brave the seas for a plenitude of untranslated texts. Once the war ended, she would sail home to Mouchy.

She left in early August with additional possessions. The Panchen bestowed on her the robe of a graduate lama and an honorary doctorate from the Tashilhunpo university. She took with her, too, the warm regards of both the Incarnated Buddha and his mother, the latter of whom continued to write to her. In return, she frequently nagged Philip to send the elderly dame postcards with views of the desert, as well as dried figs and dates.

Alexandra and Yongden wended their way back to Sikkim, stopping off at Narthang, Tibet's largest printing establishment. She admired the casual style of the printers, who did painstaking but beautiful work with primitive wood blocks. They chatted and drank tea as though their deadlines were in the next life. How different it was from the feverish agitation of a Western editorial office. Finally, exhausted, the pair arrived home at De-chen. They found their hermitage sacked, turned inside out, and the Gomchen in retreat, seeing no one.

The mystery was soon cleared up when Alexandra received notice she had two weeks to leave the country. Her trip across the forbidden border had become known to Charles Bell, who "exploded like lightning on the villagers." The Resident levied a heavy collective fine on them for letting the foreigner pass. In turn these "vicious animals"— Alexandra's phrase—pillaged her house in hopes of finding valuable belongings. Bell fined her, as well, but although he was "burning with envy," this "billious personage" couldn't lay hands on her. However, he fined and "terrorized" the Gomchen, who couldn't afford to antagonize the ruling power. Alexandra felt that at bottom was personal jealousy, in particular that of the missionaries.

These good souls chafed at being barred from the mission field of Tibet, rife with infidels. They resented Alexandra's free access and her espousal of the native religion. Through their converts they learned of her journey, then "burned the ears" of the Resident. This was David-Neel's view, of which we have no confirmation. As for Bell, he had considerations of state; the British were suspicious of any unauthorized traveler in Central Asia. They remained worried that, like the Mongol

Dorjieff who also claimed to be merely a devout Buddhist but acted in the Russian interest, Alexandra might be the agent of some European power. Bell's reprisals were harsh, and he may have felt personally betrayed. Nor could he fail to resent the Frenchwoman's opportunity to gather material, since he himself wasn't allowed past Gyantse. That she was the sort of woman who disobeyed the rules and consorted with magicians didn't weigh in her favor.

British suspicions were not entirely unjustified. In the secret files we find the following dispatch from the Gyantse Trade Agency (1917):

Mme David-Neel, the Belgian [sic] who . . . was expelled from Sikkim for having paid an unauthorized visit to Shigatse, maintains a correspondence with the mother of the Tashi Lama and *also with the Lama Chensal Kushab, the confidential adviser of the Tashi Lama.*

Bell once described the Panchen (or Tashi) Lama as "England's oldest friend in Tibet." He could scarcely afford Alexandra's meddling in Tibetan affairs, and since the correspondence referred to has been lost, we can only guess whether she was in fact butting in as she had done in Sikkim. Willfully or no, "the Belgian" had become an influence on Central Asian politics.

Alexandra instantly understood the seriousness of losing the goodwill of British colonial officials. "I have lived my last adventure," she sighed. So upset she lost track of time, she complained of the freezing Himalayan nights, of trying to make fires with yak dung that wouldn't burn, of eating wooden vegetables or preserves. A dream of Philip's in which she appeared to him as "a little old lady in gold-rimmed glasses" must have been a premonition: she was returning to France promptly but via Japan, "a wise, peaceful, restful, civilized country with railroads . . ."

Aphur Yongden accomplished the packing of his employer's twenty-eight cases. From this moment he moves to the forefront of Alexandra's life, indispensable in many ways. A lad of sixteen from a modest background—his father was a petty official—he had served a Sikkimese nobleman in return for a little education. In spite of being a novice monk, the youth had ambitions to become a man of the world. He was sure this was possible in the Philippines, of which he'd heard. Alexandra noticed him at the nobleman's house. Promising him travel, adventure, and six rupees per month, she took him into her service. The lad got plenty of what he was promised but no pay. Yongden was short, attractive in a plain way—he wore rimless glasses—and quite capable of learning. One day he would become a lama in his own right and a considerable help to Alexandra in writing her books. What was more, he carried an invaluable British passport.

Frightened by the Resident's wrath, Alexandra's other boys snuck off, while Yongden stuck. He refused to heed his family's threats, and even when they offered him a wife and house if he left the foreign she-devil, he turned a deaf ear. No mere adventurer, he came to reverence Alexandra and was willing to do every sort of menial task for her, while she soon came to prize him. Eventually she legally adopted him.

However, now the pair had to descend the mountain into the bustling world denounced by the Buddhist and of which the lad of seventeen knew nothing. The threadlike path wound lower and lower, until Alexandra glanced back one last time at her shanty. The villagers, like "a cloud of venomous mosquitoes," hovered around, ready to set the wooden structure ablaze. Her life in the hazy blue heights was already a dream, "water slipping through clenched fingers." The might of the British Empire had triumphed. Silently, the lone woman swore revenge, but a witty revenge appropriate to her beliefs and to the spirit of her birthplace, Paris.

On February 6, 1917, Alexandra and Yongden arrived at Kobe, Japan. She had gone first to Calcutta, then steamed to Burma where she admired the enormous Buddhist statuary at Penang. Back on board, she had despised the slow voyage via Vietnam across the South China Sea, or at least her fellow passengers. French with provincial accents, these people spent their time dancing the tango, unfortunately likened by the observer to "a Sioux Indian scalp dance." How could they be so frivolous when the monster Germany was menacing civilization? Thus had the Roman Empire fallen to barbarians.

The hotel at Tokyo was still worse: neat, spotless, antiseptic. Guided by Zen Buddhist D. T. Suzuki and his English wife, Alexandra took in temples as well as popular sights: Mt. Fuji, noh plays, and the bustling, commercial streets. Alexandra had boasted that she was going to be a tourist: "It is simple-minded but easy; I have played this game before." But she felt as though she were seeing Japan from behind a glass window. Brought face to face with the rapid industrialization of an Asian country, she loathed the result. A mechanized din filled and fouled the air, and the Japanese were in love with everything new and shiny. Both the soberly dressed people and their houses, which she pronounced "frightfully cold and sad," struck her as lacking in individuality. "Japanese food is simply abominable," opined the former gourmet. Ceaseless ceremonies took up endless time. The *tatami* mats constantly had to be cleaned and aired, a task that fell on uncomplaining Yongden. Furthermore, the rainy weather aggravated Alexandra's rheumatism, and worse, it reminded her of Belgium.

In a denunciation of Japanese militarism, the Frenchwoman dubbed them the Germans of the Orient. More tellingly, she predicted that one day they would seize Indochina from France, then occupy Manchuria and perhaps Tibet. China they would turn into a vast protectorate. At this time Japan was one of the Allies, scarcely regarded by the European powers who snatched up Asian ports and territories as they chose. Alexandra's view of the coming geopolitical revolution was remarkable yet typically astute. She anticipated Japan's infamous Greater East Asia Co-prosperity Sphere by some twenty years. She claimed they had spies in far-off Lhasa, and in fact the Dalai Lama was communicating with the Japanese, whom he admired as good and powerful Buddhists. Certainly Alexandra proved more keen-sighted than the French, British, or American politicians who woefully ignored the first rays of the Rising Sun.

Depressed, feeling she had failed, Alexandra relapsed into a morose period. Longing for the Land of Snows cut her like a whetted knife. She admitted:

I have homesickness for a country that isn't mine. The steppes, the solitudes, the eternal snows and the big skies up there [in the Himalayas] haunt me. The difficult hours, hunger, cold, wind that cut my face, that left my lips swollen enormously, bleeding, [the] sleeping in the icy mud and the stops among the unbelievably filthy population, all mean little. These miseries pass quickly [and] one remains permanently engulfed in the silence where only the wind sings, in the solitudes almost naked of greenery, the chaos of fantastic rocks, dizzying peaks and horizons of blinding light.

The scholar worked through the winter comparing Zen methods of meditation with those of India and Tibet, but she had to fight hard to temper her bleak mood. "I feel myself without a country and miserable," she moaned to her husband. She had been a fool to cross that forbidden line, driven by ambition to write books and to always see new places. "I understand I have lost what I will never again find," she continued. "I ask—where to go?" She wasn't nearly so bewildered as she led Philip to believe. Already the explorer was consulting cartographic maps of Central Asia, searching for a name in tiny characters that would be hardly visible among the shadow of mountains. This was Kum Bum, fabled birthplace of Tsong Khapa and the real-life model for James Hilton's Shangri-La. The monastic city was located in Tibet's Amdo province, not France or North Africa.

Voilà, a miracle! Despite deteriorating postal communications, and censors, a bank draft from Mouchy made its way out of war-torn Europe and arrived in August 1917. Alexandra barely paused to store her trunks, then sailed from overly tidy Japan to Korea. Living in a monastery on Diamond Mountain (Kongo-San), breathing fresh air "amid a savage decor of sharp peaks," she began to feel fine. She slept in a bare cell, awakened at three in the morning to meditate, and spent the rest of the day tramping the mountain paths to visit hallowed shrines, finally to admire the dazzling sunset. That is, when it didn't rain, which it did for three weeks straight. This caused a "sneaky gout" to kick up, and sometimes when she walked it felt "like lashes from a whip."

It was no matter, for as Alexandra pointed out, "I am infinitely more agile in all this climbing than when I was twenty, and so much more hearty against fatigue." At the end of September, she and Yongden renewed their passports in Seoul: she at the French and he at the British consulate. We presume she proudly stated her correct age, forty-nine, since in her case will and training had triumphed over the supposedly inevitable failings.

By early October Alexandra had reached Peking. China's former imperial city was not her goal but a way-stop. She found it large, flat, and well kept, and as usual she took quarters in the precincts of a monastery. Her project was to leave for Mongolia before spring in order to continue her studies where the lamas spoke and read Tibetan. Her "Mongol soul" yearned to breathe "the natal air of my distant ancestors."

Peking proved agreeable—Alexandra usually spoke well of the Chinese—but, because she didn't have a grasp on the language, she was lumped with the other Westerners whom the people hated. They were aware only of foreign diplomats, soldiers, and missionaries, who were "intimately linked with one another." The Buddhist denied association with this "swarm of fleas" feeding off the helpless elephant China, and she dreaded the "official teas" of the well-meaning missionary wives. However, her plan to travel to Mongolia by auto misfired. The one car, garaged at the railroad station, never left because it cost a small fortune to hire.

Alexandra explained all this to Philip while asking for more money. She didn't neglect to praise him as "good, affectionate and intelligent beyond all expression." He had improved with age like a fine wine. She was going to trust him with a secret concerning her very last journey before returning home: she intended to cross Western China to Tibet, then travel across the steppes of that country so different from all others to the northern reaches of the Himalayas. Finally, she would descend once again through the high passes to India.

If her program sounded like a crazy dream—and she would find out it was riskier than she knew—why, she would accomplish it simply by putting one foot after another. It was less dangerous than crossing the Place de la Concorde in Paris, where you were apt to get run over. But Philip must never mention Tibet, neither in their correspondence nor in casual talk in Algeria. "An indiscretion could cause me great problems and put me in danger," his wife warned him. She was making the trip against the will of the Dalai Lama at Lhasa and the Resident at Gangtok, Charles Bell. She had learned that British intelligence had long ears.

Through the French Ambassador at Peking, Alexandra met a rich

Tibetan lama from the Koko Nor district in northeastern Tibet, administered by China. He acted as a Chinese official and was in the capital to collect a large sum due him from the treasury. Tall, strong, imposing—uglier still than the Gomchen—the lama was well read, the author of a grammar. Attired in a luxurious yellow silk robe over purple velour, attended by servants, he reminded the Frenchwoman of a Roman cardinal. When he played the tambourine and sang a sweet Tibetan air, he quite charmed her.

The lama was quick to invite the foreign Buddhist to join his caravan on its return to Kum Bum, central to the Koko Nor. He even offered to supply her with wood and water, both scarce, while she studied at the monastery. In return he expected Alexandra to help him with his major ambition: to write a book on astronomy. Knowing very little about planets or stars, she jumped at the chance. It constituted the first leg on her route, and with civil strife and the accompanying black plague endemic to western China, the protection of an armed caravan seemed esential.

China, after the collapse of the Manchu dynasty, weathered a terribly chaotic interregnum until the final victory of the Maoists in 1949 when they were able to unify the country. Until his death in 1925, the Republican leader Sun Yat-sen usually held sway in Canton and much of the south, while other personalities or local generals ruled over various provinces. These warlords printed worthless money, extorted provisions and labor from the people, and sold concessions to any foreigner rapacious enough to buy. Measuring their wealth in soldiers, the warlords were never secure, and when not battling one another they would combine to march on Peking to topple the kaleidoscopic, almost imaginary, central government. China was so "lamentable to see, it makes one cry," but it didn't dim the adventurer's desire to plunge right in.

The lama never recovered his money. By the end of January 1918 he'd decided to leave anyway. A draft from Philip arrived in the nick of time, along with news that Alexandra's senile, paralytic mother had died a full year earlier. Her daughter claimed to be deeply moved by memories, and coincidentally her own depression had set in about then. Now a woman of property, which was out of reach until after the war, she quickly sent Philip her will. He was left the bulk of her modest estate after debts were paid and her library was donated to the Buddhist Society of London. Alexandra instructed her husband to provide for Yongden. She admitted that "Aphur is not brave by nature," but by defying his family he had amply demonstrated his loyalty. She confessed to growing very attached to this "petit Jaune."

Then she was off to the railroad station for a big send-off. An elaborate hospital car stuffed with medicines was appended to the train because of the pestilence raging in the countryside. To this display of fear and to those protecting themselves by wearing face masks, Alexandra replied, "Bah!" She was pleased when the fancy car became detached by mistake.

At the railhead the party switched to mules and wagons. Alexandra found the armed guards atop the lama's baggage to be worthy descendants of the Golden Horde of Genghis Khan. For herself and Yongden she fashioned a large French flag from three appropriately colored strips of cloth. This she intended to fly in the face of a battle, a talisman of neutrality. But at first the caravan faced only delay, hung up for days in a squalid village on the border between Honan and Shensi provinces.

Here Alexandra became ominously ill. Philip had begged her not to expose herself, that she was all he cared about in the world. The plague was of the fatal pulmonary variety that had ravaged Europe in the Middle Ages. Initially the symptoms were no worse than the grippe—fever, dizziness—but if on the fourth day you coughed up blood, you were doomed to an excruciating death. Most likely there would be no one to tend you in your last agonizing hours. Yongden stayed close by, but Alexandra was determined not to infect him or others. She resolved that, on the sight of blood in her sputum, she would take the revolver she slept with and blow out her brains. On the fourth day she felt much better.

In spite of the archaic politeness of the armed men to the foreign woman in their midst, whom they addressed as "Your Reverence," tension filled the air like a thunderstorm about to burst. One morning Alexandra awoke to find a few severed heads impaled on a wall in front of her door. Bandits, she was told, but their contorted faces looked no more guilty than those of the government soldiers. She heard that in the warfare between Tibetans and Chinese troops that continued sporadically along the frontier, the winners of a battle made a stew of the losers' hearts—they ate them with rice.

"To set oneself up in presumptuous judgment seems absurd in our chaotic world," wrote the Frenchwoman of atrocities witnessed. "The best moral for poor humans, without doubt, is to make ourselves charitable." In Europe, too, war was stripping the thin veneer of culture to reveal humanity's instincts for murder and revenge. Perhaps, this would prove a step forward, if it brought closer "the reality of ourselves." Still, she shuddered at "the coming realm of brutes."

In practice, the Buddhist usually managed to ward off impending violence. Achingly slow progress through filthy villages made the lama-official irritable and brought out his shady side. One evening at an inn, Alexandra was surprised to see young women clad in green pants and pink jackets enter his room. They reminded her of "a family of Tom Thumbs going into the ogre's den." After noisy haggling the harlots emerged, leaving the youngest to stay the night. This failed to appease the lama, and he fell into a quarrel with a Chinese officer. Soon heavily armed soldiers burst into the inn. The lama called his men to come running, guns in hand. It looked like a miniature war was about to erupt.

The foreign woman, aided by an interpreter, saved the day. Alexandra convinced the Han captain it was beneath his dignity to take notice of the ravings of a barbarian from the Koko Nor wilds. Then she remonstrated with the lama in Tibetan. How could he condescend to tussle with swinish soldiers? The quarrel evaporated and the caravan resumed its laborious trek toward Tibet's Amdo province.

The company Alexandra was keeping had turned into a liability. Taking Yongden, she detoured via Tungchow where a small colony of Swedish missionaries—"big devil albinos"—offered her shelter. Immediately the walled town was assaulted. Bullets sang through the air, and the pastor and his family retreated to their chapel to pray with fervor. Alexandra jumped into a hot tub. She supposed the rebels would storm the city and take her prisoner. She thought, "I might be obliged to endure a journey without a bath, which makes me very disagreeable." Fortunately, the attack was beaten off for the time being. The Swedes, convinced God had heard them, loudly gave thanks for their deliverance. Alexandra muttered that God should have prevented the attack in the first place.

The fighting continued with the invaders using ladders to scale the high walls, while the defenders, short on ammunition, hurled stones down on them. Alexandra couldn't help being roused by this classic panorama, a painting by Delacroix sprung to life. Sabers were unsheathed and blood flowed in the ditches, but compared to mechanized warfare and poison gas, it looked quaint.

The city's defenses held, and in April lilacs bloomed in the gardens. The missionaries gave Alexandra accounts of earlier Western explorers to read, which incensed her. These interlopers, speaking neither Chinese nor Tibetan, had embarked with dozens of camels and horses, dozens of servants, all of which entourage needed to be equipped. Naturally things went wrong, and about such misadventures the bunglers wrote their books. Worse, they had turned the natives against all foreigners by tricks such as slaughtering the pet animals of monasteries, stealing horses from nomads, and carving their initials into sacred trees. Alexandra traveled as a pilgrim, not a conqueror. Once the civil war cooled, she was ready to resume her jaunt.

Sian, capital of Shensi, was appointed as the meeting place with the lama. It was essential that Alexandra enter Tibet in his caravan. Ignoring the military governor of Tungchow, who pleaded with her that leaving meant certain death at the hands of bandits, she snuck out through the gates in a train of three creaky carts, each drawn by two mules. The terrified drivers whipped their beasts through a scorched countryside, "not a single peasant in the fields, nor a traveler on the road." A tempest broke, and in the dark, pouring rain, the party approached a river beyond which they supposed themselves safe. They hallooed for the ferryman and were answered by a hail of shots. Somehow, they crossed the river on a raft, then bedded down with the fleas in a hovel; next day they continued on. Finally, looking up, Alexandra saw a wagon loaded with baggage and piled still higher with Mongols—Sian, the lama, they had come through!

Nearing Koko Nor, the impatient pilgrim began to walk. She had followed a tough regimen—sleeping on the ground, gulping bad food, burned up by the sun—one she couldn't have borne in her youth. How preposterous were "the pretty tales of feminine fragility, [of] the eternal sufferers" perpetuated by mountebank writers. Robust and hearty, after "eat[ing] many kilometers," one day she surmounted a ridge to gaze down on the great Kum Bum monastery. The golden-roofed temples and flat, whitewashed houses of this Shangri-La gleamed in the mountain-rimmed valley.

"Ouf!" exclaimed the weary traveler. "Here I am!"

In July 1918, 1,600 miles from Peking and gloriously distant from Europe, Alexandra and Yongden settled into a comfortable house to begin the more mundane task of translating Buddhist manuscripts. "Ah, Asia is marvellous and diverse," the wife wrote to her husband. "We have conquered, duped and stolen from them. [Yet] Asians live in a world of beauty whose door remains closed to the West."

It was Alexandra's mission to help pry open that door, to introduce us to our fellow humans on the other side.

Book Three

THE PILGRIM

Far hence in Asia
On the smooth convent roofs
On the gold terraces
Of holy Lhasa
Bright shines the sun.

—Matthew Arnold

CHAPTER 14

A Paradise

Before the onset of dawn in Central Asia, the conchs sound their eerie wail. Under a vast dome of sky in which the stars, soon to gutter out like spent candles, burn the brighter, shadows gather on the flat roof of the assembly hall. Novices, wrapped in togas against the bitter cold, are assigned to waken the slumbering monks of Kum Bum. Each begins to blow into his shell, and while one rests to breathe, the others continue to bellow forth rising and falling waves that crash against the far corners of this monastic city of hundreds of dwellings. Although the age-old call is insufficient to raise the dead, it does rouse the living.

Lights flicker in the windows of the princely mansions of grand lamas, and domestic noises indicate stirring in the humbler quarters as the summons slowly ebbs. The sky pales to gray, rosy day breaks. Doors are flung open, and from every side some 3,800 *trapas* (monks of basic degree) stream toward the imposing hall with its ornate tiers in Chinese style. With shaven heads and in uniform robes, the monks are reminiscent of tamed mice scurrying to their accustomed spots. In a few moments the morning prayers will begin to ascend toward peaks so mighty even the sun has difficulty in scaling them. The Religion—the cumulative forces of light—once again will banish the demons of prehistoric darkness. As the wail of the conch drifts into space, albeit fainter and fainter, so the Doctrine when proclaimed echoes throughout the universe.

This *was* the unvarying routine of monastic life in Tibet. For centuries each one of the myriad monasteries scattered the length and breadth of the Lamaist domain—the immense territories of which Tibet itself is but a small part—had greeted the typically chilly dawn in the manner described. Such is the case no longer. Although the conch still sounds sporadically over the Central Asian steppes, it is in lament. The dozens of major *gompas* (monasteries) of the heartland, each a town in itself, have been sacked and even demolished; their tens of thousands of monks are scattered, murdered, silenced. The Fourteenth Dalai Lama, defender of the faith, lives in exile in India and speaks openly of perhaps being the last in his line. "Is there a world in another country equal to this one?" wondered David-Neel, of Kum Bum.

We are fortunate to have this inquiring witness to the ways of an ancient culture that, even at the time, appeared threatened with extinction. On the second-floor terrace of her house in the Pegyai Lama's palace sat the doughty Frenchwoman during the frosty mornings of autumn 1918. Neglecting the rigors of *tumo*, Alexandra dressed snugly in warm robe and high yak-hide boots in order to watch the daily pageant of life unfold. At 9,500 feet, she wrote to Philip, "The air is excellent with that special taste of high altitude." She could glance from the temple roofs burnished by sunlight to knots of yaks foraging for grass to a camel caravan of Mongols starting for Lhasa. Or she might draw within to savor "the voluptuous subtlety of isolation and silence."

Alexandra wasn't permitted to attend the usual matins service, one of the few acts common to the entire brotherhood of a monastery, nor to share communal meals. The only exception was at important holidays, when the woman lama joined in with the "shabby, ill-smelling crew, offering a strange contrast to the sumptuousness of the gold brocade vests worn by the dignitaries and the jewelled cloak and rod of office of the . . . ruler of the *gompa*." Here again we find the juxtaposition of the tawdry with magnificence.

Alexandra recreated the scene:

Hanging from the high ceiling, from the galleries and against the tall pillars, scrolls of painting show countless Buddhas and deities, while a host of other worthies, saints, gods and demons, may be vaguely discerned on the frescoes which decorate the walls of the dark edifice.

At the bottom of the hall, behind rows of butter lamps, shine softly the gilded images of former Grand Lamas and the massive silver and gold reliquaries which contain their ashes or mummified bodies. A mystic atmosphere envelops men and things, veiling all vulgar details, idealizing the attitudes and the faces. Whatever knowledge one may have acquired regarding the shortcomings of many of the monks assembled there, the sight of the assembly itself is most impressive.

Soon chanting would begin, deep toned, punctuated by bells, drums, and roaring trumpets. The little novices seated on the benches in the back rows hardly dared to breathe for fear of the "hundred-eyed *chostimpa*"—the official disciplinarian—and the rod and whip that ostentatiously hung from his elevated seat. This fellow was always a dark, strapping Khampa (native of Kham to the south) who overlooked the assembly with majestic disdain. Once Alexandra saw three men toward the rear, well hidden from view, make slight signs to one another. Up rose the *chostimpa* and, whip in hand, strode across the hall like an avenging angel.

Stalking past the foreigner, he tucked his toga above his elbows, brandishing the knotted cat-o'-nine-tails in his large calloused fist. The malefactors shook but sheepishly awaited their punishment. With the panache of a hangman, the *chostimpa* lifted each man by the scruff of his neck, depositing him in the aisle where the poor fellow prostrated himself forehead to the floor. Whack! went the whip on each one's back, then the fearful personage resumed his dignity and his high place, looking for new offenders. Sometimes it was convenient to be a woman and not subject to the rules.

For the most part, Alexandra stayed aloof, if observant, from the routine at Kum Bum. She described her day for Philip, to let him know she wasn't wasting her time or his money. After a bracing hour on the terrace during which she might walk or meditate, a boy arrived to light the stove and boil water for tea. This she took in Tibetan style, with salt and plenty of butter. She did her *toilette* and read until taking an English breakfast at nine. Alexandra claimed to be fortunate in that she had good bread from a Moslem baker in a nearby village. Until noon she translated into French and English rare manuscripts the lamas loaned her from the monastery's extensive library. She needed help with the ancient literary Tibetan, but since these texts of Nagarjuna's (an early Buddhist philosopher, the Father of Mahayana) had been lost in the original Sanskrit, the scholar was elated at the find.

Midday meant a break—not for lunch but a hot tub—followed by more work. At four the former gourmet dined on a thick soup of locally grown vegetables. Dessert might be a compote of stewed fruit. Again Alexandra bent to deciphering the texts until she retired to bed at nine. She had given the larger, lower room to Yongden, because the bright frescoes on the walls disturbed her rest. No hint of neurasthenia kept her from sleeping wonderfully well, and it seemed but a moment until the conchs woke her, proclaiming another dawn.

Alexandra's only complaint was that her eyes bothered her. She was far from bored and could go on living in this manner for a thousand years. Of course there were occasional diversions. Lamaism is a form of Buddhism that can be actively practiced only by monks. The laity supports the religion, in practice the *gompas*, which is best done by bestowing gifts. At Kum Bum, greatly revered as the birthplace of Tsong Khapa, the founder of the Yellow Hat reforms, wealthy pilgrims frequently made an offering of a special feast for the brethren. It was a welcome change from the routine *tsampa* and more-or-less buttered tea, and although Alexandra couldn't attend the banquet, she was always brought a portion of the meal. She particularly relished "a certain Mongolian dish made of mutton, rice, Chinese dates, butter, cheese, curds, sugar-candy, and various other ingredients and spices, all boiled together." Savory *momos*—meat enclosed in a ball of baked *pâté* and steamed—were another favorite. These gave the lie to an old Tibetan proverb, "To eat lama's food requires jaws of iron."

At the end of November 1918, Alexandra wrote to Philip with tears in her eyes. It wasn't because a letter from him had finally reached her four months after mailing, nor even due to worry over Yongden, dangerously ill with influenza. She was tenderly nursing him, although she had a high fever herself. "I am not in bed," she scoffed, "because it is not my custom." No, the rush of sentiment came at learning of the Armistice from some English missionaries who heard the news before she did.

Once the flu ran its course—so far from Western civilization, the pair caught their share of that deadly worldwide epidemic—Alexandra and Yongden sewed a huge French tricolor and trooped it to the top of a nearby mountain. The valley below showed green but patchy, the slopes splashed with touches of golden poplars. The sun shone "clear, warm and blinding in the blue sky which compares with that of Africa." Ceremoniously, they unfurled the banner, which had embroidered on it a common Tibetan prayer of thanks: "*Lha gyalo! De tamche pam!* Victory to the Gods, the Demons are Vanquished!"

Alexandra watched with satisfaction as the flag flapped in the breeze. Kum Bum was surrounded by a score of lesser monastic establishments occupying various mountain nooks and crannies. The monks, nuns, and hermits understood the efficacy of sending a message to the universe. But the Frenchwoman had the more practical intention of informing others that the mighty Allies had defeated the dread Huns. If the great struggle in Europe was done, the little war for Tibetan independence was being waged more fiercely. The monks, who didn't shrink at fighting, were arming to defend Kum Bum and its treasures. Recently a nearby *gompa* had been pillaged and burned by troops. The brethren fled and took revenge by killing a Chinese interpreter, dicing his body in pieces and serving his heart as a morsel for some laymen. No wonder Alexandra slept with a loaded pistol under her pillow and kept two fast horses always saddled in the stable.

Neither fear nor temptations provoked by watching trains of yaks driven by men of "mute, enigmatic faces heading towards the high, mysterious hills" would lure Alexandra from her cell until she was quite ready. In fact, she went into retreat for the next six weeks to further her studies. She was out and about by mid-February when, a hint of spring in the air, the New Year celebration took place. Kum Bum, located in Amdo province to the north of the villages and grazing lands of Kham, was accessible to the relatively populous Tibetan speaking portions of Kansu and Szechuan (China) to the east, and it could be reached by the Mongol horse breeders to its north and west. For this festive holiday, pilgrims and nomads poured into the monastic precincts to view its marvelous tree and simply to have a good time.

Legend held that after Tsong Khapa's birth, attended with portents, the umbilical cord was buried and from it grew a tree that became an object of worship. Pious visitors arrived to make offerings of ornaments and jewelry, a monk built a hut, and so the famed *gompa* began. In the 1840s the clever and learned French priest Evarist Huc sojourned there, writing of the tree, grown large and venerable, "We were filled with an absolute consternation of astonishment at finding that . . . there were upon each of the leaves well-formed Tibetan characters, all of a green colour, some darker, some lighter than the leaf itself."

The abbé and his companion were eager to convert the natives to *their* brand of the miraculous, and so they minutely examined the leaves for fraud and tore off some bark. But the young bark also exhibited the "outlines of characters in a germinating state, and what is very singular, these new characters are not infrequently different from those which they replace." Indeed, Kum Bum means "ten thousand images."

As usual, Alexandra was indifferent to miracles, and she scarcely mentioned the tree. But she observed with interest the pilgrims who arrived at the site hoping to see some wonder. The surroundings, especially at night, added a touch of magic. Snow covered the mountains and the monastic city, and soaring many-tiered temples and humble homes alike sparkled in the glow from innumerable lamps and candles. Red-garbed *trapas* carried resin torches, which glinted steadily in the frosty air. The populace surged through the streets, and all, both rich and poor, were dressed in their best. The women proudly showed off headdresses of 108 braided plaits, gleaming with butter and bedecked by red and green ribbons. The Golog women—nomads from the mountain fastnesses—added a kind of mantle of large cups of silver, turquoise, and coral, as well as a bowler hat resembling those worn by Bolivian Indians. They clanked as they moved with the deliberation of treasure galleons. Most amazing were the many statues of butter upon which the folk gaped and made endless comments.

These tableaux, composed of flour pasted over wooden frames and then drenched in butter of various colors that quickly froze to give a glassy sheen, could be images of famous kings or sages or fanciful dragons or other mythical beasts, even a scale model of Lhasa complete with a tiny Dalai Lama about to enter his palace. Executed with great care by the temple artists, the figures were to be admired for only the night of the fifteenth of the first month, which culminated the New Year celebration. They were destroyed by daylight and the butter sold as healing salve.

Whatever its potency, it couldn't compare with a blessing received from the incarnate *kandoma* (roughly "fairy" or "spirit," always female) who was ushered about the exhibits with all the pomp of a visiting archbishop. Resplendent in the flowered robe given her by the Panchen Lama, Alexandra moved in state, the crowds furiously attempting to prostrate themselves or kiss her hem. She could do no more than nod in appreciation to her worshipers, since a cordon of guards continually beat them off. The folk seemed grateful for the blows. As for the skeptical Frenchwoman turned *dakini* (mother goddess), she was reminded of an incident in the career of *Madame* Du Barry, Louis XV's favorite, when she was first presented at Versailles. Of her descent from her carriage, gorgeously attired, she later remarked, "I would have liked to have been at a window to see myself pass."

What caught up Alexandra and took her outside herself was not adoration, which she regarded as a touching proof of the aspiration of the common folk to higher things, but the trill of a Mongol flute accompanied by the irregular clang of copper cymbals. In the midst of a fawning mob, this "music of the wind among the solitudes that surround the camps lost in the desert . . . that accompanies the caravan proceeding slowly across the immense plains" thrilled the former diva "to the depths of [her] musical soul." The far distant steppes called to her, and although she couldn't account for the mystery of her enchantment, she was bound to succumb sooner or later to her lust to roam. After all, she informed Philip in a reflective mood, "Sensuality is to each in his own way . . . To me, it is being alone, silence, virgin land not disfigured by cultivation, vast spaces, a rude life under the tent . . ."

In the spring of 1919, the civil war heated up. The central government at Peking, which had long ruled over Amdo and Kham (referred to on some maps as Inner Tibet), although weakly and thus benignly, was losing its grip altogether. The Tibetan tribesmen, good fighters, were in continual revolt. Breakaway armies fought one another and brigandage flourished, especially among the fierce mountain Gologs (literally "heads on backwards"), who delighted in stealing mules from the Chinese generals. The Dalai Lama seized this opportunity to demand the total independence of all Tibet. But realistically, he had few troops to send to the frontier, a month's forced march from Lhasa over the world's worst roads. So along the Sino-Tibetan marches anarchy reigned, and to paraphrase Hobbes, life was short, brutish, and chancy.

Alexandra was inspired to go on some delightful jaunts. At a day's walk lived forty nuns in their "Fortress in the Sky," a poverty-stricken *gompa* atop a high mountain surrounded by other needlelike peaks of somber red hues. Alexandra and the cheerful nuns got along well. These women thought nothing of tramping over the entire country on a pilgrimage. Their absolute faith and quiet courage helped to fortify her resolve. Although she refused an offer to take up residence, they went together on hikes climbing slopes so steep that the middle-aged adventurer had to be hoisted along like a package. She found it exhilarating to attain ruined temples and shrines where hermits had meditated centuries ago. "The world seems strangely far off," she sighed, "a whirlwind of atoms." On the way down, Yongden, proud as a ram leading his flock, entertained the party with songs. He even flirted with the prettier nuns.

Summer found Alexandra at the head of a small expedition—including Yongden and several armed servants—headed for the barren but entrancing region of Lake Koko Nor to the northwest of Kum Bum. This was a year of pilgrimage—every twelfth—and caravans might arrive at the lake from farthest Mongolia, circumambulating its considerable breadth. This going around sacred mountains or lakes is essential to what the French scholar R. A. Stein has called "the nameless religion," by which he means the matrix of age-old popular magical beliefs and practices covered over by a Buddhist patina. The clear, high lakes were particularly employed for divination, peering into the future, and within their depths they concealed a variety of spirit beings, so that Tibetbans were fearful of eating one in the guise of a fish. Alexandra's journey to the lake lasted ten days and was not without mishaps, including getting lost. But with the aid of a rudimentary map and a pocket compass, she led the way to Koko Nor, this "miniature ocean in turquoise."

The Koko Nor area was a rugged plain lacking even a single village. The great salt lake, together with mountain ranges on the horizon near and far, broke the monotony of the steppe, which was scarcely fit for grazing. Alexandra adored the solitude, the loom of a snowcapped peak reflected in the wavery blue water. Here was a landscape she knew deep down in her soul. Yet camping on the banks of this icy sheet had its drawbacks. It was impossible to buy or beg food, and although one shivered with cold at night, the mosquitoes were ravenous. Then there was the threat of bandits.

In 1864 Dutreuil de Rhins, mariner and explorer, had been murdered in this vicinity. Some years after Alexandra's visit, two Frenchmen, Louis Marteau and Louis Dupont, disappeared without a trace. So the little party, as it circled around the flat expanse, kept a sharp watch, alert for danger. The American missionary Robert Ekvall, who lived in Amdo in the 1930s, wrote in *Tibetan Sky Lines,* "A hairlike rift in the blue may mean a lance, and the fork of a gun rest . . . enemies and a raid. The bold outline of a distant mounted figure is sure to bring a sense of uncertainty, even menace."

According to Alexandra, there was an invariable etiquette followed when one party approached another. For example, she was jogging along placidly when one of her retainers cried out, "Six guns!" Quickly, she reached into her saddlebag for a revolver, while Yongden and another man rode forward in a show of force. Alexandra's horse took off, and when she tried to dismount, she found herself stuck in the saddle. Luckily the intruders decided they were weaker, or less certain, and they beat a hasty retreat. Strength was measured by a party's num-

ber of weapons and their quality—many guns were old blunder-
busses—and its determination to fight. A common greeting in this region was, "No closer, friend, or I'll shoot!" But what if two armed
groups should meet suddenly due to uneven terrain? The weaker must
advance slowly and explain itself; to run would mean a hail of bullets
in their backs, no questions asked.

At the sacred lake on the border of Tibet, Mongolia, and China,
Alexandra met more pilgrims than bandits, when she met anybody at
all. The water, deepening in shade from azure to turquoise to lapis as
the sun waned, compelled her gaze for hours on end. One evening
three odd-looking characters planted their tent next to the traveler's.
Dressed in shabby oranges and reds topped off by faded sheepskins,
they were Bon priests, necromancers of the ancient faith who knew
charms to kill a fetus in the womb or conversely to animate dry bones.
Life in the open, and the practice of their strange rites, had given the
men the knowing, crinkled faces of sages.

Alexandra merely enjoyed the reflections of their warm colors on the
shimmering, darkening lake, indulging in the sort of refined sensuality—an ardor for the sights and sounds of the barbaric—that at times
raised her writing to the pitch of a Romantic poet. On a different occasion, in Kansu on the edge of a primeval forest, a Bon disciple joined
her company for protection against robbers. The man wore his long
hair, wrapped in a piece of red material, as a turban. She fed him well
and learned that he was going to join his master just then performing
a great ceremony on a hill some distance away. The rite was designed
to "coerce a malignant demon who habitually harmed one of the small
tribes which live[d] in that region."

Alexandra was ravished by the desire to observe the *ngagspa* (sorcerer) at his trade, but his disciple assured her it was impossible. The
Bon priest couldn't be disturbed during the lunar month it took to
perform the rite. The always curious orientalist wasn't about to be put
off, for the ways of the ancient religion were little known and much
feared. She made the Bonpo into a sort of prisoner, having her servants
tend to him but watch him carefully. He went on feasting, saying with
a grin, "Do not fear that I shall run away. You may bind me with ropes
if it pleases you. I need not go ahead to inform my master of your
coming. He already knows all about it. I have sent a message on the
wind."

Sure enough, once their party crossed the Kunka Pass and came out
on the Tibetan plain, a troop rode up at full speed, dismounted, and
offered Alexandra presents of ceremonial scarves and butter. The
ngagspa had sent them to beg the foreign lama not to visit him. None
but his initiated disciple would be permitted to approach the spot where
he had built a secret shrine. Alexandra wasn't boorish enough to per-

sist, especially since the *ngagspa* had so vividly demonstrated his powers of telepathy and his excellence in instructing his disciple.

Such seemingly magical occurrences were frequent in Tibet. Alexandra recorded them as they happened, usually providing a rational explanation for the phenomena, although not always strictly scientific in the narrow terms of her day. She speculated that the country was hospitable to these psychic sports because of its consistently high altitude, the great silence in which it was bathed—permitting one to hear another's thoughts—and, above all, due to the absence of cities, crowds, and mechanical or electric devices. These caused whirlpools of distracting energy. Then, too, the Tibetans were placid and open; their spirit world seemed as commonplace as mountains, steppes, and lakes. But later Alexandra herself delved deeply into the arcane.

The journey to Koko Nor had been a fine test of endurance, a warm-up for the big trip about which Alexandra dropped hints in her letters. By September 1919, she was pleased to be back in her comfortable house at the monastery. "For those who love books," she wrote, "Kum Bum is paradise. . . . [R]ecessed in the hollow of a valley . . . with beautiful decorated roofs furnished with ornaments and flying banners, it is a feast for the eye."

Possibly, Kum Bum served James Hilton as a model for Shangri-La in *Lost Horizon*. His hidden lamasary would have been located to the west in the Kun Lun range, where in fact there is nothing. Abbé Huc, on whose writings Hilton drew, resembled the fictional Father Perrault, abbot of Shangri-La. Huc came to dispute with and convert the lamas, but he succumbed to the lure of study. Unlike Perrault, he never lost his Christian vocation, and rather than don a Buddhist robe he left. Of all the early travelers to Tibet, Huc was the most inquisitive, and he blandly reported strange goings-on.

Alas, the abbé gave no hint of any elixir of immortality or fountain of perpetual youth, associated with Shangri-La. (It is disappointing that Hilton attributes Perrault's living for a couple of centuries to "drug-taking and deep-breathing exercises.") Yet at Kum Bum, Alexandra enunciated her own formula for longevity: "There is no more effective fountain of youth than travel and intellectual activity." Winter was not the season for gadding about, and so, in the manner of a small class of erudite monks, she took to her reading. She informed Philip she would need one more year at the monastery to complete her translations . . . Would he please send more money? Otherwise his wife might have to wander about like a nomad or beggar.

Kum Bum had long since ceased to be a vital center of thought. True, it had a notable school of medicine, specializing in the collection and preparation of curative herbs. Abbé Huc noted that "the pilgrims who visit Kumbum buy these remedies at exorbitant prices." He was very picturesque in describing the Tibetan physicians' methods of urinalysis: "They examine [the patient's urine] with the most minute attention, and take the greatest heed to all the changes undergone by its colour; they whip it from time to time, with a wooden spatula, and they put it up to the ear to ascertain how much noise it makes."

Alexandra remained surprisingly silent on any aspect of Tibetan medicine. She was afflicted with what she called "hereditary arthritis" and sciatica, but her remedy was to ignore the pain. When it became unbearable she dosed herself with patent medicines likely containing some narcotic. But she was intrigued by the disputations engaged in by the novice lamas before receiving their higher degrees. These were as elaborately staged as a Japanese Noh play, although rather more lively. While the entire faculty looked on, a master would question his pupil on the intricacies of Buddhist doctrine, standing over the seated, anxious young man, teasing him by alternately proffering or withholding the huge woolly ceremonial cap of a graduate. Or two candidates would debate philosophy, clapping hands or jumping up and down to emphasize a point. All went according to ritual, and questions and answers consisted of memorized portions of scripture. Still, the emotions of the participants were real, for the loser, in disgrace, had to carry the winner of the debate on his shoulders throughout the grounds.

This was much preferable to the outcome of religious contests in historic times. Then to finish second-best could cost a philosopher his life. Kublai Khan—in the manner of the Mongol rulers—held theological debates between Tibetan Buddhists, Taoists from China, and Nestorian Christians, and those who failed to win royal patronage for their creed had to flee the court or be imprisoned. The great reformer Tsong Khapa initially won fame as a disputant, and in 1408 the emperor invited him to display his learning before the Celestial Throne. The first of the Yellow Hats prudently sent a disciple, who won such favor he was enabled to found the huge Sera monastery near Lhasa. At Kum Bum, Abbé Huc argued so effectively against the lamas that they packed him off to Lhasa, where he nearly succeeded in converting the Regent (the Dalai Lama was a child) to Christianity.

However learned, Alexandra, a woman, couldn't engage in debates with the male lamas. So when translating manuscripts had lost its charm, she turned to a deep form of meditation, shutting herself in *tsams*. Specifically, the term refers to certain small boxlike structures that used to be maintained on the outskirts of every monastery. Here monks who were already trained to isolation shut themselves up for months or years at a time, or forever. David Macdonald described the cells as tiny, filthy, devoid of any light whatever. Once a *trapa* took the vow of lifelong retirement, it was unbreakable. The door through which he entered was bricked up and a little food placed outside a trap once a day. If this lay untouched for several days, the cell was broken up, to disclose a withered corpse. According to Macdonald, "Many of the hermits become mentally afflicted, while others become fanatics." Their view was that the virtual denial of life assured them of eternal bliss.

The French orientalist had nothing so glorious in mind. The *tsams* she entered in the winter of 1919–20 was not so strict as customary and took place in her own quarters. Alexandra's purpose was experimental: she meant to create a *tulpa*, a phantom being voluntarily produced by powerful concentration of thought and the repetition of prescribed rites. The incident, but not the process, is described in *Magic and Mystery*. She did succeed, although in a way that frightened her thoroughly.

A *tulpa*, unlike a successive incarnation of a particular personality (such as the Dalai Lama), is a temporary phenomenon willfully created. It may take any form whatever but is most often in human shape. Usually, it is sent to perform a definite mission. However, "Once the *tulpa* is endowed with enough vitality to be capable of playing the part of a real being, it tends to free itself from its maker's control. . . . Sometimes the phantom becomes a rebellious son and one hears of uncanny struggles that have taken place between magicians and their creatures, the former being severely hurt or even killed by the latter." Other cultures speak of similar unnatural creations, and we are reminded of the fictional Dr. Frankenstein's monster.

In traditional Eastern thought, there is no hard line between the real and unreal. A dream or a vision is as actual or illusory as a mountain, the perception of which depends on the viewer. Alexandra intended to manufacture an entity that hadn't existed previously, a lama, "short and fat, of an innocent and jolly type." She related in *Magic and Mystery*, "After a few months the phantom monk was formed. His form grew gradually *fixed* and life-like looking. He became a kind of guest, living in my apartment. I then broke my seclusion and started for a tour, with my servants and tents."

The monk tagged along, walking by her when she rode and stopping as they made camp. Sometimes the illusion rubbed against her, palpably touching her. Worse, "The features . . . gradually underwent a change. The fat, chubby-cheeked fellow grew leaner, his face assumed a vaguely mocking, sly, malignant look. He became more troublesome and bold. In brief, he escaped my control."

What Alexandra had feared, but disregarded, came to pass. To make matters more complicated, others began to see the fellow and to speak to him, and although he didn't answer, his presence had to be explained. Years later, Alexandra wrote calmly of the experience, but at the time she was quite beside herself. Her only hint to Philip was a statement that an "incident of very bad luck" had happened to her. It called into question her time spent and her motives in studying tantric Buddhism. Was she destined to take the left-hand path of the sorcerer?

With her usual determination, Alexandra forcibly decided to dissolve the phantom. But the mind-creature clung tenaciously to life, and he only disappeared after six months of hard struggle, presumably after she had performed the appropriate meditations. How to explain the affair? The orientalist admitted that learned Tibetans disagreed among each other, some holding that it was all due to the power of suggestion, and to projecting that suggestion to another's mind; she herself simply didn't know. She was unwilling to dwell on it.

The year's crops had failed, and by fall, 1920 there were outbreaks of famine and pestilence. At Chengtu in nearby Szechuan one hundred people a day were dying of cholera. The peasants were starving, and even honest folk had turned to murder and robbery. Talks between China and Tibet had failed, local governors were turning into warlords, fighting and pillaging one another. Alexandra wrote to Philip:

You will think that in these current exceptional circumstances the best thing to do would be to stop my Asiatic peregrinations and rejoin you in Algeria. To this I respond in all frankness that it would mean my death. . . . No matter how much I wish to see you—a desire that grows day by day—I can't tear myself away from Tibet. . . . I am chained, nailed. I can't help it.

Alexandra realized that her stay at Kum Bum was drawing to a close. Nearly penniless, she felt ashamed in front of the lamas. However, she had sworn to go where no white woman had been before. She would reach Lhasa, capital of Buddhist Central Asia, traveling on foot and without a tent if need be, begging her way. Akin to the simple herdsman of the high grassy steppes, the peasant on a small plot in Kham, or the Golog bandit in his mountain fastness, a splendid vision of the mysterious holy city rose before her eyes: "I have dreamed the same dream since I was a kid of six," sighed the Parisienne. "It's that drop of Mongol blood sprung to life after so many generations."

CHAPTER 15

Misadventures

Through the early winter of 1921, Alexandra and Yongden bent to their studies. The young man of twenty-three, who had been made a novice at fourteen, wished to become a *gelong,* or proper monk. Because he hadn't undergone the usual training, he was obliged to pass a special exam. Meanwhile, with the aid of a pair of magnifying spectacles, Alexandra worked through the nights translating texts by Nagarjuna. The Tibetan books from which she copied were actually collections of block-printed single sheets. Nagarjuna's most famous work, *The Diamond Sutra,* is contained in one hundred such volumes of a thousand pages each.

If the task seemed daunting, Alexandra was glad to be counted as practically the sole female member of—in Evans-Wentz's phrase—"that noble band of translators and transmitters who in our time have added fresh effulgence to the Light born of the East." Flourishing in the second century A.D., Nagarjuna was "the first teacher publicly to teach the supreme doctrine of the Voidness," which, though it dated to Gautama himself, had been previously elucidated only to "highly advanced disciples." Nagarjuna formed the bridge from Sanskrit to the northern languages, from the select few to the aspiring many.

Marpa, the guru of Milarepa, acted as a human bridge in a more literal sense, tramping over the Himalayan passes in all weathers, loaded down with sacred books, carrying on his back the wisdom of India to Tibet. Alexandra, too, would span not only grand distances on the map of Asia, but more importantly the cultures of East and West. She was able to leap the frightening chasm between meditation and action. "I have been taken for a *kandoma* (goddess or genie)," she informed Philip, "and for all I know, I may be one."

The peasants and nomads of Amdo could not fathom the foreign lama's researches, but when she stepped forth from her cell, they worshiped her person. These folk were labeled "people of the extremes" by the more sophisticated inhabitants of Lhasa. They looked romantic at a distance, skin shining like bronze. The men draped themselves in capacious cloaks that brushed the earth; the women sported vivid cottons of red, blue, and green, scarves dangling from their waists. Both sexes wore round or pointed bonnets trimmed with fox or lamb skins. Up close, they were grimy and unwashed, although inexplicably pleasant smelling.

It was common for bystanders to prostrate themselves as Alexandra passed. They were convinced she had solved the mysteries and could foretell the future in a bowl of water. Particularly when she donned her yellow vest embroidered with gold and silver flowers, a gift from the Panchen Lama, the effect was electric. Hordes of folk clamored for her healing touch, and the local Moslems equally came in droves, certain she must be a prophet. Thubten Norbu, brother to the Dalai Lama and former abbot of Kum Bum, writes of being put into a similarly embarrassing position:

Sometimes, because I am recognized as the reincarnation of [a venerated] Rimpoche, people came to me and asked for my blessing. I used to tell them that I had no power to give them a blessing . . . and that perhaps I was more in need of blessing than they were. . . . But they would reply that what I thought of myself did not matter, that *they* believed I must be a great person to have deserved such a high rebirth. Then I used to say a prayer with them . . .

Thus Alexandra, in the minds of the common folk, was elevated to the lineage of beneficent incarnations. More willingly, indeed decisively, she herself stepped into the ranks of a more questionable lot—the varied explorers of Tibet. Because they generally came to the Sacred Realm against the wishes of its rulers, or the foreign power that ruled over it, Peter Hopkirk has aptly termed them "trespassers" and "gatecrashers." Always they headed for the near-legendary capital of the Dalai Lama.

The first European to visit Lhasa, he claimed, was a Friar Odoric in 1324. He set out from the Franciscan mission to the court of the Great Khan at Canbaluc (Peking) to return to Italy via uncharted Central Asia, a route home not so different from Alexandra's. However, on the way he hoped to find the lost Christian kingdom of Prester John. There were Nestorians among the Mongols, although the followers of this fifth-century Syrian heresy had adopted abominable practices, unheard of in Europe, such as "washing their lower parts like Saracens." They probably influenced the ritual of Tibetan Buddhism, which Abbé Huc declared to be similar to the Catholic.

Odoric wrote an account of his journey in which he stated:

I came to a certain great kingdom called Tibet, which is on the confines of India proper, and is subject to the Great Khan. . . . The chief and royal city, Lhasa, is built with walls of black and white, and all its streets are well-paved. In this city no one shall dare to shed the blood of any, whether man or beast, for the reverence they bear a certain idol which is there worshipped. In that city dwelleth the Pope [Dalai Lama] who is the head of all idolaters.

The friar reached his home in 1330, and his tales of Tibet were embroidered and retold by the plagiarist who called himself Sir John Mandeville. All Europe thrilled to this imposter's account of *his* journey to fabled Cathay. This is the first instance of the recurring fascination with Tibet shown by Western missionaries, dreamers, and scholars. It is also a fine example of an armchair author filching travelers' tales for his own use.

Interest died down until the seventeenth century when Portugal planted a colony at Goa, India. Jesuit priests struggled over the snowy Himalayan passes, still searching for lost Christians. The Tibetans welcomed them, and a mission was established at Shigatse. In the eighteenth century, the Capuchins founded a mission in the Buddhist capital. The young Italian priest Ippolito Desideri, a Jesuit, lived and studied at Sera monastery, learning about the religion he hoped to show as false. He witnessed a Mongol sack of Lhasa in 1717 and subsequently the invasion of a Chinese army to drive out the barbarians. Once this was accomplished, the Chinese claimed Tibet for the Celestial Empire. Eventually, the lamas grew to resent the influence of both the Jesuits and Capuchin fathers at the Dalai Lama's court, and by mid-century their missions had disappeared with scarcely a trace.

The British, after securing rule in the Indian subcontinent, sent a different sort of envoy north over the mountains. Warren Hastings of the East India Company dispatched a young Scotsman, George Bogle, to open up trans-Himalayan trade and to gain intelligence of Russian and Chinese influence in Tibet. The Panchen tried to turn Bogle away, claiming he was subject to the Chinese Emperor "whose will it was that no Moghul, Hindustani, Patan or Fringy be admitted to his realm." *Fringy* was the Scotsman's corruption of *philing,* or foreigner. Bogle won the Panchen's friendship for Britain, but both he and the Lama died soon after of smallpox.

The eccentric English scholar Thomas Manning, a friend of Charles Lamb, accompanied a Chinese general to Lhasa in 1811 and had an interview with the Dalai Lama. Although Manning dressed as an Oriental, he was contemptuous of Buddhist custom, infuriated the lamas, and had to flee Tibet. In contrast, Abbé Huc succeeded in 1846 in becoming the first missionary to Lhasa in over a century. Huc came in from eastern Mongolia, and after a sojourn at Kum Bum, he took the direct caravan route to the capital. He lived there unmolested until, jealous of his influence on the Regent, the Chinese Amban ordered him out. When Huc published two volumes of his firsthand experiences, set down in a lively, open style, the pedants of his day denounced him as a credulous fool.

Toward the end of the century, feeling threatened by both the Russians and British India, the decrepit Manchus connived with fearful lamas and greedy nobles to keep the people of Tibet, and indeed the Dalai Lama, in total ignorance of events in the outside world. The Land of Religion was closed to disturbing foreign influences. The policy invited evasion, and the British took to dispatching Indian secret agents across the border. These pundits, disguised as traders, carried concealed compasses and chronometers, and by counting their paces they managed to survey much of the frontier country.

Alexandra, too, on her journey to Lhasa, lacked proper scientific equipment for map making; nor was she as methodical as the most famous of the pundits, Sarat Chandra Das, a Bengali who found his way into Kipling's *Kim*. The high Tibetan official who unwittingly helped him to attain the capital was flogged and then drowned in the river. His family's properties were confiscated, his soul condemned to hell, and even his reincarnation—a small boy—was persecuted. The frontier officials were severely punished. This made their fellows desperate to catch any *philing* rash enough to clamber up to the roof of the world.

The prohibition only made Tibet seem more mysterious and alluring. The formidable geographic barriers that surround the country are not insurmountable. Lhasa may be approached from any point on the compass. The Russian Colonel Nikolai Prejevalsky made two attempts to reach the capital from Siberia. On the first he lost fifty-five camels to the harsh winter before turning back. On the second try, in 1879, he had the support of the czar. "Nor was he going to take any truck from bandits," writes Peter Hopkirk, "being accompanied by an escort of seven carefully chosen Cossacks, all expert rifle shots, who had sworn to go through 'fire and water' with him." As a secret weapon, he brought pictures of Russian actresses to seduce officials.

A week's march from the holy city, Prejevalsky's expedition was stopped by two officials backed by thousands of warrior monks ready to die to defeat the Russian invasion. When the colonel demanded to know why he could not proceed, an official replied, "All the laymen and monks of this Tibet of ours have frequently had sad experiences when we extended kindness to foreigners. Together we have sworn a sealed covenant not to allow foreigners to enter Tibet."

Usually, the authorities were content to let the extreme climate and harsh terrain—the endless wastes of the Chang Tang in the north, the Himalayas to the south—impede and wear down travelers. But if the curious ones approached too close to Lhasa, roadblocks were thrown up. The Tibetans were often willing to negotiate terms of withdrawal, beginning sternly but ending by heaping supplies on the chastened adventurers. Neither officials nor commoners could afford to let foreigners pass, at risk of their own lives.

If masculine bluster failed to clear a way, what of womanly determination combined with evangelical zeal? The missionary Annie Taylor, who resembled Alexandra in spunk and diminutive size, got on well with the cheerful Tibetan travelers whom she hoped to convert, but she had set herself the goal of bringing the Christian gospel to the Dalai Lama in person. She endured a four-month journey from western China over a tortuous road of ice and snow; she crossed high freezing passes and nearly starved to death, only to be intercepted a few days short of her destination, betrayed by a former servant. Annie demanded provisions from a military chief, then trudged back the way she had come. When she arrived at Tachienlu, Szechuan, in April 1893, she had covered 1,300 miles in seven months and survived the rigors of a Tibetan winter. Although the plucky missionary spent many years in Sikkim serving God and awaiting another opportunity, she never attained Lhasa.

While Annie was affiliated with the influential China Inland Mission, Suzie and Petrus Rijnhart were free-lance missionaries heeding an inner call. They spent several years on the Sino-Tibetan border ministering to the natives (Suzie was a doctor) and learning languages. They, too, felt compelled to preach the Christian message in the Buddhist holy land. Dressed in native garb, the Rijnharts set out for Lhasa with a few servants and ponies in the spring of 1898. They brought with them their eleven-month-old baby, Charles. Hopkirk puts it bluntly, "Of all the attempts by westerners to reach the holy capital, theirs was perhaps the most foolhardy."

After three grueling months passing through bandit-infested regions and vast marshes, handing out tracts to illiterate nomads, and agonizing over little Charlie's teething, the missionaries came within two hundred miles of Lhasa. Then, in dreary mountain country, the baby died. They buried him at once, fearing the Tibetans would dispose of his tiny body by cutting it up for the vultures. Saddened, they pressed on but were halted by soldiers who ordered them to turn around. However, the *pombo* (governor) proved friendly, supplied them with food and ponies, and allowed them to take a more direct route back to China. But the bandits of Kham stripped the Rijnharts, then afterward shot down Petrus because they supposed he had found them out. Two months later, Suzie, "emaciated and with frost-bitten feet . . . stumbled into a mission station on the Chinese-Tibetan frontier." Incredibly, she would marry again and return to these same borderlands, but she never did reach Lhasa.

Colonel Francis Younghusband was more fortunate. "This brilliant young Indian army officer [who] seemed to possess all the qualities of a romantic hero of the late Victorian or early Edwardian era" forced his way to Lhasa, under orders from Lord Curzon, the viceroy, to negotiate a treaty with the Dalai Lama. He found that the Thirteenth had fled, but the Regent ultimately signed for him. Younghusband was an intriguing character who would have preferred to go alone in disguise, and although he was in charge of the crucial 1904 expedition, he did not command its well-equipped army.

The opposing Tibetan soldiers, convinced by their lamas that prayers had made them bulletproof, threw themselves in front of machine guns, even cannon. Accompanying correspondents were sickened, and through their reports to their papers turned Parliament against the Anglo-Tibetan Convention. By the time Younghusband arrived home, Curzon was out of office, and the young officer had become a hero to the British public and a scapegoat for the Cabinet. Nonetheless, the empire had scaled the Himalayas, and southern Tibet was open to the British and firmly closed to others.

There remained the time-honored method of deception. The Indian pundits had donned disguises, and so had the Japanese Buddhist Ekai Kawaguchi, who sojourned at a Tibetan monastery in 1901. These were Asians, and it was a more difficult task for the Swedish Sven Hedin to impersonate a Buriat Mongol. That same year, starting from Chinese Turkestan (Sinkiang), he came within a five-days' march of Lhasa before being detected. In 1906 he arrived in India with the intention of crossing into Tibet. Curzon, from London, privately backed the already famous explorer's mapping expedition. But the new government at Whitehall turned thumbs down, ordering the Swede arrested. The house of Rothschild had alerted them to Hedin's being a czarist agent in search of gold fields.

True or no, the Swede slipped in through Ladakh. He spent two years in southern Tibet mapping rivers and mountains, discovered the source of the Indus, and eventually published twelve volumes of mundane prose and exquisite maps. The British knighted him, to which he replied by supporting Germany in both world wars. Traditionally explorers have been male, domineering, and neither especially imaginative nor pleasant.

The most successful incognito previous to Alexandra's was that of Dr. William Montgomery McGovern, a canny British professor of oriental studies who passed himself off as a native caravan porter. Climbing up from India, he slept in cowsheds with the other men, lived on jerky, and struggled through heavy snows to reach Lhasa a full year before Alexandra, also at the lunar New Year. There he became ill and rather terrified of a hostile mob. He gave himself up, and due to the pro-British bent of the Dalai Lama's chief minister, he was kept under protective guard for a month while he recuperated. Then McGovern was sent down to India with an escort. He had seen enough to write a book—in Alexandra's wry phrase—of his misadventures.

However, the most bungled journey to Tibet was made by an American, Edwin Schary. A slight, active young man, he absorbed theosophical ideas in San Francisco before the First World War. Courageous and foolhardy, he set out via India to find the mahatmas ensconced in their caves in the Land of Snows. As David Macdonald wrote, "Schary must have been endowed with extraordinary powers of pertinacity and endurance, for nothing less would have carried him through the hardships and privations to which he was exposed."

He knew no Tibetan, little about Buddhism, and less about the ways of the people. After a servant made off with his possessions, he was penniless, and he did not understand how to beg. He headed for the Nepalese border but was turned back. Somehow Schary, crawling on his hands and knees, got back to Gyantse where initially he was treated no better:

One evening, at dusk, a begrimed and filthily clad figure, covered with festering sores, crawled up to the main gate of the Gyantse Fort. In Hindustani he asked the sepoy sentry to let him in, but the latter, taking him for a Tibetan beggar, refused, and ordered him away from the post. Sinking down on a stone nearby, the man said "I am a white man, you must let me in."

When all else failed, there was always the color of skin. Due to the kindness of the half-Asian Macdonald, Schary regained his health. Back in America, he wrote his opus, *In Search of the Mahatmas of Tibet*. It is sufficiently rare not to encourage many others to play the fool, and it is not likely that Alexandra knew of it. However, she had read or heard of most of her predecessors in what we may term "the little game" of sneaking to Lhasa. From their failures she learned what not to do.

Sometimes Alexandra sounded rather envious, as when she complained to Philip about lacking "a good store of fuel and a stove in [my] tent like Sweed Hadin [*sic*] and the others." But she was wise enough not to grow too dependent on servants and to avoid showing anything of value. When she requested her husband in Algeria to construct a camp bed for her, she ordered it be made severely plain. She was already used to travel along unknown roads, avoiding even peasants, many of whom were descending to banditry. She had the flexibility to change her itinerary instantly, to appear where least expected. "If things get really serious," she wrote matter-of-factly of the civil war, "I'll go to Mongolia on foot with Aphur [Yongden]."

Still, Alexandra worried about her poverty. Although she didn't wish the lamas and perhaps other Europeans to see her in tattered garments, ultimately rags would prove her best protection. It was only gradually she took the mental steps necessary to attain her goal, in the process shedding her identity as a woman of Paris.

CHAPTER 16

The French Nun

In the thin light of a Tibetan dawn, a small caravan exited through the gates of a venerable monastery in Amdo province. A few mules carried baggage, but the four native "boys"—one a "dish of a little boy," the others older—went on foot. Wrapped in crude sheepskins and wearing fur hats, yak-hide boots encasing their feet, their breaths steamed in the painfully dry air of midwinter. Across their chests were slung bandoliers of ammunition, and they carried single-shot rifles with pride if not military precision. Ahead of the pack strode a short, square lama in a red cloak lined with fur, face nearly buried in a huge fur bonnet. The temperature had sunk to below zero Fahrenheit. After marching awhile into the hills, the lama turned to stare at the white buildings and red palaces of Kum Bum, its roofs molten with the fire of sunrise. She understood she might never again see this sight. Yes, *she* . . . for the bulky figure was Alexandra David-Neel, "off on a great adventure."

"Temperamentally, there is nothing of the Don Quixote about me," wrote the woman who called herself "a rational Buddhist." She added, "But although I don't seek out adventures, they are never long in coming." No sooner had Alexandra's party taken to the high road—actually, a low road between steep earthen walls—than they ran into a long caravan of camels and drivers. The road was so narrow, either she or the camels would have to back up for at least a mile. The Mongol drivers felt, and Alexandra agreed, that it would be far easier for her. But her boys took this as a loss of face and refused. She was obliged to back them, or they would lose all confidence in her.

While Alexandra hesitated, the situation quickly deteriorated as the camels fell to biting one another. A Mongol lifted his gun—"That armed challenge made it impossible for me to give way, even had I wished to," noted the *capitaine*. She scrambled to the top of the bank for an overview, then signaled to her boys to unsling their rifles. The Mongols, impressed with their opponents' rank, or their weapons, backed down. They had a job to turn the camels around, tied as they were nose to tail in strings of ten. Once the cumbersome maneuver was completed and the passage left free, Alexandra climbed into a small cart and traveled with assumed dignity along the road. She had convincingly won the loyalty of her men. On the sly, she slipped the Mongols two Chinese dollars for their trouble.

By noon the temperature had soared fifty or sixty degrees and the sun shone brilliantly in a sky of delft blue arched over clay yellow earth. The party slowed to shed some clothing, but since they were determined to cover forty kilometers during daylight, they wouldn't rest until dark. Their leader set the pace, and when they came to a treacherous ford across a stream she didn't hesitate to plunge in first. As the barely visible western mountains turned somber gray, sunset dying out behind their peaks, the travelers searched for a safe spot to camp. Perhaps in the lee of a hill they would be sheltered from the bitter night winds, and bandits, growing ever bolder, couldn't easily surprise them.

This evening they were lucky to fall in with a friendly clan of nomadic shepherds. Alexandra scoured the plain for yak chips—good fuel—while the boys gathered a little wood, lit a fire, and put up the tents. Yongden, the most trustworthy, tended to the animals, which had to be guarded. Then the former opera singer, clutching her bowl, made the rounds of the camp, shamelessly crying out, "Give milk to a nun who eats no meat and may your sheep and yaks become as numerous as the stars in heaven." She would sleep peacefully tonight, delicious curds in her belly, head cradled on folded clothes beneath which nestled her revolver.

Thus passed a typical day on the road to Lhasa, a journey that, with detours but not really tangents, was to take three full years and end in spectacular success. By February 1921, Alexandra had lived at Kum Bum for over two and a half years. Law and order were fast disappearing throughout the district, and she herself was growing older and more troubled by rheumatism. Although she yearned to see Philip, first she intended to accomplish what she supposed no other European had. There were many reasons to go to Lhasa: prestige, fame, the pleasure of revenge on those who forbade it. Besides, what a story it would make! "I wanted to show what the will of a woman could do," claimed Alexandra.

However, something deeper called to her from this everlasting goal of travelers and pilgrims. In one sense she was content to wander over the steppes like any nomad. "The wilderness speaks with a different voice than the boulevards of Paris," she reminded Mouchy. "Hasn't everyone the right to the music that pleases him best?" But Lhasa drew her, just as it still draws pilgrims from distant Mongolia who, in greasy rags, advance the whole way by prostrating themselves full-length on every third step, until each forehead is one big bruise while eyes sparkle from the light within. "It doesn't matter how, without comfort or enough food or on foot disguised as a beggar," Alexandra had determined to make the journey.

Then why did she take so long to reach her goal? The traveler moved concentrically, Kum Bum as approximate center, along a wheel within a wheel over the face of so-called Inner Tibet, western China, Mongolia, and Burmese-bordering southwestern China before making a last dash across the treacherous Po country to Tibet's capital. She didn't plan this but responded to events, specifically setbacks in trying to reach Lhasa. Her inner gyroscope stayed on course, and the long, roundabout journey would prove its own reward as well as eventually successful. But it began badly.

At Sining, the first sizable town en route, Alexandra was told by the chief of the Christian mission, the Reverend Ripley, that a money order sent to her by Philip had been lost. She supposed the Chinese postal authorities had pocketed the sum, ten thousand francs, more than enough to keep her going for a year.

This greatly aggravated her chronic shortage of money, and she fell back on any hospitality she found, including that of brigands. The traveler wasn't above sharing a campfire and a bowl of hot buttered tea with these gentlemen, who must be distinguished from common thieves. Their calling was considered honorable and they followed a code of ethics. Punctilious brigands announced their attack beforehand, allowing victims room to defend themselves. Although they tried not to kill anyone, they appreciated a spirited fight, after which they left the losers a mule and enough food to reach safety. Times were so hard in parts of Amdo and Kham that all the men of a village went out to rob, while the women defended their homes. Euphemisms arose to describe the trade: pillage was termed "making commerce" or "gathering roots." A gentleman brigand, before stealing a mount, might inquire, "My horse is tired. Would you mind lending me yours?"

In *Grand Tibet* (in the English version, *Tibetan Journey*), a fascinating book on her wanderings in the early 1920s, Alexandra described attending a festival of bandits at their mountaintop shrine, nominally Buddhist and containing such offerings as spears, broken guns, and flapping prayer flags. Each highwayman added a colored banner auspicious to his birthdate. The group, which surely included some murderers, showed no signs of bad conscience but enjoyed themselves by intoning chants exalting the deeds of mythic knights who roamed primeval forests slaying demons and rescuing maidens. Time was kept by striking an iron rod on a large caldron of bubbling soup. A photo taken by Alexandra shows a strapping young Khampa, jeweled dagger hilt in evidence, staring unabashedly into the camera. He is not a fellow to fool with. However, in old age brigands often atoned for their deeds by going on an arduous pilgrimage or becoming monks. One rich and respected man who entertained the traveler had given up the trade only when his son was discovered to be the incarnation of a Grand Lama.

Alexandra had to keep her wits about her. Once, camping with a questionable bunch, she strung a rope across the bottom of her tent and during the night tripped up a robber. Another time she took a whip to a sturdy Khampa intent on having her knife. Because not all brigands were honorable and conditions went from bad to worse, outright ambush was a real danger. In 1922 the saintly Dr. Albert Shelton of the American mission hospital in Batang was senselessly gunned down on the road, although he was traveling with the prince of the region and an armed escort.

In uncertain country, Alexandra kept well ahead of her party, dressed in a dirty old robe like a Chinese peasant woman. Hobbling along, she looked too poor to rob, and she could scout for her men who followed. These were outfitted like soldiers and made a great show of their arms. Although the warning signal was a pious chant, the Buddhist dubbed this "war conduct."

The penchant for disguise—in particular as a harmless old crone—combined with an occasional judicious show of force reminds us of the tactics often employed by Lawrence of Arabia in his campaigns. Granted the large disparity in the size of the forces they led, both these warriors preferred using wiles to guns, and they were willing to expose themselves to harm before jeopardizing their men. They appeared where least expected, thought always ahead of the enemy's moves, and never lost sight of their distant but realizable goals. These are classic guerilla tactics which necessitate a feel for the country and its natives that Lawrence manifested in the deserts of Arabia and Alexandra on the steppes of Central Asia.

Of course, the comparison ought not to be stretched. Alexandra, a Buddhist and a woman, better understood the consequences of violence. She claimed that she carried arms while traveling only to satisfy the desire of her boys "to swashbuckle," with "guns on their backs and swords at their belts." She tells us, "As for myself . . . I cannot imagine any danger I could not successfully circumvent by my wits alone." Yet while traversing a dense forest known to be unsafe, Alexandra recorded "the sharp little thrill that the Lama [Yongden] and I experienced . . . when loading our weapons before a start and thinking of the brigands who might show themselves . . ." Is that not Lawrence setting out to dynamite a Turkish railway train?

As Alexandra's party traveled south along the border of Amdo and Kansu, famine prevailed and cholera raged; tigers and leopards were coming out of the woods to eat corpses. Yongden played tunes on a tin whistle to keep away the beasts, and more practically, he spread word through the villages that his mistress was an ancient sorceress.

Donning her necklace of 108 pieces of human skull, she adopted a grim air. Peasants appeared with their horded morsels, anxious to reverse the plagues afflicting them. Alexandra had to work for her and the boys' supper, blessing the new barley crop, the sheep and goats and pigs, exorcising the house where they put up, and divining for its owner where a recently deceased relative would be reincarnated. She "officiated with the solemnity of an archbishop," performing the rites while biting her tongue. It was useless to declare such business to be rubbish. Once when she had done so, the locals suspected her of being a Christian missionary.

Alexandra usually received all the hospitality a visiting dignitary might expect. Abbots of both Buddhist and Bon monasteries welcomed her, while the peasants plied her with fresh eggs or barley flour. But on one occasion, when her party arrived at a village soaked after a day's trek in the rain, the folk were rude and only grudgingly assigned her a campsite. It turned out this was the common toilet. Alexandra, growing furious, spat three times and solemnly cursed the villagers, "Because you have sent a *kandoma* to an impure place, the demons will visit you and in your next lifetime you will eat shit!" She strode off, declaring that she was going to sleep in a field and, to do so comfortably, would stop the rain. Within an hour the sky was filled with stars.

Next morning the headmen arrived to offer an excuse, but Yongden seized a flashlight, warning, "Watch this and tell the others." He snapped on the light, terrifying the simple peasants. Then he invoked "the sacred fire" within the lamp to do the bidding of the angry *kandoma*. The village was cursed and not even their lama's prayers could save them. Leaving the poor folk in consternation, the party marched off. Alexandra felt they had gone too far, saying, "It is rather a wicked joke." But Yongden, like a son to her, refused to countenance any slight. Her servants were sad, certain their mistress's curse would take effect.

By summer 1921, the wanderers were tramping through the forests of western Szechuan, braving downpours and mudslides—Alexandra praised her rubber-soled American boots—and crossing swollen rivers on rickety bridges of braided bamboo rope. One such span looked so unsteady, they spread planks atop it. They began to inch across, rocks falling from a cliff almost on their heads. Yongden called to hurry up, and no sooner had people and mules got over then the entire bridge crumbled into the rushing water. Up they went into the perpetually white mountains, trudging along the steep, narrow paths hemmed in by walls of snow.

In her published works, Alexandra liked to present herself as hale and hearty, "a *voyageur* in a Fenimore Cooper novel." The "sacred fire of adventure" kept her "morally and physically warm." But to her husband she was more candid, writing at about this time:

I'm not doing very well. While I'm riding or walking it's not too bad. But as soon as I stop, rheumatism and, strangely enough, my old neurasthenia return.
  Will I see the end of my projected trip?

Failures of body and spirit were not usual, but the indications of them in her letters were the very items Alexandra demanded that Philip, and later her secretary, destroy. Fortunately, except in one important instance, they failed to heed her wish, knowing better than the imperious one that she was only human. She was not, as she has been presented, an Amazon, but rather a normal although gifted woman. Will, and the power of an idea, drove her onward.

Officials caused more problems than did bandits, often being one in the same. The Chinese merely tried to fleece the travelers, but the Frenchwoman could threaten the wrath of her consulate at Chengtu—known as "Capital of the West"—or in a pinch invoke Yongden's British passport. When a Chinese petty bureaucrat refused to let them leave his village without an official stamp, that is to say a bribe, Alexandra refused, threatening to report him to Peking as an abuser of lamas. He backed down. However, the Tibetans were thornier to deal with.

In early September, the party was well entertained by the rich abbot of Dzogchen *gompa* in Kham near the Yangtse. Alexandra, who had been reduced to eating a dried sheep's head that gave her boils, delighted in feasting Chinese style with the cultivated abbot. Dessert came first, followed by dumplings, stews, fish, and meat and finally soup. Perhaps she dined too well, since soon after they left she came down with digestive difficulties that she termed enteritis.

In her own words, "While traveling in Kham, I fell ill and wished to proceed to Bhatang [further south on the Yangtse] to be nursed there by the foreign doctors at the mission hospital." The American Dr. Shelton, held in high regard, presided over a clinic for the natives. However, on a grassy plain Alexandra spotted two mounted men who were playing a fanfare and carrying an immense flag displaying a heraldic lion. Behind them rode a fat, ostentatious official (*gyapon*) in whom she sensed trouble.

Lhasa had newly asserted its authority over this area, and the *gyapon* was sent from the capital to investigate thievery. In a moment, his force of twenty-five soldiers appeared, headed by a sergeant. The officers informed Alexandra that foreigners could proceed no farther into Tibet without a special passport. She must return to the monastery to await one. Very likely they supposed the *philing* was bound for Lhasa, and to let her pass would cost them dearly. Alexandra demanded they let her proceed. She described her illness in graphic detail, reveling in the richness of Tibetan terms for describing the manifestations of dysentery. The *gyapon* was sympathetic, but Alexandra quickly discovered that he lived in dread of "the great man at Tachienlu"—the British consul in Szechuan.

We cannot be sure just how influential the British were in this anarchic region. But if Alexandra had known how interested the Government of India remained in her whereabouts, she would have grown even angrier with them. The Foreign and Political Department of the viceroy's office issued the following communiqué on October 21, 1921: "Perhaps the minister at Peking may be able through the Chinese government or his French colleague to secure return of the French nun who is reported to be trying to enter Eastern Tibet."

Alexandra's disguise as a *kandoma*, while impressing the peasants, doesn't seem to have fooled the Tibetan or British officials. However, it was not until December 6 that the viceroy's office learned it was the woman on whom they kept a careful dossier: "We did not realize that the French nun was the well known Mme. Neel who crossed the frontier of India some years ago despite orders to the contrary. We hope she still can be turned back."

On the spot a standoff ensued. Alexandra was determined to press forward and the official and his soldiers to stop her. Fear of being banned altogether from the country made her act cautiously. All right, she declared, she was willing to leave the district, but by her own route. She now intended to go northwest to Jyekundo. This alarmed the *gyapon,* because not only did that town lie on the direct caravan route to Lhasa, it was headquarters for a dangerous enemy, a Moslem Chinese general who was waging unrelenting war on the native tribes. The official, ordering the sergeant to draw up his men, insisted that Alexandra return to the monastery.

"Let them shoot me in the back as I go!" threatened the traveler, secure in her right *and* in her race. For the Tibetans were frightened at the thought of killing a European. "Long life! Long life!" cried the men, while the *gyapon* burst into tears. Still they kept her surrounded. Grasping her sturdy walking stick, the dumpy Frenchwoman attacked with the dispatch of a grenadier—Slap! Bang! Smack!—she cleared a path.

"Bring my revolver," she called to Yongden. "I'm going to shoot myself, and the crime of my death will fall on you [the Tibetans]. You'll suffer the consequences!"

Alexandra strode toward her tent, but poor Yongden was equally taken in by her performance. He quickly hid the weapon and the drama fell a little flat. Still, the *gyapon* was sufficiently cowed to permit her to travel where she pleased. He gratefully acquiesced to her terms: yaks, supplies, an escort. Alexandra felt satisfied with her victory, temporary though it might be. Alas, the gymnastics had interfered with her digestion.

One day from a distance high on a snowy perch, the adventurers looked down to a valley with over two thousand yaks in line, divided in groups, hastening to the shrill cries of the cowboys who drove them, "Dzo-eee, Dzo-ess!" Large fierce dogs circling the yaks emphasized their masters' commands.

"There at last is the road I have seen so often on the map!" exclaimed Yongden. "When I reach that road, I'm going to bow down three times."

It was a caravan bringing tea to Lhasa.

CHAPTER 17

An Officer and a Gentleman

Jyekundo, under the control of a Chinese Moslem warlord, was as much military garrison as town. Its nondescript baked mud houses straggled up a bare hill toward an overlooking *gompa* of no distinction. The place failed to boast a single indoor toilet. At twelve thousand feet, set among frosty mountains on the edge of the Chang Tang, "Desert of Grass," it had a moderate summer climate. But winter promised to be bitter, and Alexandra, low on funds, was living in a leaky shack on a roof. She fought off the temptation to make a dash for Lhasa, some six weeks away. She was leery of another clash with Tibetan officials, who had been alerted by the British and were on guard. So she and Yongden vegetated while water leaked from the roof onto her books and the wind whistled through crevices to torment her joints.

In late October Alexandra wrote to Philip that, although her heart bothered her, it would be "better to get out under canvas . . . to launch ourselves up into the steppes." It was "infected" here, and "the people [were] of an unspeakable dirtiness." She was headed northwest to the Mongol camps in Chinese Turkestan (Sinkiang). She intended to rent a warm felt-lined *yurt* from the shepherds and winter there. The summits she saw from her roof were already whitened, but perhaps the snows wouldn't block the passes for another month.

The attempt lasted ten incredible days and failed. The pair couldn't struggle through drifts to their waists, and their horses' hooves froze. Big gray wolves tracked the little party, and although Alexandra showed her usual fearlessness of wild animals and wished to tame their leader, she couldn't spare even scraps of food. She saw also small bears and troops of wild goats and wild mules (*kyangs*). Back they came along the route they went out.

Yongden turned up three rooms in a better house, but by midwinter Alexandra was seized by what Alaskans call "cabin fever." Firing a little stove, she kept her room at a tolerable forty degrees Fahrenheit during the day, but at night it grew much colder. Outside the weather was dry and the sun shone in an azure sky. Alexandra, sick of stiff joints, decided they would fight their way through to the warm valleys of the south where orchids bloomed the year long.

Returned once again to Jyekundo, in early spring the explorer recounted to her amazed husband, who would receive the letter four months later, "I walked for forty-four days with only one of my domestics [Yongden], crossed a dozen peaks with snow up to my knees, slept in icy caves like a prehistoric woman, without food, almost barefoot, the soles of my moccasins being worn out by the rocks in the road." Unfortunately, once more they were intercepted by Tibetan officials, who when they found a camera on Yongden, demanded that the pair turn back. This time Alexandra exacted horses, fuel, and money for the return trip. At Jyekundo she wanted to start immediately for the Gobi Desert, but the Moslem commander implored her to wait for warmer weather. The Parisienne had a way with generals.

A second general, Sir George Pereira, arrived at Jyekundo from Peking on June 23, 1922. He was a well-bred gentleman after Alexandra's own heart. If she in her fifties had rheumatism, he, nearing sixty, limped from a childhood riding accident. His record in combat in the World War was heroic, and in spite of a troublesome digestion, he loved to roam the wild, far corners of the Orient. This splendid representative of the mature British Empire, a charming unassuming scholar educated under Cardinal Newman, had experienced a rough journey. He was weakened by hunger and thirst, his pack animals perished, and he had survived on the generosity of a passing caravan. Nonetheless, Sir George was as eager as Alexandra for further adventure.

The pair often met to take tea, and the Frenchwoman put on her best robe to show the Englishman the few sights of interest. The fellow explorers shared their most recent exploits. Pereira had hunted through the mountains of Szechuan in hope of bagging a giant panda, at that time a rare animal that no European had ever shot. He missed the prize, coming down with frostbitten toes instead. However the Buddhist Alexandra felt about such useless slaughter, lately she herself had acted more from desperation than good calm sense. Stymied by petty bureaucrats, she was getting no closer toward the elusive goal.

Sir George was bound straight for Lhasa. He was suspected of being on a secret mission for Whitehall, and at any rate he stayed in touch with the Government of India through Sikkim. He left at the end of the month, waited at Chamdo until early September for permission to continue—granted due to Charles Bell's influence—then journeyed for six weeks over a difficult mountainous route to the capital. He was well received and granted an interview with the Dalai Lama. In spite of deteriorating health, Geneal Pereira traveled during the next year along the wild Tibetan-Szechuan frontier, where he died at Kanze of a bleeding ulcer. He was a careful surveyor, and had he lived would have received the gold medal of the Royal Geographical Society. Surely he felt his end was near, because he did a thing uncharacteristic of explorers: he shared his maps with a perfect stranger. Alexandra, who often navigated by instinct, now possessed more definite guidance. In return, she plied the general with information on the area where he was to lose his life.

Both travelers were intrigued by the poorly known country of southeast Tibet, lying between Yunnan and the capital. As Alexandra told it:

One afternoon, after having had tea together, we were speaking . . . A map remained open on a table, and with the tip of his finger Sir George Pereira followed the thin line marking the supposed course of the Po [River].

"Nobody has ever been there," he said. "There may be several accessible passes above the spring of the river. . . . It would be an interesting way to Lhasa."

It would be a way fraught with danger. For the inhabitants of the Po country were deemed savages, maybe cannibals, and anyone foolish enough to enter their domain supposedly never came out. After dropping this hint, and providing Alexandra with a rough sketch map, Sir George departed. To Major (soon Colonel) F. M. Bailey, who in 1913 had explored part of the Po region and lived to become the new Resident officer at Gangtok, Pereira wrote on July 28th: "I met Mme. Neel, the French Buddhist lady, at Jyekundo, she had gone from Kansu via Kantze to Jyekundo and [she] left the day after on her return to Sinning and Lanchow."

The latter two destinations were to the northeast past Kum Bum and the Koko Nor Lakes, and in the *opposite* direction from Lhasa. True, Alexandra was headed that way at first. But Sir George couldn't have been ignorant of her ultimate goal, nor of the wish of the Government of India to keep her from it. It strains credulity to suppose Alexandra deceived him. Rather, the chivalrous war hero covered for her, deceiving his own government not by lying but by relating only part of the truth.

Meanwhile, Alexandra made good use of her time "stuck in this hole," waiting for money. She continued to acquire Tibetan books, which she sent on to Peking. "Albert and I are in rags," wrote the despairing wife to her husband on May 25. Who was "Albert"?—merely Yongden with an anglicized name to suit his position, if not his attire. By now in his early twenties, although slight and scarcely taller than Alexandra, the boy had grown into a man of many talents. Besides acting as secretary and helping with translations, he was obliged to bake bread, cook, wash linen, gather wood, sew together the remnants of their clothing, and perform any other task called for at the moment. In return he received not a rupee in salary, thus raising him from the class of servant to that of gentleman. Yongden, like his mentor, was celibate. "He has decided to live with me as long as I live," Alexandra informed Philip. Therefore, her husband must adopt and provide for him, because according to French law she herself could not. "You will be happy to have him once you know him," wrote the proud mother-to-be. That was a fond assumption on her part.

Alexandra spent nearly a year at Jyekundo scheming to leave. Blocked from her goal by Tibetan officials and low on funds, she had run out of momentum. While she and Yongden were stalled, they could watch caravans of yaks trundling by on the route from Tachienlu across the Desert of Grass to Lhasa. Even their mad dash south through the frozen mountains had failed. At a loss, the frustrated adventurers wandered the muddy streets when the weather, often snowy or rainy, permitted. One day a huge Khampa, brandishing an antique sword, dashed from a house and was quickly followed by a score of fellows trying to catch him. Alexandra inquired of some women and learned that the warrior took himself for an incarnation of Dickchen Shenpa, minister to Gesar of Ling, the hero of the Tibetan national epic of that name. Because Gesar's enemy the King of Hor had also reincarnated in town, in the form of a young lad, Dickchen, when he'd downed too much *chang,* roared off in search of the evildoer. The men always stopped him from harming the poor boy.

Alexandra was delighted to learn that Dickchen was a wandering minstrel who sang passages from the long poem. The next day she slipped in among the women gathered to hear him; the men sat opposite, everyone on a bit of carpet on the dirt floor. The madman now appeared composed, chanting, gesturing, all the while staring at a sheet of blank paper. Alexandra, who hadn't lost her admiring eye, "found him to be a very fine man . . . [having] the stature of a giant and the figure of an athlete. . . . His proud bold features, and his big luminous brown eyes that at times flashed fiercely and imperiously and at other times seemed to reflect a whole world of marvelous visions, gave him a remarkable expression."

Singing in the Kham dialect, the bard played out the numerous roles of the colorful epic and even provided his own accompaniment by imitating trumpets and other instruments. The audience, who had listened to the story many times before, interrupted on occasion with cries of, "*Om mani padme hum!*" (Hail to the jewel in the lotus!) The blank paper was put in front of the performer because on it he envisioned what he was about to sing. The minstrels of the poem appear to have committed it to their subconscious memories, able to call up passages when they wished. This large Khampa proved to be an extraordinary seer.

Alexandra invited the minstrel to perform the epic in private, to which he agreed only after she assured him that King Gesar would not be denigrated. As the man chanted, she and Yongden both scribbled, and in six weeks they had produced the most complete written copy in existence. Alexandra realized the minstrel lived more in the time of Gesar (the Tibetan "hour of glory" towards the seventh century) than in the present. He would often disappear to wander over the grasslands dreaming of his old life as companion to the great champion of right. But in earnest, he insisted he *was* Dickchen and could transmigrate back and forth between past and present.

Once, in midwinter with temperatures down to below zero Fahrenheit, the Khampa brought the foreign lama a fresh blue flower—sent to her by Gesar himself. The ground was frozen, the nearby Yangtse covered with ice six feet thick, and this species of flower normally bloomed in July. Where on earth had he gotten it? Equally puzzling was the prediction by "Dickchen," based on the epic, that the Panchen Lama would flee to China in exactly two and a half years. Alexandra scoffed, but on her way to Lhasa in 1924 she was shocked to learn that her friend, fearing for his life, had indeed taken refuge in Chinese territory. Even the boy supposed to be the evil King of Hor, then a novice monk of ten, seemed to possess an appropriately vicious nature: he delighted in killing birds with stones and pummeling his fellow novices.

There were too many local versions of the epic for Alexandra to produce a definitive text. But since the historical Gesar had been a Khampa, their version was the most comprehensive. The tale of heroism, of knight errantry, is nominally Buddhist but pervaded by an earlier spirit of magic and wonders. Gesar, an incarnate god, rides a golden, winged stallion into battle against the demons of the four directions. He is the great hero, the tiger-god of consuming fire, sometimes fitted out in gold armor and at other times all in turquoise, including helmet, shield, bow and arrows. He is fond of quick changes and appears indifferently as a humble blacksmith's apprentice or the god Namthig Karpo, clad in white and riding a goat, or in the more suitable guise of the handsome, irresistable king who uses his soulful black eyes and enchanting smile to seduce his worst enemy's wife.

For there is a touch of Rabelais about this rambling tale, sung not in classical Tibetan but the dialect of whichever region the bard finds himself. Gesar, like Buddha, comes to banish ignorance, but he is not squeamish about using force. After he has slept with the queen, and she has fed him dainties and quickly hidden him when her husband the King of Hor comes home—not under the bed but beneath the kitchen floor—Gesar cleaves the cannibal-demon-king's head in two. Then he gives the villain's spirit, which is wandering in the *Bardo* (purgatory), precise instructions on how to avoid hell and reach the Western Paradise. Sinners are to be redeemed.

The epic, Homeric in its proportions, functions on several levels. The simple folk love to hear it over and over, for it both reflects their concerns and transports them to magical realms. But as made clear by Chögyam Trungpa, this is a serious treatise on courage: "Gesar represents the ideal warrior, the principle of all-victorious confidence. As the central force of sanity he conquers all his enemies . . . who turn people's minds away from the true teachings of Buddhism . . . that say it is possible to attain ultimate self-realization."

The enemy, then, is to be found in one's own mind; it is cowardice. Alexandra's attraction to Buddhism, allegedly a passive faith, can be better understood if we see it in this light. Once she overcame her doubts and fears, she attained her birthright, her self. Then no official, no army, no empire could stop her from going where she pleased.

In early August 1922 Alexandra, after selling two mules to reduce her cavalry to five, headed a small party traveling northwest toward the Gobi in Chinese Turkestan (Sinkiang). The Moslem general loaned her a couple of soldiers as an escort and a two-wheeled baggage cart. Writing to Philip, she hinted about following an old caravan route, rich in Buddhist lore, to Samarkand, Russia, from where a railroad ran to Paris! It isn't likely she was serious. The czarist empire had startled the world by becoming the Soviet Union, and its eastern provinces were the scene of civil strife and epidemics. On this occasion, Alexandra typically wrote little about her actual destination, instead vaguely admitting, "Just now I am zigzagging, returning on my steps, tripling or quadrupling the distance." Her letters might be intercepted and read at any time. Earlier she had warned Philip that he might not hear from her for lengthy periods of time; she was bound "beyond the post offices." No matter what, he mustn't send out a search party. The notoriety would put her life in great danger.

Alexandra proceeded at a leisurely pace. She spent November and December at Kanchow on the edge of the Little Gobi just below the Great Wall. In a drafty house where they often had to sleep without a fire while the thermometer plunged to below zero, she and Yongden polished their version of the Gesar epic, consulting several texts. Curiously, she complained that many of its incidents were too risqué for her, and the edition that she finally published in English in 1934 is (alas!) properly Victorian. The scholar had high hopes for her progeny and rather mistakenly supposed that the *Superhuman Life of Gesar of Ling* would make a best-seller.

In January 1923, with a light sprinkling of snow on the ground, the temperature barely rising to the twenties Fahrenheit in the glare of the noonday sun, the party saddled up their mules and set off across the desert. Occasional low dunes were followed by stretches of spiny grass. They saw almost no one, and it is likely that somewhere in this region

Alexandra had her finest opportunity to observe a *lung-gom* runner. One day, peering through field glasses, she picked up a moving black spot far in the distance. As she watched, this turned into a man heading toward them with incredible rapidity. The orientalist was thrilled as she realized she would be the first Westerner to verify the remarkable feats of these adepts, who are sometimes said to fly. She reached for her camera.

"Your Reverence will not stop the lama, nor speak to him," warned a trusted retainer. "This would certainly kill him. These lamas when travelling must not break their meditation. The god who is in them escapes . . . and when thus leaving them before the proper time, he shakes them so hard that they die."

The French skeptic doubted this, but she knew she must respect even the grossest superstition if the people believed it. Reluctantly, she took no pictures but contented herself with the following description of a *lung-gom-pa:*

I could clearly see his perfectly calm impassive face and wide-open eyes with their gaze fixed on some invisible far-distant object situated somewhere high up in space. The man did not run. He seemed to lift himself from the ground, proceeding by leaps. It looked as if he had been endowed with the elasticity of a ball and rebounded each time his feet touched the ground. His steps had the regularity of a pendulum. He wore the usual monastic robe and toga, both rather ragged. His left hand gripped a fold of the toga and was half hidden under the cloth. The right held a *phurba* [magic dagger]. His right arm moved slightly at each step as if leaning on a stick, just as though the *phurba,* whose pointed extremity was far above the ground, had touched it and were actually a support.

My servants dismounted and bowed their heads to the ground as the lama passed before us, but he went his way apparently unaware of our presence.

Lung-gom-pas were not expected to make a fleet dash but to continue in their even, ground-devouring stride for days on end without stopping for food or water. In the vast, nearly empty countryside of northern Tibet, such a feat might be termed practical. Only certain lamas indulged in such traveling, and their training was as curious as the accomplishment. Not really athletes, they were mystics who had meditated for years in a dark hole. Breathing exercises, chants, and visualizations were repeated until the adepts were able, from a seated posture, to leap straight up out of the hole. Another portion of the training consisted in going about for long periods in heavy irons, so that when the chains were removed, the practitioner felt feathery light. Like *tumo* breathing, skill at *lung-gom* was occasionally necessary to the few who meant to brave the immense difficulties of the Tibetan wilds. Soon Alexandra would have to call on both these arts to survive.

After traversing barren country that reminded her of the Sahara, and reaching Anhsi in Sinkiang, Alexandra wheeled her party around for a grand flanking move. She wasn't deterred by the cold, for although the occasional inns were miserable, sleeping on their Mongol-style *kangs* was comfortable. This was a cement platform upon which bedding was placed and, more important, under which horse dung was burned. It smelled bad but kept the sleeper warm. But a turn around Mongolia was ruled out by the hostilities between pro- and anti-Bolsheviks and lack of time. In early April the expedition arrived back in Lanchow, where Alexandra took decisive steps. She sent on her books, certain valuables, and good clothes to the French Bank of Indochina at Shanghai. She dismissed her loyal Tibetan retainers, gave up the camp bed Philip had sent her, and her snug tents as well; not even her beloved tub was spared. From here on the once-particular Parisienne would travel lean, depending on her adopted son to do the tasks she couldn't manage.

In May Alexandra crossed the dry land of Kansu—"mountains of yellow earth, meager fields and dust"—under a scorching sun that raised the temperature to nearly ninety degrees Fahrenheit. When night came, it plummeted forty or fifty degrees to leave her and Yongden shivering in their sheepskins. Since she was taking quinine, she likely had a touch of malaria, but she worried more about her son's violent fever until it abated. On they traveled, Alexandra carried in a sedan chair by two porters—like riding in an upright coffin—while Yongden brought up the rear. Still in poor health, he prodded a couple of mules with baggage.

Through the narrow gorges of Shensi, the poor woman sweltered in her bouncing black box. The inns were filled with vermin, and often she preferred to spend the night dozing outside the front door in the chair. She informed Philip that she was sending him two articles for the *Mercure:* one on "Socialism Among Primitive Tribes," the other a humorous aside on how to travel cheaply in China.

Toward the end of June, held up by seemingly random fighting, Alexandra arrived at Chengtu, Szechuan, "Capital of the West." Typically, she lodged with missionaries, in this case French Catholic nuns who ran a hospital. Again she was sick with dysentery and saw a doctor at the Institut Pasteur. He insisted that she live there so he could begin a course of treatment. The weary traveler moved in, reveling in good food and a lush garden. But she declined a series of injections of "a new infallible remedy." She admitted, "I really don't like the hypodermic shots, I never had one before." Living genteelly, she mended, helped along by the sizable French community showering praises on her head. The consul gave a reception in her honor, which she attended with a slight fever, and he demanded that she accept a loan of money.

Alexandra also dined with the Catholic bishop at his palace, where she and Yongden were offered such unaccustomed luxuries as wine, cigarettes, coffee and cake. The clergymen present never spoke of religion, but they nevertheless encouraged their countrywoman to join forces with the church. "You are so nice," sighed the bishop at the conclusion of the feast, "what a pity!"

Fearful of being thwarted, Alexandra concealed her destination from everyone. The allegedly Republican government at Peking—still referred to as "the Emperor's household"—held the allegiance of a wavering number of Chinese provinces. From Canton, Sun-Yat-sen influenced much of the south, while most larger coastal cities were dominated by the European powers. Japan was powerful in the north, and the situation in the west was bloody and anarchic. The governor of Kansu was making war on the rebel governor of Szechuan, who had called on Yunnan to send troops to his aid. Alexandra wrote to Philip, "It is total confusion, a chaos that sweeps in sudden tempests, brigands all over, officials [who are] just as bad; at any moment you can be caught up in a wave and have no recourse but to run or hide in a corner. Oh, I assure you, for those who love adventure, there is no better place!"

In mid-July Alexandra took to her sedan chair, traversing muddy roads, torrential rivers, and a combat zone in southern Szechuan. She found herself in the midst of the retreating northern army. The soldiers tried to stop her, but she chatted with the general and got a pass. Next she came to the rear guard digging in to impede the enemy advance. She felt sorry for the men, boys really, some holding parasols or fans. It reminded her of a scene from *Madame Butterfly*. At a deserted village, her coolies rebelled and laid down the chair. Madame hopped out and threatened to beat them, if not worse, and so they carried her onward. She wanted to stop to watch the battle, but the shrieking coolies persuaded her to go around through a rice paddy. She found the mosquitoes a nuisance.

More serious were the native bandits formed into sufficiently large armies that they defeated the regulars. The Lolo tribe had the nasty habit of kidnapping foreigners for ransom. So with much evading and maneuvering, trekking in paddy mud up to their knees, Alexandra and Yongden reached Likiang in late September. This last Chinese town in northwest Yunnan was dominated by another tribe, the Mossos. Burma was to the south, Tibet to the north, and already there were Tibetans nearby. Staying at a Pentecostal mission where she was cordially received, although the food was plain, Alexandra wrote to her husband, "I begin the difficult part of my journey."

She must cross the Mekong River by a preposterous rope and pulley. Then, after paying a call on an isolated French abbé, "I attempt a new and final adventure." Mouchy would hear from her in the spring.

Think of me from time to time, my very dear. Imagine a tiny tent in the recess of a mountain at night when the cold wounds and the hard earth crackles underfoot, a fire of cow dung in front of the tent with a kettle of tea balanced on three rocks, and two travelers with caps pulled to their eyes seated next to this primitive hearth.

Tell yourself they are mad. But whatever you may think, you have to admire their courage. If it happens that their strength fails them and they don't return from their adventure, keep in your mind a miniature portrait of these explorers who tried something their glorious confreres, with famous names, didn't have the heart to undertake.

But don't worry, things will go well. It's a long walk, that's all.

CHAPTER 18

A Long Walk

From Alexandra's farthest penetration of the Gobi at Anhsi in March 1923 to the northwest corner of Yunnan province, adjacent to where she designed to slip into Tibet, is a distance of over a thousand miles north to south across western China. That is as the crow flies, but she and Yongden had proceeded more like turtles, maturing their plans as they went. By the time the pair arrived at the Abbé Ouvrard's parish on the right bank of the Mekong in late October, they had likely covered at least twice that mileage. They were on the march since leaving Jyekundo in August of the previous year. They had traversed desert, jungle, and rice paddy, enduring scorching heat and freezing cold— often in the course of a single day. Although the travelers were worn out and undernourished, health shaky, one could never tell from the author's upbeat tone in *My Journey to Lhasa.* "Farewell!" she opens. "We have turned the corner of the road, the Mission House is out of sight. The adventure begins."

Rumor was Alexandra's most feared enemy. If Tibetan officials got wind of her intentions, they would guard the few roads to Lhasa with greater care. The abbé had proved warmly cordial to utter strangers; still, she fooled him with a story about going on a brief search for rare plants. Inspiration had come from a chance meeting with the American botanist Dr. Joseph Rock, who tendered her an offer, naturally refused, to plant hunt with him. His large expedition, with its comings and goings, nevertheless provided good initial cover for the two outlanders to stray across the border. Amusingly, Rock would be responsible for spreading the erroneous idea that Amne Machin, in the region of Koko Nor, was a peak higher than Everest. His article in *National Geographic* in 1930 contributed to the mysterious, Shangri-La quality of Tibet, where even the supposedly highest mountain on earth could go un-remarked for centuries.

One bright autumn morning, his guests bid the ingenuous Father Ouvrard *adieu* and headed toward the Kha Karpo range. Rather than "the dread guardian of an impassable frontier," the glittering snow mountain "looked more like a worshipful yet affable deity, standing at the threshold of a mystic land." The explorers wore typical Chinese dress, while two coolies carried provisions for a week and a light tent made by Yongden. It would have been unthinkable for a European woman to carry her own pack. Alexandra, after evading the curiosity of botanist and priest, now had to rid herself of servants.

The party spent its first night in a vultures' cemetery where on occasion the locals slaughtered an old mule in order to lure scores of the winged scavengers, which they would bludgeon to death for their feathers. The site was littered with bleached bones, but Alexandra had eyes only for the highest of the mountains, "towering in the clear sky and lighted by the full moon." She knew it was the season for pilgrims, come from the four directions, to tramp the long way around the sacred Kha Karpo. Upon these various folk depended Alexandra's scheme to disappear.

She dispatched the coolies one after the other on specious errands. Paid and fed, they were sent in opposite directions to meet eventually and share their confusion. But in directing one of the boys to a mission bearing a package of clothes for the poor, Alexandra gave away most of their wardrobe. "We had not even a blanket with us," she later recalled. Still the travelers had too much to carry, and they had to sacrifice a waterproof groundsheet.

Their kitchen equipment consisted of the following: one aluminum *marmite*—to do duty as kettle, pot and saucepan—a lama's wooden bowl for Yongden, an aluminum bowl for Alexandra, a case containing a knife and chopsticks, and two cheap foreign spoons over which the Frenchwoman was to nearly kill a man with her new automatic pistol. They took so little because they meant to pose as *arjopas,* "mendicant pilgrims who, by thousands, all the year round, ramble across Tibet, going from one to another of its sacred places." Many of these, while keeping back a few coins or a purse for Lhasa, often begged for their supper. It was considered meritorious to aid them. However, Alexandra was greatly attracted by "the absolute freedom of the *arjopa* . . . liberated from care."

The pair headed for the Dokar Pass, gateway to Tibet proper, and at first they walked only at night through the heavily forested district. "I knocked myself against sharp rocks, I tore my hands and my face in the thorny bushes," the author would recount. "I was dead to all sensation, stiffened, hypnotized by the will to succeed." Something more palpable kept her going, since she was taking small doses of strychnine for energy. When used homeopathically, this deadly poison is a central nervous stimulant. Unfortunately, a slight overdose can result in a condition in which one's senses become overly acute and one sees and hears what isn't there. This partially explains why at first,

Alexandra peopled the forest with spies, and identified with "the scared game dreaming of the hunter." Then came an odd series of incidents.

"Born from fever, from the play of the moon rays between clouds and branches or from more mysterious causes, strange mirages rose before us." When the pair spotted black birds, probably crows, perched on a tree branch, the creatures circled around them, making high-pitched noises like laughs. Yongden declared these were really feathered demons "who play[ed] tricks at night with fire and music to delay us." The orthodox young lama admitted that his great-grandfather had been a renowned magician. Then Yongden, to disperse the mysterious birds, recited formulas and made the appropriate ritual gestures.

Alexandra's unease only deepened, accentuated by tramping through the darkness, as though in a coma, to the accompaniment of panthers roaring in the bush. Her bones hurt from sleeping by day on the ground hidden under a pile of moldering leaves. Even a pleasant morning during which the interlopers approached the Dokar through a beautiful valley white with frost turned bitter as they commenced their ascent. They reached the pass by evening, the threshold of the guarded region. Tibetans had planted around it the usual flags inscribed with prayers. "In the failing light they looked alive, belligerent and threatening, like so many soldiers scaling the crests."

The two were welcomed to the Land of Snows by a sudden blizzard of sleet. Missing the path down, they began to slip and each had to fix a sturdy staff in the ground for support. They squatted on their haunches until two in the morning while snow fell, but when a faint moon rose they were able to descend. These staffs were furnished with sharp iron tips and were *de rigueur* for treks through the Tibetan wilds. By now the travelers had donned heavier clothes more suited to the weather. Yongden dressed in lama's robes, while Alexandra put on suede boots from Kham, a coarse, heavy dress in layers with long sleeves, and an old red sash twisted about her head. None of this could compare with the fleecy sheepskins worn by natives to keep out chill blasts.

On the far side of the Dokar, bizarre happenings continued. In a glade by a river a leopard came by to sniff. Yongden was asleep. Alexandra, remembering her tiger, wished "the little thing" well and sent in on its way. That same day the travelers stumbled upon a village unmarked on any map. They saw "villas and miniature palaces surrounded by small yet stately looking parks!" They retreated to cover till evening. "I sank on the moss and fell asleep, feverish and raving a little," wrote Alexandra. When they awoke the strange town was entirely gone. Yongden insisted that it had not been a product of both their imaginations. A vision, yes, but real in its own way, which he had dispelled with magic words and signs. Perhaps it was the work of someone who wished to hinder them.

Alexandra took the affair with a grain of salt. Feeling more herself, she wasn't given to worrying about distant threats. They were leaving the Kha Karpo woods, and when Yongden worried they must soon "confront true villagers . . . and true men, officials, soldiers," who would be suspicious of strangers, Alexandra reassured him. "I will make *them* dream and see illusions," smiled the *kandoma*.

She was perfecting her disguise as they moved along. She made braids out of jet black yak's hair and to match that color rubbed a wet stick of Chinese ink on her own brown hair. She wore huge earrings in native style and powdered her face with cocoa and crushed charcoal to darken it. Her hands she blackened with soot, greatly helped by a proficiency with make-up learned in her operatic days. Equally important was the role she ought to play, and quick-thinking Yongden devised one. When a group of pilgrims wondered aloud if the silent old woman—transfixed by dazzling white peaks jutting into a cobalt sky—were a *pamo* [a medium], he calmly replied, "Mother is with the gods." Elaborating, he said his father had been a *ngagspa* (sorcerer), and therefore his old mother was a *sang yum* (literally "secret mother," the spouse of a tantric lama). This instilled caution in the simple folk they had encountered. The pilgrims dreaded to offend even the consort of a wizard, whether he were living or dead. After offering mother and son *tsampa* and butter and even dried meat, they hurriedly went their way. The food was welcome, since the travelers carried only a small supply.

Yongden's strutting as a lama skilled in the occult arts was bound to get complicated. For a while they continued to avoid villages, skulking through before dawn and concealing themselves at daybreak, watching the stream of pilgrims flow past. "We saw, from behind our hiding-place, a most picturesque procession of men and women from different parts of eastern and northern Tibet . . ." Yongden tried to cadge food, tea, and information from these sojourners, and in return they often demanded he perform *mo*. This fortune-telling by means such as counting beads or staring into a bowl of water had as its object anything from predicting the future to discovering a lost domestic animal. It would have been unthinkable for a Red Hat lama to refuse an honest entreaty, and besides he was sure to reap a reward. Between mother and son positions were now reversed: *He* was courted for his knowledge, while *she* dumbly scoured their pot or did some other chore.

Ten days out, they reached the majestic Salween River, where they accepted a kind lama's hospitality for the night. Alexandra was beginning to gush over the countryside:

In this country autumn has the youthful charm of spring. The sun enveloped the scenery in a rosy light that spread joy from the river of opalescent green, flowing swiftly in the depths of the gorge, to the top of the cliffs, on which a few hardy fir trees pointed to the sky. Each pebble on the path seemed to enjoy the warmth of day, and chatted with suppressed laughter under our feet.

Nature's "deceitful magic" had seduced the skeptic to feel the thrill of being alive.

The travelers spent a delightful few days loitering along the beautiful river valley. Having left behind the pilgrim route around Kha Karpo, they needed to invent a new excuse for their wandering. A minor loss briefly shook their confidence. Alexandra carried a small compass that she took pains to conceal. After a night spent in a cozy cave, she was putting on her overdress, which served as a blanket, when she discovered the instrument was missing. If so foreign an object were found, it would give them away to officials who might hunt them down. Frantic, Alexandra finally located the compass nearby, although she admitted the mishap set her heart to pounding.

"Travelling in Tibet is a constant going up and down," she related in understatement. After ascending the Tondo-la (*la* means pass) at 11,200 feet and once again descending, the weary walkers pitched their small tent by a stream. Now they dared to use it but only under cover of darkness. In the morning a large party of anxious pilgrims overtook them and begged Yongden to tell their fortunes. One countryman wanted to know how his cattle were faring during his absence. More serious was the plight of a young girl with sore feet who feared being abandoned on the trail. Such was the fate of those who failed to keep up on the arduous tramps; they might fall victim to wolves or perish of hunger.

The Red Hat lama was both compassionate and clever, in Alexandra's words, "really gifted for such ritualistic work." He slowly counted the beads on his rosary, tossed pebbles in the air, and consulted the auguries. He concluded that a wicked demon had swelled the girl's legs and that it must be exorcised by stopping for three days at a *chorten* (a burial monument containing a relic) they would soon encounter. Here the pilgrims were to observe a particular ceremony, which they "strained their brains in a mighty effort to understand." The simple folk had to recite a spell which concluded "Bhaah!" Yongden made them practice "Bhhaaah!" many times over until they got it right.

At least the girl would enjoy a much-needed rest. The bumpkins, deeply impressed by the lama, only reluctantly allowed him to leave and began to spread stories about his magical powers. At a nearby village, Yongden enthralled the whole population and monks from the *gompa* with tales of faraway places and his making of *mo*. The peasants brought him gifts, which he graciously accepted, while Alexandra, squatting in the dust, grew uneasy and jealous. She uttered a pious expression—Tibetans were always dropping them—but one that secretly meant, "Let's get out of here!" Yongden had to surrender his newly won celebrity and a comfortable lodging to tramp off with his mother. The scolding she gave him made him sulky for days. However, it was his turn next to berate her for a potentially fatal misstep.

The pair had stopped in midmorning to boil tea beside a primitive aqueduct. A dozen villagers gathered to watch, muttering, "Who are these people?" Yongden, stolidly chewing on *tsampa* flour, refused to utter a word. Alexandra grew flustered and hurriedly washed the teapot. She forgot that the water would reveal her white skin. "Her hands are like those of *philings!*" whispered a farm wife.

Tibetans held odd ideas about Europeans. Doubtless these folk had never seen one in the flesh, but they felt sure they were tallish demons with white eyes and gray hair. Nothing could be more ugly or dangerous. The people of Tibet were naturally friendly and helpful to strangers, especially pilgrims, but they had been led to believe that all *philings* wished to destroy their religion. So it was no joking matter when three soldiers joined the crowd. They demanded to know where the travelers were bound.

Yongden calmly spoke up, saying that he and his mother had made a pilgrimage to Kha Karpo and were returning to their own country, Amdo. They loaded up and started off on the road to Lhasa. "*Philings* going on a pilgrimage!" mocked one yokel. The villagers broke out laughing and good-naturedly decided that the strangers must be Mongols. This was still funnier, because the natives of the south supposed the nomads of the northern steppes to be half-wild savages. Alexandra breathed a deep sigh of relief.

Mother and son trudged on through a bucolic landscape, cultivated and green along the hillsides although it was nearly winter. The valleys of southern Tibet are so favored climatically that they can grow a winter crop. Food was for sale at the monasteries, which often owned the land worked by the farmers. But ironically, monks were more worldly than the common folk, and they might recognize Alexandra as a *philing*. So the travelers liked to hurry by the walls of a *gompa* in early morning darkness and camp in the woods; then at dawn, Yongden would return for supplies and intelligence. In one instance, becoming hopelessly muddled in a pitch black night, they decided to lie down where they found themselves, without shelter or a fire. "Small heads of rocks piercing through the earth made a really painful couch," admitted Alexandra, "even for me, who from youth upwards had been accustomed to the bare boards affected by the Greek stoics."

The first rays of light revealed they were camped directly beneath the walls of a *gompa* in which lodged an important official. While his mother scurried off to the nearest field, the lama went in to barter. He returned loaded down like a mule, and they breakfasted luxuriously on broth thickened with wheat flour and then continued to a pilgrims' camp. The good-humored folk came forward to be blessed, and all of Alexandra's reserve melted:

I delightedly forgot Western lands, that I belonged to them . . . I felt myself a simple *dokpa* of the Koko Nor. I chatted with the women about my imaginary black tent in the Desert of Grass, my cattle, and the feast days when the menfolk race on horseback and show their cleverness as marksmen. I knew by heart the region I described, for I had lived there long, and my enthusiasm for my so-styled mother country was so genuinely sincere that no one could have guessed my lie . . . After all, was it entirely a lie?

Soon thereafter, Alexandra found "an old fur-lined bonnet such as is worn by the women of Kham" thrown away on the trail. It would both complete her disguise and warm her head on the cold heights rising between them and Lhasa. But Yongden warned her against touching it. Tibetans believe that to pick up a hat, although it falls off one's own head, insures bad luck. The Frenchwoman thought otherwise: here was a gift from "some milliner goddess." She stuck the greasy fur onto her pack.

Their luck did change, and for the better. A close encounter with a *pombo*, posted by Lhasa to guard the road and interrogate suspicious characters, turned out well. Officials, soldiers, and monks were all on the alert against foreigners. This *pombo* carefully scrutinized Yongden but ignored his mother squatting in the dust, then gave the pilgrims a rupee as alms. Alexandra was so nervous she felt that needles were piercing her brain. She needn't have worried, since her son's twice-told tale was becoming as polished as a jewel.

Congratulating themselves, the pair hurried upward toward the next pass, the To-la. At the gusty summit, prayer flags flapping, they shouted to the ice blue sky, "*Lha gyalo! De tamche pam!* Victory to the Gods! The Demons are Vanquished!"

Alexandra soon found herself, for the first time, "the guest of Tibetans in my role as a beggar." Already she had adopted certain habits of the country, such as blowing her nose with her fingers, sitting calmly on a dirt floor spotted with grease and spit, or wiping her soiled hands on her dress. Now, however, she would face additional affronts to her ingrained sense of cleanliness, offered out of hospitality. "I was to live near the very soul and heart of the masses of that unknown land," she tells us, "near those of its womenfolk whom no outsider had ever approached." At the home of a wealthy villager, she had to eat anything that came her way. It was unheard of for beggars to turn down food put into their bowls. Here, at least, the householder was too frugal to offer the Tibetan luxury she most dreaded: maggoty meat.

The travelers gained valuable information at this place. Later, Alexandra, when creating her own legend, claimed, "I profoundly despise everything connected with politics, and carefully avoid mixing in such matters." In fact she was, and had to be, a shrewd political observer. Her sympathies lay with the Panchen Lama, who had treated her kindly and whom she found more philosophical and open-minded than the Thirteenth Dalai Lama. Thus she seemed ready to believe the worst of the government at Lhasa. She listened attentively as the farmers complained of arrogant officials sent from the capital and of taxes levied to pay for the new, modernized army. The latter idea she entirely blamed on the British. She was quick to inform her readers that the men of the border regions were trusted only with old, outmoded rifles. Some of them secretly preferred the governance of the defunct Manchu Empire, which had been distant and light. The Khampas particularly were independent to the point of anarchy, and it was for good reason Alexandra was able to impersonate one.

Well briefed on where the *pombos* held sway, the pilgrims tramped on. Feeling confident, they sought out habitations where the lama could tell fortunes or the mother beg from door to door. One housewife called them in for a meal and poured into their bowls curds and *tsampa*. Alexandra began to mix the two, forgetting her fingers were dark from wet ink recently applied to her hair: Black streaked the milky *tsampa*.

"Eat quickly!" hissed Yongden, as the good woman approached. Alexandra hastily swallowed the entire bowl of nasty tasting stuff.

Far less appetizing was a meal served by a poor couple who extended the hospitality of their hovel on a bitter night. These folks were no better off than beggars, so Yongden offered them the rupee given him by the generous *pombo,* in order to buy something decent to eat. The man exited and triumphantly returned with a parcel. By the embers of the tiny fire, Alexandra made out a stomach. She explained further, "The Tibetans, when they kill a beast, have a horrible habit of enclosing in the stomach, the kidneys, heart, liver, and entrails of the animal. They then sew up this kind of bag, and its contents go on decaying inside for days, weeks, and even longer."

The housewife made a stew from this gelatinous horror, the children fell upon the scraps, which they devoured raw, and then bowls of the foul soup were presented to the guests. Alexandra had already crawled into a corner, groaning.

"The old mother is ill," announced Yongden, growling beneath his breath that she always escaped the worst of it. But he bravely gulped a full portion of the nauseating liquid. Not surprisingly, he too fell down sick. The family joyfully feasted on the rest, smacking their lips, while the numbed travelers drifted off to sleep.

The pair had become true Tibetan wayfarers. If the trail led down and then up several thousand feet, it was gladly climbed. Officials and their retainers, each more arrogant than his fellows, combed the villages to tax the folk. The two beggars dodged them or, half-smirking, pleaded for alms. They lingered along the "graceful yet majestic" Nu Valley, chatted with its farmers, struck out into unknown, barely explored country. "Autumn leaves blaze[d] in their golden and purple tints around the dark greens of the fir trees." Sometimes a fine snow sprinkled the grass to lay down a magical carpet. But this fairyland aura could be shattered by the suspicious stare of a nosy lama, or the whispered rumor that *philings* had been seen in the neighborhood. Alexandra and Yongden reverted to nighttime tramps, once again fearful of discovery.

The total lack of privacy among humble Tibetans caused the retiring Frenchwoman problems. Once so fastidious, a hot bath struck her as a memory from a former life. Going to the toilet in front of others remained trying. Aside from the embarrassment, she couldn't afford to divulge the articles hidden beneath her voluminous dress. She had to complete her arrangements in the early morning darkness before their hosts stirred. She darkened her face with soot from the bottom of the cooking pot, then poked Yongden awake. They would position their heavy money belts containing silver coins—the accepted currency—and, in Alexandra's case, gold jewelry given to her by the late maharaja of Sikkim. This hoard was sufficient to get them murdered many times over. Next they tucked away compasses, watches, and maps, and finally each secured his or her pistol, always kept loaded.

Alexandra wanted to carry a camera in her pack, but it meant added weight and if found would have made her position very precarious. She had been turned back earlier on that score, and her precautions had grown meticulous. She recorded everything she did bring, never mentioning a camera. Most significant, there exist *no* photos of the four-month journey, an opportunity for documentation the traveler would have seized. Then what of the various photos of Lhasa erroneously credited to Alexandra? More on this later, although it is worth mentioning that when she did pack a camera, it was as likely to be up-to-date as her seven-shot automatic.

At the house of a well-off farmer on the bank of the Salween, the usual difficulties were compounded by his incredible stinginess. The man, having lost a cow, demanded that Yongden predict where he should find her. After much hocus-pocus on the part of the lama, and to his astonishment, the cow turned up on schedule. The farmer was so impressed that he insisted the lama bless his household and every one of his cattle and pigs. Yongden had to read scripture and sprinkle holy water throughout the extensive stables. Finally, the travelers' reward was served up—a thin soup of dried nettles. Then they were shown to their sleeping places on the dirt floor far from the fire. Out of respect, the lama was given a bit of ragged carpet on which to curl himself.

Tibetans, except for the highest class, traditionally slept naked, "doubled up . . . almost in the form of a ball." Often the peasants crawled into the same verminous sheepskins worn during the day. Alexandra watched as the daughters of the household performed this act, first stripping to the waist to reveal upper arms and breasts encrusted with dirt. But the weary pilgrims comforted themselves with thoughts of a warm breakfast next morning. It was the custom to reward a lama lavishly for making a successful *mo*.

At break of day the imposters had scarcely finished secreting their gear when the mistress appeared. She kindled the fire and poured into their unwashed bowls the remains of the greasy broth.

"Let us shut our eyes and drink off our soup though it is even more nauseating than last night's," groaned Alexandra. To add insult to injury, the old miser demanded an additional blessing from Yongden, obliged to grant it.

Once on their way, the cheated lama hurled a ferocious curse at the farmstead: "May the wool never grow on your sheep's backs, your cattle prove barren, and your fruit trees be blighted!"

Mother and son burst out laughing, echoed by the babble of the Salween, which seemed to chime in, "That's the way things are done in the fine country of Tibet, my adventurous little strangers; you will see many more such!"

CHAPTER 19

A Long Walk, Continued

"If you look at the map of the country north of Burma," wrote the British officer Frederick Bailey in his *No Passport to Tibet,* "you will see a strange physical formation. Following from north to south are three enormous rivers, close to each other, the Yangtse, the Mekong and the Salween. . . . Now look at Tibet [i.e. to the west] and you will see a large river, the Tsangpo, flowing due east through the southern and most populous parts of the country." So much a terra incognita was this land that geographers, knowing the Tsangpo originated in distant western Tibet around Mt. Kailas, were puzzled as to where its waters eventually flowed. This and other geographical mysteries were finally solved by intrepid explorers such as Bailey, nearly all of whom were trespassers.

The Tsangpo becomes, in the tangled mountains of eastern Tibet, the Brahmaputra, which before it joins the Ganges to debouch into the Bay of Bengal, forms the heart and veins of present-day Bangladesh. Similarly, the Yangtse constitutes the main artery of China, while the Salween descends through Yunnan and Burma to the sea. The Mekong, of course, snakes down through Vietnam to widen into a marshy delta no American of this generation is likely to forget. While flowing in the Land of Snows the rivers are more rapid and not so broad. Because they are older even than the Himalayas and rise in what Sven Hedin dubbed the Trans-Himalayas, deeper into Tibet, the rivers have had to cut their ways through the massive mountains to the seas, creating steep, impressive gorges. Tibetans have devised a variety of hairraising schemes to cross from one bank to the other.

Bailey, who presently would act as host to a triumphant Alexandra, told of crossing above a river in 1913 while tied to a sort of saddle that slid along two twisted bamboo strands. He did not care to repeat the strange sensation. To cross the Mekong, Captain Kingdon Ward, a noted botanist, had to tackle a contraption similar to one Alexandra described: kicking off on the higher bank and vaulting down a single bamboo rope to the lower. Descent was mercifully rapid over a roaring torrent. On calmer streams yak-hide coracles were used to float over up to six passengers. Impossible to steer, the craft might get swept away in the current. When the American missionary Robert Ekvall, in the mid-1930s, rowed a high lama across the angry Yellow River in his inflatable rubber boat, it caused a sensation. The rest of the amazed pilgrims headed for Lhasa were ferried by stages in a barge pulled by horses attached to ropes. This boxy contraption nearly tipped into the swift water. Typically, the pilgrims couldn't swim, trusting rather in prayer.

To David-Neel must go the prize for the most frightening reported transit of a Tibetan river. On the way to the town of Zogong, she and Yongden were overtaken by two lamas acting as couriers for the governor of the Mekong district. Alexandra realized they were suspicious of her, and after getting away, she altered her route to traverse the sparsely populated country of the Giamo Nu River, the upper course of the Salween. They reached the station on a glorious day, and because a lama and followers also wished to cross, they were lucky to find a ferryman at this out-of-the-way spot. The blasé traveler was not put off by the sight of "the narrow glittering ribbon" at the depth of the gorge, but the device looked worrisome: "There was but a single cable fastened to poles fixed at the same level on either bank, and it sagged terrifyingly."

Alexandra, still disguised as an elderly dame, and a young Tibetan girl were unceremoniously bound together to a wooden hook meant to glide along the leather cable. A push sent them swinging into the void, dancing like puppets on a string. Down they went to the middle of the sag, from where ferrymen on the far bank jerked on a long towrope to haul them in. It snapped and back they slid to the dip. Their lives were not in danger—unless one succumbed to giddiness and, letting go of the strap fixed under the hook, fell backward. In that case both of them would tumble into the gorge. "My nerves are solid," boasted Alexandra. "I could stand there even for hours."

However, her young companion, turning pale, fixed her eyes above. "The strap is coming loose," she quavered.

Alexandra could see nothing wrong with the knots, but the girl's terror began to communicate itself. She probably knew more about these contraptions than did a *philing*. It seemed a question of whether the men would repair the towrope before the knots unraveled. What a fine subject for a wager! The determined traveler refused to countenance failure. Steadying the lass by telling her she had called on secret powers for protection, she watched a workman slowly crawl out the cable, "hands and feet up, the way flies walk on the ceiling."

Attached once again, the couple were hauled to safety, fearing the strap might come undone with each jerk. On the far side, crones fussed over them, the ferrymen cursed the hysterical girl, and Yongden, cool as ever, demanded alms for "his aged mother, who had suffered such agony while hanging to that rope." In truth, the pilgrims were about to enter on an episode that would come close to killing them both.

To reach the Po country, Alexandra had to choose between two roads. She had a sketch map of the first, which clung to valleys and passed by villages and monasteries. Tramping through inhabited places no longer troubled the pair, for as soon as they approached a settlement they began crying for alms. This helped to keep off the huge, fierce watchdogs and often led to a simple meal with humble folk and a berth in the corner. From monasteries the beggars sometimes purchased such extravagances as molasses cakes, dried apricots, tea, and butter. Still, back in Jyekundo, General Pereira had been more enthusiastic over a large blank spot on the map of southern Tibet. "Nobody has ever been there," echoed in her mind.

There were problems with this route through an uncharted wilderness. Any travelers met on the path were likely to be brigands setting out to rob in more settled country. They might murder witnesses to shut their mouths. Worse, a high pass led into the long valley, then another out. If heavy snow fell after they managed to get in, and the second pass were blocked, the travelers would be trapped to freeze or starve to death.

Alexandra was drawn by the lure of the unknown. She struck out across an icy stream in weather sufficiently cold that, when the ice splintered and she got her feet wet and dried them with her woolen skirt, the skirt stiffened and froze. They had been warned in the last village to take ample provisions, but due to the exactions of the local *pombo* in his fort, the folk had nothing to spare. So to warm themselves, she and Yongden cooked a soup out of a piece of dry, dirty bacon, a pinch of salt, and *tsampa*. "My father's dogs would never have eaten such a thing," chuckled Alexandra, demanding a second bowl full.

Up they climbed until "the sun set and a sharp cold wind arose." They found shelter for the night in an abandoned herdsmen's camp. Nothing could be more comfortable, since it had a roof, a hearth, and plenty of dung to burn. "We had reached a paradise!"—where they had to string a rope just inside the door to trip any brigand that wandered in. Given warning, Alexandra was ready for anyone. First she would try "the 'winged words' of the divine Ulysses and the artifices of the goddess Juno." If these failed, she reached for her revolver.

They faced more climbing the next day. On the lookout for a *latsa*—the jumble of prayer flags that marks the summit of a pass—they stumbled over a high ridge without finding one. They had hoped to begin descending. Instead,

Quite suddenly an awe-inspiring landscape, which had previously been shut from our sight by the walls of the valley, burst upon us.

Think of an immensity of snow, an undulating tableland limited far away at our left by a straight wall of blue-green glaciers and peaks wrapped in everlasting, immaculate whiteness. At our right extended a wide valley which ascended in a gentle slope until we reached the neighboring summits on the sky line. . . .

Words cannot give an idea of such winter scenery as we saw on these heights. It was one of those overpowering spectacles that make believers bend their knees, as before the veil that hides the Supreme Face.

The trail was obscured by snow, and the pair didn't know which way to turn. It was three in the afternoon, and to miss the path meant being caught on the heights through the night. "Let us proceed straight forward," determined Alexandra, quite in character. Fortunately, her bag was light, but Yongden was weighted down by carrying the tent and pegs. She forged ahead quickly through knee-deep snow, goaded by worry, then wondered if the lad had fallen behind. She glanced back.

Far, far below, amidst the white silent immensity, a small black spot, like a tiny Lilliputian insect, seemed to be crawling slowly up. The disproportion between the giant glacier range, that wild and endless slope, and the two puny travelers who had ventured alone in that extraordinarily phantasmagoric land of the heights, impressed me as it had never done before. An inexpressible feeling of compassion moved me to the bottom of my heart. It could not be possible that my young friend, the companion of so many of my adventurous travels, should meet his end in a few hours on that hill. I would find the pass; it was my duty. I knew that I would!

Alexandra's love for her adopted son spurred her on to greater efforts. She plowed upward and, where the snow appeared too deep to walk, used her long staff as a pogo stick. In waning light, she discovered a white mound with a few branches protruding, and from them hung ice-covered scraps—the *latsa* at the top of the pass. She waved to Yongden who slowly joined her. She wrote later, "The moon rose as I looked around in a trance of admiration. Its rays touched the glaciers and the high snow-robed peaks, the whole white plain, and some silvery unknown valleys toward which I was to proceed."

Relieved, the pilgrims didn't forget to offer a blessing to all creatures, ranging from the tiny "elves of the frozen waterfalls" to the towering "giants whose heads wore helmets of cold radiance." Then they descended from the 19,000-foot Deo-la, hoping to come upon shelter and fuel. By moonlight they roamed an eerily beautiful valley bisected by a frozen river, winds whipping them. To stop without a fire meant death.

The pair had been tramping for nineteen hours straight, nothing to eat, when at two in the morning they halted. They weren't tired, only a little sleepy, but they had found cow dung at a camping place near the stream. *Lung-gom* had taken over where even the strongest determination faltered. Trance walking—fixing the mind on its distant goal—enabled the travelers to disregard fatigue, hunger, and cold. Because these objective conditions still posed a danger, it was vital to start a fire at once. Fuel wasn't enough; the flint and steel upon which they depended were soaked through.

"Jetsunma," said Yongden, addressing his mother honorifically, "you are, I know, initiated in the *tumo reskiang* practice. Warm yourself and do not bother about me. I shall jump and move to keep my blood moving."

Alexandra regarded herself as out of practice in this occult art. She had given up the strenuous *tumo* exercises in favor of warm clothes and a hearth. But now was the time to remember the teachings of the Gomchen of Lachen. She sent Yongden to collect cow droppings, and then, tucking flint and steel and a pinch of moss beneath her dress, she sat down to begin. She drifted into a doze, or really more of a trance because her mind remained concentrated. "Soon I saw flames arising around me; they grew higher and higher; they enveloped me, curling their tongues above my head."

The loud report of ice cracking in the river startled Alexandra awake. The vision of flames subsided and she felt the cold wind against her heated body. Her fingers were like live coals. Confident, she struck steel against stone. Sparks leaped onto dry grass, spread to a hearty blaze. When Yongden returned he was amazed, not least by his mother's fiery face and glowing eyes. Although they enjoyed their fire, she feared her health might be affected. But the touch of the morning sun on the little tent roused the pair from a refreshing sleep. Alexandra never felt better.

At times, the travelers had been suspected by the populace, but more usually helped. Tibetans tried to improve their karma by giving aid to pilgrims bound for holy places. However, the few poverty-stricken herdsmen that they encountered wintering in the valley between the two high passes were downright rude. They learned that the Aigni-la to the Po country *might* still be open if they hurried. Yongden, glib as Ulysses, had a religious talk with one of the *dokpas* and not only persuaded him to guide them to the summit of the pass but to bring a horse for his aged mother. They accompanied the cowboy to his camp where they were lodged in the chief's own dwelling: dark, smoky, the dirt floor spotted with spittle.

Once Yongden stepped out to beg for alms, the hospitality included an attempt to rob his poor mother. Nearly any of these bumpkins thought of banditry as good clean fun. Nothing was wrong with it unless, perhaps by accident, someone was killed. Rather, shame fell on the victim for not defending his property. In this case, Alexandra was curled up before the hearth, pretending to sleep but keeping an eye open to guard their packs. "What can they carry in their bags?" demanded the chief of his fellows. With the host on the point of plunging into Alexandra's, she rolled around, calling on her son in her supposed sleep. Then up she popped, claiming the lama had warned her from afar to awaken. Just then he returned and immediately fell in with the game. The superstitious *dokpas* were frightened and behaved themselves.

They all dined on broth made from yak's innards, and Alexandra gulped three bowls of it. She was distressed by talk of *philings* at the Kha Karpo. Had these rustics heard about them, or was the story several years old? In Tibet there was no knowing. News might travel with surprising swiftness from village to village via "yak telegraph," or it might linger in some out-of-the-way camp, being savored like ripe cheese. Next morning, the travelers were glad to get going, and the guide proved true to his word. At the *latsa* that marked the Aigni-la, Yongden offered the *dokpa* a few coins, but he wanted only a blessing.

"As for the money," said the humble fellow, "if I accepted it I would lose the merit of having served a lama. . . . I like better to keep the merit. It is useful for the next life as well as for this one."

Thus the pilgrims stood at the summit of the first and only pass they attained without the usual hard climbing. But under a lowering sky, both were filled with foreboding. "It will snow," said Yongden, looking grave. "Let us go quickly."

The herdsmen had been concerned about the grazing come spring. The ground held insufficient moisture to grow healthy grass. To gain their goodwill, Yongden promised them snow if they would perform a simple rite, but only after he and his mother passed over the Aigni-la. Now the two wondered if the *dokpas* had succumbed to impatience. The air was laden with humidity as the travelers descended across barren pastures to a marshy stream. Alexandra realized she had discovered one of the springs of the Po Tsangpo, a tributary of the river that flowed placidly to the south of Lhasa. She suddenly assumed the role of explorer, hoping to trump the professionals at their game. Despite Yongden's laconic warning that they were low on food, Alexandra determined to range farther in search of additional feeder springs. She considered there remained enough *tsampa* for three meals: "Three meals meant three days, for we had not come to these Tibetan wilds to indulge in gastronomy." So she led the way forward into the upper valleys.

"After sunset the snow began to fall, lightly at first—just a few butterflies whirling among the black trees. Then it gradually became more and more dense, one of those slow snowfalls, whose flakes descend from some inexhaustible heavenly store, shrouding the mighty peaks and burying the valleys." The explorers pitched their tent in the form of a shelter sloping against a rock, boiled tea, and went to sleep. Alexandra was awakened by a sense of painful oppression. She instantly realized they were being buried alive under an immense weight of snow. The pair stayed calm, turned on their stomachs, and, heaving upward, broke free. They had to tramp the rest of the night, since another shelter would be similarly smothered.

Next noon they discovered an earthen cave where they holed up, sleeping until the following dawn. Still the huge, wet flakes came down. Undaunted, the adventurer strode out on the whitened terrain. Yongden, trailing behind, mistook snow for solid ground and plunged into a ravine. His companion hurried to reach him, finding him "lying in his ragged lama dress on the white snow stained with drops of blood." That was only from bruises, but, more importantly, he had badly sprained or dislocated his ankle. With Alexandra's help, he crept for hours back to the cave.

In the morning, Alexandra woke to the sight of Yongden leaning on his staff, trying to walk. His foot was swollen out of shape and could bear no weight. What was to be done? Turning back was impossible, and so the mother wished to hurry to the nearest village for help. But this was Po country, and the Popa inhabitants were famous as bandits, even cannibals. Leaving Yongden alone in the cave was dangerous. At night wolves, bears, or a leopard might attack him. Staying put meant starvation.

Alexandra, deciding to take action, plunged into the snow in search of a *dokpas'* camp. She walked the whole day under falling flakes without meeting a soul. She started back with cow chips from an abandoned hut, wrapping them in her upper dress. Her Chinese underdress became soaked, and the bitter wind turned it to ice. Night fell and she couldn't find the cave. She had an urge to cry out in the darkness but suppressed it for fear that, if she heard no answer, she would go mad. Finally, a glimmer of light higher up showed the way, and at last she was reunited with Yongden, who was half dead from fright.

A bowl of hot water and tea dust cheered them, and the lama turned philosophical. "Perhaps I shall be able to walk tomorrow. If not, you must go away and try to save yourself. . . . All that happens comes from some cause. This accident is a result of my previous deeds." Thinking thus, the pair slept soundly as the snow continued to fall until it had done so for sixty-five hours straight.

Next day they struggled through knee-deep drifts. Alexandra had fixed her son a primitive crutch from a stout branch and an empty provision bag for padding. With the weather clearing, she was able to enjoy fine alpine scenery and the prodigious stillness of the strange white land. Unfortunately, her right big toe was peeping forth from its boot, and as the tear grew, her foot began to freeze from the fresh snow. "No trace of cultivation, no cattle were seen, and it also seemed that we would find no shelter."

Darkness came and with it snow once again. They couldn't take another night in the open. But the pilgrims' luck—call it karma—hadn't
run out. Alexandra, ahead, bumped into a fence. She grabbed it, afraid
it was illusory. She had stumbled upon a herdsmen's summer camp,
complete with a snug cabin and firewood and dry dung under the
shed. By the time Yongden hobbled up, Alexandra had a fire roaring
in the hearth and was preparing dinner: boiled water sprinkled with
tsampa. "After the nigths spent in the [cave]," she would write, "the
warmth that spread into the closed room thrilled voluptuously in me
the epicure which is always lurking in the corner of the most ascetic
hearts."

The travelers stayed on for a lazy, hungry day in the cabin. Yongden
patched his mother's boots, and they dined on tea dust. Next day they
started before dawn under snowy skies through a holly and oak forest
of the sort pictured on greeting cards. It was Christmas Eve, and Alexandra broke off a small branch of berries, meaning it for a friend
in Europe. In this manner she reassured herself that the weakening
pair would live to present it one day. Ironically, by the time the Frenchwoman had returned home the intended recipient had died.

About noon, when the travelers realized they had taken the wrong
path, their chances looked grim. They retraced their steps to the camp,
boiled snow, and drank the water. Yongden went to scout, while his
mother reflected how her European acquaintances, in her place, would
surely give themselves up for lost, blame each other, and curse fate. A
snatch of Buddhist verse came to mind: "Happy indeed we live/ among
the anxious, unanxious." But when Yongden returned, she grew
quickly worried. "He was pale, with glowing and feverish eyes."

That night was a trial. By the dim light of embers, Alexandra awoke
to see the lama tottering toward the door. She intercepted him, but he
mumbled that the snow was piling up and would bury them. They had
to start out right away. Burning, wracked by starvation, Yongden
lunged for the door, showing white drifts against the blackness.

"You will die, Jetsunma!" he raved. "Come quick!"

Alexandra shoved him inside and wrestled him down. While he
fought with feverish strength, she recalled that the clearing outside
ended abruptly in a precipice a few feet away. She tossed an armful
of branches on the fire and the sudden explosion of light startled the
young man to his senses. He ceased to resist her efforts to make him
lie down. Dozing with one eye open, Alexandra watched over her son.

Christmas morning the pilgrims arose to the gnawing of their bellies.
Yongden looked sane, but when he said that he was a mountain god
bearing a gift, his mother wondered. Promptly the lama produced a
bit of bacon fat he'd employed to waterproof their yak-hide boots, and

some leftover leather from the soling. Into the pot went the goodies, and in true Tibetan style, they drank a beggar's feast.

The day was an auspicious one on which to meet their first Popa. As they proceeded, he emerged from a cabin and invited the travelers to warm themselves. Inside they found a dozen men seated around a fire—burly fellows with a mass of free-flowing hair and Mongol features. They questioned Yongden, who admitted he and his mother had crossed the Aigni-la. The men, who thought the pair had come this moment across the snow-blocked pass, were astounded. They must have flown over it! The Popas immediately demanded that Yongden foretell the answer to a burning question. They were more or less in rebellion against the *pombo* representing Lhasa, who had sent to the capital asking for reinforcements. In turn, the rebels had dispatched a band to intercept the courier, and now they wanted to know how it would turn out. The lama stalled, knowing the ruffians would treat a false prophet summarily.

"No harm will be done," muttered Alexandra from a corner. "All will end well."

Her butting in caused the men to wonder if she were a *pamo*, a medium. Yongden went through the story of his mother being the consort of a sorcerer. The Popas plied their guests with generously buttered tea, then slunk out, afraid of such powerful magicians. Alexandra and Yongden slept well and in the morning tramped on to Cholog. Soon the whole village gathered around the magical beggars who had flown over the Aigni-la. They were presented with a true miracle—a thick turnip soup. The two gulped down bowlfuls to break a week's fast.

It was rumored that travelers foolish enough to enter Po country never came out. Alexandra and Yongden discovered one reason why: vicious watchdogs. As they reached the outskirts of a village at dusk, farmers fled from them, warning their neighbors that pilgrims were approaching. Every house was barred, and at a prosperous dwelling they were attacked by several furious mastiffs. J. Hanbury Tracy, an Englishman who mapped the Po in the mid-1930s, described these hairy beasts, each weighing up to 150 pounds, as being "the size of a small pony" and having "a crusty disposition." Fearless, they could easily pull down a grown man. The dogs were trained to maul strangers, and when they were let out at night even their masters had to beat them back. Alexandra defeated these yapping beasts in time-honored fashion—raining blows on their muzzles with her staff and jabbing them with its iron spike. But the pilgrims got neither alms nor a spot by the hearth at this place.

After crossing a dense forest, they arrived at Sung Dzong. Originally *dzong* meant "fortress," but by Alexandra's day, a *dzong* included any dwelling on a height that housed an official. Although the town was at the junction of two rivers and important to the Po, it hadn't appeared on the map. The French orientalist regretted that her disguise, and the need to be vigilant, prevented her from doing any serious map-making. She claimed that the discovery of scientific instruments in her pack could have doomed her and Yongden. But her watch or ther-mometer, if spied by a native, was instrument enough to cause her unmasking. And the Indian pundits of a previous generation had car-ried simple concealed implements for determining distances. Alexan-dra's thermometer, if boiled in water—the method is described by Bai-ley—could have indicated approximate altitudes from sea level. Rather, the itinerant preferred to remain wholly in the role she had chosen, to become and not merely to act the mendicant pilgrim. In that way the *philing* disappeared, most of all to herself. Then, in the last instance, when menaced by desperate characters, Alexandra had to be willing to employ the ultimate tool, her revolver.

The Popas hated the Chinese for devastating towns and countryside during the invasion of 1911–12, when they also murdered their king. The scorched-earth policy had further impoverished an already prim-itive district. But still New Year's was celebrated in mid-January ac-cording to the Chinese calendar. On this day the pilgrims passed an isolated farmhouse, and from it emerged a number of drunken, rau-cous men. "All of them carried guns across their shoulders," Alexandra calmly recalled, "and some made a pretence of shooting at us. . . . [W]e proceeded as if we had noticed nothing." There was no more trouble until, in the morning, a Popa showed up at the cave where they had slept. He quickly grew fascinated by their two cheap foreign spoons.

To be rid of him, Yongden asked if he had any local cheese to ex-change for sewing needles—a kind of currency. He did and would bring a sample right back. Instead the man fetched one of his cohorts, a bold rascal who first fingered and admired their tent, then seized the spoons. The other grabbed the tent, while both cast impatient glances toward the farm, as if expecting the rest of their gang. When the Popas found out what these supposedly poor *arjopas* carried, in-cluding gold and silver, they would be obliged to murder them.

"Let that tent alone at once!" commanded Alexandra, mustering what height she could. "Give the spoons back!"

The robbers laughed in her face, turning to pillage their packs. The "old mother" pulled out her automatic and coolly grazed one fellow's scalp. Flinging the stolen goods on the ground, the pair took off like scared rabbits. Probably a battle was about to be joined, but luckily a band of thirty pilgrims arrived. They were from the Nu Valley and had already been attacked by, and fought off, Popas. But their monks, who did the fighting, were armed only with swords and spears. They were delighted to meet companions with a gun and demanded to see the marvel. Yongden showed them an old revolver, claiming that *he* had fired the shot. Alexandra was pleased to have the pilgrims hail him as a hero, because an automatic pistol wielded by a woman spelled *philing,* if not demon.

These people were friendly and Alexandra enjoyed their company for a few days. Then she let them race ahead, while she preferred to revel in the mild winter climate and to loiter amid spectacular scenery and lush vegetation, including orchids. Kingdon Ward commented on the "many kinds of small ground orchids, some of them deliciously scented" that he found in southern Tibet. This was the land of purple iris, yellow primrose, and the blue poppy. The Frenchwoman had attuned herself to the "queer psychic atmosphere peculiar to places consecrated to Nature's gods." Everything about the landscape, from towering snow-clad peaks to waving fields of barley and the colorfully garbed monks, told "of times long past when men's hearts were young and naive."

A brief stay in a hut with a simple couple touched her own heart. They had invited the pilgrims to share their meager hospitality. Neither young nor beautiful, the two were as tender toward each other as first lovers. The man had a goiter on his neck—common among Popas— and the woman was wrinkled with a wen on hers. Once considered a beauty, she had been the mistress of a rich merchant until she ran off with her Romeo. Now the penniless pair lived *en famille* with a cow, her suckling calf, and a litter of baby black pigs who didn't hesitate to manure the floor. The lovers had no regrets and, rare for Tibet, didn't desire children, so wrapped up were they in each other. They shared turnip soup with their guests and gave them *tsampa* for the road. During the night, Yongden put a few rupees in a pot on a shelf. The snoring lovers, when they found the money, would think the gods left it there.

Alexandra started before dawn to tramp to Showa, the Popa capital. Here she reverted to form, begging loudly at the gate of the Po king's dwelling. In those days each of the border regions of Tibet was a semi-independent principality. This particular ruler was then in Lhasa but would eventually fall out with the central government. A chief of brigands, he was defeated by the Dalai Lama's new army and died wandering in the mountains. His stewards heaped the lusty beggars with butter and eggs to get rid of them.

One last major hurdle stood between the interlopers and their goal: a toll bridge across a gorge at Tongyuk, where a *dzong* was placed to watch over travelers proceeding toward the capital. A bridge-keeper controlled a gate, and as the pilgrims knocked on it, he set it slightly ajar to regard them. They pounced with the eagerness of cats on a mouse.

They demanded to know the whereabouts of the large party of their friends from the Nu. The keeper said they'd passed through in the morning. What, hadn't the monks left a bag of dried meat for them?

No! That wasn't like them. He, the keeper, hadn't stolen their meat? On they went in this vein until the keeper, forgetting they needed permission from the *pombo* in the fort to pass, waved them ahead. He was glad to be rid of such pests, while Alexandra silently gave thanks to her friends the pilgrims who had proved useful on several occasions.

Crossing forest country containing only scattered villages, staying out of sight by day, the travelers supposed their journey would surely succeed. They emerged on a stretch of land partly cultivated and partly pasture, "exceedingly beautiful . . . like some landscapes in the French or Swiss Alps." One evening, while Alexandra toyed with the idea of exploring to the north, a simply dressed lama appeared at their camp. He wore a rosary made from human bone and carried a staff surmounted by a trident. He sat down and stared hard at Alexandra. The man, who carried no provisions, not even a bag of *tsampa,* made her nervous. He did produce a skull fashioned into a bowl and took tea.

"Jetsunma," he demanded, "what have you done with your rosary and with your 'rings of the initiate'?"

Yongden began to spin a tale, but the tantric *ngagspa*—a genuine one—ordered him away. Alexandra understood that deception was useless. The lama knew her, she couldn't say from where. "Do not try to remember, Jetsunma," he half-teased, reading her thoughts. "I have as many faces as I desire, and you have never seen this one."

There was nothing to do but settle down into a long conversation about Buddhist philosophy and Tibetan mysticism. Finally the mysterious lama arose and vanished into the woods as silently as he'd come. Alexandra was sunk in fear: she had been found out. Yet she soon reassured herself that the *ngagspa* would keep her secret. He and she were of the same breed. Still, she would take the more direct route to the capital.

One day in February 1924, four months after starting from Yunnan, the pilgrims crossed into Lhasa territory. Here, the year before, General Pereira had been greeted by officials bearing cakes and peaches. Even poor exhausted Montgomery McGovern, dressed as a porter, "ran into a swarm of beggars, who followed our party for more than a mile gesticulating and clamoring for alms." But no one took notice of this pair of dusty, weary *arjopas,* no different from scores of others come for the New Year festivities.

Alexandra, giddy from excitement, spotted the Potala palace. "Now we could discern the elegant outlines of its many golden roofs. They glittered in the blue sky, sparks seeming to spring from their sharp upturned corners, as if the whole castle, the glory of Tibet, had been crowned with flames." With a suddenness peculiar to the roof of the world, "a furious storm arose, lifting clouds of dust high into the sky." The palace was obscured, the trespassers hid from any prying eyes.

This omen was both good and helpful, since the plain usually teemed with life. Alexandra again assured herself that none of the inhabitants of the holy city dreamed it was about to be invaded by a *philing*—a woman! Equally miraculous, as the pair entered the sacred precincts, unsure where to find lodging during the crowded holiday season, a young woman approached. She offered them a narrow cell in a beggar's hostel. Remote from the center of town, it would make a perfect hideout. It even provided a fine view of the Potala.

Inside, Yongden dared to declaim—in whispered triumph—"*Lha gyalo!* The gods win! We are at Lhasa!"

CHAPTER 20

"The Potala Is the Paradise of Buddhas."

—TIBETAN SAYING

In 1949 the American Lowell Thomas, Sr.—broadcast media's original anchorman, although he rarely stayed in one place for long—and his son Lowell Thomas, Jr., were invited by the Fourteenth Dalai Lama, or really his Regent, to visit his capital. The spur was fear of Red China, victorious over Chiang Kai-shek's Nationalists and already massing an army of invasion on the vulnerable Sino-Tibetan border. Thomas was granted this unusual privilege through intermediaries in India. Clearly, no other newscaster of the time had so wide an audience and was personally familiar with important government figures. If help were to be extended to Tibet, whether diplomatic or military, it must come from the dominant Western power, the United States.

Fortunately, both father and son were hardy, adventurous types, used to life in the outdoors. The Sacred Realm remained as closed as ever. "The peaks are our sentinels," runs an old Tibetan saying. Reaching Lhasa twenty-five years after Alexandra David-Neel made her heroic effort had become only slightly easier. The means of travel hadn't changed in hundreds of years: horse, mule, or foot, or camel from Mongolia. "Tibetans absolutely forbid travel by air, by car, or even by carriage or cart," wrote the younger Lowell in the engaging account of his journey to Lhasa. Since the situation was urgent—Chinese radio was calling for the "liberation" of Tibet—the two Americans had to start from Calcutta in July in the midst of the rainy season.

Once inside the Sikkimese frontier, the expedition was halted by a giant landslide: "an immense wall of rock, dirt and stripped tree trunks . . . The whole side of a mountain had collapsed under the monsoon rains." The Thomases overcame this difficulty and others ranging from obdurate mules to leeches that attacked their coolies' bare legs to the serious danger of sodden, crumbly mountain trails. Up the forested slopes of the Himalayas they climbed, hoping to make it from Gangtok to Lhasa in the usual three weeks. They crossed the Tibetan border—near where Alexandra had caught her first glimpse of the Forbidden Land—at 14,800 feet under a yak-hair rope fastened to two boulders and festooned with hundreds of flapping prayer flags. They frightened off three bushy-tailed wild yaks.

Despite the biting cold of the plateau, incessant rains worked through the Thomases' rubber suits. In a pine forest they met their first inhabitant: a huge white monkey with a long tail and black face. Tibetan myth holds that humans are descended from monkey ancestors. Naturally, the natives will not harm these or other of the photogenic creatures inhabiting this land of strange, magnificent scenery. Here Alexandra learned to admire the many-faceted yak, the sure-footed blue sheep of the peaks, and the furry black-and-white panda of the eastern mountains. Here she befriended the bear, the wolf, and the elusive snow leopard.

Tibetan manners are as striking as their animals. Because the Thomases were guests of the Dalai Lama, provincial officials were careful to extend a warm welcome by sticking out their tongues and hissing at them. When they offered to shake hands, they found a white silk scarf draped over their outstretched arms. This was nothing compared to the misunderstanding that arose when, during World War II, several U.S. airmen had to bail out of their plane over the Tsangpo Valley. Spotting house doors decorated with swastikas—the Tibetan symbol for prosperity—the Americans thought it was Nazi country and held off the friendly natives with their pistols. The nasty situation was not resolved until the arrival of a Ladakhi who spoke some English. Then the villagers feasted the airmen on incomprehensible foods and plied them with *chang* (barley beer). Although the natives were sorry when the British rescued the party, the G.I.'s were relieved to get out of such a funny country.

The end of all journeys in Tibet is one. Lowell, Jr. wrote, "Late that evening . . . we suddenly caught a glimpse of our goal—Lhasa, far off, under a range of dark mountains—sparkling in the sunset; and the Potala, standing out above the city, its golden roofs beckoning like a far-off beacon." Montgomery McGovern, too, wrote of "a great and sudden thrill" on sighting the Potala: "I knew that on the other side of the hill on which the palace was perched lay Lhasa, the abode of the gods." McGovern, by turning himself in once he reached the capital, got to hobnob with the more enlightened Tibetan officials. He even achieved a clandestine interview with the Thirteenth Dalai Lama. No such secrecy was necessary for the Thomases, who received a royal welcome. Of course, their journey, although grueling, can scarcely be compared to the rigors and frights undergone by the earlier, disguised desperados.

Oddly, it was Alexandra who played down her own triumph. In her published account she insisted, "I had endeavoured to reach the Tibetan capital rather because I had been challenged than out of any real desire to visit it." This Olympian pose suited the image she wished to create. Still, she was delighted to have arrived during Monlam, the great festival to celebrate the New Year, and she was determined to keep her incognito and to enjoy herself to the full. "All sights, all things which are Lhasa's own beauty and peculiarity, would have to be seen by the lone woman explorer who had the nerve to come to them from afar, the first of her sex."

What did this so-called "Rome of the Lamaist world" look like? Then it remained a small city, of at most twenty thousand people, "prettily situated at a little distance from the bank of the river Kyi [tributary to the Tsangpo], in a large valley with a commanding horizon of high barren mountain ranges." A hill to either side marked the town's extent, and on the smaller, more pointed one was situated the medical college, while stemming from the other, surrounded by its own little village, rose the magnificence of the Potala. However, Lhasa, a collection of flat-roofed, whitewashed houses of sun-dried brick, revolved around the Jo Khang cathedral, the St. Peter's of Tibetan Buddhism. The cathedral was there before the town, which, in a way, constituted its outbuildings. The market ran right around it, and twice daily each pilgrim circumambulated this Holy of Holies.

Despite certain artistic reservations, Alexandra determined to visit the Potala first. She admitted its imposing appearance, "a red palace capped with golden roofs, uplifted high in the blue sky, on a shining pedestal of dazzling white buildings." But she sincerely felt that "Tibetan architects . . . succeed only in expressing might and wealth and fail to reach beauty." On the other hand, McGovern, when he finally came to face the Potala, "halted almost dumfounded by its splendor. . . . [I]t possesses a simplicity and yet a stateliness of style that cannot but impress even the most sophisticated." Apparently the Potala, like beauty, is in the eye of the beholder.

To avoid suspicion, Alexandra wished to enter the Potala in a group. Outside the palace gate, she spotted a couple of plain border folks loitering. Yongden was sent to inform the "dear, good, stupid fellows" that they were to have the honor of "meeting"—a Tibetanism—the holy Potala. They replied they had met it already and were headed for a *chang* house before setting out for home. Yongden, with an air of compassion, brushed aside their objections and offered to take them on a tour, explaining to them the names and meanings of the myriad deities. Surely that was preferable to getting drunk? Fortunately, the pair turned out to be as religious minded as most Tibetans. A theory holds that it is because they are so close to heaven that people from the roof of the world are given to piety.

Curiosity drew Alexandra to the Potala. She still did not approve of the worship of graven images, nor giving fees to priests for opening doors to chapels and sprinkling a few grains of *tsampa* on the altars within. Yet she would appear the humble suppliant, head lowered and eyes cast down, as she toured the huge complex, really a cluster of buildings and wings, which included not only tombs, temples, and chapels but reception and ceremonial rooms, schools, and offices. As Alexandra told the story, "The three men walked in first, strong in the superiority of their sex." The doorkeeper, a gnomish boy lama in an ill-fitting robe, insisted that she remove her bonnet from Kham. This was an unmitigated calamity. Because at the rooming house every act was public, she couldn't ink her hair, and it had resumed its natural brown shade. Worse, it looked incongrous next to the braids of black yak's hair grown thin as rats' tails. Just such a nonsensical accident— the barking of a tiny pet dog—had caused the unmasking of McGovern the year before.

Alexandra, infuriated at "that horrid little toad" of a doorkeep, was obliged to trudge through the Dalai Lama's palace feeling like a clown. But the other pilgrims ignored her, and she became absorbed in the labyrinth of corridors and galleries and especially in the wall paintings, depicting "the legends of gods and the lives of saintly men . . . in millions of tiny figures full of lifelike animation." In the shrine rooms were enthroned statues of the many deities of Mahayana Buddhism, bedecked with gold ornaments and inlaid with coral, turquoise, and precious stones, before them smoldering solid gold butter lamps.

If these houses of the gods were bright with the glow of lamps and festooned with silken banners in white, green, red, blue, and yellow— the five mystic colors—Alexandra could also veer off to investigate darker recesses where she found altars to "the aboriginal gods and demons of the pre-Buddhistic religion, which Tibetans have never been able to forsake." These entities had fought tooth and nail against the missionaries from India bearing the new teachings, harming their converts, until they were subdued and themselves converted by the superior magic of the holy men. Then they, too, were adopted into the Tibetan Buddhist pantheon of benevolent forces.

Far worse beings, hideously malevolent but invisible, were supposedly kept chained by the power of magic charms in special buildings. They were fed symbolic sacrificial offerings and watched with great care lest they escape and devour humanity. Such aspects of Tibetan ritual as vulgarized saddened Alexandra. She was displeased by the superstitious awe demonstrated by the horde of pilgrims before the huge golden statues of departed Dalai Lamas. She pitied the humble souls who "led by ignorance [of Buddha's teachings] tramp for fathomless ages the sorrowful road to renewed births and deaths."

Nevertheless, once atop the palace—which, including its mount, reaches to two-thirds the height of New York's Empire State Building—Alexandra felt master of the domain before her. Wisps of smoke rose from innumerable sacrificial altars. Colored paper dragons sent up from rooftops danced in the crisp air. The triumphant traveler "enjoyed the beautiful sight of Lhasa, its temples and monasteries, lying at our feet like a white, red, and gold carpet spread in the valley." Scattered among the surrounding snowcapped mountains were what appeared to be toy monasteries, some clinging precariously to rock cliffs like eagles' nests. The two peasant lads were anxious to depart, and reluctantly the "old mother" trailed after, reminded that her stay would be limited.

The once-upon-a-time Parisienne found this capital to be a lively place inhabited by jolly folk who loved to loiter and chat outdoors. She described the streets as "large, with broad squares . . . and relatively clean." This conflicts with the accounts of certain other Westerners. Millington Powell, who went with the Younghusband expedition, portrayed Lhasa as "filthy beyond description, undrained and unpaved." It must have been "the scene of unnatural piety and crime." Montgomery McGovern quailed before its "brawling monks" and "the fanatic populace." To Spencer Chapman, who arrived with a British diplomatic mission in 1936, everything seemed "mean and gloomy . . . repellent and sinister." The Lowell Thomases were far more relaxed about their adventure, and so was Hugh Richardson, who also accompanied the 1936 mission. He has written, "There was one terrible street near the public latrine but the main square was broad and quite well kept. I never found Lhasa either gloomy or sinister and for most of the year the intensely dry air kept down smells." The appeal of Lhasa, then, was also in the eye—and nose—of the beholder!

Alexandra went often to the Jo Khang, wandering from the cathedral to the shops that fairly ring it. The Lhasans were and are very fond of bazaars, and in their capital, as in the Jerusalem of Jesus' day, temple and marketplace are hopelessly intertwined. Interestingly, most retail trade lies in the hands, or better the laps, of women. Alexandra frequented the market for its color—cunning traders, sheepskin-clad Khampas, turquoise-bedecked nomad women, Moslem merchants from Kashmir, and for the holiday season hundreds of monks let loose from the three surrounding monasteries of Drepung, Sera, and Ganden. However, she was disappointed by the show of cheap aluminum ware and other shoddy goods from abroad. This she blamed on the restriction of trade with China in favor of inferior goods imported from India and England.

One incident that turned out to be amusing put her in grave danger, perhaps more than she realized. A policeman at the market made the browser nervous by staring at her. Instead of a uniform, these gentlemen were distinguished by a slouch hat and a single dangling earring. They were not known for their honesty and, under cover of dark, sometimes turned robber. Alexandra, reacting quickly, selected an aluminum saucepan and began to bargain for it loudly.

She offered the tradesman an absurdly low price. At first he laughed, saying, "Ah, you are a true *dokpa* [peasant], there can be no doubt of that!" The other merchants and customers joined in to ridicule the stupid woman who knew nothing beyond her cattle and the grasslands. But as she continued her ceaseless twaddle, the tradesman was ready to crown her with the pan. After the chuckling policeman had passed on, the "old mother" bought the loathed thing and scuttled away.

Had Alexandra been slower of wit and were she caught, she would have been taken not to the civil authorities but to two abbots from Drepung monastery. For the three weeks of the festivities they had absolute rule over Lhasa and could reprimand even the Dalai Lama. The ancient custom of their rule was necessitated by the streaming into town of up to twenty thousand *trapas* from the three great monasteries, many of them "brawling monks." No one else could control these bullies, who were worldly types given to drinking and quarreling. However, the Drepung abbots were known to be fiercely antiforeign, and they might have turned the interloper over to an outraged mob. Her sex would not have protected her. McGovern watched from a roof as a naked woman was whipped in the marketplace to within an inch of her life for the illegal sale of fireworks.

The atmosphere at Monlam was more solemn than gay. As a religious festival it commemorated Lord Buddha's victory over the malicious spirits that tempted him during his meditations. Yet McGovern reported heavy drinking, rowdyism, and rather more innocent activities: "The whole morning [of the first day] the marketplace was full of revelers of both sexes and from every part of Tibet. These were singing, shouting and dancing." He was charmed by the colorful outfits and how the women would "begin to sing, and stamp their feet rhythmically, at the same time jangling the bells which they held in their hands." The men joined in, and slowly the frolicking groups circumambulated the sacred Jo Khang.

Of course, what one saw depended on one's point of view in the literal sense. In 1921 Charles Bell had been the personal guest of the Thirteenth Dalai Lama for the festivities. From a privileged seat he watched spirited pony and foot races, wrestling matches, cavalry processions, and the beggars known as "white devils" who amused the crowd with bawdy jokes. Outside the gates, Bell sat in the reviewing stand with the highest officials to take in the scene of sparkling blue and white tents that dotted the plain. Men dressed as traditional warriors competed in contests of archery and displays of horsemanship to win prizes of Chinese silk or bricks of tea. The Khampa nomads in their fox fur hats and heavy beads looked for all the world like a detachment of Genghis Khan's horde. These picturesque horsemen were fine subjects for photography.

More available to the pair of pilgrims were the events that took place in the Par Kor, the wide avenue running around the Jo Khang. Normally it was the scene of devout Buddhists gaining merit by circumambulating the cathedral, reciting prayers, and making obeisances. The shrine contained as its chief treasure a venerable image of Siddhartha Gautama as a youth, supposedly painted from the life. However, on the evening of the full moon of the first month (March), a festival unfolded with its roots in equally ancient times. Alexandra described the setting:

Light wooden structures of a large size are entirely covered with ornaments and images of gods, men, and animals, all made of butter and dyed in different colors. These frail frameworks are called *tormas*. About one hundred of them are erected along the Par Kor . . . and in front of each one, a large number of butter lamps burn on a small altar. That nocturnal feast is meant to entertain the gods, just as are certain concerts on the roofs of the temples.

By the lurid light, Alexandra and Yongden pushed into the midst of an enormous crowd. Previously, attendants had always cleared her way, so this was her first experience at being crushed by the mob. Waiting for the appearance of the Dalai Lama, the excitement grew. Sheepskin-clad giants, forming a chain, ran for sheer joy although they knocked others down. Proctors from Drepung wielded long sticks and whips to no avail. Everyone pressed toward the center to get the best view. "At last the arrival of the Lama-King was announced," Alexandra recalled.

The knocking, beating, boxing increased. Some women screamed, others laughed. Finally there remained along the walls of the houses that confronted the *tormas* only a few rows of people, more tightly pressed against one another than tinned sardines. I was amongst them.

First the new-model garrison of Lhasa marched past to an English music hall tune, then the Dalai Lama was carried by in a sedan chair covered with yellow brocade. The awestruck crowd couldn't have caught more than a slight glimpse of the Compassionate One. After the formal procession passed, nobles in their silks paraded by proudly, surrounded by attendants holding Chinese lanterns; high lamas with monk followers marched along, and then came rich merchants with their women in elaborate headdresses displaying their finery. Finally the populace joined in, catching up the pair of interlopers in the madcap joy. They found themselves "running, jostling, and pushing like everybody else, enjoying . . . the fun of being there in Lhasa, feasting the New Year with the Tibetans."

On the whole, the atmosphere of Monlam—the "Great Prayer"—was dignified and religious. People shied away from the monastic proctors with their sharp eyes and long staffs. Since she was quite short, Alexandra usually hid among tall, strapping herdsmen and let them take any indiscriminate blows. One day she happened to trespass where "quality only were admitted." Without warning her, a policeman hit the "old mother" with his truncheon. The confidante of high lamas and maharajas was so tickled that she wished to give the lout a tip. "What a wonderful incognito is mine," she confided to Yongden. "Now I am even beaten in the streets!"

Although the pilgrim missed her meditations among the tranquil steppes of Amdo, she couldn't deny that Lhasa was the hub of Tibetan life. She must view the doings of its lamas and officials from the level of a plebeian, one among the many, a role to which she was unaccustomed. In compensation she was able to penetrate deeply into the intimate lives of common folk. The hostel where Alexandra and Yongden occupied a narrow cell, with scarcely any privacy, turned out to be a caravansary of talented, eccentric beggars and ne'er-do-wells. Dirty and ragged but unashamed, they often slept in the open courtyard. All of them survived "as birds do, on what they could pick up daily." Still, they were joyful, under "the bright life-giving sun."

Preeminent was a tall, handsome, former officer ruined by drink and gambling. Contemptuous of work, the captain each day strode out of the hovel, his bearing erect, courier bag slung over his shoulder, to chat with his many acquaintances. His conversation was lively and those better off gave him what he casually requested. He returned in the evening with a full bag to feed his wife and children. However, affairs in these lower depths didn't always run so smoothly; stealing and quarrels, adultery and accusations flourished. The neighbors would butt in, debating the right and wrong of the matter until the wee hours when everyone went away drunk. In one instance, the captain's wife received a blow meant for another woman, and the captain threatened to bring suit and to call Alexandra as a witness. This hastened her departure from the capital.

The set of miscreants lived in a manner totally foreign to lay and clerical dignitaries, and they even spoke a different tongue. McGovern distinguished sharply between "the elegant language," that is, proper Tibetan, and "Coolie talk," the language of servants and the lower classes. Alexandra relished her unique opportunity, musing, "I really lived in a novel whose plot was slum life, but what amusing and exotic slums!"

Alexandra's rascally friends loved to sing the songs of the rebel Sixth Dalai Lama, nicknamed Melodious Purity by the Lhasans. She owned, along with a variety of other Tibetan songbooks, a book of the Sixth's lyrical verses, devoted to his affairs with his sweethearts. One verse of the Sixth's runs, "They call me the Profligate/For my lovers are many." Yet in her *Initiations and Initiates,* Alexandra related that, "A sort of unofficial and half-secret cult is paid to him by the good folk of Lhasa. . . . [And] a mysterious red sign marks houses [where he] met his fair friends." She saw Lhasans, as they passed by, touch their brow to these signs—a mark of deepest respect. Until the advent of the Fourteenth, the Sixth was alone among the Dalai Lamas in linking the pinnacle of Tibetan society with its humbler elements. He had more than a little in common with the sojourner from afar who, in disregard of naysayers all her life, came to view his forbidden capital 250 years after he had passed into a new incarnation.

One curious custom uniting all clases of Lhasans was that of the scapegoat, who was a man who willingly assumed the misfortunes, the karma, of others. By being driven out of town on the appropriate day, he purged the citizens of their collective guilt. During the week preceding the ceremony, the scapegoat was expected to wander about carrying an enormous hairy yak tail. He could demand money or goods of anyone, and woe betide the one who refused. Alexandra spotted the fellow in the market; if the offering were too meager, he threateningly raised the yak tail, and the shopkeeper quickly gave more. A curse from the scapegoat was certain to ruin a merchant's trade.

The volunteer gained a small fortune during his allotted time. Then one day, after a ceremony performed by the Dalai Lama, he had to flee to a nearby wilderness. Crowds along the route out of town were denser than any Alexandra and Yongden had got mired in, and the police more preemptory in beating them back. They clapped and whistled—to chase out evil—as the scapegoat in a coat of genuine goat's fur, face painted half white, half black, was hurried past by officials. Although his exile would be temporary, the bad luck accrued by taking on others' sins nearly always proved fatal to the greedy one. The previous scapegoats had died promptly and painfully of no apparent cause.

That evening Lhasa celebrated its deliverance for another year. "Everybody was outdoors," recalled Alexandra, "chatting, laughing and, especially, drinking. The most hideous beggars, deaf and dumb, blind, eaten up by leprosy, rejoiced as heartily as the wealthiest and noblest citizens." She met acquaintances who insisted on treating the "old mother" and son to a variety of dishes in a restaurant. Alexandra, a great fan of Tibetan cooking, pronounced herself pleased.

The final grand ceremony of Serpang occurred next day. Weeks in preparation, it took place around the Potala but especially in the vast courtyard at its base. Thousands of monks carried hundreds of large multicolored silk banners. Dignitaries proceeded in state under canopies, while drums beat and bands played, including fifteen-foot-long trumpets borne on the shoulders of several men. A "solemn impressive music . . . filled the whole valley with deep sonorous voices." Elephants plodded along, escorted by paper dragons performing all manner of antics. Young boys danced ritual steps whose origins were lost in antiquity.

Perched on the rocky mountainside, Alexandra, one among many, took in this array of barbaric splendor under "the blue luminous sky and the powerful sun of central Asia [which] intensified colours of the yellow and red procession, the variegated hues of the crowd's dresses, the distant hills shining white . . . All these seemed filled with light and ready to burst into flames." Lhasa lay at the beggar's feet, and she felt amply repaid for all the fatigue and danger she had undergone. Here indeed was a scene worthy of Shangri-La, a moment that has disappeared from earth. Since the Chinese invasion in 1949, the festival of Serpang exists only in cans of film stored in archives and on the pages of Alexandra David-Neel's writing.

In *The People of Tibet*, Charles Bell translated the blessing that officially closed the New Year revelries: "Lhasa's prayer is ended. Love is now invited." In early fall 1921, after nearly a year, his sojourn came to an end. It had proved no paradise for the canny diplomat, whose curly hair was turning white. He had encouraged the building of a small but modern army and in the process received threats on his life, possibly inspired by the Chinese. He returned to his estate in England to write his books on Tibet. Because their basis is more political and official, they nicely complement those of David-Neel, who was more concerned with Buddhism, the techniques of mysticism, and herself.

After two months of gadding about, Alexandra left the capital as quietly as she had entered. "No one suspected that a foreign woman had lived there," she wrote. We shall see that is probably *not* correct. Still, there is no quarreling with her boast, "[F]or the first time since the world began a Western woman ha[d] seen the Forbidden City." The only man who could make a remotely similar claim, Montgomery McGovern, departed Lhasa in March 1923, the year before Alexandra, under armed escort to protect him.

Alexandra took the prudent step of promoting herself to a respectable station: a middle-class woman who owned two mounts and was accompanied by her manservant (Yongden). She had bought numbers of books and intended to hunt for old manuscripts in the south. The horses were needed to carry the luggage. The sun shone brightly the last time the pair rode past gardens where the trees were dressed in April's pale new leaves. According to Alexandra's *My Journey to Lhasa*, published three years after the event, after she had crossed the Kyi River and ascended to a pass, nostalgia gripped her. She stole a final

glimpse at the shabby, splendid capital, above which floated the Potala—"a tiny castle suspended, it seemed, in the air like a mirage." The
pilgrim, who in six months would be fifty-six, called down blessings
"on all beings visible or invisible" who lived there. Then she set her
face away from the holy city.

The newsmen, the Lowell Thomases, would spend only a few weeks
on the roof of the world, guests of the Fourteenth (and current) Dalai
Lama. At the time he was a young man of fourteen, already very impressive. In September 1949, it was their turn to leave Lhasa, bearing
an urgent message for the president of the United States. This failed
to impress the spirits that guard the passes to the forbidden land. The
party had scaled the 16,600-foot Karo-la and were traveling in caravan
when Lowell, Sr. was thrown from his horse and badly shattered his
right leg below the hip.

The injured man was wrapped in a sleeping bag and borne along
on an army cot until the cold, windswept darkness fell, when fortunately the party reached shelter. Lowell, Jr. wrote:

That first night was one of the worst Dad has ever experienced. The shock
and exposure brought on high fever and frequent fainting. . . . Sleep was impossible. It was a long gasping night of agony and worry in just about the most
out-of-the-way spot you can find on this planet. Imagine being stricken in a
land where the people don't believe in doctors, relying on the lamas to cure
their ills through herbs, incantations and ceremony.

The Thomas expedition struggled for days to get its wounded member to Gyantse, where they knew there was a doctor. They crosed the
same monstrous terrain as had Alexandra twenty-five years earlier. It
seemed "like a sea, the gigantic waves of which, driven by northern
and southern winds, have been changed to stone at the moment of
their worst fury." Tibetan bearers carried the elder Lowell's improvised
stretcher over "the steep rocky trails, which skirted chasms and swift
streams," while he roasted under a burning sun, then froze when the
winds blew. As we shall see, Alexandra, although she gave no hint of
it to the public, made this leg of her journey while nearly as ill, and
without servants.

At Gyantse the Thomas party rested, befriended by the Indian garrison. They continued by mounting the patient in a sedan chair, the
poles of which were set on the shoulders of ten strong men. It took
sixteen grueling days to traverse the two hundred miles over the Himalayan passes to Gangtok, and Lowell, Sr. was cruelly bounced and
jostled the whole time. From there the Thomases would fly to Calcutta
and the United States.

The senior Lowell's leg, healing incorrectly, had to be broken again
and properly set. His son delivered the Dalai Lama's diplomatic note
to President Harry Truman. The dignified plea for assistance was

handwritten in Tibetan characters with a bamboo pen on paper made from shrub bark. The president, who was soon to order American troops into Korea, refused to help Tibet or, consistent with the policy of his predecessors, to recognize its independence. Landlocked and isolated, the Sacred Realm could not count on American support.

Ironically, Truman, the level-headed politician, sighed wistfully as Lowell, Jr. pointed out the route of his journey on a map. He had long dreamed of visiting Lhasa, but he supposed it was too late.

Book Four

THE MASTER

Full of charm is the forest solitary for the yogi with a heart empty of desire.

–*Buddhist Saying*

CHAPTER 21

The Dream of Repose

"Alexandra David-Neel has never gone to Tibet." So wrote Jeanne Denys in her scandalous *Alexandra David-Neel au Tibet* (1972). A retired medical doctor with an interest in the East, Denys was hired by Alexandra in the summer of 1958 to catalog her extensive library of Tibetan books. The famous explorer, recently bereft of Yongden, lived quietly at her home, Samten Dzong ("Fortress of Meditation"), in the south of France. The two women struck sparks at once. Denys quit and confronted her employer with an assertion that her successful account, *My Journey to Lhasa,* was sheer fiction. "Prove it," responded the crusty, canny ninety-year-old. "You will give me publicity."

The enraged Denys spent the next decade trying to make the case that Alexandra was a charlatan, the latest in a considerable line who had claimed to visit Tibet but who garnered their tales from other travelers or thin air. Denys's methods were similar to those of a nineteenth-century orientalist. Afraid of the hardships of travel, she sat in Paris and cast her net. However, unlike Alexandra's later French biographers, who have uncritically repeated the David-Neel *mythos,* she thoroughly read the accounts in English of explorers who had covered similar terrain. Unfortunately, this enabled her to quote wildly out of context, a fate Alexandra seems to have invited. Denys's mainstays were Colonel Frederick Bailey and Hanbury Tracy, the former of whom had explored in Tibet ten years earlier than the Frenchwoman, the latter ten years after. But in the main these two knowledgeable writers do support David-Neel's *Journey to Lhasa,* with differences in description accounted for by their traveling in summer in well-equipped parties, while Alexandra and Yongden went in winter, disguised, fearful, and often desperate for a meal.

Denys criticized her *bête noire* for vagueness on dates and places and for not displaying maps of Central Asia on her walls. But this sojourner had learned not to trust the often false assurance given by maps and preferred to follow the information she could glean from natives.

Uniquely, as a Buddhist she was an insider. True, she told Lawrence Durrell in the interview for *Elle* in 1964, "I am foggy about dates." It wasn't a question of her age but a constitutional aversion, since she also loathed clocks and never cared about the exact time. Certainly, there were contradictions in the woman's character, which Denys played upon, calling her derisively "an actress" and pointing out that, instead of discussing philosophy, she complained about illness or pored over the latest stock fluctuations on the Paris Bourse.

Denys was assiduous in carrying out her vendetta. She corresponded with French diplomats in Asia and with Christian missionaries who had known the traveler in the Sino-Tibetan marches during the Second World War, both Catholic and Protestant. Their memories had faded somewhat, and besides, they could know nothing of her earlier journeys. One valid point made by Denys is that, while Alexandra often poked fun at the missionaries, she would turn to them for help in times of need, rarely to be refused.

Alexandra's travail in the Po country came under Denys's closest scrutiny. She stated that the Popas spoke a different dialect from other Tibetans, and so how could Alexandra and Yongden have conversed with them without an interpreter? Colonel Frederick Bailey answered the question, since he mentioned that many of the Popas had been to the capital, and a traveler could get along easily with a knowledge of Lhasa Tibetan. This Alexandra spoke well, and when it was of use she was also able to adopt the dialect of Amdo where she had lived for years.

Admittedly, Alexandra's geography tends toward the hazy, and her findings are at slight variance with those of Bailey, who did meticulous cartographic work in the Po. In fact, he had with him a British army surveyor. The Frenchwoman knew early on of Bailey's efforts, since she referred to a British officer who had been to Showa, the Popa capital. After her adventure, she met the man and swapped stories with him. Had she wished to, she might have borrowed wholesale from the professionals. Instead, because the subterranean nature of her trip made a travel log impossible, she had to cull details from memory. Strictly speaking, Alexandra was not an explorer, since she carried no measuring equipment and made no maps. As Peter Hopkirk has noted, "[H]er contribution to the scientific exploration of Tibet has been nil." But the gentlemen of the exploring profession, including superbly trained British officers, had no difficulty in accepting her as one of them.

A further mystery remains. The English version of *Journey* includes eight photographs allegedly taken by Alexandra in and around Lhasa; these have turned up in recent books and museum shows, credited to her. One, of petty traders from Lhasa, she may have snapped elsewhere. Alexandra developed a flair for capturing the wild yet genial looks of nomadic types. But she took no photos in Lhasa because she carried no camera. Braham Norwick, a Tibetanist of long standing, points out that in the French version of *Journey,* published a few months after the English, the author admits to not bringing a camera because it would have been too bulky and dangerous.

Norwick suggests, "They [the photos] had been taken by Tibetan photographers in Lhasa, and this explains . . . how they were made without exciting suspicion." However, it is not likely that there were any Tibetan photographers at that time, especially with access to a dark-room. We do know of at least one resident Nepali photographer, about whom we are told by Montgomery McGovern: "He was somewhat ac-quainted with the mysteries of photography, and while I was cooped up as a prisoner he went around the city and took several pictures for me." The Nepali, a member of the good-sized artisan community at Lhasa, may have had ties to Johnston and Hoffmann of Calcutta, a commercial studio that also had agents in Nepal and southern Tibet.

Another related mystery is that of the curious photo of Alexandra, Yongden, and a little Lhasa girl posed against the backdrop of the Potala, which appears rather like a stage set. Denys, certain it was faked, made much of the shot, while other, more reliable writers have sug-gested it may be a composite. But if the photo is viewed in the original larger size in which it appeared in 1926 in *Asia* magazine, before it was shrunk to suit a book format, it regains its natural depth. Moreover, the traveler sent this single photo to her husband as his Christmas present for 1924. It is an additional item of proof, as intended, that her journey took place in the real world.

Jeanne Denys was a would-be orientalist who preferred to carp rather than seek knowledge in the field. Much of her tirade consists of a long, fatuous digression on Eastern themes. More ominously, an apparent anti-Semite, she became convinced that Alexandra's father and mother were Jews who spoke Yiddish at home! Her attitude was typical of the French ultraright, but because Denys was accurate on other personal matters, we cannot dismiss the suggestion out of hand. The librarian of the Paris Alliance Israelite has stated that a search of their files turned up no mention of Louis or Alexandrine David. Still, Alexandra used to speak of "my ancestor, King David," and as with Genghis Khan she seemed to be referring to blood lines. Toward the end of her life, she became intrigued with the theme of Jesus as the culmination of the Hebrew prophets. That, and a couple of other hints, are all we pres-ently know of the matter.

Even in her extreme old age, Alexandra remained reticent about her early or personal life. Forgotten, in the image that she projected, were days as a student radical, a bohemian, an opera singer. To one person alone she entrusted the secret of her excursion on the left-hand path of Tantra. For her readers she adopted the slightly cold pose of a reporter. They had no way of learning she had a husband until the posthumous publication of her letters to him, a juicy portion of which she had destroyed. Nor do the letters entirely reveal the hidden woman. Jacques Brosse was correct to write, "She feared to say too much." Ironically, in writing privately of her achievement, the traveler told a still more hair-raising tale than she would present to the public.

Alexandra wrote to Philip from the Tibetan capital on February 28, 1924, her first opportunity since she set out from Yunnan the previous October:

My dearest great friend . . . I'll tell you at once that I have *completely* (as completely as I might have dreamed) succeeded in the "promenade" I undertook when I sent you my last letter. This excursion, considered rough for a young robust man, was pure madness for a woman my age. My success is complete, but if I were offered a million to begin the adventure over again, under the same conditions, I would refuse it. . . . Know only, today I have arrived at Lhasa reduced to the state of a skeleton. When I pass my hand over my body, I find only a thin layer of skin covering the bones.

Alexandra was not greatly worried by a case of influenza that, mixing with the crowds of the capital, both she and Yongden had contracted. More bothersome was the "general emaciation and debility I had scarcely felt until now, thanks to [taking] the stimulants" (that is, homeopathic strychnine). Alexandra's thoughts leaped ahead to concerns of a practical sort: she intended to cross the Himalayas into India, but her baggage—sixty parcels of rare books, ancient manuscripts, and *objets d'art*—were strewn across China in the keeping of French banks, officials, and especially missionaries. How could she ever collect them? She would be arriving in India broke, dressed in "sordid Tibetan rags." At any rate, first she needed "a month of rest, eating and sleeping."

It is evident that this remarkable confession was not mailed, or even wholly written, on the day it was dated, nor was it likely mailed from Lhasa. Alexandra ended by stating, "This letter is not ready to be sent, though there is a post office here, [because] the latter offers no guarantee of discretion." The Tibetan postal system, only a year or so old, was indeed peculiar. There were twelve branches, and these, in the words of McGovern, "[a]re employed as the most efficient means of keeping the unofficial European intruder out." Both letters and telegrams were used to dispatch warnings from the capital to border stations. Further, not stamps but "a small present to the postman" made the mail go. As far as Gyantse, at any rate, where it would have to be transferred by a friend to the British post office in the fort overlooking that city. From there a letter could be sent to the outer world. Had Alexandra mailed her letter to Philip (in Algeria!) from elsewhere in Tibet, he never would have received it, and she would have been quickly detected.

On March 12 the interloper began another lengthy letter to her husband. She warned him that the flu had worsened. Both she and Yongden were painfully coughing up blood, and their condition was so miserable that for a while they thought they had the pulmonary plague. Their fears were now dissipated, and Alexandra assured Philip:

I count on leaving Lhasa with only a brief delay. The town is without great interest. . . . The famous temple of the Jo [Khang] is nothing marvelous. The palace of the Dalai Lama, despite its richly decorated interior . . . is nothing in particular. . . . I have no curiosity about Lhasa. I went there because the town was located on my route, and because it was a really Parisian joke to play on those who tried to stop me.

This is a side of Alexandra, weary and cynical, totally absent from the heroic personality she presented to her readers in *Journey*. Along with this unattractive realism came demands of a practical sort couched in a manner almost conniving. This time, she assured Philip, she really was coming home. On his next trip to Algiers he must ask the governor to use his influence with the press on her behalf. He should stress that her father had been an influential publisher and a Deputy in 1848. As for herself, "I would like to become Far East correspondent for a large circulation daily."

On April 2 Alexandra wrote again, describing a trip she and Yongden had taken to Ganden monastery. Not as large or politically influential as Drepung, nor noted for the propriety of its rites as was Sera, Ganden (holding around 3,300 monks) held a certain preeminence because it had been founded directly by Tsong Khapa and was the fountainhead of the Yellow Hat reforms. It should have taken the pair an easy day to travel out and another back, but because only Yongden could sleep within the walls, they had to camp out at night. Windswept and without covering, they grew much sicker by morning, and the young man could not move. Alexandra made her obligatory visit and then the pair dragged their way back to town.

In the same letter the traveler informed Philip that she had purchased a couple of scrawny horses to help them negotiate the treacherous snowy passes of the Himalayas in spring. She felt that "at my age it is not wise to prolong the enormous effort I have made." This was an understatement because a trek through the mountains on foot would have finished her and Yongden both. She also insisted that she was running out of funds, which was simply untrue. Alexandra wore a necklace of graded, nearly solid gold coins given to her by the late maharaja of Sikkim. It could be spent piecemeal and was meant to serve as money of last resort. But whether out of sentiment or for other reasons, Alexandra kept the necklace secret.

Alexandra's indifferent reaction to Lhasa is understandable. Aside from the normal letdown of having achieved a long-cherished goal, she was seriously ill throughout her stay, and Yongden was at death's door. They had taken so many pains, gone so roundabout, to reach Lhasa Nyima ("City of the Sun") that only Shangri-La itself would have answered her expectations. Besides, because of the disguise in which she took such delight, Alexandra had barred herself from the high life of the capital or its continuing educational and intellectual traditions. There is a bite to Charles Bell's comment about her: "Travelling . . . disguised as a beggar, her opportunities were limited."

On her way out of town, the foreign Buddhist passed the Jewel Park, the Dalai Lama's summer palace. She was certain he knew nothing of her presence in his capital. "Had I given my name, and had he been free," she mused, "he might have liked to see me again." There is evidence that the Omnicient One was aware of her feat and that he looked the other way. Alexandra's disguise as a mendicant had worn pretty thin, and even before she reached Lhasa the mystery lama had divined her identity. Hugh Richardson related to us an anecdote told him by Tsarong Shappe, commander-in-chief of the Tibetan army, about a woman he supposed was David-Neel. One of Tsarong's servants anxiously reported to him "a strange nun who actually had a towel!" Unmistakably this was Alexandra whose obsession with cleanliness had overcome her prudence, marking her as a *philing*.

At that time most Tibetans did not bathe at all. Montgomery McGovern discovered the reasons when, against his host's protests, he attempted the experiment. "The joke really was on me, for [after the bath] I did suffer more acutely from two things, lice and cold." Deprived of the secure protection of layers of dirt, McGovern came down with a vicious flu similar to that suffered by Alexandra. Tsarong sent him medicine and clandestinely interviewed him. A reformer and self-made man, he was secretly working to open Tibet to the world. Because he was personally close to the Dalai Lama, he would have reported Alexandra's presence to the Thirteenth. But, especially during Monlam, they both dreaded the wrath of the reactionary monks of Drepung. Best to ignore the interloper lest they create a nasty incident.

One must not take Alexandra's pretence at studied objectivity too seriously. Her route, with all its detours and circumambulations, had clearly aimed at Lhasa—since her first glimpse of the Sacred Realm a decade before. By early April, however, she was as determined to leave as she had been to invade it. She boasted to Philip that, of all the European travelers, "I am the one who knows Tibet best." Then, recalling her tramp through the Po, she wrote in a more winning style:

I was really enchanted by my visit to the hot valleys in a cold country. I saw a Tibet unknown to explorers, contemplated extraordinary countrysides that surpassed in splendor all I had seen in the Himalayas, and I could during the month of January pluck a flowering branch of wild orchids.

So special is this country that some Tibetan students of the ancient texts hold it to be the location of Shambala, or paradise, known to Westeners as Shangri-La. But they do not consider it imaginary; rather, ringed by massive snow mountains glistening with ice, spiritual powers are needed to find the way there. Travelers here will find food and shelter and, if they have eyes to see, sacred images and mystical texts. Knowing the boons of perpetual youth and health, they will not wish to leave. Alexandra, although decided upon the goal of her journey, had felt something of this, and she tucked deep within her the secret of the lush, carefree valleys. She set her gaze toward the snowy peaks standing between her and acclaim. Burning with a long-nurtured ambition, Alexandra had little to gain by delay. "[I am] finished with dreams of repose," she announced.

An uneventful journey of three weeks over rugged terrain included a stopover at Sanding monastery to visit Dorjee Phagmo, the "Thunderbolt Sow," a personification of female power, who unfortunately wasn't at home. The ragged pair descended in early May on David Macdonald, the British Trade Agent at Gyantse, while he was calmly dozing in the fort on the hill overlooking town. To the weary adventurer, their meeting was a crucial moment. She later claimed that instinct caused her to reveal her identity to the British. Really, she had no choice but to throw herself on the mercy of her old antagonists. Neither she nor Yongden had got much better, and exhausted, ragged, they couldn't go on without help.

Macdonald, who had served under Bell, knew his duty. He questioned Alexandra and then wrote hastily to the viceroy:

Mme. informed me that she left Yunnan seven months ago and entered Tibet by an unknown route disguised as a Tibetan lady [sic]. . . . She appears to have avoided Chamdo and other places where Tibetan troops are stationed. She traveled through the Po country[,] Gyamda [and] thence to Lhasa, and remained there for two months in disguise. . . .

Questioned why she visited Tibet she simply states that her object was to collect religious books and see the country, but otherwise she is very reticent in her reply. She now intends travelling to India via the Chumbi valley . . . [S]he proposes visiting America.

There in the terse wording of a communiqué is the essence of *Journey to Lhasa*. Had Jeanne Denys read those words, she might have spared herself a decade of furious effort.

Behind the scenes Alexandra had not only opponents but powerful friends. Was she aware that, as early as 1922, the French Foreign Ministry had intervened on her behalf? At first this simply made the Foreign Department of the viceroy's office more suspicious. They wondered how the French government knew of her whereabouts, since, in her own phrase, she had gone "beyond the post offices." In fact the French were confused, placing her in the Pamirs on the border of

China and the Soviet Union. In a memo labeled, "For use by the department only," a nameless bureaucrat complained,

Mme. Neel is a lady of somewhat doubtful antecedants. . . . She was said to be contemplating a journey to Lhasa. . . . It is not quite clear what the French government expect the Government of India to do. The latter cannot be expected to go to trouble to provide . . . facilities for a lady with Mme. Neel's record. Possibly all that is expected is that the G of I should refrain from arresting her as an undesirable.

In any event, the daring of Alexandra's exploit overcome bureaucratic scruples, and the British extended their hospitality. Macdonald sheltered the wayward traveler, fed her at his table, expedited her mail, and even loaned her the sum of four hundred rupees. The Trade Agent was not a wealthy man, and after retirement his family was obliged to run a sort of boarding house at Kalimpong for the British stationed there. (This has become the Himalayan Hotel, well known to travelers from many nations.) More important than money or the gifts by his daughter Victoria of clothing, so that Alexandra might arrive in India in style, was Macdonald's agreeing to verify his guest's stay at Lhasa. He knew the capital and would have been impossible to fool. However, the half-Scottish official waited until August 21 to actually sign and date a letter to that effect. The reason is readily apparent: it was then he was repaid his loan!

The travelers took most of May to mend. Alexandra was sick and dispirited for days. Although the handful of Britons at Gyantse—including Captain Perry, Macdonald's son-in-law—were clearly in awe of her, she felt foreign among these whites and their stiff manners. Once again she had turned her back on Tibet and was beginning to regret it. "Re-entry into the so-called civilized world gives me no pleasure at all," she sighed. Over dinner at a table covered with linen, porcelain, and silverware, everyone seated demurely and chatting about nothing, the veteran of the steppes had to struggle to keep from tears. Still, by the end of the month she was ready to leave for India, "back in [her] old plumes again."

Crossing from the windswept plain of Gyantse to the flower-filled Chumbi Valley, home to the Macdonald clan, Alexandra and Yongden dawdled for nine days. They stayed in comfortable *dak* bungalows along the way. Macdonald's wife, informed over the telegraph line, pampered the adventurer and clothed her in suitable European attire. Although Alexandra would pose in pilgrim's garb for a photographer in Calcutta, her explorings were at an end. It was reassuring to learn from Victoria Williams that she treated the young woman kindly and kept her sense of humor, because her letters to Philip were raspy and demanding.

"I desperately need money at once," the intrepid one fired at her husband from Gyantse on May 16. She had already written to the newspapers and others concerning her great success. Philip must employ the Argus press agency to clip articles certain to be written about her. He should also keep not only her letters but envelopes postmarked Tibet. Let anyone who wished doubt her, she would have the proofs handy. So absorbed was Alexandra in self-promotion that when she heard her friend General Pereira had died in the mountains of western China, she casually remarked, "He died like a true traveler on the march."

While resting at Chumbi, Alexandra was overcome by "chills of fear thinking about what I've done." Neither the emotion nor the candor to admit it were usual for her. Lonely nights concealed in solitary forests frightened her in retrospect. "We climbed and it became colder and colder," she recalled. "There was nothing but a mute countryside of rocks and snow, and we were so little, so lost in this immensity, my boy and me . . ."

Although she rejoiced in modest comfort, Alexandra could not regain the strength necessary to attempt the Himalayas, even mounted. So Macdonald's older daughter, Annie (Perry's wife), loaned her a dandy and porters to carry the conveyance. This hardy woman had to be toted out of Tibet like a package, in little better shape than Lowell Thomas, Sr., an experienced traveler in his own right. It was nothing to be ashamed of. The Land of Snows, forbidden then and still a difficult country in which to travel, does not yield its secrets lightly.

Alexandra put behind her the stinging plateau, the blizzard haunted mountains, and like Conway, the hero of *Lost Horizon,* reentered the world of everyday. She came down to the fetid air of the tropics at rainy season to be the guest of the British Resident at Gangtok, Sikkim. This was now Colonel Frederick Bailey, the explorer, who held court with his wife Lady Irma. Alexandra was well received, and she was correct to claim, "Everyone admires me." If she detected an air of reserve in the Resident's treatment of her, it merely expressed the ambiguity felt by agents of the Government of India. They had to laud her but wished she would go somewhere else.

Bailey himself—a tall, handsome man of bearing who spoke in a soft voice—had been a daredevil as a young officer. He had disobeyed orders by entering Tibet and charting the course of the Tsangpo. Tramping a portion of the same ground as Alexandra, he was more methodical if less imaginative. Badly wounded in the Great War, Bailey managed to carry off a secret mission in Russian Turkestan; employed by Bolshevik intelligence, he was searching for the British spy, Captain Bailey! By 1924 the colonel had settled down to administering Sikkim and pursuing his passion, collecting rare butterflies. His important books on Tibet were written later.

Alexandra sensed that most of the British officers were jealous of her. They couldn't fathom how this diminutive, frail Frenchwoman and her ordinary-seeming Asian (to-be-adopted) son had beat them at their own game of heroics. Their wives, such as Lady Irma the only child to Lord Cozens-Hardy, were intelligent, charming, and decorative. But whatever his personal feelings, Colonel Bailey was the man best able to comprehend Alexandra's achievement. Reversing the expulsion order of his predecessor, Charles Bell, he invited her to stay as long as she liked at Gangtok.

The Resident couldn't help the weather in his Lilliputian capital, which at two thousand feet was hot and sticky. Prices had shot sky-high. Worse, "The natives, previously polite and respectful, have become arrogant and don't hesitate to ridicule the Europeans." Alexandra wondered why the British tolerated such behavior. Due to her isolation, she hadn't realized how the war sounded the death knell of the old colonial society. As well, she was troubled by memories of friends she had known from a time that seemed long past.

The old maharaja and Dawasandup the interpreter were dead. All she had left of Prince Sidkeong were gold trinkets, valuable but of cold comfort. Gangtok no longer struck her as "a romantic and delicious hideaway." Desperately, she hoped for a letter from her "dearest Mouchy," from whom she hadn't heard in a year. Her inquiries about his health were truly anxious.

Alexandra was overjoyed when, on June 9, 1924, she received word from her husband. In replying, she couldn't resist attacking a French novel by Pierre Benoit—a book she hadn't read—set in the Sahara. It was the current rage in Paris, and she wished to hear of no triumph but her own. Impatiently waiting through the rainy season for funds with which to return home, she accepted the invitation of French Franciscan missionaries to occupy a bungalow at Padong in the Darjeeling district. The altitude was somewhat higher, and she hoped to breathe more easily, as well as to "put together a whole parcel of merchandise to place with editors." Once again the missionaries would provide her with shelter free of charge.

Monsoon rains fell through the summer, turning the streets of the village to mud. The bungalow, a former post office, was small and leaky. Alexandra felt like a prisoner. "When one has accomplished something," she fretted to Philip, "it has to be served to the public piping hot." While he delayed in answering her, she claimed to be reduced to a shameless beggar. "How much have you sent and when will I get it?" ran the refrain.

To this sort of demand the engineer was accustomed. In mid-June— received by Alexandra a month later—he wrote from Paris of his lucrative affairs. But he was nonplussed by his wife's declaration that she wished, most of all, to rush home to him. He stalled, writing once more, "I must know where you are going and your exact needs." On August 15, Alexandra responded irately from Padong, "It seems to me that I explained to you my travels are finished. Where am I going? . . . [T]o our place, where I plan to write the books American editors have asked for. Only the itinerary of my return remains in question."

Alexandra was just beginning to face the reality that, after an absence of nearly fourteen years, she had abdicated her marriage. Soon letters arrived to cheer her exile: first one from the president of the Geographical Society of Paris, then one from the French ambassador to China, an old acquaintance. He was seeking a government subsidy to be made available to her at Peking. Professor Sylvain Levi, the great Sanskritist, sent his warm congratulations and an offer for her to lecture at the Sorbonne. More immediately, he referred her to his son Daniel, consul at Bombay. Only Philip remained aloof, nor had funds arrived to pay her debts, about which she was scrupulous, and passage to France. "I can walk across Tibet," she growled, "but I can't cross the water like Jesus Christ."

Toward the end of August, Alexandra received a sufficient sum along with a note from Philip, taking the mineral water cure at Vichy. Elated, she assured him she intended to spend the winter at *"chez nous"* in Bone, but she hoped he would help her to give conferences at Paris in the spring. What was really on her mind is evidenced by the following astounding declaration:

I plan to join the Franco-American Society. . . . I'm attracted to America, first for financial reasons, but also, strange as it may seem, [because] it better suits my character and affinities to move among the Anglo-Saxons than the French. Among the latter, I feel like a woman without a country. . . . I wasn't raised in France, I have lived there very little time, and my maternal lineage is not Latin. I will succeed in America . . .

Philip, even had he wished it at this late date, could never hold onto his comet of a wife. No wonder he felt melancholy and hypochondriac. Alexandra promised that once she and Yongden arrived home, they would "chase away the black butterflies." Her star in the ascendant, she didn't consider how Philip had blocked her out of his emotional life. Worse, she didn't care to realize that bringing home another man—no matter how related—was more of an affront than her husband could swallow.

While Alexandra prepared to leave the Himalayan region for Calcutta, after hearing from several New York publishers eager to read her manuscript, she did feel regrets of a sort: "Oh, the beautiful, unique journey . . . I wonder sometimes if I didn't dream it?"

CHAPTER 22

Success at Paris

In his autobiography Alan Watts wrote of "that incredible and mysterious Russian lady Helena Petrovna Blavatsky, who founded the Theosophical Society in—of all places—New York City in 1875." Fifty years later Alexandra David-Neel dreamed, perhaps, of emulating her predecessor's feat. At least she instructed Philip Neel, bearer of a Protestant name, to obtain from the French president, a Huguenot, a letter of recommendation to the consul at New York. Circumstances, including a lack of ready money, would alter this plan. Unfortunately, much of the American interest in Tibet, conditioned by Blavatsky, centered on fantastic "Tibetan prophecies concerning heroes who are to come from the North," and their alleged similarities to the Bible.

Alexandra received acclaim in Calcutta, a welcome contrast to her husband's continued coolness. "The newspapers are filled with me," she exulted in October. As she arranged for her valuable belongings to be shipped from Shanghai via Colombo to Algeria, she was beset by many small problems. Government of India officials, surrendering, went out of their way to help. The governor of French Indochina presented her with a parcel of land on which she might build a house, so that she would have a *pied-à-terre* in the Orient. At Benares in January the explorer sighed, "I adore Asia, it is an innate passion." Partly by way of compensation, she commenced outlining the story of her journey to Lhasa, in the larger sense, in three hefty volumes.

At Bombay, which she reached in early February 1925, Alexandra had to concentrate her thoughts. The *Revue de Paris* urgently cabled for her Tibetan memoirs, and the American magazine *Asia* promised an advance of 375 dollars (18,750 francs) for three articles. The cash settled the matter of how Alexandra's adventures would first appear: serially, aimed at an audience interested in the East but by no means specialists or necessarily inclined to Buddhism. The appropriate tone—detached yet open to the wondrous—when once she had mastered it, infused the author's most successful and influential books. Her original account—in English and published in five monthly installments the next year—is travel writing at its most compelling.

When the adept of tantric mysteries met the Indian poet Rabindranath Tagore, he reinforced her decision to write for a wide if literate public. At a "big lunch" to honor the Nobel laureate, Alexandra managed to become the center of attention. The director of the Musée Guimet, present because he was returning from Afghanistan, insisted she install at the museum a genuine Tibetan Buddhist chapel. Since it was at the Guimet she first started down the road to Lhasa, the suggestion gave her particular pleasure. Tagore, too, proved encouraging, and at a private interview during which Alexandra found "the poet [to be] very much a businessman," he offered to help place her articles in Latin America, where he had recently toured.

Ironically, Professor Sylvain Levi actually launched David-Neel's worldwide reputation, but by reminding her, "All success begins at Paris." His son Daniel, whom she knew as a boy, seconded his father's urging that she proceed directly to the French capital. Levi was working hard to assure Alexandra's triumph in her natal city. He could scarcely wait to delve into her collection of four hundred rare Tibetan books and manuscripts, and he requested a catalog at once. Only Philip remained aloof, claiming he lived in too small a house to accommodate her souvenirs, especially a certain young man. "We will meet again and embrace like two old faithful friends," replied the unrepentant adventurer.

On May 4, accompanied by Yongden and mounds of baggage, Alexandra landed at Valencia, Spain, hoping still to rendezvous with her husband in the south of France. Spanish customs, after taking a look at her books, robes, masks of the supposed devil dancers, and other unusual mementos, indicated they would prefer she continue to Le Havre. This meant she wasn't to see Philip until months later, but it placed her at the door to Paris. She responded to the challenge reluctantly: "I fell sick again, [and] for several days I suffered painfully from fever and facial neuralgia." However, on landing, her admirers were many, congratulations poured in, and then she—and surprisingly, Yongden—became the talk of the town.

From the moment of Alexandra's arrival at the railway station, she had to suffer the pop of flashbulbs and the intrusive questions of reporters. Although she clung to her stated aversion to the worldly life, the returned pilgrim handled interviews with aplomb. She permitted the men and women of the Paris press to see in her what they wished: French heroine in the mode of Joan of Arc, magician, studious orientalist. The most amusing, and telling, of these interviews—by one Simone Tery—was not published until March 31, 1926, in *le Quotidien:*

Mme. David [*sic*] has the air of a very tranquil woman. She wears well a high bonnet of black velvet, strange, pushed down on her head, which serves to bring out the pallor of her face—but, this detail aside, she resembles the average French housewife [literally, "all the mothers of families"]. She speaks in a soft voice, a little sharp, without ever raising her voice, as though she were telling her neighbor about the illnesses of her children or [trading] kitchen recipes. Mme. David has a horror of "chic," of lyricism and easy success.

For journalists of her day and would-be biographers of ours, the handiest means of coping with this character *formidable* who had broken the implicit rules against a woman thinking and acting heroically was to domesticate her, to pretend she was like other women after all except rather bizarre, a bit freaky. Along with this view goes the notion that Alexandra was the plaything of some imperious Destiny. Indeed, Philip Neel lamented that for his wife, "It would be difficult to resume the role of a *petite bourgeoise,* with its domestic preoccupations and cares." But he understood it was because she had freely chosen a life of study and discipline, of adventure and loneliness.

Tery's remarks on Yongden were, as we might expect, racist:

He is dressed in a monk's habit, small and squat, with an impassive face, a small flat nose and narrow and alert eyes. He speaks of things in Tibetan, moving very rapidly his ten sharp fingers. Then he intones some weird chants to make your skin crawl, interspersed with inhuman cries.

The article concluded by suggesting the duo ought to have ahead a stunning career in music halls. In this regard the reporter perceived a bit of the truth. For two years after her reentry, Alexandra became once again a performer, although in the guise of an itinerant lecturer. First, worrying over Mouchy's health and the misunderstanding between them, she pressed for a meeting with her husband. This was finally achieved shortly before Christmas 1925 in a side parlor of the Hotel Terminus, near the railway station at Marseilles, neutral ground.

Indirectly we know a good deal about the "very unfriendly conversation" that ensued between Philip and Alexandra. Yongden was a witness, along with whomever else happened to overhear. The engineer, in his midsixties, retained a dapper appearance. His hair had turned completely gray, although he blackened his mustache. However, *monsieur*'s boiled collar and stickpin-in-the-cravat elegance was hopelessly out of date in the 1920s. Albert—the anglicized version of Yongden's first name—usually dressed in a more *au courant* striped suit and tie, which fit his stubby frame without grace. Only in the guise of a tantric lama, a *tulku,* did he appear handsome, slightly resembling the late Maharaja Sidkeong.

These days when traveling, Alexandra favored a prim suit, starched white blouse, and a beret set squarely on her broad forehead. Beneath the amply cut clothes her body remained slimmer than it had been. But the coquettishly plump figure that could be enhanced by the latest

Parisian mode remained only a distant memory of Philip's. This woman, strange to him, her face deeply lined from exposure to harsh weather, eyes keen but hard, resembled some errant uncle returned from a voyage to far shores and set to relate his lengthy, incredible tales.

After meaningless kisses on both cheeks and the obvious exchanges, Alexandra would have to break the ice. She began to extol the virtues of the younger man. "It is eleven years that we have been together in the wilds. A number of times we have seen death whiz by our heads. As a matter of honor, you must help me adopt the boy who I already treat as my son."

"I won't stop you," Philip replied—as he later insisted. "I can't think it a good idea from any point of view, but I don't uphold this law that demands you obtain my permission."

"I thought to have a son would give you pleasure," Alexandra reminded him. "Albert could accompany you on your walks; he is very amusing."

What the young man of twenty-five said, or what he felt, has been nowhere recorded.

"I never opposed you," Philip insisted to his wife. "I gave you complete freedom to leave me, to roam around the world. I have helped you to satisfy your imperious taste for things Asiatic."

The Frenchman's glance toward Yongden showed he regarded him as a rival. Alexandra, aware her husband was concerned about "the misery of old age," may have turned wily. "Albert has proved his loyalty," she argued. "Isn't he to be preferred to some strange servant?"

Philip, writing about this memorable incident from Bone on March 23, 1927, claimed that he had surrendered in the precise words, "Do what you wish, I will give you the necessary authorization." Perhaps the negotiations broke down over the question of money. Alexandra, putting aside thoughts of America, was demanding a large sum to buy a house in the south of France. Philip may have taken umbrage at her offer that he could "come to stay in it whenever it pleases you." At any rate, the discussion flared into a quarrel, spilled into the lobby to the astonishment of the hotel guests, and ended out in the street with bitter words back and forth. Fortunately, Marseilles was not the sort of town to care greatly about a husband and wife fighting over a young man.

Did the street fight come to curses or blows? We can't know because Alexandra, embarrassed, had much of the correspondence from this period burned along with other material she considered compromising. We have this on private but impeccable authority. At any rate, the storm had blown over by March of the following year when Philip agreed to wire her six thousand francs toward her living expenses. Her inheritance had already been eaten up by the postwar inflation. Alexandra thanked Mouchy from the bottom of her heart and added the following significant words: "I need to have a free mind to compose a work far more complex than a mere recounting of an adventure."

To make ends meet, and for the publicity, Alexandra was obliged to give a series of conferences. These began at the Sorbonne in the autumn of 1925, under the sponsorship of Professor Levi, and they proved both colorful and enormously successful. In the same lecture hall where she had sat as a student, an overflow audience listened breathlessly as "the first white woman to reach Lhasa"—the phrase is hers—told a tale of daring, disguise, and hardihood, and even let drop morsels of information on the secret, exotic tantric rites. Still, she was careful to strike a dispasssionate pose.

To Alexandra's surprise, Yongden upstaged his mother and brought crowds to their feet cheering his improvisations of Tibetan poetry. She claimed he had picked up his style from watching Tagore. Declaiming in his lama's outfit, his poetry—which she would translate—was filled with "mountains red as coral, skies blue as turquoise, conch-white palaces . . ." Or the young lama would enthrall his listeners with an anecdote of *ngagspas* grinding human bones into life-prolonging powders.

That winter the pair toured the south. They packed the large municipal casino at Nice, then went on to Marseilles and Toulon. Handsome in colorful, flowing Tibetan robes, Alexandra received from her audiences all the acclaim bestowed on a renowned diva. But she did not bask in her triumph. She hated living in hotels, and the rooms were expensive. At Paris she had solved the problem of accommodations by setting up her yak-hair tent in the garden of the Guimet and moving right in! The best she could do in the provinces was to pull the mattress off the bed and sleep on the floor.

Returning to Paris in the following spring, Alexandra spoke before standing room crowds at the Collège de France, the Guimet, and the Theosophical Society. To vary the show, and likely put Yongden in the shade, she introduced slides made from her striking photos of nomadic men and women, merchants with wares, so-called devil dancers in masks, monasteries like fortresses, and the huge snowcapped Himalayas. Alexandra had taken hundreds of photos and had asked Yongden to snap many of her, in order to document their travels. Perhaps viewing these made her homesick, because although she was off to Lausanne, Brussels, and London for additional conferences and more applause, deep down she felt bereft. Dr. A. d'Arsonval of the Collège de France, a leading psychologist and at once the orientalist's academic sponsor and her doctor, diagnosed the malady as colitis brought on by "nostalgia for the country and life [she] left." Or as Alexandra put it to Philip, "I am a savage, my dearest . . . I love only my tent, my horses and the wilds."

Neurasthenia threatened once again, even while the author recounted "the happiest days of my life when . . . I wandered as one of the countless tribe of Tibetan beggar-pilgrims." She wrote up to sixteen hours per day in various nondescript hotel rooms. The initial article for *Asia*—her most effective short piece—appeared in March 1926. The five-part series, collectively titled "A Woman's Daring Journey into Tibet," formed not only the skeletal outline of Alexandra's first important book but its heart and soul. She was working so diligently to complete the full-length work that in March 1927, at Toulon, she contracted an eye inflammation that blinded her for a week. Then, peering out of one eye, she resumed editing the proofs. *My Journey to Lhasa* was supposed to be issued simultaneously that spring by Plon in Paris, Heinemann in London, and Harper in New York. Actually the English language editions appeared in early fall, the somewhat abridged French in November.

Luree Miller has pointed out that *Journey* "has a style and spirit never excelled in her [Alexandra's] next twenty books." She wisely observed:

Included were all the ingredients of a fantastic adventure: traveling in disguise; mistaken identities . . . a faithful companion . . . dangers to Alexandra's life . . . miraculous escapes accomplished by cleverness and an almost supernatural good luck; final victory over every obstacle; and her happiness secured.

Contemporaneous reviews of *Journey* were universally favorable but more mundane. The *New York Times* declared that "as a traveler she [Alexandra] has performed a brilliant feat." In London The *Saturday Review* found the work "a thoroughly absorbing tale," while in more sober style The *Times Literary Supplement* felt certain the author had imparted "a considerable measure of useful and trustworthy information." Sir Francis Younghusband reviewed the book for the *Journal* of the Royal Geographical Society from a unique perspective. Just two years earlier he had compiled General Pereira's diaries into a consistent narrative entitled *Peking to Lhasa*. Few Westerners knew Tibet better than Sir Francis.

The "short, stocky, and warmly gruff little man with a bristling moustache"—Alan Watts's description—who in 1936 was to convene the World Congress of Faiths, and who leaned toward mystical ideas, appears to have missed the essential nature of Alexandra's writing. After the obligatory praise of her daring and courage, he complained, "The geographical results are very meagre, for there is no map attached to the book and no means of knowing exactly what route she took." In contrast, Pereira traveled over six thousand miles continuously, mapped every step of the way, and died of exhaustion. It was no accident that his precise map of Tibet and western China was sent to the British War Office and reproduced by their permission. This exploring by military officers was no mere academic avocation, and it is ironic that the British should have supposed Alexandra to be a spy.

Journey, recently reissued in both Britain and the United States, has become once again the subject of reviews. The feminist element is clearer now, an appreciation of the lone woman's winning out over nature and empire. Alexandra's example has inspired women to take to the rugged out-of-doors and even to scale Himalayan peaks. Unfortunately, feminists too have treated this seminal work as "the sort of thriller-yarn that keeps you up all night and is too soon over." Perhaps, her readers have been overly taken with Alexandra's "I will not be conquered!" pose.

Journey to Lhasa is a pilgrim's tale, and if we would travel there, especially today, we must do so in the realm of the spirit. This is a book of exploration but only secondarily of terrain. The pair of pilgrims on their way to the holy city, forbidden to outlanders, plumbed the depths of their physical endurance, their wit and comprehension, their faith in anything at all. On a deeper level, *Journey* is of the genre of spiritual autobiography, comparable to the tales told by and of the enlightened souls of other religions. The eighteenth-century Hassid Rabbi Nachman also overcame disaster after disaster—some of his own making— to pilgrimage to Jerusalem. He too donned disguises, lied or cheated when necessary, but always he was careful to perform the proper rites to propitiate a God jealous of outlandish success.

Madame David-Neel, Asian son in tow, voyaged to the most austere regions on earth and within the self. She loved the lad with the fierce love of a mother tiger for her cub. On the edge of the hostile Po country, unknown even to explorers, the pair had to hole up in a cave while Yongdon nursed his badly dislocated ankle. They hadn't a morsel to eat, and wet and shivering, they wondered when the snow would stop falling and if they would end as a meal for the wolves. Yet, Alexandra wrote,

Had it not been for my concern for my young companion, I should have found a peculiar charm in my situation. Indeed, that charm was so powerful that it triumphed over my preoccupations and my physical discomfort. Until late that night I remained seated, motionless, enjoying the delights of my solitude in the absolute silence, the perfect stillness of that strange white land, sunk in rest, in utter peace.

The snow continued to fall as the voyager sat, making no effort to peer beyond its gauzy curtain into the uncertain future. Mind stilled, for a timeless instant seer and seen became one. Finally, at this desperate juncture, Alexandra reached the *samadhi* sought by the yogi through meditation, the union devoutly prayed for by the mystic Christian. Seeing by the clear light of wisdom, she glimpsed the Void from which all stems and into which all dissolves.

Still, there is a limit to the spiritual intimacy that Alexandra allowed her readers. Rather than truly follow Emerson's dictum "My life is for itself and not for a spectacle," the former opera singer stage-managed what she was willing to show. In matters delicate or profound, she often employed the "twilight language" typical of the Tantra, symbols with a double meaning. All in all, *Journey* is a voyage in space and self that bears comparison with Lanza Del Vasto's *Return to the Source* or Gurdjieff's *Conversations with Remarkable Men*. These seekers through exploring the world about them illumined an inner terrain. They do not provide the usual sort of guidelines, but if maps of their wanderings were drawn they would resemble the mariner's charts of the early ages of exploration: colorful, lacking detail, and slightly fantastic. The intent, rather than to mislead, is to direct the reader to unexpected places.

Sales of Alexandra's seminal work were healthy—nine French editions within two years—and translations were made into a number of languages, including German, Czech, Italian, and Spanish. The Americans, who compared this supposed Amazon with the conquerors of the North and South Poles, were especially partial to the book. "[They] can appreciate my sort of courage," she boasted. Instantly she thought of sailing to New York to reap more laurels and enormous royalties. Not so incidentally, the dollar was very strong in relation to the franc, in the ratio of one to fifty. However, the web of events was drawing the author in a different direction.

The French were quick to applaud their own, awarding honors and subsidies to Alexandra. First came the silver medal of the Belgian Royal Geographic Society, then the Chevalier of the Legion of Honor and the gold medal of the Société Géographique. To the latter was attached a much-appreciated six thousand francs. One award that Alexandra accepted tongue-in-cheek was the grand prize for feminine athleticism from the French Sports Academy. A great lover of the outdoors, she couldn't consider herself an athlete nor trekking through Tibet a sport. Ironically, she received the medal in May 1927 when, hobnobbing with the literati in Paris, she felt she was suffocating and her heart troubled her. Her feet grew red and swollen from wearing high heels. "What a horror these big cities are!" she complained to Philip.

As long ago as her "Huron hut" in the Himalayas, Alexandra had dreamed of acquiring a home with enough land on which to grow vegetables. Turning, for the time being, from thoughts of America, she focused on the south of France, although not the coast, which she considered overbuilt. In the fall she went on a walking tour of the Basses Alpes above the Riviera—prescribed by Dr. d'Arsonval to regain her health—and there the keen-eyed traveler discovered a likely spot. The German edition of *Journey* had netted ten thousand francs, and in addition she was able to sell several articles, the most noteworthy being a contribution to *Man and His World*, a reference work edited by Paul Reclus. He was the nephew of Elisée, Alexandra's old mentor from student days. For a change she had money, but she was careful to keep

Philip informed. According to French law she might buy a house on her own, but if she wished to sell she would need her husband's permission.

Not just any location would do. Occasionally Alexandra liked to damn civilization and its works—"There is nothing good but wild plants, mountains, the sky and the clouds." Yet she insisted that her new home be accessible by rail and served by electricity. "It's necessary for my success," she reminded Philip, "that my dwelling can be seen by people, journalists and foreign visitors . . . on whom it must make a good impression. . . . I needn't remind you our time demands publicity, a certain appearance . . ."

In May 1928, outside the quiet spa town of Digne, ninety-five miles northwest of Nice, Alexandra purchased a small villa on a hill with a good view of the surroundings. She named it Samten Dzong, Fortress of Meditation. Her description of the locale was succinct: "The countryside is very pretty and my property is admirably situated. In front of my door the road to Nice, lined with trees, offers me a beautiful promenade overlooking the river below, with mountains in the background." She quickly installed herself and Yongden, and it made her proud to inform Philip, "In my house you are equally at home as in your own."

Samten Dzong did become a refuge for the sixty-year-old orientalist, although for work rather than contemplation. The series of books on Tibet she was planning to write nearly fell victim to a surfeit of approbation. French president Gaston Doumergue, a moderate elected in 1924, became a great admirer of his redoubtable countrywoman. "I believe that our century belongs to Asia," he wrote, urging her to hurry along her writing so he might read her books. The president made available to the author sixty thousand francs to undertake a mission through Siberia into Mongolia to study the tribes of Soviet Central Asia, in particular the effect of the revolution on women. Additionally, she long had been fascinated by the interaction between Buddhism and native shamanism.

Turmoil in the areas she needed to visit caused Moscow to refuse Alexandra a visa. Stalled, she appealed to her friend, the writer and internationalist Romain Rolland, who interceded with the Soviet delegation to the League of Nations at Geneva. Their Minister of Education Lounatcharski seemed more kindly disposed, and gleefully forgetting all else, the would-be traveler began to make arrangements. Shortly the minister fell from grace and was shot. In the end, the applicant received the famous Russian *nyet*.

This apparent setback proved fortunate. Alexandra had to swallow her disappointment, while she kept open her contacts with the French government; she would need their backing for future expeditions. No more eager to chain herself to a desk than many other authors, she surrounded herself with her unique collection of Tibetan books, her superb, demonic masks, and other souvenirs of fourteen years of wandering on the roof of the world—not least of these being Yongden. Alexandra commenced on the next decade of fruitful study and writing.

CHAPTER 23

The Short Path

Digne, a small cathedral town of winding streets, is best known from a memorable episode in Victor Hugo's *Les Misérables*. Here the exconvict Jean Valjean stole silver candlesticks from the bishop who had befriended him. Out of pity, the good cleric lied to the police, saying he gave the candlesticks away. Digne has thermal baths dating to Roman times, and at eighteen hundred feet, a nearly perfect climate. The waters are said to be beneficial for chronic rheumatism.

During the summer of 1928, once she settled into Samten Dzong, Alexandra's misgivings cropped up. She let Philip know the surrounding mountains were too skimpy for her taste. "These are Himalayas for Lilliputians!" she quipped. There were trees on the property, but she and Yongden would plant additional ones: cherry, pear, chestnut, and lime. If the neighborhood wasn't wildly picturesque, at least the sun shone year round and she could sleep on a rug on a roofed-over terrace.

The country around Digne could boast of magnificent wildflowers. With Yongden, Alexandra explored the mountain paths, admiring gentian, edelweiss, and marguerites, but especially fields of lavender. She endorsed the air over that of the seaside, and she begged Philip to visit before the winter. People were scarce; only a couple of houses stood anywhere near, and their inhabitants gave the woman and her Asian son a wide berth. Pen and paper were the company she most desired.

Alexandra planted a vegetable plot at her new hermitage. Her first crop would turn out to be a bumper one and she could sell the excess. Growing her own food suited her pioneering nature and appeased an increasingly frugal streak she inherited from her mother. In the East, she became used to pinching pennies, and although currently prosperous, she didn't forget the lean years. Once her Eastern acquisitions were thoroughly installed, she intended to work with the speed of a *kyang* bounding over the Tibetan plateau.

The householder ordered Philip to ship various "*objets orientaux*" that he saved for her, including her voluminous letters, the only true *journal de voyage* she had made. Surprisingly, she had kept a meticulous inventory of every object sent to her husband, down to numbering each of the hundreds of photos. Where was the quilt from her student days, and books by her favorite authors Flaubert, Anatole France, Jules Verne, and Tolstoy? He might dawdle over these but he must immediately send her bicycle. "The roads here are pretty," she admitted, "and I would love to once again pedal a little."

By the end of the year, Alexandra was as snug in her sun-dappled retreat as she had been at snowy Lachen. She wrote Philip that "the site where I have planted my tent" pleased her better. Alexandra was growing more distant from her academic mentor, Sylvain Levi, who was chiding her for not devoting herself entirely to works of philosophy. He had suggested she do a philological study of Tibetan literature, not unconnected with his own labors on a dictionary of Buddhism. The orientalist realized that the authority of her statements rested on how well she stood with the professors, never mind they didn't dare venture into Tibet. But works for a select audience failed to pay expenses, and these were mounting alarmingly as she renovated Samten Dzong. Without a university salary, the author deemed it impractical to write "for the love of art."

Levi was also angry that his former pupil didn't turn over to him certain rare manuscripts. D'Arsonval, who had superseded him as Alexandra's patron, wrote her amusingly, "Levi . . . cares for you very much and is put out that you won't give him some old papyrus to gnaw. These library rats periodically suffer from lack of vitamins." The author, ignoring the rivalry between the two men, worked diligently. In 1929 Plon brought out the French version of the book that would be titled *Magic and Mystery in Tibet* when published in New York in 1932. This has proved David-Neel's most durable, popular, and widely translated work, being rendered into Portuguese (Brazil), Hungarian, and Annamite (Vietnam), as well as the Scandinavian and other European languages. Here, despite an assumed air of detachment, the author discussed those "spiritual sportsmen" close to her heart, adepts of the Short Path to Deliverance who risk its dangers in order to win enlightenment in one lifetime.

The Short or Direct Path, according to Alexandra, "is considered as most hazardous." The results of failure "mean a spiritual fall leading to the lowest and worst degree of aberration and perversity to the condition of a demon." Clearly, this doctrine of complete freedom can be subject to abuse, especially since its founder, or really its translator to Tibet, Padma Sambhava, was a tantric magician of the Left Hand. Alexandra found that those who claimed to be on the Short Path ranged the spiritual and even the social spectrum: "Sorcerers, soothsayers, necromancers, occultists from the meanest beggarly class to those of high social standing, can be met with among them." Fortunately for us, she was acquainted with every sort of Tibetan, from the Dalai and Panchen Lamas to the lowest cutthroat brigands.

Alexandra was not the first Westerner to discuss the arcane lore of tantric Buddhism. The British officer L. A. Waddell had written on its cults, symbolism, and mythology, and although an untiring researcher, his obvious prejudices tainted his findings. Supposing that in Tibet he had come upon the work of the devil, Waddell found it all the more fascinating. To our knowledge the Frenchwoman was the first to actively participate in Tibetan tantric rites, including those of the Left Hand, and to report back on them. The *chod* rite, for example, an extremely hazardous practice, was known but spoken of in a whisper. David Snellgrove and the Italian scholar-explorer Giuseppe Tucci wrote about it only from hearsay. Alexandra, meanwhile, actually performed a mild version of *chod*, and we believe continued to practice it after her return to France.

She began to experiment with elements of the rite under the supervision of the Gomchen of Lachen. Although she understood its symbolic nature, an incident from *Magic and Mystery* shows how Alexandra's detachment fled when she witnessed a practitioner go berserk while acting out "the dreadful mystic banquet." The rite is a one-person drama, chanted while dancing ritual steps to a drum made from two human skulls, skin stretched over them and pellets attached; it is played with one hand like a rattle. A trumpet made of a human thighbone is also played, and magical implements are manipulated: the *dorje*, or thunderbolt symbol, and the *tilpu*, a small handbell, as well as a three-sided dagger used to stab demons. Coordination is essential, and the performance must be rehearsed to go according to formula, because a misstep or hesitation could prove fatal.

Traditionally, ascetics from Kham, *naljorpas* whose hair plaited into a single braid fell nearly to their feet, were masters of *chod*. On her travels through the borderlands, Alexandra had watched them dance under an infinite starry sky to the throb of drums and wail of the trumpets. They looked like the demons they called upon as they strained every sinew into intricate contortions. Their faces shone as they ecstatically trampled down their own feverish egos, daring death itself in the effort to halt what Buddhists term the mad race toward mirages. The initiate understood that the demons envisioned were imagined, but in the trancelike state these symbols became realities to the practitioner. An old lama told Alexandra, "One must know how to protect oneself against the tigers to which one has given birth, as well as against those that have been begotten by others."

Once, camped among cowherds in northern Tibet, Alexandra happened on a funeral. She stayed to witness the ceremonies, but she was even more intrigued by a nearby ascetic, Rabjoms Gyatso, who had established himself in a cave and was attended by two disciples, one nearly a skeleton. Alexandra guesed that the emaciated lama was performing *chod* as part of his spiritual practice, and she knew it was best acted out in a cemetery or other wild spot where a fresh corpse had been disposed.

Along with a large gathering of Tibetans, the foreign lama ate and drank copiously before the corpse, which was placed in a seated position in a large caldron. Friends of the deceased arrived from all directions to bring presents to the bereaved family. Rabjoms Gyatso's disciples read religious books over the dead man, after which he was carried to a likely spot in the mountains. The body would be "cut into pieces and abandoned there, as supreme alms to the vultures."

Alexandra, herself dressed in the costume of a *naljorpa,* waited until dark, and walked to the place to spend the night meditating under a full moon. She was musing on "the strange mind of the race that has invented *chod* and so many other grim practices," when on approaching the cemetery, she heard hoarse cries rising above an insistent drumbeat. "This language was clear enough to me." Hiding in the cleft of a hillock, she recognized the tantric master's wasted-looking disciple. Playing his role in the macabre drama on an apparently deserted stage, he jerked his frame into frenzied postures. He accompanied this dance with aggressive staccato yells, which summoned the demons to feast on his carcass.

Having rehearsed, the *chod* celebrant is acting in a sense. He is to imaginatively create a feminine deity who, sword in hand, will cut off the actor's head, while troops of ghouls hover around clamoring for their banquet. Then the merciless goddess severs his limbs, flays his torso, and rips open his belly. Bowels falling out, the aspirant must urge on the hideous beings to attack with invocations of surrender. No doubt, as Thubten Norbu, former abbot of Kum Bum, has pointed out, the ceremony derives from human sacrifice in early times.

"[F]or the adept performing the rite of *Chod,*" adds Norbu, "there is a very terrible reality to the demoniacal form that advances upon him to sever his head." The celebrant may easily lose hold of himself and the ritual, acutely feeling the pangs being recited. Should the actor, weak from fasting, drop the thread, he would likely go mad or die indeed. A celebrant hopes to follow through the ritual, to see himself as a heap of charred bones, to let go of the illusion of existence.

Alexandra watched as the emaciated monk adopted a defiant stance. She heard him exclaim, "I, the fearless *naljorpa,* I trample down the self, the gods, and the demons." He whirled, genuflected to the four corners, and stamped wildly as he followed the formula to vanquish anger, lust, and stupidity. All the while he stared at pieces of the previous day's corpse strewn before him.

The disciple soon became muddled. He entered the small tent he had erected, leaving the corpse to a natural wolf come down from the hills to feast on it. But the apprentice wizard, hearing the animal growl, took it for a demon. "I pay my debts!" he cried out. "As I have been feeding on you, so feed upon me in your turn!" Furiously blowing his trumpet, he jumped up and collapsed the tent on top of himself. When he struggled free, face madly contorted, he was howling with the pain of being bitten. Even the wolf became frightened, staring as though it too saw the host of ghouls surrounding them.

Alexandra felt that the young man had lost his mind and her pose as disinterested observer wouldn't do. Giving way to sympathy rather than compassion, she rushed toward him. "Come, angry one, feed on my flesh!" he howled. "Drink my blood!" The poor fellow took her for a hungry ghost from a Tibetan hell.

Intervention had already made matters worse. The lad tripped on a tent peg and fell heavily to the ground. Alexandra ran off to inform Lama Rabjoms, although as she makes clear, it was because "*I* could not bear it any longer." Guided by a feeble light from an altar lamp high on a nearby hillside, she found the cave. She saw the master seated cross-legged in deep meditation but still let fly her news about his disciple.

The *naljorpa*, smiling calmly, asked, "You appear to know *chod*, Jetsunma. Do you really?"

When Alexandra insisted that the lama's disciple was on the point of dying from the illusion of being eaten, he replied, "No doubt he is, but he doesn't understand that he is himself the eater. Maybe he will learn it later on."

Alexandra began to regret her impetuous action. The lama, perhaps telepathically, had anticipated what she would say. He proceeded to lecture her good-naturedly, although they both agreed she had been trained in methods of the Short Path. Rabjoms reminded her of how hard it was to free oneself from illusions or the mind from fanciful beliefs. He was sure her path, although more refined than his disciple's, was equally difficult. "Did your spiritual teacher not inform you of the risks and did you not agree you were ready to run these three: illness, madness and death?" Chastened, Alexandra agreed, and she stayed on for several days to study with this tantric master.

The unwillingness of the Frenchwoman to suspend her faculty of criticism, to in a sense lose her mind, whatever obstacle it may have presented among the Tibetans was hailed as admirable once she returned to Paris. In his introduction to *Magic and Mystery*, Dr. d'Arsonval wrote of her, "This Easterner, this complete Tibetan, has nevertheless remained a Westerner, a disciple of Descartes and of Claude Bernard, practicing the philosophic scepticism [that] should be the constant ally of the scientific observer. Unencumbered by any preconceived theory, and unbiased by any doctrine or dogma, Madame David-Neel has observed everything in Tibet in a free and impartial spirit."

D'Arsonval, a professor at the elite Collège de France, was president of the Institut Général Psychologique, and his imprimatur on Alexandra's work was intended to remove it from the realm of the mystical or occult. So in her lectures at the Collège, the orientalist donned the mask of detachment, of the reporter rather than the participant, summing up with the remark, "Psychic training, rationally and scientifically conducted, can lead to desirable results. That is why the information gained about such training . . . constitutes useful documentary evidence worthy of our attention."

Fortunately, *Magic and Mystery* is written in a far more sprightly style reminiscent of the traveler's original articles in *Asia*. It introduces us to a gallery of intriguing real-life characters: Dawasandup, the learned scholar but hopeless schoolmaster; the Gomchen of Lachen, who despite his frightening apron of human bones was a pushover for a pussy cat; and the maharaja of Sikkim, handsome, dashing, and vulnerable. We meet a whole gallery of lamas, *ngagspas,* and *naljorpas,* wise, magical, and sly. Of these the wearer of the rings of the initiate, our "learned lamina," is not the least subtle. About her own deeper self Alexandra would drop hints throughout her writings, but they are largely symbolic and must be watched for with the keenness of a cat eyeing a suspicious mousehole.

"My success is not a flash fire made from straw," the author informed her husband in March 1934. "It endures and is growing." During the years 1928 to 1936, except for an occasional conference in London, Belgium, Switzerland, or Eastern Europe, Alexandra remained at work at Samten Dzong. Other than Philip she didn't encourage visitors. Some came anyway, including a reporter from Milan dispatched at the behest of her old friend Mussolini to interview her. In April 1931 she responded to an invitation to visit the Italian dictator at the Villa Borghese, Rome. Professing no use for politics of any sort, she apparently was able to maintain a distant friendship with a clear conscience. Even Adolf Hitler took an interest in the orientalist's work. She claimed *der Führer* planned to attend one of her conferences, held in Berlin in 1936, but had to regretfully cancel at the last minute. The swastika, we may note, is an ancient symbol of lightning found in the ruins of Troy, among native American tribes, and especially in Tibet.

Hitler's fascination with the Land of Snows was of long standing, and as a mere corporal he was assigned to infiltrate a German cult concerned with Tibetan magical rites. According to Otto Rahn, his interest in David-Neel's investigations had a more practical side: he wished to learn more about *tumo,* the breath of inner heat. Was Hitler thinking of equipping his storm troopers with, in Milarepa's phrase, "the best clothing" in order to facilitate their invasion of the icy wastes of Russia? If so, the Nazi dictator failed to grasp the essentially spiritual nature of the practice.

Initiations and Initiates in Tibet appeared in its French edition in 1930, published by a smaller house, Adyar. Following so close on the heels of *Magic and Mystery,* it failed to achieve an equal popularity, and indeed Alexandra complained that foreign editions were being held up by the proximity of publishing dates. *Initiations,* denser and less anecdotal than its predecessor, remains indispensible to the serious student of tantric lore or even the do-it-yourself occultist. It contains far more precise observations and specific methods of Tibetan mysticism. Many of these mysterious and arduous practices were elucidated for the first time in the West, and by one who was herself an initiate and had intensely practiced several of them.

Alexandra was at pains to dispel the misconception that an initiation meant "the revelation of a secret doctrine, [or] admission to the knowledge of certain mysteries." True, it was usually preceded by lengthy preliminaries and testing of the disciple by his guru, sometimes nearly to the point of death. Also, initiations were accompanied by particular esoteric teachings. But, Alexandra insisted, "The *angkur* [initiation] is, above all, the transmission of a power, a force, by a kind of psychic process." It represents a step on the path to enlightenment. "The fruit of the initiations is the gift of being able to see more than the mass of men, to discover in all things what remains unperceived . . . to find out who *really* is the person we think ourselves to be and what really is the world in which we move."

Alexandra's knowledge of esoteric tantric methods was hard won, and because so much of traditional Tibet lies in ruins, it is improbable that her experience could be duplicated today. "Most initiates do not teach what they have learned," she wrote; "they even keep secret the fact that they have been initiated. They have taken an oath of silence regarding both these points, and this oath contains such dreadful imprecations that the perjurer would be reborn in hell." Did Alexandra take such an oath, and did the Gomchen of Lachen, her tantric master, give her permission to reveal to the world a cornucopia of secret knowledge, almost always passed on orally to a chosen few? Lama Govinda supposed that he had, and we must presume so.

However, Alexandra received along her way certain warnings. The mysterious lama who accosted the pilgrims just before they reached Lhasa demanded, "What have you done with your rings of the initiate?" In fact, she had hidden them both with her other jewelry in a small leather case. In *Initiations* she described them: "The *naljorpa* initiates wear rings adorned with these two emblems: a *dorje* [thunderbolt] on the gold ring worn on the right hand; a tiny bell on the silver ring worn on the left hand." The masculine *dorje* symbolizes method, the feminine handbell knowledge. It is their union that is represented by the statuary of intertwined couples in Tibetan Buddhist temples.

In the eighth century the great Padma Sambhava wielded only the *dorje* to tame and convert the native demons to Buddhism. Alexandra's possession of these rings stamped her as an adept, aspiring to be a *naljorpa,* which she herself defined as "He who is possessed of perfect serenity." Yongden, although ordained, was not permitted to listen to the conversation between his mother and the mysterious lama. Luree Miller implies that the lama was a fiction, or perhaps a projection of Alexandra's fears. At any rate, he reminded her of who she *really* was. They talked Buddhist metaphysics through the night, and after the lama departed, Alexandra initially hesitated but then marched on to Lhasa.

If *Initiations* may be thought of as elucidating in more technical guise the themes introduced in *Magic and Mystery,* then Alexandra's fourth book after her return, *Grand Tibet* (Paris, 1933), harks back to her first success; indeed, its English title *Tibetan Journey* makes the relationship quite clear. This is an account of the author's adventures upon leaving Kum Bum in 1921 to travel among the merchants, brigands, and varied desperados of the Sino-Tibetan borderlands. It is straightforward and enormously enjoyable and deserves a wider audience. We have recounted the period's more hair-raising episodes, and it remains to emphasize that Alexandra's daring was equally matched by her understanding of, and empathy for, the wild souls among whom she journeyed. Her responses to their aggressions were cool-headed and correct, leaving the boldest of brigands her admirers.

Captivated by the sensuality of "solitude, silence and virgin land, not parent to any culture, huge open spaces and [a] rude life under the tent," Alexandra came into her own. In an experience more archetypically American than European, the highly cultured woman, who yet was able to relate to the wildest of beasts, came face to face with brute uncaring nature, indeed became one with the primeval forces. No wonder she refered fondly to her childhood reading of James Fenimore Cooper, in whose novels, imperfectly executed though they may be, the overwhelming shock of the primitive on the civilized is made manifest. According to Jacques Brosse, a kind of Cooperian haste already had begun to show in the author's writing. In order to meet contract dates she fell into mistakes of orthography and other sloppy errors. But Alexandra worked best when under the pressure of a deadline, and each of these early books was written from an inner compulsion. We find no evidence of the patched-together quality of certain later works.

Of her several shorter efforts, "Women in Tibet" was an unmitigated triumph. She wrote to Philip concerning it in March 1933, immediately after returning from a highly successful conference at the nearby health resort of Gap. The proceeds of the talk, incidentally, went to fight tuberculosis, and this charitable side of Alexandra, which she herself kept quiet, is not well known. However, she didn't hesitate to boast that the widely published article "went all around the world." Female readers from countries as far apart as America and China were writing to her craving more information.

The piece analyzed the means by which Tibetan women mastered an exceptionally harsh environment and gained sway over their men. The women had achieved a de facto equality despite law and scripture unfavorable to them, this by virtue of innate independence and physical stamina. Tibetan women were clever and brave and therefore valued by their husbands. The tenor of the article showed that Alexandra remained a firm feminist—no less than during the period 1906 to 1908 when she had crusaded for the legal rights of housewives and unwed mothers, still more for their economic independence.

The most intriguing aspect of the article was the author's assertion that polyandry was widespread, if unadvertised, and that the women involved didn't necessarily suffer in body or status because of it. David Macdonald, in corroboration, mentioned certain cases among the peasantry where a woman married all the brothers in a family despite there being five or six! She would be expected to bear each a child, and the offspring would treat the eldest brother as father and the rest as uncles. Thubten Norbu contends that the custom exists to keep land in one family and is harmless. Clearly, it has helped to keep the population low, which proved disastrous for Tibet in confronting China.

Alexandra, with the help of Yongden, was at work on more abstruse topics. Their version of *The Superhuman Life of Gesar of Ling* appeared in 1931 in France and 1934 in London, published by Rider, the venerable purveyor of titles occult and Eastern. The author, writing first in French, had found a new translator, Violet Sydney, who remained her collaborator. Although Alexandra thought of her as a snob and sometimes criticized her translations, their relationship proved fruitful over the course of several books.

Gesar, recently reissued in English, ought to be better known, in particular to Americans, who in the course of this century have managed to fight three Asian wars. Alexandra, aside from repeating the long, flowery epic of chivalric heroism that she heard in Jyekundo, related a prophecy of deep importance to the Central Asian peoples. Gesar— so goes his legend—is bound to return in some guise and, at the point of his sword, first sweep the white man from Asia and then conquer his homeland. A well-educated Mongol monk, acting as secretary to a merchant at Peking, told Alexandra toward the close of World War I,

We have slept long, while he, the Invincible, was resting; but we shall waken for his return. To the conquest of the world, he will lead the millions of Asiatics who, today, are drowsing. On the one hand, we shall throw back into the sea those insolent Whites whom the Chinese have so weakly allowed to establish themselves with them as masters; on the other hand, we shall invade their countries in the West, and everywhere the cleansing army will have passed nothing will remain, no, not even a blade of grass!

She was stunned by this vision of a new Genghis Khan, although Mongols, Tibetans, and some Chinese concur in the certainty of his return. The prophecy may be fanatical, but after Mao's revolution, after Japan's rise to industrial preeminence, who would say it is out of the question? Millions of Asians believe in this bloody second coming, and the Soviet Russians appear to fear it.

In a very different vein is Alexandra's *Buddhism: Its Doctrines and Its Methods,* which appeared in France in 1936 and in English in 1939, and which once again is in print in the United States. In his foreword to this edition, Christmas Humphreys, the respected British Buddhist, has written, "This is an outstanding work almost unknown to the Western student of Buddhism. . . . In it they [*sic*] may see . . . the principles of the oldest school of Buddhism, that of the Theravada as practiced in Sri Lanka, Burma and Thailand, viewed by a mind learned in one of the later traditions, that of Tibet." Humphreys added that, since she had authored several books on Tibet, he was surprised when David-Neel turned back to the first principles of her adopted faith.

Humphreys met Alexandra in 1936 on the occasion of one of her conferences in Nice. They discussed the work at length, yet he apparently did not realize that it was mostly a rehash of her *Modern Buddhism* published previous to the Great War and her sojourn in Central Asia. The tract was ignored at the time, and as early as 1926 the triumphant orientalist thought of redoing it. Editors in several capitals were clamoring for any manuscript of hers. By the midthirties demand had waned as Europe was faced with the rise of fascism. That Alexandra was able to squeeze in this project during her busy decade is in itself remarkable. However, she merely borrowed much of the text from the earlier work, interlarding Tibetan variants concerned with the central themes of Buddhism. The result is as dry as melba toast save for the faint flavor of youthful idealism.

Here is Alexandra the rationalist. We can find no tales of anchorites performing wonders in rude caves high above the earth, no dashing brigands or celebrants in gorgeous robes performing ancient rituals, no *naljorpas* meddling with cadaver pieces in wild places otherwise inhabited by vultures. Instead we are treated to Alexandra's distillation of the Buddhist doctrine into a two-page chart. Her lengthy discussion of karma is useful, emphasizing that the concept has nothing to do with the Western idea of destiny, but rather depends on free will. It may be summarized in the Buddhist admonition: "By pure deeds man becomes pure; by evil deeds he becomes evil." This was a message the world needed to hear.

Toward the close of *Buddhism*, apparently swept away by her Tibetan memories, Alexandra lapsed into a spirited discussion of the *Bardo Thodol*, said to stem from Padma Sambhava himself, the magician savior. *Bardo* means "between two" and refers to the state between death and rebirth. "In Tibet," wrote the tantrist, "the art of dying skilfully—and, I will add, profitably—is considered of the highest importance." It is held that the last thoughts of a dying person determine whether he or she will be reborn propitiously and may wipe away a lifetime of selfish or even bad acts. Thus a lama will whisper directions on which course to take into the ear of an expiring person, who will strive mightily to remain conscious to the end.

In *Buddhism* Alexandra wrote, "My old travelling companion and fellow student, the scholarly Tibetan, Dawasandup, in whose company I have ridden so far in the Himalayas, going from one monastery to another, has made an English translation of one of the versions of the *Bardo Thodol*." After Dawasandup's passing away from the heat in Calcutta, Evans-Wentz published the translation with commentary as the well-known *Tibetan Book of the Dead*. But according to the Oxford scholar, Alexandra not only made fun of the Tibetan but stole from him. In *Tibetan Yoga*, discussing another rare manuscript called "The Precious Rosary," he noted, "Copious extracts from our own version or from a very similar version of this work were published by Madame A. David-Neel in the appendix to *Initiations and Initiates in Tibet* (London, 1931)." It might have been coincidence, but these texts were exceedingly rare and prized. Dawasandup had obtained several, and most of his knowledge, from his guru, a venerable and learned hermit in Bhutan, where it may be recalled the Frenchwoman was forbidden to enter. Had she taken her revenge by plagiarizing the relatively obscure Tibetan? This appendix was dropped from later editions of *Initiations*.

Two significant reconciliations occurred during Alexandra's middle years. The first was with her origins and unhappy youth. In the summer of 1934 she visited Brussels in order to pay her respects at the grave of her parents. Perhaps she was moved to weep; she never said. She admitted that the rancor of an earlier time had gone: her father, despite his reserve, she always loved, and now she could see her mother as a victim of circumstances. Next, possessed by nostalgia, she visited her old boarding school, and then a seaside village where as a teenager she had been taken on vacation and from which she sneaked away to England. How fervently she had wished to explore the wide world! Presently, she told Philip, "I find Belgium rather unsightly, but she stole my heart and I recognized my native land."

More urgently, Alexandra achieved a rapprochement with "dear

Mouchy." Their correspondence had gone on unabated during her travels, at least whenever there was a post office, and it ran the gamut from affection and concern to raging hostility. Philip appears to have given as good as he got. In the end, he sent the money and his moral support. Now their letters back and forth waxed mellow. On occasion the aging, still debonair gentleman traveled from Algeria to visit his wife at Digne.

Alexandra urged her husband to make more frequent and longer stays. In an invitation dated October 7, 1934, she assured Philip, "You will find your customary bedroom well-heated." She insisted he spend the entire winter at Samten Dzong. If he became bored with their walks and chats about old times, he could take the train down to the casino at Nice. Alexandra signed off "very affectionately" and meant it.

During the same year the orientalist, feeling she must accomplish a more scholarly work to enhance her reputation, but begrudging the time and lack of recompense, set Yongden to roughing out a translation of a major text by Tsong Khapa, founder of the Yellow Hats. The result she meant to dedicate to Sylvain Levi, who hadn't long to live. Yongden bogged down in the archaic Tibetan and Alexandra decided they needed help. "I must hurry," she informed Philip, a bit incongruously. "The Italian Orientalist, Prof. Tucci, is working on the same book, obliging me to beat him to the book stores."

Alexandra attempted to solve the problem by declaring she and her son would leave at once for Peking. In the Tibetan temple there they might find a well-versed lama to assist them. If not, they could look elsewhere. Surely this was an excuse to return to Asia, which she had been plotting since 1926. She had even considered crossing the steppes with an expedition of mercy funded by Citroën, the Yellow Cross, which was to encompass thirty cars and trucks, two hundred pack camels, and dozens of French volunteers. She abandoned the scheme, admitting it struck her as more dangerous than going alone.

It took Alexandra nearly three additional years to complete her work at Digne and to raise funds through her royalties and a grant from the French Ministry of Education. On January 9, 1937, a glacially cold night, the pair of pilgrims boarded an express at the Gare du Nord bound for Berlin, Warsaw, Moscow, and the Far East. "Without a whistle, in the surrounding silence, the train slipped from the station . . . and we penetrated a deep gloom, a night of low sky lacking a moon or stars where only the pale gleam of individual snowflakes falling on the fields and rooftops of invisible houses pierced the darkness."

CHAPTER 24

Storm Clouds

"I have left many times without ever arriving," wrote Alexandra, the indefatigable traveler, "and the great departure that each [passing] day brings closer will certainly not lead me to any definite place where I may rest forever." Such words might have made the motto for this woman, a perpetual seeker both physically and intellectually. Yet beginning on her new, and final, great adventure brought her no comfort. Rather, on the train she chafed at having to wear pajamas and to sleep under blankets that had covered countless others. She raged at the passport requirements that had replaced letters of introduction to local notables.

Alexandra and Yongden stopped briefly in Warsaw, "under a grey, leaden sky," to see pictures of themselves in bookstore windows. This did not lessen her feeling of impending doom, of menacing influences. Considering the destruction that soon enough would overtake this city with its crammed Jewish ghetto, Alexandra may be forgiven for her morbidity. But in fact she was preoccupied with the *Bardo Thodol,* the Tibetan *Book of the Dead,* and certain of its occult theories, which she applied to herself. "When the 'soul' has left the body," she noted cryptically, "the person is really 'dead,' though the body may for a time accomplish the habitual acts of the living."

Russia, next, at this season was hardly likely to bring cheer to the pilgrim's heart. As a small child, its snowy immensity had fascinated her. As a young radical in Paris, tales of czarist cruelty had reached her through exiled intellectuals. Then, after the revolution, the Soviet Union became the mecca for those desiring drastic social change. Thus it was out of a long-held curiosity that Alexandra booked a day's tour of Moscow—at the depth of Stalin's purges.

She found the station heavily guarded and the porters wooden and mute. Her female Intourist guide, who spoke perfect English, brushed aside her suggested itinerary in favor of a rushed tour of factories, capped by Lenin's tomb and accompanied by a recital of the party line.

Afterward, the guide deposited the weary travelers at a fancy hotel where indifferent waitresses served up overpriced ham and eggs. Alexandra understood immediately that the average Russian couldn't afford these prices and that the revolution by no means had abolished the antagonistic classes of servant and those who could afford to be served.

The entire population appeared weighed down by a lassitude of spirit. With only a couple hours left before their departure, the pair were kept busy filling out a multitude of forms. Alexandra had not expected to find a heaven on earth, but daily life in the socialist republic impressed her as a poor comedy, with worse food and no manners. She was delighted to claim her seat on the next express bound for Vladivostok. "Ah, enchanting Asia," she sighed as she settled in for the long ride across Siberia, "I want to squeeze you in my arms, friend of my youth!"

Indeed, China was an old, deep love of hers, but she should have known such affairs are difficult to renew.

On the next to last day of 1937, Alexandra was having a pleasant lunch on a terrace with a French doctor in Hankow, a port city up the Yangtse River. It had been nearly a year since she and her son had boarded the trans-Siberian express, bound east. Six months earlier the simmering tension between Japan and China had burst into the flames of war. Forces of the Rising Sun, already in control of Manchuria, advanced rapidly south of the Great Wall. Europeans caught deep in the country generally headed for the seacoast cities where their home countries maintained concessions with extraterritorial rights. Those remaining within the folds of the stricken giant, whose power seemed paralyzed, found themselves glancing toward the skies from which death might descend with the swiftness of a thunderbolt.

Both Alexandra and Yongden (because he carried a British passport) could have been evacuated on a special train reserved for Europeans. It would leave Hankow the next day, and no Chinese were allowed aboard. The train, bound for Hong Kong, wouldn't even stop at Canton but would proceed directly to Kowloon within the Crown Colony. The consul had urged them not to miss this last opportunity. Each car would have the flag of its occupants painted on the roof, a talisman to ward off Japanese bombs.

The day before, Alexandra had written to Philip, retired in the south of France:

I won't speak to you of the events in China, [because] you know them from the newspapers. What they don't tell is the horror of this war that takes us back to savagery. The Japanese are killing young Chinese civilians in the streets to diminish the number who could become soldiers. They're killing the wounded in the hospitals . . . As for prisoners, there are none taken by either side. The Chinese officers, most of them, only think of getting out of the fighting in one piece.

For that matter, she complained, the Europeans were showing no courage in face of the Japanese onslaught. The Chinese now thoroughly despised their former masters, and servants, if you could obtain them, were opium smokers or drunkards.

Why didn't the orientalist and her son board the train and escape? She informed Philip that, were she to reach Hong Kong, she lacked sufficient funds to sail to Europe. The excuse appears lame, since her husband's drafts could more easily reach her in British territory than wartorn China. In reality, the traveler, although nearing seventy, sensed adventure, and she had no interest in returning to tame France. Instead, she decided to journey from Hankow on a rickety steamer up the Yangtse to Chunking, then to travel farther west and perhaps reenter Tibet via her old route, as Yongden was urging. She gave her next address as in care of the French consul, Yunnan-fou.

While Alexandra chatted at lunch, she heard the scream of warplanes diving down on the airfield. Bombs exploded to rain debris and spread black smoke over the neighborhood. She wondered about the steamer, which was anchored in the river with Yongden, their baggage, and many others aboard. It made a tempting target for the Japanese planes. The worried mother instantly commandeered the doctor and his car and they sped to the dock, but they could see no boat. The woman's heart sank within her till she learned that the savvy captain had maneuvered his tub a few kilometers upstream. After the attack was over he dropped back down, and mother and son were happily reunited. Next day the steamer, packed with fearful humanity, mainly Asian, departed for the upper reaches of the Yangtse.

How had the usually prescient Alexandra mananged to get herself booked on this floating sardine can as vulnerable to rocks in the riverbed as to stray aircraft? She and Yongden had arrived at Peking, via Manchuria, in midwinter 1937, anxious to get on with their research. She was impressed by the assured behavior of the Chinese and still more by their capital. "Peking, rejuvenated, had become one of the most picturesque and fascinating cities of the world." Alexandra was a guest of *Madame* Rosen Hoa, a friend from Paris, who with her Chinese engineer husband lived in a charming villa surrounded by gardens.

Yet each time the Frenchwoman left the villa to be pulled through the city in a rickshaw, she felt "an inexpressible sadness [and] that tears were going to flood my eyes." She did not mind the police spy who followed her everywhere, but the people themselves seemed menacing, more antiwhite than anti-Japanese. At the end of June that same year the orientalist gladly quit the capital to head for Wu Tai Shan, the sacred Mountain of Five Peaks, slightly to the southwest but just below the Great Wall. The trip by train and mule was arduous; however, Alexandra declared, "The sight of the summits brought me real joy."

Wu Tai Shan provided a rugged yet hospitable setting, eight thousand feet above the North China plain, for a stunning complex of hundreds of monasteries, temples, and shrines. Its history went back to first-century missionaries from India who had arrived bearing the treasure of Buddhist texts. It was the object of an annual pilgrimage for the devout from China, Mongolia, and Tibet, and Alexandra and Yongden joined in observances with thousands of their coreligionists. While staying at Pou sa-ting, the largest monastery, she mused, "Possibly this was the last time in my present life I would live in a *gompa*. The idea impressed me. . . . I compared myself to a woman gluttonously, yet sadly, savoring the joys of a love affair about to terminate, since her age made another similar one unlikely."

The Mountain of Five Peaks, decked with flowers and surrounded by additional green and purple mountains, nonetheless had a decidedly occult atmosphere, perhaps because of the many Tibetans come to pay homage to Manjusri, wielder of the sword of wisdom. While the pair searched the libraries for ancient texts, they also explored for a secret passage, open only to the pure of heart, that would lead one to Lhasa in five days. They did not find it, although talks with Tibetan lamas brought them there in spirit. From the lamas Alexandra obtained "pills containing flesh taken from the cadaver of a Tibetan hermit considered a superman." These supposedly made her immune to all maladies and assured a long life. She would have need of them to survive the gathering storm.

In July, after a provocative skirmish at the Marco Polo Bridge, Japanese troops stormed into Peking. From the Nationalist capital at Nanking, Chiang Kai-shek temporized, but an August attack on Shanghai forced him to defend the nation. Unannounced, World War II had begun in the Pacific. Shanghai fell to the Japanese in November and Nanking the next month. The troops "proceeded to signalize their triumph by an orgy of rape and murder." Chiang responded by shifting his government fifteen hundred miles inland to Chunking, Szechuan. Fortunately, instead of immediately pushing on to Hankow, the Japanese consolidated their position by taking control of the railroads. Military lines began to stablize with the Rising Sun flying over the north and the coast, the Nationalists ruling the mountainous southwest, and between and behind the lines, circulating among the mainstream of the peasantry, Communist partisans spreading Mao's message.

Alexandra hoped that Wu Tai Shan, although within the Japanese sphere of influence, was sufficiently remote to be ignored by the soldiers. She was only sorry she had left her baggage at Peking. "Counting on a long stay in China," she complained, "I had brought a veritable library." Now she was cut off from her books. Forgetting about scholarly works, the author turned to the novel, to elucidate a theme constant in her mature thought.

Back in September 1934, Alexandra received from her publisher comments on the manuscript of a—supposedly first—novel she had sent to them. The editors found it "filled with charm and color" and were certain it would make at least a "*succès d'estime.*" She cut it down and the next year Plon brought out *Mipam, or The Lama of Five Wisdoms.* Allegedly it was the work of Lama Yongden, who in a brief note complained about Europeans who wrote "books which in the form of novels claimed to describe Tibet and the customs of its inhabitants." These attempts he supposedly found hilarious, and so he had put pen to paper to correct the rampant misconceptions of his native land.

Certainly, Yongden supplied the story line (from folk sources) for *Mipam,* and likely did a draft in Tibetan. The novel was at first ascribed solely to him, and was referred to by Alexandra as "Albert's book," but to judge by style, he wrote neither the French text nor the author's note. Alexandra was annoyed by the astonishing success of *Lost Horizon,* issued in 1933. It instantly swept America, where President Roosevelt named his vacation retreat Shangri-La. She must have supposed that a novel authored by a genuine Tibetan lama would trump a fabricated tale by a Briton who had never set foot in the Land of Snows. *Mipam* sold well enough despite the hard times of the Depression, and it was soon translated into a half-dozen languages.

Mipam, an unrecognized incarnation, is a fascinating, carefully drawn character, but his conflicted psychology is simply not Tibetan; he is a David-Neel alter ego. His adventures are compelling, including communion with a snow leopard reminiscent of Alexandra's meeting with various wild animals. His determination and fearlessness echo Alexandra's own comment, "It is not in my nature to admit defeat." Yongden lacked the psychological resources to create this dogged fighter who, despite his unlikely origin, ascends to a higher spiritual plane. We shall see that Alexandra little by little smothered her adopted son.

Encouraged by their initial success, the pair decided to cooperate on a second novel, *Magie d'amour et magie noir.* Its name rightly suggests a tale of black magic, lust, and murder. Alexandra, trapped in a paradise threatened from all sides, turned to the genre now termed "horror-occult." *Mipam,* written with a wry sweetness, has an upbeat resolution: Dolma, the hero's love since childhood, by sacrificing herself helps to elevate him to the throne of the Lama of Five Wisdoms. They knew each other from previous lifetimes and would meet again in the next, this time as guru and disciple. In contrast *Magie noir* is a wartime story, bitter and bleak, as it presents a nearly identical theme: romantic love between man and woman is an illusion and obstacle to the enlightenment of both. While *Mipam* is suffused with the light of the steppes, *Magie noir* plumbs the inner depths of unreasoning desire.

Briefly, its hero Garab, a dashing brigand, falls madly in love with the beautiful, kind-hearted Detchema, who reciprocates his passion. Garab, whose father was a demon, makes a pilgrimage to Mt. Kailas in western Tibet to investigate his paternity. But a little piety undoes him, as Detchema is ravished by the very same demon. Garab's jealousy leads to murder, followed by an attempt to give up the world as disciple to an anchorite, then to murder once again to protect Detchema who has sought him out in his solitude. There is a sub-plot concerning "[C]ertain black Bons who engage in strange and cruel magical practices . . . the hollow table with the heavy lid, underneath which live men are left to starve to death and putrefy, thereby producing an elixir of immortality." Tales of such practices were confirmed for Alexandra by Tibetan lamas visiting Wu Tai Shan. In *Magie noir* she described techniques she herself employed to determine if one were the victim of a more subtle vampirism. The author seems to have been undergoing one of her periodic dark nights of the soul.

This gloomy yet brilliant brief novel clearly reflects the circumstances under which it was written. The monks of the Five Peaked Mountain conjured demons to keep their enemies at bay. They engaged in the wildest rumor mongering, such as that an armed, Japanese-trained column of orangutans was bearing down on the sacred mountain. Alexandra, since she never knew when she might have to dash for safety, not only composed on the run, she and Yongden packed the manuscript on the day hikes they took to keep fit. "Many times we burst out laughing to see our robes so stuffed with papers," she noted.

Their Chinese paper money soon became nearly worthless, and cut off from Peking, they had no way to cash a check or draft. The hardy travelers were reduced to eating boiled rice and roots they dug up, seasoned with a little vinegar. Alexandra claimed to fatten on the excitement of wartime. "My sleep is just as good as my appetite," she would boast to her readers. "Neither let themselves be troubled by circumstances."

Still, as the Japanese advanced and bombed Pou sa-ting, the Frenchwoman decided to head for Taiyuan to the south. Evidently she supposed *Madame* Rosen Hoa had fled there, and she hoped to borrow some good hard money. Alexandra and her son finally obtained mules and servants and set out. Disclaiming any personal animosity toward the Japanese, she still took the precaution to drape herself in a French flag.

Predictably, the route was infested by blackmarketeers, bandits, and assassins. The laws, applied erratically, were apt to be enforced with a sudden severity. The pair watched as a handsome young soldier was shot by a firing squad because he married without his captain's consent. The Chinese proved more of a hindrance than did the invaders. One petty official detained Yongden, accusing him of carrying a forged

British passport; he must be an imposter because he didn't have fair hair and eyes. The pest summoned his cronies to substantiate his brilliant detective work. He made Yongden write his name and the word *London* in the Roman alphabet. Astonished by the lama's facility, the officials regretfully let them pass.

At the first sign of danger, Alexandra's muleteers deserted. There were no trains, no trucks, but the pair obtained space in a cart that bumped along. Not far from their destination, she was violently hurled from the cart to the ground, limbs askew like a rag doll's. A box of books that struck her in the head knocked her into a semi-coma. While Yongden tried to help, she moaned, "Leave me alone, I'll never move again."

Alexandra had to be lifted back into the cart and endure its jolts. Yongden covered her with a piece of greasy oilcloth of the sort used over corpses being returned from the front. But the woman's training counted for something. "I abandoned myself to that special state yogis call 'exteriorization,' during which it seems that one is outside one's body." As the vehicle trundled in and out of ruts, the ancient formula of the Stoics came to mind, 'Pain, you are but a word.'"

After nine days on the road, hurt, exhausted, and filthy, Alexandra arrived at Taiyuan to find it under attack by the Japanese. Her European friend was gone, and her entire fortune consisted of four Chinese dollars. However, the French consul loaned her money, and in time Philip would cable her a considerable sum. As usual, the seventy-year-old spurned any thought of a hospital or medical treatment. She could not be so cavalier about the daily air raids, which had to be sat out in cellars. Even this she turned to advantage, toting the manuscript of *Magie noir* with her in a suitcase. "There are not many books," she commented dryly, "that have been written under such singular conditions."

Alexandra could not return to Peking, and without the library of books she had stored there, scholarly pursuits were difficult. For the first time she was able to observe detachments of gray- or blue-clad Communist troops. Their discipline and willingness to fight the Japanese marked a sharp contrast with the Nationalists. With her typical political savvy, the Frenchwoman predicted a civil war once the Japanese were beaten, an outcome she didn't doubt. For the moment, Alexandra once again found herself obliged to missionaries, Baptists this time, who received and conveyed money to her.

Alexandra and Yongden boarded a train at Taiyuan bound for the southern city of Hankow, still in Nationalist hands. The trip lasted three days and nights, and the two were crammed in among refugee families under squalid conditions. The train was bombed and some died. "The besieged people don't know how to save themselves," observed the writer, already at work on a new book. "Those from the villages of the south flee toward the north and those from the north toward the south. . . . Flight . . . it is not important where, only to flee."

By the time of her arrival in Hankow in December, Alexandra had been accidentally spat on by peasants, urinated on by infants, and stepped on by soldiers in their boots. Due to the milling crowds and changes of train, she had lost additional Tibetan books, copies of rare manuscripts and extensive notes. In this strategic but threatened port city on the Yangtse, her choices were clear: east by the special train for Europeans to Hong Kong and then by ship to France, or west into the unknown. Alexandra felt disposed to laugh at it all, at least until she supposed Yongden and her baggage had gone down on the ferry moored in the river.

"Then I became a fugitive," noted the observer, more soberly, "like the millions of Chinese."

In January 1938 the travelers' voyage up the Yangstse from Hankow to Chunking went smoothly enough at the pace of earlier times. At each port passed on the way thousands of people were jammed onto the dock, "standing around like sheep, pushing against one another." They stared mutely as the ferry steamed by without stopping. Although the winds blew bitterly, Alexandra was able to marvel at the majestic beauty of the Yangtse gorges. The temporary Nationalist capital, and focus of resistance to the Japanese, proved another matter.

Chunking, crammed with officials, troops, and refugees, had turned filthy and ill-tempered. Formerly picturesque flights of stairs mounting the hillsides from the river became "infected cesspools." More disturbing was the openly manifested dislike of Europeans. "For the first time you hear kids screaming [at you] in the streets, 'Foreign devil!' " wrote Alexandra. It made her nervous to need Yongden by her side to keep them from pelting her with stones. For the police it was open season on any foreigner's purse.

"War undoes the manners of civilization," declared Alexandra, "returning us to savagery." Certainly this war without a face, signalized by the seemingly random violence of air raids on the civilian population, frayed her nerves. After a few miserable weeks in Chunking she grew morbid. The river was too low to proceed farther up by boat, an airplane to Chengtu was prohibitively expensive, and a chair and bearers could not be found at any price. Soldiers, deserting from the inept Nationalist army, were pillaging the countryside, nor did they act in the chivalrous fashion of brigands of old. "These brave types . . . are a lot better armed than they used to be," Alexandra informed Philip. "They have machine guns and even airplanes."

Nonetheless, the resourceful Frenchwoman was writing to her husband from Chengtu by early March. She and Yongden were comfortably installed in a small, detached pavilion near the extensive French medical mission, precisely where they had stayed a decade and a half earlier. They watched dubiously while the doctors and nurses painted huge tricolors on the roofs of the buildings. Alexandra had learned the flags would make fine targets for the Japanese, determined to drive all Europeans from Asia.

Good tidings awaited the weary, impecunious travelers: dear Mouchy had sent them ten thousand francs. Alexandra immediately mailed *Magie noir* to Plon, instructing Philip to inform them it was on the way. The remark with which it opens, "I have hesitated a long time, in fact for several years, before deciding to publish this book," is more fictional than the novel itself. Alexandra was avid to have Plon bring it out, only hoping the manuscript would get through to them. During most of the war, while armies marched and countermarched, the Chinese national post office continued to function after a fashion. *Magie noir* arrived safely in Paris eight months later.

Never far from the front, Alexandra had begun working on a more immediate account, *Sous des nuées d'orage*, or *Under the Storm Clouds*. She wrote about events in China at the time they were happening. In Paris her editors were convinced the book would sell. Ironically, had it appeared earlier, the French might have found in *Storm Clouds* a warning of their own impending doom. At any rate, the author needed a more peaceful place to write about the hostilities. Chengtu, crammed with refugees, attracted Japanese bombers. Food and fuel were scarce and dear. "Such preoccupations are really painful when one is no longer young," signed the aging Amazon.

Alexandra fled toward Tibet, hoping to take up residence in a monastery. In mid-June, once the snows had melted, the travelers rounded up porters and two chairs to carry them westward over a pass 13,500 feet high. Ten days later they arrived at the middle-sized, frontier town of Tachienlu, buffeted by spring rains but elated to be in the Tibetan-speaking (if Chinese-ruled) world. Alexandra didn't know the town, but she was familiar with the mixed, seminomadic population of the borderlands. At 8,000 feet, the air crisp, Tachienlu occupied an attractive cuplike valley. Alexandra took comfort in realizing that just ten miles on the other side of the western hills Tibetans were grazing their sheep and goats where the forests allowed.

Unfortunately, the previously tranquil place was busy with refugees, and Alexandra could not find accommodations. The monasteries held more troops than monks. Families camped in the steets braving weather chilly at best. English missionaries befriended the orientalist and offered her shelter. By midsummer she was pleased to escape to a hermitage on the plain of Pomo San, some miles out of town. The pair liked to stroll about the neighborhood, Alexandra in baggy suit and cloak, a battered man's hat atop her head, stout stick in hand, while

Yongden trailed after. She would jot down notes and he would snap photos to send to Philip Neel or her publishers. Not surprisingly, they aroused the suspicion of the Nationalist authorities. The Chinese officers forbade Alexandra from gazing at the nearby mountain passes through binoculars. They even ordered the foreign devil not to stare out her window at passing columns of troops.

Alexandra hoped to make the best of a deteriorating situation. She purchased fur robes in anticipation of the harsh winter, but by November she and Yongden were practically freezing in the unheated hermitage. Bothered by arthritis, she was too rusty to attept *tumo* breathing. Like the other foreigners, she felt hemmed in by events, adding, "I don't know where to turn."

The clever observer had sense to recognize that the convulsions shaking Asia would lead to the expulsion of the European powers and a worldwide realignment. Emblematic was an attack in the street by a screaming mob on the French Catholic bishop, nearly killing him. Meanwhile, Japanese bombers were penetrating deeper into the west, hitting Chengtu three times a week and, to the south, Yunnanfou, on Alexandra's possible escape route to Burma. The Japanese "included among their victories a massacre at the elementary school for boys," she wrote to Philip, after inquiring about his health. When he informed her of the capitulation to the Nazis at Munich, she shot back, "All the ignominies of the toad Chamberlain and his cohorts, abasing themselves under Hitler's boots, won't save us." Her joints might creak but her tongue stayed tart.

In late November after she returned to the mission, snow fell for fifty hours straight, and shortly thereafter the English missionaries kicked *Madame* David-Neel and son and their baggage into the street. "A real brick fell on my head," she said, metaphorically. Jeanne Denys, who corresponded with the missionaries, claimed that Alexandra tried to sublet her dwelling to a tenant, perhaps to live more cheaply elsewhere and pocket the difference. We don't really know the cause of the quarrel, but in fact space was desperately short at Tachienlu. Alexandra was fortunate in being able to turn to her countrywomen, an order of Catholic nuns who rented her an old granary. The wooden shed had several rooms and its own courtyard. After a good cleaning and airing, she was able to create a cozy apartment for her and Yongden.

Alexandra settled in to write about China, or what she had seen of it, because for all else she was dependent on rumors. By midsummer 1939, she had completed *Storm Clouds,* and in September Violet Sidney arrived to translate the manuscript. This she accomplished between air raid alerts, when much of the town gathered in a nearby cemetery. Chinese and Tibetans, Buddhists and Bons assembled in an atmosphere of camaraderie and indifference to danger.

In November, Alexandra was able to send off her French manuscript by diplomatic pouch from Chengtu to Paris. But Sidney got stuck, with "no practical means of crossing a chaotic country." She "suffered from ennui" and the author's carping about her translation. How the woman in her midsixties eventually made her escape from western China in May of the next year is unclear, but certainly no English version of *Storm Clouds* has ever appeared. In an unusual step, Alexandra apologized to Philip for having written this work so hastily. She lived amid uncertainty, "in dread of a possible sinister moment."

Storm Clouds is really a personal form of journalism, of reporting events as they occurred to the writer. Because of her own undoubted importance she was able to endow the often trivial with significance. Still, this account of Alexandra's travails as once again she crossed China from east to west, although it may evoke sympathy and admiration, lacks the truly heroic. No longer able to order her environment, more at the mercy than in command of her servants, the sometime orientalist, sometime *dakini* (literally "sky walker") had been reduced to a refugee. An everywoman, Alexandra like countless others could only flee before frightening, impersonal forces. Her saving grace was that she saw far more clearly than the leaders of the day. "In order to escape the evil their madness has created," she wrote, "men will soon have no other refuge but death."

By the time *Storm Clouds* appeared in the spring of 1940, France was on the edge of a devastating defeat. Poland had fallen to Hitler's blitzkrieg and Europe was in disarray. China seemed too distant to worry over. In May the French army crumbled in Belgium, by June the Germans marched into Paris, and this book written and dispatched with such a sense of urgency disappeared into history. "It's odd that once again I find myself in the Orient during the war, just as I did during the first one," Alexandra wrote to Philip, who had retired to Gard in the south of France. She was occupying herself and Yongden with work on an erudite project, their grammar of spoken Tibetan. Desperately in need of official aid, she was hopeful that the grammar, which she regarded as drudgery, would bring her funds from the French Foreign Ministry.

Alexandra preferred to devote herself to a book more in her freewheeling style, *A l'ouest barbare de la vaste Chine.* We like to translate the title as *In China's Wild West.* The work, which would meet with some popularity after the war, is a study of the borderlands and the native tribes that inhabited them. Alexandra, although lacking any anthropological training, always had a feel for writing about the anarchic nomads of the Sino-Tibetan marches and the status of women among them. She had hopeful things to say about the relations between the Chinese and Tibetans. In this region the two peoples had married and intermingled for centuries and were mutually tolerant if not entirely respectful. Still, the author had her blind spots, and she did not foresee—in response to the Chinese invasion of Tibet—the fierce guerilla warfare of the late 1950s and 1960s, nor the even fiercer Maoist repression of peoples primitive in all but the ability to fight. For the grazing grounds to the north and west would attain an infamy equal to, although lesser known, than the Soviet Gulag. In the words of John Avedon, "These two provinces [Amdo and Kansu] contained a vast sea of prison camps housing up to 10 million inmates, a 'black hole' from which little information ever reached the ouside world or even the rest of China."

Alexandra's reporting was no longer firsthand. "It is out of the question for me to travel," she informed her husband. "Foreigners run the risk of being arrested." Despite her later claims to the contrary she did not cross into Tibet. She wished to remain within reach of the French consul at Chengtu, the Catholic missionaries who could be counted on to befriend her, and above all the post office, her link to Philip Neel.

During the early 1940s Alexandra hung on at Tachienlu, complaining about the nasty weather and her lack of funds. The war always threatened to bring destruction closer, but correspondence with France remained possible, if tardy. She fretted about Philip's safety under the German occupation and sent him the usual advice about keeping up his health and spirits. There could be no disguising that the elderly engineer was failing; he informed her of his will, adhering strictly to their marriage contract. He did express his gratitude toward Yongden for being such a help to his wife. On February 14, 1941, Alexandra received a tattered, grimy envelope containing a telegram. She sensed that Mouchy had died weeks before. Once she saw it came from his niece Simone, who had nursed him, her fears were realized.

From youth, Alexandra hardened herself against any show of emotion. She had slept on a board, read the Stoics, then discovered the subtle philosophy of Gautama Buddha. She had consorted with magicians and brigands, not hesitating to make of love an experiment. Now she stared unbelieving at the slip of paper, reading it again and again as though it were in a foreign language. Tears welled up and spilled over. Yongden, nearby, was amazed to watch his mother weep unashamedly.

"I have lost the best of husbands," she moaned, "my only friend."

Alexandra was not aware that just the month before Professor D'Arsonval, her academic sponsor, had also died.

CHAPTER 25

The Wife of the Chinese

From 1938 through mid-1944, during a prolonged albeit vicious stalemate in the war, Alexandra and Yongden were paying guests of the French Catholic hospital at Tachienlu. They suffered more from uncertainty than serious privation. King rumor ruled, and the orientalist candidly admitted she had no sure means of learning what was happening elsewhere in China, let alone Europe. She kept in close touch with the consul at Chengtu, and she read, wrote, and collected information for her books. What she could not easily do was to shake off the effect of Philip's death.

Alexandra's familiar enemy, neurasthenia, stalked her. She quit eating, vomited, lost weight. During August 1941 she noted, "For three weeks I've been suffering violent pains in the kidneys and in my bowels on the left side. The Chinese doctor said it is caused by an inflammation of the nerves." The skeptical one had her own remedy for the problem: she got up and beat a servant, then Yongden. "Marvelous! The exercise took away the pain."

Such acting out could not assuage the inner hurt. Expressing love or feeling grief were opposed to Alexandra's view of herself, and so she tried to suppress these unseemly emotions. The result was rancor against those closest to her. She found fault with Yongden, who to escape her ill humor spent much of his time in little tea shops, chatting with the owners and customers. Formerly an abstainer, he may have turned to drink. Although everyone found him helpful and agreeable, his mother was displeased.

In November 1943 she vowed, "Today I resolve to separate myself from Albert. The lad is getting older, approaching fifty and becoming insupportable." She added, "I have assured his future, he remains my heir." Still, we get the sense that the woman of seventy-five has a growing fear of age, a suspicion that Yongden, too, may predecease her, leaving her alone and in many ways helpless. "It's a sad thing to grow old," she sighed. "I should have died in my tent in the Tibetan solitudes."

Instead, Alexandra soon would have to respond to new challenges. In 1944, once the snows had melted, Japan launched a final desperate drive to sever China and secure an overland route to southeast Asia. The Nationalist armies melted before the onslaught, profiteering increased, and the police turned more brutal. Inflation soared, ruining the horde of teachers and students who had migrated to the west carrying their universities on their backs. Many joined the Red Army, under the firm direction of Chairman Mao Tsetung, nipping at the heels of the advancing Japanese. Alexandra, although she is alleged to have read the poems of this political genius based somewhat to the north, gave no clue of it in her published writings of this period.

Japan's kamikaze offensive was bound to fail, if only because of the increasing presence of American forces in the Chinese southwest. "Vinegar Joe" Stilwell commanded—along with his arch-rival Chennault and his famous Flying Tigers—while thirty-five thousand G.I.'s built and ran the world's busiest airport near Kunming, Yunnan. From India over the hump of the Himalayas came more men, material, air support. In a decisive step that spring, one more fateful than she might imagine, Alexandra abandoned her converted granary at Tachienlu and returned to Chengtu.

In the capital of Szechuan, Alexandra encountered John Blofeld, a cultural attaché to the British Embassy at Chunking. Blofeld has written to us, "I happened to run across her at a very comfortable hotel. . . . Jokingly, I asked why she chose this luxurious abode in preference to the exhilarating hardships of a lonely mountain cave. In reply she gave me a highly detailed description of a recent journey into Tibet, during which she had been robbed of her possessions and thus forced to return immediately to a city where she could obtain credit and hope to receive funds from France. Only later did I discover that the whole long story, doing much credit to her self-image, was pure fiction!"

Why did Alexandra deceive a young man whom she knew from before the war as a dedicated Buddhist? We are verging on speculation, but we do not suppose it was a matter of self-image. How did Alexandra afford an expensive hotel in the midst of World War II when she could not tap either her own or her late husband's funds? Her French biographers relate that through their consul at Chengtu the French Foreign Ministry paid Alexandra a stipend of thirty thousand francs per annum (about six hundred dollars). According to Jacques Brosse, the consul "asked nothing of them [Alexandra and Yongden] except to render them a service." Jean Chalon insists that the money was support for writing their Tibetan grammar, a text that after the war no publisher or government agency showed the slightest interest in and that was finally privately printed after Alexandra's death.

We must recall this was the Vichy (or profascist) government that was allegedly making these funds available for a recondite project on the Sino-Tibetan border, while the occupying German troops and the French resistance slaughtered one another, and the Allies bombed military targets in France. To us this appears a taller tale than Alexandra's feigned journey into Tibet. We suggest her story may have been told to Blofeld, a British official, as a deliberate cover-up by a woman embarrassed to have been in the pay of Vichy, and who with her usual political acumen realized it might soon prove a real liability. We cannot blame her for accepting the money, without which she would have fallen on hard times indeed. The question remains—did Alexandra supply the consul at Chengtu with information in return? Certainly, the Chinese military authorities supposed that she had. We are left on the edge of what may be a thrilling spy story, but biographers may only peer over its precipice.

Alexandra and Yongden spent a little over a year in what Blofeld has described as "a walled grey-bricked city affectionately styled 'Little Peking.' Its residential lanes bordered by low grey walls pierced with bronze-studded lacquered gates . . . and the charming courtyards lying behind produced a sometimes startling resemblance to the Empress of Cities." Here Alexandra completed her grammar and also *China's Wild West*, spending odd hours listening to Hitler's final insane broadcasts relayed via Radio Saigon in Japanese-controlled Indochina. Here she learned of the end of hostilities in May 1945. In late July, courtesy of the new Gaullist government of France, she and Yongden were flown to Kunming. After spending two months there, she flew over the Hump to Calcutta, again at government expense.

Alexandra spent the next nine months based at the Grand Hotel. Her coming return to France loomed like a Himalayan peak on the horizon. Later she told intimates that she undertook it solely to settle Philip's estate, and that she had been unable to return to Asia because of her rheumatism. In any event, she could no longer live the life about which she wrote. Without Neel as an intermediary, she needed to be closer to publishers, the newspapers, the adulation of admirers. The south of France was the right distance from Paris.

We have glimpses of Alexandra's state of mind while waiting for conditions in France to improve. She calmly watched through her hotel window as, on the eve of Indian Independence, Moslem and Hindu mobs alternately burned, pillaged, and murdered one another. Troops with tanks and machine guns were sent in to end the carnage. She didn't suppose the Europeans were any more moral. Writing from the Grand Hotel on the occasion of a celebratory dinner, Easter 1946, she was gloomy but incisive:

In this dining room . . . filled with defenders of Christian civilization, this on the evening of Saint Vendredi [i.e. Good Friday] . . . I have doubts. I must be the only one to think of Him [i.e. Jesus], I who am not a disciple, I who have rejected Christianity. . . . Men don't wish the realm of God [i.e. the millennium].

He is abandoned. The Pharisees triumph in the Temple . . . It is the downfall of the Holy Ghost.

Alexandra went to musing on Jesus' "Father, why hast thou forsaken me?" She interpreted the word *Father* as externalizing and objectifying an inner need for love, of which Jesus felt bereft on the cross. She called this special plea "very Jewish," but we need to keep in mind her own desire to be loved by her father and his inability to outwardly reciprocate. She may have been speaking of her own early wounds, which had not healed.

If Alexandra didn't care for the attitude of the waning colonial class, she positively disdained their attire: "Khaki uniforms and women who show their legs, if not their thighs." The brief military shorts worn by handsome young officers infuriated her. These are the complaints of a woman born in the middle of the nineteenth century, the heyday of hypocrisy. It is the sad song of a wife who has lost her husband, the man who knew her youth and beauty and whose existence, never mind at what distance, made her feel perennially attractive. The once-coquettish Parisienne was not above crying of sour grapes.

Alexandra always showed at her finest in the mountains. On a trip to Darjeeling, she rose before dawn to stand in the brisk air, watching the sun burst into flower over five-crowned Kinchinjunga. She recalled how some thirty-five years ago this had been her first enticing view of the Sacred Realm, forbidden to her race, her sex. Yet she had dared to enter, to travel and learn. Now she had decided to return to Europe.

She smiled to herself, "They can never take from me the soul of a Tibetan."

Alexandra's actual departure from the Orient occurred at the Calcutta airport on the rainy morning of June 30, 1946. She boarded a "very ugly and monstrous" airplane. As it took off with a roar and glided into the clouds, she bade "*au revoir* to the India of my youth, India where so much of my life has unrolled. *Au revoir* . . . or isn't it goodbye?" She felt numb to the core. "Am I living or already dead, [despite] having a fleshly body, as the Tibetans believe [possible]? Am I wandering in the shadow of the *bardo*? No, I have left, it is true."

The return of Alexandra and Yongden to Paris did not go unnoticed in the press. However, the journalists were still referring to her in terms of "the first white woman to enter Lhasa," or "the great traveler and explorer," episodes of her life that were past. Her brief stay in the capital, still suffering from many shortages, was dominated by nostalgia, as she looked up old friends, many of them no longer living. Yongden, who understood French far better than he spoke it, liked going to the cinema. He was not so pleased as his mother to return to Digne.

They found Samten Dzong in good repair except for the furniture, damaged by the police who occupied the villa during the war. Alexandra, turning in her pilgrim's staff for a sturdy cane, could still hobble about the countryside. Nearing eighty, her stride had slowed but her mind was busy with projects. *China's Wild West,* appearing in 1947, looked both forward and back. The author, noted Lowell Thomas Jr., "[w]as a keen observer [who] learned a great deal about China's far west and the intrigues of the border country."

Prophetically, Alexandra warned the West to stop thinking of Orientals as passive. "The Chinese, even the most obscure shopkeepers and peasants, are not inert people as we have described them. They possess a strong latent energy, good sense and ability." Asia was going to be ruled by Asians, she stated flatly, a good portion of it from Peking. She advised Europe and America to initiate diplomatic, cultural, and commercial relations with whatever regime emerged from the postwar turmoil. This came at a time when the United States unequivocally backed Chiang Kai-shek, and the Soviet Union, taking advantage of the civil war, had seized the former Japanese railroad concessions in Manchuria.

The nostalgic element in this work leavens rather than obtrudes. The author scornfully remarked, "There are now autos on what used to be picturesque [dirt] roads. The contemplative silence is shattered by the feverish activity of civilization." She was pleased to have explored Central Asia before its colorful, mysterious way of life was ground under the rails and wheels of progress. Interestingly, Alexandra was under no illusions as to the conditions faced by China's minorities. She wrote, "It is ridiculous for the Chinese to talk about equality when they oppress the Tibetans and other native peoples." She understood that the Han "consider[ed] the old occupants of the soil as inferior to them." Unfortunately, in certain later works she chose to disregard what she knew so well.

The late 1940s and early 1950s proved a wonderfully productive time for Alexandra. However, her next two books were neither financially nor critically very successful. *Nepal: The Heart of the Himalayas* appeared in 1949 and *India Yesterday, Today and Tomorrow* in 1951. The titles are translated but the books (other than into German) were not. The books were useful in educating some Europeans to a deeper sense of the Indian reality during the time the Subcontinent was achieving independence and splitting into three major nations. The author had significant ties to India; still, she failed to make it hers as she had with Tibet. What is most intriguing about these works are the personal anecdotes, in particular Alexandra's rather detailed descriptions of *pancha tattva,* or tantric sex rites. Although the events described took place in the period 1912 to 1914, she never would have published her account of them during the lifetime of Philip Neel.

"I myself have been a witness three times to the complete celebration of the rite of five elements," wrote the adventurous one. She disdained merely reading about Tantra, because "the texts are archaic and customs disused." But her experience in Nepal under the aegis of a sorcerer had proved disagreeable. It was in Calcutta, no doubt while she was close to Sir John Woodroffe, that Alexandra took part in one symbolic tantric ceremony and witnessed another in all its material actuality. She found both enlightening.

At the first, to which she was invited by a guru, ten upper-class Hindu men attended, each accompanied by his wife and a *shakti,* or adored female. In an opulent house the richly attired threesomes formed into a *chakra* (mystic circle) seated on cushions on the floor. Alexandra, herself a *shakti,* wrote, "This whole ceremony took place slowly, in deep silence." Neither meat nor fish nor wine was indulged in, but rather there was prolonged chanting in Sanskrit while incense burned, the lights of oil lamps flickered over smooth, chiseled faces, and bronze bells tinkled. The traveler recalled, some thirty-five years after the event, "A subtle perfume of adventure mixed with the odors of the room, and adventure is my only reason for living."

This audacious statement of Alexandra's creed, had it been made while Neel lived, would have been brutal. In this instance, the fifth element—sex—was replaced by a curious union as each man wrapped himself in his wife's sari. The couples sat immobile for a long time after which they emerged each to adore their *shakti.* "I felt rather humble," commented the Frenchwoman.

The third instance of *pancha tattva* witnessed by Alexandra took place in an isolated pavilion in a garden, while jackals howled without. She had bribed the gardener whose patrons worshiped the goddess, or female power, on certain moonless nights. Alexandra was secretly installed on a stairway leading to an unused terrace, and from here she looked on undetected. She was dressed in a dark blue sari like those worn by women of a low caste. By craning her neck, she was able to view the proceedings.

First a goat was slaughtered, then the attractive, well-off participants, seated in the *chakra,* drank a lot of wine from a communal jug. Then each of the ten men "brought his *shakti* toward him." This was his "wife in the cult," or as Alexandra had written in an earlier work, "any woman *except* one's legitimate wife." The couples assumed the pose of tantric statues, and the observer concluded, "The fifth element presented itself with perfect decency."

Of course both *India* and *Nepal* contained a great variety of recollections from Alexandra's amazing storehouse of experience. If they did not sell to any extent, perhaps it was because the French in the lean postwar years were preoccupied with keeping body and soul together. But conditions were not too hard in Digne, where other houses were beginning to encroach on the neighborhood of Samten Dzong.

Alexandra, her legs growing worse, purchased a car, a Citroën 4CV. The good burghers, watching Yongden chauffeur her around in this mechanized tin can, dubbed her "the wife of the Chinese." That he was her son and Sikkimese never made any difference to them.

On the town's main square, nowadays named Place Général de Gaulle, sits the Librairie Sicard, which sells books and stationery. The proprietor, *Madame* Sicard, well remembers the frequent occasions when Yongden and his mother would putter up in the Citroën. Yongden, rather squat and nearsighted, would come in with the order, and the clerks would scurry around to fill it. If they proved too slow for the imperious one waiting in the car, she would loudly honk the horn and everyone would scurry faster. Later, when she grew too arthritic to leave the house, Alexandra would order by telephone the writing materials dearer to her than food.

Across the square from Sicard stands Lorion Photo. Here Alexandra had developed, and in some cases rephotographed, her old glass plate negatives for illustrations for *Nepal, India,* and other works. The proprietor recalls the shot of her and Yongden against the backdrop of the Potala and is certain it is genuine. What bittersweet memories these photos must have evoked in this voyager becalmed! The traveler, stranded, reached out for companionship.

She sought out Judith Jordan, teacher of English, in order to speak the language that had stood her in such good stead in Asia. She heard of a woman, Maria Borrely, who for years had been studying Sanskrit texts on her own. She asked her to come visit, and her son Pierre drove his mother. "Alexandra," he told us, "wanted to get to know the other bird in the countryside." At Samten Dzong, while the women talked, he was left with Yongden. It was very awkward, "because he spoke only English."

A few years later, in 1954, Pierre was a student at the university of Marseilles. His professor of philosophy, Gaston Berger, suggested he ask *Madame* David-Neel for an article for the college review. She recalled the handsome, curly-haired young man and agreed to see him. She received him in the garden at Samten Dzong dressed "in a light green two-piece Italian summer dress topped by a hat with a big bird feather." She greeted the nervous student with the remark, "*Voilà, mon bon monsieur,* I am about to end a miserable life."

When Alexandra demanded what he wanted, Pierre hesitatingly replied, "I am a student of philosophy."

"Philosophy, what do you want with that, *monsieur?* Presumption! Vanity! Don't you know this Western culture is a vacuity? It is . . . *insipide! insipide!*"

Pausing for breath, Alexandra returned to the attack, "Bergson! This Bergson was a cretin, Immanuel Kant mentally ill, nuts. They have written books and books up to here [she gestured with her hand] to fill them with nothing. But, *monsieur*, thousands of years ago the [Sanskrit] poet Valmiki said it all and much better."

The intrepid student pressed on, requesting an article for the *Revue d'etudes philosophiques de Marseilles*. The orientalist broke into a loud laugh. Poor Pierre reported to Professor Berger that Alexandra was too tired to write anything for the review. Although she was eighty-six, her productive capacities in fact had not dimmed. *Monsieur* Borrely, who kindly related the above anecdote complete with gesture and intonation, has recently retired from his post as professor of philosophy.

During the 1950s Alexandra edited and translated into French previously unknown (to the West) Sanskrit and Tibetan texts. These were published quietly and had a limited circulation. She was able to cull them from her magnificent personal library, which included over four hundred rare Tibetan books and manuscripts. Considering the holocaust that has taken place in Tibet and the wanton destruction of Buddhist artifacts, this collection of an adventurous lifetime has become all the more valuable. Certain of the books were priceless in a more material sense, including a Tibetan-Mongol dictionary written in gold dust.

In 1954 Alexandra and Yongden published a third folk novel, the title of which in a recent American edition (1982) has been rendered as *The Power of Nothingness*. Originally the brief tale of suspense appeared under Yongden's name alone, but this was likely the repetition of a device we have seen before. The translator, Janwillem van de Wetering, well known for his mystery novels, credits Yongden with creating its plot, characters, and general outline. This appears a fair estimate, and certainly the main character, a loyal but not especially brave Tibetan monk named Munpa, has feelings close to Yongden's own.

Munpa finds himself tracking the murderer of his guru, and the tale ranges over the Sino-Tibetan borderlands so familiar to its authors, even to the Gobi Desert. In the manner of Eastern storytelling, while the plot opens outward it simultaneously spirals down toward the core of reality, at once empty and dazzling. Munpa doesn't exactly fall into a landscape, which Alexandra was warned against in her youth, but in solitary meditation he is obliged to paint a colorful epic upon a blank wall with the brush of his thoughts. Unwilling to believe the imaginary mural has a reality equal to any other aspect of his life, the monk becomes frightened, in fact, by his own mind and runs away. Later he accepts the proposition, "The world is nothing but a series of pictures, painted on a wall." This cleverly constructed piece is amiably, yet deeply, Buddhist.

However, Munpa has aspects of a character compelled to piety that remind one of Yongden. In 1938, replying to a letter from Philip praising her (and his) adopted son, Alexandra confided:

I consider him always to be the fourteen-year-old kid that I took close to me in bygone days. But the years have passed and the kid will be thirty-nine at Christmas. Happily he has remained a child in many ways, perhaps because of the manner in which I have directed him. I acknowledge my egotism. I wanted to have someone useful to me no matter the circumstances and who would bend to my desires. This has been to the detriment of the boy's development . . . I preferred to keep him dependent. This isn't very nice on my part, but the thing is done.

The boy had grown into a thickset man wearing thick glasses and traveling in somber European clothing that scarcely flattered him. At Digne he was popular, going about his errands in a beret and striped shirt and blue pants. When a café owner offered him a glass of beer, or a patron a cigarette, he didn't refuse. He learned to speak adequate café French. Tongues wagged that he was interested in women but afraid of his "wife." Certainly, he wished to live in or even visit Paris for the amusements it offered. Alexandra preferred to write of her remembrances of times past.

Yongden made the best of things. He rose early and accompained his mother on her increasingly painful walks. When these became impossible, he grew roses, wrote, and sometimes meditated, performing a thousand helpful tasks. In early October 1955, a Saturday as Alexandra recalled:

It was the last time Albert drove the car to get groceries. He returned, we ate a veal cutlet. He insisted on my having the larger piece. We listened to the radio. . . .

He went to bed. During the night he took ill . . . The servant knocked at my door to call me. . . . [She] said, "Monsieur is very sick.

Yongden died next morning at Samten Dzong, the diagnosis, uremia. He was fifty-six. "He ended up an alcoholic," according to Dr. Marcel Maille. "Completely depressed because he was thoroughly uprooted." Interviews with several *citoyens* of Digne who knew Yongden elicited a similar response. In the end, it was the cautious Philip Neel who proved correct about the unwisdom of transplanting the young Asian man from his native soil.

Alexandra's adopted son once complained to her that she treated him more like a servant, just as did the British and French their colonial underlings, as though she had a right to boss him. Indeed, she had written, "Where would he be without me, this wretched Sikkimese?" It came as something of a shock to learn from General George Pereira— surely not from Alexandra, who kept this as quiet as she had her marriage to Neel—that "she had adopted as her son a young lama of the red hat sect who was a minor 'living Buddha' from South Tibet." Perhaps the *tulku* will be freer to express his innate talents in his next incarnation.

The statement by a recent biographer that Yongden "smiled a lot" and felt at home anywhere is another instance of the European desire to believe their Asian servants really enjoy their lot. Jacques Brosse understood better and relates a telling incident. After Alexandra returned from Tibet to De-chen and learned that Charles Bell had expelled her from Sikkim and fined the locals, they became furious at her. Violence threatened, especially since the natives supposed the British had withdrawn their protection of her person. Yongden, then a lad of sixteen, insured his mistress's safety by reminding the villagers, "One day the Resident and Madame will be reconciled, because they are Whites. It will be us Yellows who finally take the blame." The British, if not Bell, eventually forgave Alexandra her trespasses, but we never heard that they recompensed the Sikkimese.

Alexandra was "desolated, worse than desolated to have lost my travel companion of forty years." With Yongden perished her last living tie to Tibet. She had the lama's body cremated and placed the ashes in an urn at the foot of a Buddha in the shrine room. She felt that something of his "tranquil Buddhist spirit" remained at Samten Dzong. But feelings aside, the orientalist had lost her heir, who was to have received her rights of authorship, and the guardian of treasures collected with so much difficulty. For the continuation of her work, as well as companionship, she would have to turn to strangers.

Dr. Marcel Maille lives in a small town near Toulon, a two-hour drive from Digne. In his seventies, retired, half-blind, he navigates the streets from memory. His former patients come up and begin to complain of their problems. "Ask your doctor," Dr. Maille suggests. "But I don't trust my doctor." Maille smiles, "I don't trust doctors either."

In 1953 this still dapper gentleman was in his handsome prime. His upright slimness and the way he carried himself may have reminded Alexandra of Philip Neel when he came to call on her about her health. That she had heard of him is not surprising since he was known as a Tibetanist, and there were few of those in the south of France. "She was enormously fat with swollen, painful knees and legs," Dr. Maille told us. "She could hardly walk."

Alexandra soon dropped the subject of her health. She began to quiz the doctor on his knowledge of Buddhism, in particular the obscure tantric rites. He was not abashed because he was well read in the texts and more importantly, after the war, had lived with the monks in Indochina and Burma. Alexandra quickly realized that here was a man whose passion for Tibetan Buddhist philosophy equaled her own.

The aging orientalist returned the visit, ostensibly to consult about her legs. Yongden stayed in the car, which was parked the wrong way on a one-way street. "Her legs were terrible," recalled Dr. Maille, "with varicose veins and bleeding ulcers, which she wrapped up in cloth. She would let me do nothing for her." It was Tibet Alexandra wished to talk about, especially when she learned the doctor was planning a retreat in the mountains to practice the ritual of *chod*. The term means "to cut up," and the world-famous author understood she needed to cut her ego down to size.

"Take me with you!" she demanded.

Thinking of the terrain, the doctor protested, "But I can't carry you on my back, *Madame!*"

Alexandra gave in and recommended the ideal place in the Alpes Maritimes for the retreat; it was rocky and isolated, a little dangerous but with ancient Celtic ruins. Had she done *chod* at this magical spot after returning from the East in the 1920s? It reminded her, in spirit, of a "wide, natural clearing, shadowed by giant trees . . . like a cyclopean temple meant for solemn occult rites" that she had discovered on her journey to Lhasa. Then, too, she was overcome by "the desire to perform the rite that Tibetan hermits hold in high esteem as a way of liberating the mind from all attachment." Despite the danger of detection, Alexandra had sent her son to fetch water, while she "[wove] the figures of the mystic dance . . . calling the gods and the demons." She made of grim *chod* a dance of the joy of living.

After Yongden passed away, the two Tibetanists grew closer. Dr. Maille visited as often as he could, and they translated texts together. He was very impressed by Alexandra's library and more by her excellent knowledge of Tibetan. "I would be searching for the meaning of an obscure term," he recalled, "but before I found it in the dictionary, she told me. She was always correct." She told him stories—"thrilling!"—not found in any of her books. At five o'clock a servant cleared everything away and they concluded with tea in the English style.

When Alexandra suggested that she wished to move to Dr. Maille's locale, that she would give up Samten Dzong if he could find her a house on one level, he was taken aback. "You will be my doctor," she insisted. "What doctor? You refuse to take drugs. You don't give a damn for medicine." She looked arch, "At least we could talk more often about things Tibetan."

If the doctor was dubious, it was no doubt due to the orientalist's habits. She slept badly because of pain, and she lived in a mess of newspapers, books, manuscripts. He always found her in her chair surrounded by mounds of papers, immersed in the latest projects. Then, too, she had, as she admitted, "a difficult character."

"She was a woman of authority who would not brook contradiction," recalled Dr. Maille. "She would defend her ideas, even if false, tooth and nail.

"She was *very friendly* to me and I liked her a lot, but there were times when I wanted to say, 'Enough!' I could have slapped her. Because she was so irritating, preemptory in her judgments. She never listened to your arguments."

Alexandra's scheme to move fell through and instead she took a Russian housekeeper. Dr. Maille was probably relieved, but their friendship, which continued into the 1960s, grew ever more intimate. "She didn't tell me in a formal way," Dr. Maille told us, "but she explained to me that she had practiced sexual rites . . . sexual rites of left-handed tantricism. She never wrote of it . . . She mentioned it to me because as her doctor I was not shocked. But I am persuaded she spoke of it with *actual knowledge*."

"I have translated a number of texts concerned with tantric sex," continued the doctor. "They must be read from two points of view: one actual, the other symbolic. There are certain medical observations in them. She [Alexandra] spoke of this as an adept who had actually done these practices."

Their conversation on the subject began when Dr. Maille told Alexandra that, in his university days, he had been given a hoary Tibetan text to translate for its tantric vocabulary. "My professor was an old prude, his interests were strictly academic."

Alexandra explained that the texts were not reliable because the tantric tradition was essentially secret and oral. "I assure you," she said emphatically, "there is much to be gained by *doing* it."

Dr. Maille added that she was ninety at the time of this conversation and that her eyes glowed with delight at the memory of the midnight rites. We inquired where he supposed these might have taken place. He could not be sure, but perhaps Tibet or China.

CHAPTER 26

The Sage of Digne

The *International Herald Tribune* (Paris) reported in an obituary of Alexandra, September 8, 1969, "Mrs. David-Neel shut herself away for the last 24 years in a secluded southern villa, crammed with Buddhist statues, masks, and prayer wheels." True so far as it goes, the obituary imparted the false impression of a willing, if eccentric, hermit. Jacques Brosse was more colorful, although erring in another direction, when he wrote, "She didn't die forgotten by the world . . . but in full glory, a glory that was not at all sought after, that came to her very late and that annoyed her because she didn't wish to waste her time with such frivolity." But as monuments do not topple easily, neither did this larger-than-life character. Alexandra's last decade was a battleground.

When Lawrence Durrell visited this "most astonishing Frenchwoman" in 1964, perhaps his most intriguing observation was to compare Alexandra to Prospero in *The Tempest,* and to claim that, like the Shakespearean magician, she kept hidden a shy, pretty Miranda. That retiring young woman—Marie-Madeleine Peyronnet—is now in her fifties, yet her handsome, pointed face framed by barely graying dark hair hasn't greatly changed. Although her manner is far more assured, slim as ever, she still prefers to dress casually in pants. She is the custodian of Alexandra's home, papers, and photographs and editor of her posthumous works, indeed the custodian of her memory. It is through her eyes that the world has viewed this decade in her and Alexandra's life.

The two women were cast from radically different molds. Where Alexandra was born a Parisienne, Marie-Madeleine was raised in French Algeria in a family of soldiers. The budding orientalist began her travels as soon as she was old enough to run away, while Madeleine remained at home, dominated by a father who had been colonel of a battalion in the Sahara. Still, she dreamed of faroff places, particularly Canada. In her late twenties she became nanny to a wealthy family and traveled to lovely Aix-en-Provence. Here, in 1959, she was recommended to the notice of the famous author who, due to her bad temper and bizarre habits, couldn't manage to keep a secretary—a pale description of the functions once performed by Yongden.

Earlier, Violet Sidney had remarked of Alexandra, "The woman is a genius but she is impossible to live with." Jeanne Denys, who tried in the summer of 1958, became her dedicated enemy. But by the author's behavior on their first meeting at the Hotel Sextius, renowned for its thermal treatments, Madeleine could not have guessed she was speaking with "a woman of ferocious strength, unalterable will and incommensurable despotism." Alexandra lolled on her balcony, mild as the June air. Putting aside her copy of *le Monde*—she consulted its stock tables daily with the aid of a jeweler's loupe—the ninety-year-old asked the young woman what she had accomplished in life.

"Nothing. I haven't studied, I haven't learned a trade."

Alexandra pressed her slightly to discover she had a way with children. "Wonderful!" she exclaimed. "I am in my second childhood, you'll suit me fine."

After inquiring if the applicant were familiar with housework, the author blurted out, "*Mademoiselle*, with me there will be no social security. I don't want to hear about such things." More agreeably, she described the beauties of Samten Dzong, its three terraces from which one could admire the rose garden or a sunset. The climate of Digne was always agreeable. Of course the young lady would like to come work there, yes?

Madeleine was uncertain. The Algerian war raged, and she felt guilty about abandoning her relations. She had been offered another position, with a family about to leave for Tahiti. However, the shrewd David-Neel made up her mind for her. That evening she telephoned Madeleine to come at once, she was dying. The young woman found her collapsed in a wicker chair leaning on two shepherd's crooks (on which she usually hobbled about), moaning. "Don't leave me, my child," she implored. "I only have an hour or two . . . you won't find me ungrateful."

Madeleine agreed to spend the night, and to her amazement by nine Alexandra was wolfing down her dinner. When she went to prepare the supposed invalid's bed, she learned this was an armchair padded with cushions over which would be draped, once Alexandra was in it, an old Tibetan blanket. The scholar insisted her books, pencils, and pads be kept handy. She only drowsed and a vital thought might strike at any time. "Day? Night?" she scoffed. "What do such words mean?"

Her whole life, writes Madeleine Peyronnet in *Dix ans*, a memoir, she had been searching for "a person of intellect." She had the uncommon sense to want to evolve and therefore was ready to be taught. Soon the pair left in Alexandra's battered Citroën for Digne, Madeleine driving and singing above the clatter. Her exhilaration faded when, at the end of the journey, she tried to help her employer out of the car. "Big fool!" grumped Alexandra. Needing assistance made her furious.

Madeleine's first glimpse of Samten Dzong was of the *former* garden, presently abandoned to weeds higher than the car. "It was a real jungle . . . needing only tigers." The interior of this little Tibet proved still more shocking: low-ceilinged rooms hung with grimy red tapestries. The ragged furniture looked ready for the junk heap, and the kitchen appliances might have come from there. Madeleine followed Alexandra as she clumped through on her canes, raising swirls of dust. When she shyly suggested sweeping, the orientalist growled. How could a girl of good family notice such trifles?

If the novice found the house disconcerting—"somber, damp and cold even at midday"—its shrine room terrified her. "When she [Alexandra] opened the door of her private meditation room, I was hit in the face with the smell of incense and the first thing I saw in the center of the room were little tables covered with human skulls and phallic symbols. I was afraid, but wanting to be polite, I said in astonishment, 'Oh, *madame*, it's pretty here!' "

Today, Madeleine loves to tell this story as a joke on herself. She also mistook a rare carved wooden statue of Buddha on a lotus for "a man sitting on an artichoke." Humor aside, surely David-Neel had been practicing rituals here, Tibetan and Shaivite. To the believer, the stone phalluses are not symbols but Shiva himself, the Great Destroyer of ego. With them and certain chants one invokes his power to demolish earthly suffering, to die. The skull drums are employed in tantric rituals, and so were other appurtenances of the little temple: thigh-bone trumpets, a grinning pig mask that dominated one wall, a *tanka* depicting couples wrapped in the poses of desire. Alexandra stared past them all to a tiny case in a glass-doored closet by the Buddha. When Madeleine heard this contained the ashes of Yongden, she silently made the sign of the cross.

The first night in her bedchamber she spent in a nervous sweat. A large black spider hung from a beam, but it didn't bother her nearly as much as the strange bells, butter lamps, and thunderbolts she had seen strewn about, nor the emanations from the oddest object: a *phurba*, a bejeweled magic dagger. This would-be initiate, not lacking in grit, successfully fought off her fears to become indispensable to her mentor. Later on she amused herself by scaring others with the *phurba*. But on that night, had she known how her mistress acquired the dagger, she would have fled down the road in her pajamas.

The *phurba* came into Alexandra's purview in 1921 while she and Yongden were on a journey through northern Tibet. These ritual weapons, designated "tongues of the jumping corpse," were valued as marvelous instruments of sorcery. Tribladed, fashioned out of bronze or ivory with the handle shaped as a demon, *phurbas* became permeated with occult energy after they were employed by lamas in magic rites over periods of time. Laymen who owned such objects ran grave risks.

In *Magic and Mystery* Alexandra told of her encounter with three monks who were carrying the ornate dagger from place to place in an attempt to get rid of it. The dagger once belonged to their deceased head lama, a powerful necromancer, and they were convinced it was wreaking havoc. Several who had touched it died suddenly. Then the pole that held the monastery's banner of benediction fell and broke apart. Naturally, these suspicious occurrences only intensified Alexandra's interest in the dread object.

The monks had enclosed the *phurba* in a box in order to carry it to an isolated cave and abandon it. Cowherds who lived in the vicinity, learning of its approach, protested. Monks and common folk alike feared the dagger might fly through the air to kill indiscriminately. Thus the guardians of the *phurba* were obliged to trek to the highly remote spot in the Chang Tang, where they happened upon the orientalist. Abetted by her lama's robes, she pretended aloofness, but she prevailed on the monks to let her examine the weapon. "The *phurba* was a fine piece of ancient Tibetan art," she wrote. "I was seized with a desire to possess it, but I knew that the *trapas* would not sell it for anything in the world."

Alexandra induced the fellows to camp with her, fed them well, and at nightfall took the curio to a lonely spot and stuck it in the ground. In her own words, "I had been there for several hours when I seemed to see the form of a lama appearing . . . From beneath the toga in which his rather indistinct body was wrapped, a hand came out slowly and advanced to seize the magic dagger." The dumpy woman grabbed it first and held on while the handle wriggled like a snake. When she looked about, the would-be thief had disappeared.

Alexandra raced back to camp to detect which of the *trapas*, less superstitious than his fellows, had dared to make the attempt on the valuable dagger. She demanded of Yongden which of the trio had absented himself for even a moment. "No one," replied her son. "They are half dead with fright." They hadn't even ventured into the darkness to relieve themselves. When she related the strange occurrence, the monks exclaimed together, "Surely that was our Grand Lama! He wanted to take back his *phurba* and perhaps he would have killed you if he succeeded. Oh! Jetsunma, you are a true *gomchenma*."

The monks raised their voices in chorus, begging Alexandra (the "great hermit") to accept the dagger. She permitted them to persuade her, on the rationale that, although the lama had done his worst, "I, by my superior power, became its legitimate owner." One may believe what one wishes about this curious tale, but Alexandra was not only trying to entertain her readers, she was signaling something about her own accomplishments. Those who would picture David-Neel as a disinterested reporter, a sort of cultural anthropologist ahead of her time, choose to ignore her deep involvement in the ritual core of Tibetan Buddhism. But what of the magic dagger? It resides peacefully at Samten Dzong, and we have handled it with no ill effects.

It was the very disarray of Alexandra's life that drew Marie-Madeleine to her. The former's bedchamber and office were one: a large wooden desk and a writing table—heaped with books and papers—a chair, chests containing odds and ends, in one corner a turn-of-the-century suitcase packed with camping gear ready to go. A Tibetan altar with the usual offerings dominated one wall, and *tankas* or bibelots decorated other spots. Each night Madeleine had to tuck her mistress into an armchair, prop her feet on a cushion covered with cloth from her old camp tent, and then massage her legs covered by sores. Ever vain, the older woman ordered the younger to wrap up her legs so they couldn't be seen. In fact, she should have slept with them elevated and open to the air. Her pain must have been constant.

Alexandra would drift off but often awaken to jot down an idea. Then she would ring for Madeleine to bring her tea, never mind the hour. "She made me her slave," wrote the author of *Dix ans,* "but I accepted to live the adventure." Her tasks ranged from cook to secretary. Alexandra might demand a lengthy quote from a Sanskrit manuscript, never considering that Madeleine knew nothing of oriental languages. Clomping about on her canes—"I walk on my arms," she quipped—the old explorer would check if her employee were slacking off in any department. "You will be the head, and I will be the legs," the young woman had agreed, scarcely reckoning she would spend most of every day, and a good part of the night, on her feet.

Alexandra would not hear of a holiday. Madeleine, in order to see her family, brought her mother and sister to live nearby. During the next decade her only real time off, three half-days, was to attend funerals. Throughout this period the orientalist worked with a fervor that belied her age. Wrapped in her claret robe, thick white hair plaited in a pigtail, she kept near her always a simmering tea pot, a magnifying glass to decipher small print, pens, plenty of paper, and her daily schedule and notes for current books. In the later 1960s, she saw less of Dr. Maille, so Dr. Julien Romieu, the mayor of Digne, became her physician. He advised her to get reading glasses. She answered indignantly, "Doctor, at my age one does not wear glasses!" She was ninety-seven, yet Madeleine could not be sure if she meant she were too old or too young.

Still, Alexandra did not delude herself; she was preoccupied with death and its mirror image, rebirth. In 1961 she had published *Immortalite et reincarnation: Doctrines et pratiques en Chine, au Tibet, dans l'Inde.* At long last she was accomplishing what she had felt called to half a century earlier—the comparative study of religions. But Alexandra always kept current on the news, and she allowed herself to be drawn into the crisis in Sino-Tibetan relations. *Old Tibet Faces the New China* (1953), and at greater length and more thoughtfully *Four Thousand Years of Chinese Expansion* (1964), elaborate her views on one of the nastiest political situations of our time. The titles are translations, for mercifully these two slim volumes remained in French and disappeared as quickly as they became outdated.

In 1950 elements of the victorious Red Army gingerly pushed westward into Tibet. China couldn't afford an immediate war in such forbidding territory, especially while the Korean conflict lasted. An anomalous situation arose whereby the young Fourteenth Dalai Lama was expected to act as a figurehead and the Chinese hoped to rule through their generals resident in Lhasa. However, the Panchen Lama (who befriended Alexandra) had died in 1937 and was no longer available as a counter to the Dalai. Although the Chinese put forward a reincarnation of the Panchen, he has not become widely recognized by the Tibetans.

"There is no question of invasion or even Chinese agression," wrote the author in her first book on the subject. Rather, China had "reoccupied Tibet" by right, since "it has always been part of their empire." Further, "Not a shot was fired against the [Chinese] troops in the course of their advance through Tibet, [but] they have been greeted with enthusiasm by the majority of the population." Alexandra asserted that the peasants, heavily taxed by Lhasa and burdened with ancestral debts to their landlords, had welcomed the Chinese as liberators, and that especially the Khampas, who had often intermarried with them, looked forward to the reestablishment of the old ties with Peking, which they regarded as more distant and lenient than Lhasa. "Foreigners who supposed the Tibetans were victims of odious agression were badly misinformed," concluded the author.

This did not represent a change of views on Alexandra's part. In 1927 she had written, "Tibetans have lost much in parting with China. Their sham independence profits only a clique of court officials." Because of her experience in the Himalayan border states, Alexandra was convinced that the British barred foreigners from Tibet because the empire intended to swallow the country, as it had Sikkim. In contrast, she found China weak and anarchic, yet, in a holdover from Confucian times, polite and welcoming. Even her trials during World War II could not erase these lasting impressions. She interpreted the return of Chinese generals to Lhasa as a reestablishment of the custom of Ambans, and she insisted that "the Chinese are perfectly sincere when they promise complete liberty of belief to their [minority] peoples." Only the abbots of the great monasteries, whom she dubbed "feudal lords," would object to reintegration within China. Concerning the position of the Fourteenth, he would never flee his capital. Just as the pope outside of Rome would lose his authority, "one can't be Dalai Lama outside of Lhasa."

It might be argued that much of the above is in the realm of prediction, and that although Alexandra's political sense was usually astute, here it failed her. However, she did not essentially alter her attitude in *Four Thousand Years,* written ten years later when Red Chinese ferocity in Tibet was clear for the world to see. In 1959 the International Commission of Jurists had concluded its investigation, and the General Assembly of the United Nations had voiced its "grave concern . . . that the fundamental human rights and freedoms of the people of Tibet have been forcibly denied them." While admitting China had instituted "a regime of servitude more or less masked," Alexandra insisted that Chinese domination was inevitable and unassailable. "Tibetans have never formed a true nation," she wrote. The cheerful Tibetan people were bound to adjust to the situation, and in any case the new China would improve the lot of the poor, of women, and it would develop the natural resources of the country.

Previous writers on David-Neel have either overlooked or whitewashed her stand on the above issues. In fact, her position was gravely mistaken. We needn't go into the actual tragic situation in Tibet in detail. That is expertly accomplished in the writings of Peter Hopkirk, John Avedon, the Indian scholars Suchita Gosh and P. K. Karan, the Tibetan scholars Tsepon Shakabpa and Thubten Norbu, and especially in H. H. the Dalai Lama's *My Land and My People.* Succinctly, guerrilla warfare against the Chinese occupying army broke out in the early 1950s, centered among the rifle-wielding Khampas, always certain that "One Tibetan is worth ten Chinese." But in 1959, with the flight of the Dalai Lama across the Himalayas to India, a genuine holocaust was unleashed.

One-third of the population of Tibet proper was killed outright or died prematurely from disease or starvation. Over six thousand monasteries small and large were destroyed, shelled by cannon and then dismantled brick by remaining brick by forced labor under the guns of soldiers. Religious statues were seized and removed, many melted down for their gold, silver, and jewels. Others were sold, mainly in Hong Kong. Frescoes were defaced, books burned, monks shot or imprisoned or forced to marry nuns. Hardest blow of all was the prohibition of study of the *Dharma,* the doctrine of Gautama Buddha, which early in her life Alexandra had embraced as her salvation. To practice Buddhism through study, rites, or prayer was branded treason. The International Commission of Jurists termed the Chinese atrocities "genocide," but even this horrific word falls short of the totality of destruction wreaked on the Sacred Realm.

In 1984, on "the twenty-fifth anniversary of the Tibetan National Uprising Day," the Dalai Lama reminded the world that China's policy toward his country remains essentially unyielding, as does the Tibetan will to resist:

The present campaign of terror which the Chinese have unleashed in Tibet has once again made the Tibetan people live in a state of anxiety and fear. The brutal act of playing with the lives of people by believing in the power of weapons cannot subdue the human mind, nor can it foster understanding and harmony . . . Until now the number of Tibetans killed in action, executed, starved to death, tortured to death, and driven to suicide, add up to about one million deaths.

What has been achieved by all this killing?

The essential question we must ask is how Alexandra, so identified with Tibet, could have been so mistaken about its destiny. Practically immobile at Samten Dzong, she had to depend on secondhand information. Few Tibetans had yet arrived in France, and for her sources she had only erroneous news accounts and the scuttlebutt picked up among like-minded intellectuals. For Alexandra remained a French intellectual on the Left. During the Algerian War anything that smacked of colonialism was anathema to this group. They firmly believed that China, which had liberated itself from Western dominance, would do the same for the rest of Asia. The orientalist was sympathetic to Chinese aspirations, and perhaps naive as to Chairman Mao's actual intentions.

Still, there is something deeper psychologically at work here. Alexandra's *Four Thousand Years* was sprinkled with anecdotes about the good old days in Tibet when there were no roads and picturesque brigands ran rampant. Clearly, this anachronistic world was in any case doomed to extinction, precisely as she herself was facing the end. Alexandra once compared herself to *Madame* de Pompadour, mistress of Louis XV. Perhaps she also shared some of Louis's disdain for the future—"*Après moi, le déluge!*"

This enormously egotistical woman, in many ways larger than life, was really heartbroken in her loneliness. She took a certain sad pleasure in supposing that, as she would be no more, *her* Tibet had vanished beneath what she called "the wave of Chinese expansion."

At Samten Dzong, while life went on, Alexandra ruled with an iron, if arthritic, hand. Marie-Madeleine was ordered to attack the weeds in the garden in order to plant peas, beans, parsley, and chevril. These vegetables would be cooked into thick soups reminiscent of the good meals at Kum Bum. The orientalist liked to discourse on the joys of eating homegrown produce. During her journeys in Asia she was more or less a vegetarian, and she always preferred this diet. However, according to Madeleine, drafted into cooking for her, "She had to go [i.e. trek] for days without eating. When they arrived [at a camp] she would yell at her servants to cook up everything and she gorged herself."

These irregular habits carried over and at home she had no regular habits for eating, sleeping, or working.

Madeleine found it impossible to keep up a strictly vegetarian diet, although Alexandra remained fond of pasta, boiled rice with milk, coffee, and sweets. Her favorite dish was *beignet aux pommes:* apples in batter, fried in butter and then dipped in powdered sugar. This was disastrous for a woman in her nineties given to arthritis, and her knees grew swollen, red, and deformed. For the last several years she could not walk at all, and Madeleine had to carry her from chair to chair. Fortunately, she was not quite as heavy as formerly.

One bone of contention between the two women, who developed a deep but tense relationship, was Alexandra's Buddhist reverence for all forms of life. The shrine room was a refuge for mice who were eating up the Tibetan rugs and manuscripts. Alexandra refused to put out traps and instead experimented with taming a few of the little creatures. Secretly, Marie-Madeleine poisoned the lot, just as she surreptitiously, then openly, waged war on the dirt and disorder of Samten Dzong. When it came to the realm of ideas, Alexandra turned tough and her young Algerian sentimental. She liked to force her companion to examine the framework of her beliefs. "What does 'love' mean?" Alexandra inquired tartly. "Isn't it just a word that imbeciles repeat without knowing what they say?"

In turn, Madeleine probed for the chinks in the old stoic's armor. She was a woman who deeply missed her husband. And the mention of Yongden's name brought a wounded look to her face. Madeleine was the first woman since Alexandra's youth to breach her hard shell. Three-quarters of a century before, her mother's lack of understanding left a deep scar. Since then, the orientalist had tended to measure her accomplishments against those of men, whether they were admirers, teachers, or rivals. This relationship of her last decade was more intimate, more feminine. The imperious one criticized her employee for being too slow to carry out her commands, dubbing her *"Tortue"* (tortoise). She poked fun at her, "Ah, this tortoise of bad luck, how she amuses me . . . She is ugly! She is stupid! She is wicked! She is too tall! But I like her mug."

"Intellectuals are perverse and Satanic," Madeleine confided to her diary. To her employer's face she called her "a Himalaya of despotism." The old dame chuckled. When, the last few years, she could no longer hold a pen, Madeleine wrote for her.

Curiosity seekers bombarded Samten Dzong with letters and visits, much to the overworked secretary's annoyance. Convinced of Alexandra's powers, these extravagants came from the four corners with outlandish petitions. One South American fell down and began to kiss Madeleine's feet as she opened the door. Numbers of women begged to live as celibates with one they supposed was a great medium, while others expected her to help them succeed in business, cure an illness, or accomplish a crime. A refined-looking woman was eager to learn if her dead husband were wandering in the *bardo* or already reincarnated. Perfumed letters had made her suspect his fidelity and she wanted to demand of him the truth. Another irate wife implored the wizard of Samten Dzong to kill, at long distance, her straying spouse. "If all unfaithful husbands are murdered," teased Alexandra, "there will be nothing on earth but widows."

In the 1960s caravans of hippies often stopped at Digne on their pilgrimages to the East. They idolized the sage who had lived among Tibetan hermits, but to her credit she disdained to promote a cult in the manner of certain self-proclaimed gurus. Girls in miniskirts were declared unwanted at Samten Dzong, since Alexandra considered such revealing garb inappropriate for well-bred women. Otherwise, she liked to chat with and was rejuvenated by her qualified young admirers. If they had read a book or two of hers and a little Eastern philosophy, she would entertain them like old friends.

Alexandra warned that the serious business of vagabonding wasn't for the fainthearted or faddish. First one must master the language of a country. To depart without money was a disservice to native beggars. She proposed that ten years of residence was necessary to speak of a place with real authority. Otherwise, the Buddhist set down no dictums, nor would she assign her admirers *mantras* to chant or exercises to perform beyond what could be found in her writings. To end a tedious interview she closed her eÿes and sat stock still, either in deep meditation or simply dozing.

In *Dix ans* Marie-Madeleine makes it plain that her employer was "monstrously demanding," and to us she has stated that she worked eighteen hours each day. According to an informant, the relationship between the two women was yet more hard-edged. "Madeleine wept when Alexandra insulted her, and she begged to be taken on as a disciple." She could not realize, not then, that she *was* being taught in the manner traditional to master and disciple in the Tibetan school favored by Alexandra, particularly when both are originally difficult, prideful persons. Even the myriad petty tasks heaped on Madeleine had a purpose beyond themselves, and she has in fact become David-Neel's disciple, the transmitter of her painfully acquired knowledge to future generations. Such was the relationship between the master Marpa and his student Milarepa, on whom he heaped such vexations as to make Marie-Madeleine's seem lightweight. An account may be found in Dawasandup's translation of the life of Milarepa, edited by Evans-Wentz.

It is intriguing that Marpa became the human bridge between the great storehouse of Indian Buddhism, carrying its Sanskrit texts on his back over the treacherous Himalayas to the new ground of Tibet, where in this icy clime, once translated into Tibetan, the teachings would take new root. So Alexandra brought home her wonderful collection of both manuscripts and adventures and translated them not only into European languages but a mode comprehensible to the Western mind. This, on the eve of the Tibetan holocaust, was her greatest achievement, and since the fruition is still in progress, it necessitated the entire dedication of Marie-Madeleine. Be it husband, lover, son, or disciple, Alexandra picked aright.

The ambrosia of wisdom was reserved for *Tortue* in informal sessions after the long day. Alexandra reposed in her armchair, majestic as a Tibetan oracle. Her small hands made deliberate gestures to accompany the recitations that compensated the secretary for the rigors of her apprenticeship. Sitting on a straw mat at the master's feet, the disciple imagined that it whisked her to lamas' caves amid the Himalayas. Alexandra's monologues were delivered with elan: one moment she foamed like a torrent, the next she was wrapped in Buddhist calm. The old opera singer knew how to transfix her audience of one.

Madeleine's restricted upbringing hadn't prepared her for the vagaries of genius. She hardly understood Alexandra's insistence that her success was owing to her "*mauvaise caractère*," which we may translate as "bad temper." Still, Madeleine was enthralled by the tale of one cruelly cold night on the steppes. The wind blew so strongly it blew out the fire and sleep meant death. Alexandra had to keep her bone-tired servants and animals moving, and this she accomplished by whipping them without pause or mercy until dawn. Recounting the story, the explorer gripped a cane in her delicate fist and flailed the air, crying, "*Vlan! Vlan!*" Madeleine could feel the stripes across her own back.

Of course the ancient one sometimes grew morbid. She regularly quoted the Greek maxim: "Those who die young are loved by the gods." Instead, she claimed to be paying for her sins with a cruel old age and "a filthy, stupid end in an armchair." She longed after the Central Asian plateau, cursing herself for leaving. "I should have died there," she moaned, "among the immense grassy solitudes close to the Tibetan lakes; for a bed the earth, grass or snow, for a ceiling the canvas of my tent and the great starry sky." A wise lama would have performed the proper ceremonies to insure a propitious rebirth, after which her body would be cut to pieces and scattered for the vultures—the "sky burial." She sighed, "That would have been a beautiful death . . . grand."

Alexandra realized that, due to her own choices, she had been brought full circle: hobbled, dependent on domestics. This was reminiscent of her mother's last days, a fate that in the flood of life she had despised, never dreaming it might resemble hers. Alternately she wished for deliverance and feared it, begging, "*Tortue*, don't let me die." She was especially fearful of being buried alive. She had seen supposed corpses still breathing as they were tossed on the funeral pyres in Benares. So she instructed Madeleine to observe her body for ten days before summoning the undertaker, and even then to sever the veins in her wrists.

Madeleine preferred to distract Alexandra by encouraging her to weave travel yarns or by baking a special dessert. Visitors were an unfailing tonic, but the younger ones annoyed the harassed secretary. Seeing nothing in these youthful seekers beside a lot of unkempt beggars, she once burst out that were she president of the republic she would ban David-Neel's books because of the mischief they encouraged. The explorer of outer limits, making no reply, seemed to stare into space. Was it then she thought of implicating the younger woman in the destruction of portions of her correspondence?

When Jacques Brosse inquired of Marie-Madeleine about gaps in the letters, she "confided that under the order of Alexandra herself, she had very probably burned them [the missing ones] up, without knowing what they were about." Earlier, the explorer had requested of her husband that he destroy the letters that mentioned her illnesses or repeated demands for money. He does not seem to have complied. The gaps in the record exist for several tumultuous years after the Neels' marriage, as well as a couple of other embarrassing instances we have mentioned. Alexandra's motives in demanding Madeleine commit the mysterious packet to the flames remain a matter of speculation.

Distinguished guests who arrived at Samten Dzong were regarded favorably by both master and disciple. The Bishop of Digne, *Monseigneur* Collin, was an erudite man with whom Alexandra liked to discuss everything from politics to the Bible. The iconoclast had always got on remarkably well with the higher clergy. Teilhard de Chardin was another Catholic intellectual with whom she kept in touch. Once when he visited he chided her for not believing in miracles. "I make them!" she replied.

A touching incident occurred when Alexandra entertained two explorer friends from earlier days. Bertrand Flornoy, discoverer of the source of the Amazon, had won her lasting esteem by declaring on radio, "The greatest explorer of our century is a woman . . . Alexandra David-Neel." Gaètan Fouquete was a well-known journalist and travel writer. Alexandra hadn't seen these cronies in thirty years, and she envisioned them as still young. She primped and fussed, haranguing Madeleine on how to fix her bun. The gentlemen arrived and the Parisienne greeted them with the charm and manners she showed toward those she considered her peers. But once they had left, she told her secretary to throw open the windows to rid the room of "a musty odor." Sighed the nostalgic one, "They are old men!"

It took a different sort of man to bring out Alexandra's sprightly, coquettish air. When Lawrence Durrell interviewed her in 1964 for *Elle*, he was struck by her "magnificent eyes," her "small and beautiful ears" and "delicately designed nose and mouth." Unfortunately, she was difficult at first, relating a story that is most intriguing. In brief, she claimed that, after crossing the border into Tibet, she became ill and was dying in the snows. Charles Bell, the Resident, received word of her plight, yet because she had disobeyed his order, he would do nothing to help her. "You English are not gentlemen!" she remonstrated.

We don't think Alexandra's memory was faulty, but that she told on purpose a composite story, the elements of which the reader will recognize. The incident shows how she still felt the hurt of her expulsion by Bell from Tibet, indeed the loss of what was really her native country. Besides, the old fox liked to test people. Durrell was well prepared for the eventuality. Struck by one of the postage-stamp-sized illustrations from the French version of *Journey, Voyage d'une Parisienne à Lhassa,* taken by an outmoded plate camera, he had it blown up. As he informed us, "It showed a young woman of quite exceptional beauty and spirituality dressed as a Buddhist pilgrim with beads and begging bowl and a little pointed wicker hat that I remembered from my own childhood."

To counter Alexandra's grouching, Durrell produced the photograph. He recounts her reaction:

"Yes," she said, "it was a farewell picture I had taken on the eve of my departure from Darjeeling." Then becoming grumpy once more she added most reproachfully, "I think you might have brought one for me." I replied, "Madam, I have brought four for you." At this her face relaxed into its pretty youthful lines and she took the pictures from me with delight and said, "Ah monsieur, you see that I was once beautiful." It was very touching, very feminine, and from then on we were firm friends.

So the two authors chatted amiably, and Alexandra, hair not entirely white, appeared to Durrell as a woman of perhaps sixty. Here was another triumph of will over pain by the adventurer who opened the hidden world of Tibetan Buddhism. Or was it method—did she practice any form of internal yoga? We believe she did, at least some of those silent practices concerned with concentrating the mind, sleeping, dying, and meditating on aspects of the Void. It would be impossible to prove what cannot be detected, yet even a passing knowledge of tantric methodology, as elucidated in *Initiations and Initiates,* leads to the conclusion that Alexandra had not forgotten what she so arduously acquired.

Nearing a century on earth, the woman began to crumble physically. She still had her teeth, but now and again one would crack and fall out. Her skin itched terribly, and she would scratch off pieces of flesh. "Ah, *Tortue,* I am falling apart bit by bit," she complained. However, she retained the spirit of adventure. At one hundred she renewed her passport, much to the puzzlement of the official in charge. This was no empty gesture but the prelude to a journey. Alexandra would not fly in an airplane, remarking, "To be locked up in that utensil and precipitated from one capital to another, without the possibility to contemplate anything, what's the good of traveling that way?" Still, an itinerary had crystalized in her mind.

She put the grandiose scheme to her secretary casually: they would drive the Citroën first to Berlin where she knew of a doctor who claimed to cure arthritis. Then it was on to Russia, driving the length of that vast country to Vladivostok. There she and Madeleine could embark for their final destination, New York. Did she envision a ticker-tape parade up Broadway?

Alexandra had thought it out in detail, down to sleeping in the car and cooking to trim expenses. Seeing new places would make her feel young and well again. Madeleine vetoed the proposal, and not to provoke an argument gave the excuse that her legs were too long to curl up in a tiny vehicle. This put an end to the centenarian's long-held wish to see America.

In 1969 Alexandra was promoted to the highest order of the French Legion of Honor. Scholars came to pay homage. Rene Grousset, the orientalist, praised her erudition: "She knows the depths of Tibet and speaks excellent Tibetan." He added that his Tibetan acquaintances uniformly held her in high esteem and accorded her the title *Jetsunma*. Similarly, the Fourteenth Dalai Lama from his Indian exile spoke favorably of the explorer in an interview with Arnaud Desjardins. The spiritual leader wanted to meet the woman who had known his predecessor, and added, "We have read her books and we recognize there our own Tibet."

When the French government decided to cast a bronze medal in Alexandra's honor, she refused to pose. Madeleine got this snappy reply, "When one is old and ugly one shouldn't show oneself." The medal had to be cast from a photo without the subject's cooperation. She did choose the motto to be engraved on the reverse: Walk Straight on Following Your Heart's Desire. It is from Ecclesiastes and had caught the attention of the youthful rebel three-quarters of a century earlier.

Rather reluctantly, Alexandra engaged in a television program about Tibet that devoted twenty minutes to her exploits. She acted strange, replying to the interviewer in French, English, or Tibetan as she fancied. She couldn't help but oblige the mayor, Dr. Romieu, and the councilors of Digne, who wished to celebrate her hundredth birthday with a party. She descended into a dark mood for weeks before the gala. While Madeleine, impressed by the magnitude of the occasion, tried to tidy the villa against the expected invasion of reporters and notables, her mentor took refuge in her Tibetan books, mumbling the syllables aloud.

The cameramen on the occasion shot a beatific Alexandra, chignon neatly arranged, in a robe of Chinese silk. On each hand she wore the appropriate ring of the initiate given to her long ago by the maharaja of Sikkim. She chatted with reporters as zestily as she had on her return in 1925. The municipality had contributed champagne to commemorate its most famous citizen, and the author's office was transformed into a bar that rang with toasts to her courage and longevity. Gawking locals and sophisticated Parisians made Samten Dzong teem like a three-ring circus.

The one-time hermit's goodwill eroded under the onslaught. To the cameramen she snapped, "Sirs, don't you think it is indecent to come film the death of an old woman?" Finally, she let loose at a troop of girls from the grammar school who shyly waited to present a bouquet of roses. Pulling herself up to the dignity of her five feet two inches, Alexandra barked, "Girls, have you nothing to say? Or are you simply eaten up by curiosity to see the old ape?"

After the crowd left, the scholar communed for a few hours with her Tibetan volumes. Honors were as useless to her as old hiking boots. Although sitting upright in her wicker desk chair made hot irons jab into her spine, work was her one reliable painkiller. She accepted her trials, once informing Madeleine that suffering refines the character of men and women. Then, too, as an initiated lama, she might through meditation choose her moment to exit, and according to Tibetan theory, her time and place of rebirth.

Alexandra was touched when Digne named a projected secondary school after her. Along with Dr. Romieu, she pored over the plans, sad that Philip Neel hadn't lived for this moment. How wise of the councilors to memorialize her before, rather than after, death. Even more on the scholar's mind was her will, the disposal of her invaluable library and extensive collection of Tibetan artifacts, especially the stunning masks. Dr. Maille was consulted, and he agreed to contact his good friend Professor R. A. Stein, head of the French Asia Society. Thus France's two leading Tibetanists conferred at Samten Dzong.

Alexandra wished her library and artifacts kept intact and placed where they might be studied. She hoped that Stein, a distinguished scholar but decidedly of the old school, would oversee the installation of her collections in Paris. In return he would have her ashes strewn in the Ganges. To sweeten the deal, she offered him certain ritual bone items. Professor Stein refused, commenting to Dr. Maille, "This woman is not very interesting."

Perhaps conflict was inevitable between these two proponents of rival versions of the epic of Gesar of Ling. Alexandra was stung by the rejection, but we are reminded of a saying of hers: "Who knows the flower best?—the one who reads about it in a book, or the one who finds it wild on the mountainside?"

In something of a panic, Alexandra cast about for means to assure continuity of her work. She felt that Marie-Madeleine was too inexperienced, too welcoming, to take proper charge of her legacy. In this, to the benefit of all her admirers, she would be proved mistaken. According to an informant, "Each week she wrote another will, [and] the last one was used." Her entire library of French, English, and Tibetan books was donated to the Musée Guimet, where she had begun her studies as a young woman. Her wonderful collection of artifacts was left in limbo, with the most unfortunate results. Only her letters and unpublished manuscripts were to remain at Samten Dzong under the care of Madeleine, and the proceeds of their publication would go to the municipality of Digne. The latter act proved both charitable and wise.

One of Madeleine's first experiences had been a summons to witness Alexandra's final breath. Throughout the next decade the author rang her bell persistently, usually in the middle of the night, to signal the supposed last act. Naturally, the secretary learned to disregard these false alarms. Against reason, she came to regard her mentor as immortal, a notion abetted by Alexandra's strong will, which showed no signs of withering. But in July 1969 she understood that her employer was beyond searching for sympathy. At breakfast the old explorer's pinched face had a blissful glow, the aftermath of an illumination given to her the night before.

"God, the Father, spoke to me," whispered Alexandra. "He has made a great light in my soul and I have seen the nothingness of all that was myself."

These words, at once Christian and Buddhist in tone, are a quote from Anatole France's *Thaïs*, made into an opera by Massenet. No doubt Alexandra in the role of the heroine—a courtesan converted to religion, who nonetheless seduces a monk—once had sung them.

From this point on the world-weary one showed little emotion, only a certain sweetness, an affability, that her secretary had not known from her before. She wasted neither words nor tears, only stating, "This time, *Tortue*, it's really the end. My father was right . . . You can sense it."

Her major regret concerned giving up current investigations: yoga, not as popularly conceived but as authentically practiced by true sages; and the lives of Jesus and Mao. She wished to approach the Christian savior as a typically Hebrew prophet, a patriot, and to treat the Communist Party chairman as an incarnation of the mythical Gesar, righter of wrongs suffered by the Chinese and Tibetan peoples. Her thought, like fine wine, grew more valuable with age, and we, too, regret she was unable to complete her work.

Alexandra, like Conway in *Lost Horizon*, ultimately returned from her paradise to the mundane world out of a sense of duty. She wished to educate others, to share the rare knowledge she had acquired. Putting off her personal quest for Nirvana, she took the path of the *bodhisattva,* enlisting in the common human struggle to be free of ignorance.

Toward the last, old voyages ran in her head: "I am at Marseilles and I wish to go to Peking," she mumbled. On September 8, 1969, at three in the morning, with the hard-pressed *Tortue* at her side, Alexandra ceased fighting for breath. The traveler departed on her final journey.

Marie-Madeleine felt crestfallen to be liberated from this "prideful, difficult, impossible, passionate" woman. At the same time, she was left with "a joy in living" and the tasks of editing her teacher's voluminous papers and composing her own *Ten Years with Alexandra David-Neel.*

On September 11 at Marseilles the remains of Alexandra were cremated. Madeleine and Dr. Romieu were present, along with several old explorer friends and a niece and nephew of Philip Neel. As she had wished, there was a minimum of ceremony, and her ashes were placed in an urn to be kept with Yongden's at Samten Dzong until Madeleine could transport them to the River Ganges. Newspapers, radio, and television in many countries announced the explorer's death, and most fittingly the *New York Herald Tribune* showed a photo of Alexandra riding a yak; it was captioned, "Woman on top of the world."

The sadness about Alexandra's life, inextricably mixed with her triumph, was caused by the knowledge she would have to renounce her Shangri-La, come down from "the solitudes, the eternal snows and the big bright sky of 'up there.'" After she had left her hermit's hut in the mountains to explore Tibet, and consequently had been expelled from Sikkim, Alexandra wrote to Philip,

The decor was snow white or bedecked with flowers according to the season. One was there alone with nature in a country magnetized by ancient legends and the prayers of a whole people: the Himalayas, home to the gods and sages! [A] living dream that I knew how to taste intensely, understanding from the first day that I would wake. No matter how the bitterness was predicted or prepared for, it was none the less cruel.

To help smooth Alexandra's path down from the mountain, the authors would like to perform something of what could not be done at her death. So that her spirit may not lose its way in the *bardo* but seek Nirvana, or find a favorable incarnation, we offer the following ancient verse from *The Tibetan Book of the Dead:*

When demons noise their savage call
Let me hear naught but six holy sounds
When blinded by rain and snow,
    wind and dark
Let my eyes be touched by wisdom
Unseeing, see.

Coda: The Legacy

What has Alexandra David-Neel left us all? Including posthumous works, thirty distinct titles bear her name—which was her husband's, too. While each is concerned with the East, at least in part, they vary from early utopian to the highly erudite, from the formality of grammar to the intimacy of private letters. Her books range over philosophy, anthropology, orientalism, philology, geographical discovery, historical and political nuance, and the tangle of tantric practices. Always they are crammed with adventure, the author's "only reason for living."

Born in the eye of a revolutionary hurricane, Alexandra ultimately disdained politics but remained a keen observer. Once an opera singer, she later chose to perform on the vast Central Asian plateau. A staunch feminist, she learned from men, loved her father, husband, and son, and was welcomed as a compeer by the most rugged of the lot. She explored over great unmapped distances—the ice-clad Himalayas, leech-ridden jungles, the fierce steppes—but she delved more significantly into the crevices of the human psyche. Above everything, this willful woman who could beat a recalcitrant servant, this beneficiary of turn-of-the-century imperialism who defied an empire, stands for individual liberty, for the full expression of the "I" that her Buddhist philosophy denied.

As a girl, Alexandra resisted the discipline and orthodoxy that her respectable mother tried to enforce. Her father's liberal past and encouragement provided a way out: she grouped with her peers, studied music and Eastern thought. Temporarily a bohemian in *Belle Epoque* Paris, the pretty young woman took a lover and flirted with popular occultism and chic anarchism. But for her the transforming freedom had to be personal. These were but steps, albeit slippery ones, on the path toward the significant renunciation inherent in Buddhism.

When the anarchist movement was defused, there appeared on the opera stage a certain Alexandra Myrial whose brief career held a few moments of glory. Her voice and refined looks suited the music of

Massenet but not Wagner or Puccini, the coming idols. Nearing middle age, the singer found herself tinkling piano at the casino in Tunis. A local engineer and man about town took a fancy to her, she became his mistress and more or less duped him into marriage. Once the ring was on her finger, she left to follow her heart's desire, and Philip Neel picked up the bills for his wife's Asian travels.

That is crudely put, but the time has come to demystify a life devoted to elucidating the mysteries of oriental thought. Alexandra donned the saffron robe and took refuge in the Buddha in her midforties. Her true career began at an age when others begin to think of retirement. She studied and meditated amid the snows of a Himalayan winter ensconced in a cave; most difficult, she subordinated her will to another. The Gomchen of Lachen taught her much. Then she employed the knowledge she had gained to explore, to record and explain to others. She never cut herself off from the world for long but fought for a hearing as determinedly as she battled the brigands of Koko Nor. She packed a pistol and could shoot straight, although her main weapon was a quicker wit. She strove to attain Lhasa for several reasons, not least "because it was there."

Her account of her journey recently has been reissued in Great Britain and the United States. We can't gauge what effects it will have in the future, but we do know the actual influence of David-Neel's writings on particular intrepid souls because they have told us. Lama Govinda, a German who became perhaps more Tibetanized than Alexandra, consciously followed the path she blazed. At Sikkim's royal monastery of Podang, he was pleased to occupy "the same room in which she had lived and where a strange voice had warned the young Maharaja . . . of his impending end and the failure of his intended religious reforms." Lama Govinda, like Alexandra, learned from the Gomchen that "mere goodness and morality without wisdom is as useless as knowledge without goodness." Hallmarks of this woman were her searching intellect and her refusal to surrender to a mushy mysticism.

In 1972 the naturalist George Schaller (*Stones of Silence*) and the writer Peter Matthiessen (*The Snow Leopard*) clubbed together on a journey from Katmandu to Shey near the Nepalese-Tibetan border. They were studying the habits of wildlife in terrain that was both difficult and politically dangerous. Areas along the route were inhabited by Khampa refugees, hard-bitten from years of guerrilla warfare against the Chinese army. Hampered by late monsoon rains, the pair settled into a small hotel in an isolated Tibetan village to the west of Annapurna. Rain continued to fall, the travelers needed porters, and the locals refused to carry. So they remained for days in their sleeping bags and read about Tibetan Buddhism, entranced by *Magic and Mystery*. Eventually the weather cleared, porters materialized, and the pair trekked on.

In 1978 the first all-women's rafting trip down the Colorado River through the Grand Canyon began; it was 115 degrees in the shade, if you could find any. The rafters poured buckets of water over each other to keep cool. Some rowed, others paddled, a few talked. China Galland, who has described this and other adventures in *Women in the Wilderness*, wrote, "Our group is extremely diverse . . . Still I know there must be a common thread that has drawn us all together."

In the chapter titled "How We Got There," the author recalls making a most important discovery: the life of Alexandra David-Neel. At a time of crisis in her own life, Galland identified with Alexandra's despair at successive early frustrations. Galland continues, "I ponder the change in my spirits that has come over me since beginning to read about Alexandra . . . the triumph of implacable spirit, the danger and the merit of following one's own path, and the realities of living out a dream." Alexandra inspired China Galland to explore difficult terrain, both outer and inner, and to communicate her victories.

Again in 1978, at the opposite end of the world, 18,500 feet high on Annapurna in Nepal, Dr. Arlene Blum, leader of the first all-women's expedition up the giant mountain, spoke into her tape recorder, "I keep wondering when the next avalanche will come. I'm spooked . . . Risking our lives; God, it's crazy. Why? Well, in another six days someone can be on top."

While David-Neel didn't initiate Dr. Blum's climbing career, which began during Blum's student days in the Pacific Northwest, finding a copy of *Journey to Lhasa* in a secondhand bookstore in Katmandu profoundly affected her. She carried the message of the book with her up that towering mass of ice and snow, and perhaps the Frenchwoman's dogged determination stiffened the American's will to succeed. The women conquered the world's third highest peak, although on the descent two climbers, roped together, plunged to their deaths. Dr. Blum's *Annapurna: A Woman's Place* surely counts as a fruit of the tree of many images conjured up by Alexandra.

In August 1985, sixteen years after the Frenchwoman's demise, another American woman found herself at the ornate entrance to the Jo Khang, Lhasa's cathedral, festooned with flags to celebrate the twentieth anniversary of the People's Government of the Tibet Autonomous Region, and the arrival of the puppet Panchen Lama to bestow his benediction on the occasion. Many rural folk, following age-old custom, had flocked into Lhasa for the event—complete with Mardi Gras–like floats proclaiming the new Tibet and "Twenty Years of Progress." Townsfolk, peasants, and nomads smiled broadly, only partly because they had been warned to for weeks in advance over the loudspeaker system that permeates every nook of the City of the Sun.

Tall, lanky, blond, the woman's typically Tibetan outfit of dark felt failed to disguise her nationality, and when she spoke it was with the slight twang of the western plains. Glancing around as though looking for someone, she began to circumambulate the baroque, swoop-roofed building. She told her rosary of 108 turquoise beads, chanting "Om Mani Padme Hum!" along with other pilgrims treading the clockwise path taken for centuries. Some hobbled, some prostrated themselves full-length, others were absorbed in prayer. The American's journey to Lhasa, half a century after the original, was triggered by reading and translating Alexandra's *Journal de voyage,* her letters to Philip Neel.

At Katmandu she had been informed by the Chinese consulate that she could not cross from Nepal into Tibet. But in New York they had assured her the border was open, that China welcomed tourists. Well, yes, replied the official, but a visa was necessary. She could obtain one in Hong Kong. She didn't need to point out she would have to fly there and back for a prohibitive sum. Despairing, she solaced herself by having a lunch of savory *momos* at a little dumpling shop. Fighting back tears, she realized she would get no closer to the still forbidden land.

Three young Tibetan men approached and informed the American they knew of her difficulties. One produced an air ticket from Calcutta to Hong Kong. It was hers if she agreed to deliver a package to Lhasa. But what about the return ticket? They had none, suggesting instead she cross to Canton and travel through China by rail to Kunming, Yunnan; from there a truck took two weeks through the Po country to Lhasa. That was the safest way because there would be a less thorough search at the border. She wondered if these genial lads in their twenties were anti-Chinese guerrillas. The partisans operated out of Nepal, although less openly now, and even the Dalai Lama could not always control them. Besides, what was in the package?

She was forbidden to open it, that was the stipulation. But to whom should she deliver it? She needn't worry, a person would claim the parcel; they themselves knew no more. She asked herself, what would Alexandra have done? Certainly not turn back after coming this distance. She accepted and within two days found herself in ultramodern Hong Kong, a forest of skyscrapers so dense it made Manhattan seem open and airy. At Canton she boarded the train and spent the next three and a half days crossing China in fourth class: rock-hard benches, compartments jammed with poor families, the women wrinkled, the children asleep under the seats, the toil-worn men chain-smoking cheap cigarettes, hacking and spitting. The lavatories were unusable, and the aisles soon turned into lavatories.

At Kunming the American learned the Tibetan border was closed, visa or no. Lhasa was full due to the celebrations. She might try flying from Chengtu, Szechuan. But there, too, the answer was no, although she was told to try again. But suddenly one day both the skies and Lhasa opened miraculously, and from the plane she looked down upon a range of snowcapped mountains plunging toward the horizon like a school of humpbacked whales at sea. Finally, the mountainous wave broke, and as they glided down onto the plain, the Potala glinted white and gold, changing shades like a faceted diamond ring.

The Par Kor around the Jo Khang runs through the heart of Lhasa, past the din of the marketplace, and a pilgrim must concentrate on her *mantra* not to be seduced by colorful nomads hawking their wares. Where this street widens and the peddlers thin out about halfway around, she spotted propped against a wall an elderly Tibetan woman of no distinction, a beggar, if such were allowed. She gestured to her and the pilgrim obeyed the summons. The crone deftly slipped her a rolled-up sheet of rice paper, and then, with a gap-toothed grin, motioned like a wheel. She understood she must complete the circumambulation.

At the hostel that evening when her roommates had gone out—they were democratically assigned without regard to nation or sex—the American unrolled the coarse paper. Poorly printed in Tibetan, Chinese, and English, it was the authentic cry of a people ground under the boot of history, declared abolished, yet still placing faith in the conscience of the world. "Long live His Holiness the Dalai Lama!" it began, then in a breathtaking unraveling of language:

We want to Free Tibet. We against by forc 20 celebration of [indecipherable]. Go out Red China. We against Chiness Goverment. We want to Howmen Right—U.N.O. We want to Justics. Justics. Justics. Long live Free Tibet! Free Tibet!

This sheet so thin as to be transparent, this splotched printing and mangled English, were sufficient if intercepted by the police—and their spies were everywhere—to lead to prison, torture, and finally the dawn gift of a pistol bullet in the back of the head for any number of patriots. She quickly tucked it away as her British, French, and German roommates returned.

Next day the beggar woman was absent from her spot, nor was she anywhere in sight until it was nearly time for the American to fly back to Chengtu. Each day, carrying the mysterious parcel tucked under her Tibetan robes, she went around the Jo Khang, meandering a bit obviously through the market, but in vain. The last morning she had stopped at a stall to buy a trinket from a peddler lady of Amdo, colorfully dressed and loaded with turquoise, when she felt a hand grasp her arm. Turning, she saw those withered lips curled into a splotchy smile.

She followed the crone down a narrow side alley. Without knocking she entered a door; the dimness within was further obscured by smoldering incense, but the American was able to make out several lamas praying before an altar. This was a clandestine Buddhist temple. The religion is strictly curtailed and controlled in its old home. But rites are held in secret, and lads are designated and educated as monks while appearing just like their comrades. *Tulkus,* such as Sidkeong or Yongden, are still discoverd. Over the altar hung a framed, faded portrait photo of the Fourteenth Dalai Lama beaming with youth.

One of the lamas, in broken English, asked the visitor if she would like to make an offering. She understood, revealing the package. Opened, it contained nothing more sinister than hundreds of pocket-sized photos of His Holiness, who at fifty looked better suited to the title, wiser, perhaps sadder, surely more benevolent. Under the photo was printed a blessing in Tibetan, but the American grew so excited on discovering what she had been lugging about that she missed the translation. It was given to her by the lama, a sturdy Khampa, in his ruptured English that reminded her of the "Free Tibet!" flyer. Surely the Dalai Lama, the incarnation of Chenresi, Bodhisattva of Compassion, blessed impartially Tibetans, Chinese, and *philings.*

The American left for New York. She had seen the sights: the monasteries of Drepung and Sera, slowly being restored, which hold a few friendly monks. She had "met" the Potala several times—necessary because on each occasion she was rushed through by the Chinese guide. Rather bizarre are the Dalai Lama's private quarters, kept exactly as they were when he fled in 1959. He is not likely to return any time soon. She watched as lamas prepared a corpse for the "sky burial" and chanted to guide the deceased's soul through the *bardo* as they waited for the huge vultures to swoop down. She walked several miles to the site of Ganden, more steadily than had Alexandra and Yongden. There were no crowds, as there used to be, around the imposing tomb of Tsong Khapa, made of pure gold and silver and encrusted with jewels. The tomb had been broken to pieces and melted down. Ganden, which once housed thousands of monks and Tibet's leading university, today is a heap of rubble.

The American realized that the true stream of Tibetan life flows underground, disguised, in the style of Alexandra, as a poor old beggar woman. Buddhism, back to its roots as an outlaw faith, finds expression in artists who continue to paint *tankas* with unchanging devotion; in the market folk at Lhasa, who as they deal continually chant under their breath the holy names; in pilgrims from far places who refuse to stop short of their goal. After all, Shangri-La was not made of bricks and mortar.

What of Samten Dzong, closer to home for most of us? Digne is more bustling than when Alexandra knew it, and pastel-shaded villas have crept up on the once private Fortress of Meditation. A gas station does business nearby, cars honk as they speed past on the road to Nice. Still, if you are in the neighborhood and find yourself attracted by the tree-shaded garden with its Tibetan flags, do step up to the modest two-story dwelling and ring the doorbell. Samten Dzong is now a museum and conference center.

Mademoiselle Peyronnet, who makes her home here, will be pleased to show you about. There are three scheduled tours daily. The former dreariness has been banished, light floods the place, and there are no more cobwebs. You will be facing the old dining room, presently an office for selling Tibetan rugs and other crafts. The proceeds go entirely to help refugees. In 1986 Marie-Madeleine told us, "I am in my twenty-eighth year of service to Alexandra David-Neel."

On this floor is the shrine room, really a small Buddhist temple containing an altar, offerings, *tankas*, rare statues of Buddha, various tantric implements such as a *damaru* (skull drum), *kangling* (femur trumpet), and sets of the *vajra* (thunderbolt) and *vajra*-bell, which stand for supreme wisdom and compassion. One Buddha is draped with a white Tibetan scarf; is it the same musty scarf presented to Alexandra by the Thirteenth? At any rate, there is a photo of her in the red lama's robe commented on by General Pereira.

The temple is moving, otherworldly, but on returning to the hall you will find a large glass cabinet containing articles that sum up what an American Tibetanist called "the travelogue of Alexandra David-Neel, the fearless lady who journeyed across Tibet from one marvelous adventure to another." Here you see the mementos of her journey to Lhasa: watch and compass—the one she nearly lost—cooking pot, pistol, Khampa hat—the one she found on the trail—and a leather pouch for concealing jewelry beneath her clothes.

The jewelry itself is nearby, along with several cameras, including an old Rolleiflex, high technology in its day. There is a rosary of 108 beads each from a different skull, next to the necklace of heavy gold coins given to Alexandra by the maharaja of Sikkim. Most intriguing are two delicate rings of the initiate, the *vajra* for the right hand fashioned from gold with a ruby, the bell for the left made out of silver with a turquoise. In the downstairs office—not on the tour—we have seen a photo of Alexandra in her late nineties, hands crippled with arthritis. Yet on the appropriate fingers she is wearing the rings that identify her as a *naljorpa*, something more than simply a student of Buddhist philosophy.

Alexandra's office is upstairs. In contrast to when she worked here amid a clutter of papers, the room is exceptionally neat. Books are kept in a glass-doored case against the far wall, and one or two lie open for effect on the desk in the center. Because the elderly author complained the desk was too high, Madeleine bought her a small camp table on which she wrote. The rattan chair facing it bears the imprint of her back.

On the table sits a little blue lamp which, together with a magnifying glass, Alexandra employed to assist her failing vision. "It is not a question of eyeglasses," she insisted to Madeleine. "Go into town and buy a lamp, a cheap one." Thus it happened that when Christmas Humphreys visited his fellow Buddhist, he was "impressed to find her, at the age of 95, correcting proofs without spectacles in a room made dark against the summer sun."

A second lamp stands on a bureau in Alexandra's bedroom, which is merely an armchair located across the room from her office. The short space is deceptive, because toward the end Madeleine had to carry an almost paralyzed Alexandra, of considerable weight, across it to put her to sleep. The exercise crushed vertebrae in Madeleine's back, and she is a woman well acquainted with pain. Oddly, this second lamp is covered with newspaper in lieu of a shade. The orientalist insisted that her secretary not use *le Monde* but a less expensive paper. Had Alexandra, who once knew how to spend, become a miser in her extreme old age? Not precisely, since she had in mind one last grand plan.

In her will, Alexandra stipulated that Samten Dzong was to become a true "*Centre Tibetain.*" A building would be constructed in the garden to house "Buddhists, scholars, students" at very low cost. The purpose was to combine study and meditation, to recreate the Tibetan institution of *tsams* (deep, secluded meditation) but for Westerners, as Alexandra herself had productively practiced it at Kum Bum. The building was constructed, but if its inhabitants were to be isolated, each room would need plumbing. There are building codes in Digne as elsewhere. Madeleine considered this beyond the means of the foundation, and so the building is used occasionally for conferences.

In more significant fashion, Alexandra erred in not leaving all her artifacts, and perhaps her library as well, at Samten Dzong under the care of her disciple. Shortly after her death in 1969 a truck came to carry away the rare and precious rugs, *tankas,* statues, ritual objects of bone, and wonderfully fanciful masks that the orientalist had collected, with a superb eye, over her years of arduous travel in corners of Asia where it is difficult to venture even now. Madeleine saved what she could, but "twelve huge containers of objects" were shipped to Paris. Under supervision of the executor, these were to be allocated to several museums. The Musée Guimet got its books and lists 440 of these, all Tibetan. Alexandra's personal library of French and English books—of great interest to a biographer—is not to be found.

A few things remain at the Musée de l'Homme, mainly Alexandra's Tibetan clothing. The yak-hide and felt boots are delightful, and we enjoy clomping about in similar pairs of these decorative boots. But what of the really valuable *objets d'art?* We don't know. You may as well ask the wind that blows across the Tibetan steppe. Alexandra's superb collection has been dispersed to the universe whence it came.

Her physical remains—her ashes, along with Lama Yongden's—were taken by Marie-Madeleine to Benares in 1973. She sprinkled them upon the breast of Mother Ganges, which carries the nourishing snows of Tibet to the Indian plain. Madeleine paid her respects to the Dalai Lama, and she felt a certain triumph, a vindication, when His Holiness informed her, "With my first visa for France, I will come to see the house of Alexandra David-Neel, who was an enthusiastic Buddhist and the first to make the real aspects of our country known in the West."

Surely, this praise would have been music to Alexandra's ears. Still, in her heart she preferred a different sort of end. Let her speak in words unpublished until now:

It's really too bad I didn't die in my hermitage [i.e. cave at De-chen]. I arrived there at the summit of my dream, alone, soaring like an eagle, in my cavern on a Himalayan peak. What remains for me—to do, to see, to experience— after that? Death there . . . the old lama would have come one morning, to carry my body as he promised me, to a place still higher on some rock, and he would have left it there. There are no police regulations about funerals in these solitudes. So there it was, simple, not banal, according to me and my desires.

For those who follow in Alexandra's footsteps, we can only be grateful that she did descend from the mountain to "cities where people restrict life, believing they are improving it." She took the path of the compassionate *bodhisattva.* To us personally there exists another moment—a snapshot from the travelogue of her life—that exactly captures her choice.

In 1936 Europe trembled before the extortionate demands of Hitler. Czechoslovakia would soon be swallowed by the Nazis, but that didn't prevent the orientalist, at the height of her renown, from going to Prague to give a conference. While there she visited the home of the sixteenth-century kabbalist Rabbi Loew, the building adjacent to a very old synagogue. In order to defend his people, this learned mystic had made a *golem,* or so legend held. He created it by fashioning the statue of a man from clay, then animating it via certain magical sayings. The creature possessed extraordinary powers for good or evil.

Alexandra didn't believe in *golems.* She felt the conception was too narrow, too physical. This sort of work was best done as a mental creation. Yet, when the guard left her alone in the rabbi's chambers, she scarcely hesitated:

I had the audacity to pull aside the silken cord that barred access to the antique chair where Rabbi Loew sat during his offices, and I sat there a while.

She felt the thrill of mystery, the electricity of the hidden.

Throughout her life, Alexandra sought substance behind the screen of shadows. She, too, fashioned a protector for her people: her works will help keep alive the true Tibetan spirit. After a century of endeavor, she departed for that dim shore to which we all journey one day. What she discovered there is hers.

Sources and Acknowledgments

Concerning biographers, Leon Edel has observed, "They think too little about art and talk too much about objective fact, as if facts were as hard as bricks or stones." We can think of no one worse served than Alexandra David-Neel by this state of mind. For many years the facts of her long life were obscure, largely because she preferred to conceal her intimacies, human frailties, and even illnesses, which she considered a sign of weakness. Now that the facts are mostly out in the open, they ought not be interpreted either in the spirit of attack or hagiography. We have aimed for a more objective, if equally enthusiastic, work. Above all, we have been concerned to show the significance of Alexandra's life and writings, what she continues to mean to others.

Over a decade ago we began with Dorothy Middleton's *Victorian Lady Travellers,* which stirred our interest in these phenomenal, neglected women. Becoming acquainted with Mrs. Middleton, honorary vice-president of the Royal Geographical Society, has been one of the great pleasures of this endeavor. Luree Miller, in *On Top of the World,* first shone real light on corners of Alexandra's life. She was the first to write a sensitive biography in English—although limited to one chapter in her fascinating account of women interlopers in Tibet. She has been a consistent and unwavering supporter. A third woman, Letha Hadadi of New York, came to this work later. Still, we cannot thank her sufficiently for her superb translations of idiosyncratic French, probing insights into Alexandra's character, and arduous travel on our behalf, when she wielded camera and brush to good effect. These three women became the cornerstone of our effort.

We wish to cite our equal gratitude to three gentlemen—in the full sense of the word—each British. Peter Hopkirk, author and foreign correspondent, was most generous with his time in reading the manuscript and making suggestions for its improvement. His casual remark about the India Office Secret Files led us to a mine of information. This material, never before drawn on, provides the first third-party verification that Alexandra went where she said. It shows why she took detours and evasions. Here is the key to the mystery of her roundabout route.

To Hugh Richardson, dean of Tibetanists, we are more than thankful both for his meticulous guidance and amusing anecdotes. Through his eyes we obtained a view of the actual world in which Alexandra moved. Without this precious knowledge, evaluating her actions would have been mere guesswork. Lawrence Durrell provided another sort of view of our subject, personal and incisive. We are grateful for his time, attention, and encouragement.

We are sorry to have to thank Christmas Humphreys posthumously for recounting his meetings with Alexandra. We have relied greatly on Mr. Humphreys's *Popular Dictionary of Buddhism* for both meanings and spellings. At times we have fallen back on the most commonly accepted forms, not necessarily those used by Alexandra, but contemporaneous with her. Consistent with that policy we have spelled Chinese and Tibetan names in the fashion known to David-Neel. Furthermore, the adoption of current Chinese spelling of Tibetan names would imply a recognition of their legitimacy we are are not prepared to grant. Similarly our maps—drawn by Letha Hadadi—conform to the boundaries agreed upon by the Simla Convention of 1914.

Until now, no one had thought to interview a variety of people close to Alexandra. Doing so proved both enlightening and entertaining. Our thanks to Professor Pierre Borrely for his candor (and imitations), and to Frank Treguier for his helpfulness. We are truly indebted to Dr. Marcel Maille for his deep learning and interest in Tibetan Buddhism, and his willingness to share his unique insights with us. Additional thanks to his charming wife, Michele, for her contribution to our knowledge of the enigmatic one. And to Dr. Yves Requena, physician of the soul as well as the body, for introducing us to Dr. Maille. The intelligence conveyed by these wonderful people, and by a number of tradespeople at Digne, came to us precisely when we could make the best use of it.

In a class by herself, *Mademoiselle* Marie-Madeleine Peyronnet, Director of the Fondation Alexandra David-Neel, Digne, graciously entertained us on three separate visits to Samten Dzong. Here we could get the feel of Alexandra's domestic life, and here we were introduced to the manuscript letters to Philip Neel and other rare material. *Mademoiselle* Peyronnet has done a superb job of keeping alive interest in Alexandra's work, and the current strong revival owes much to her courage, energy, and remarkable dedication. If only she had been allowed to retain charge of Alexandra's library and artifacts! Nonetheless, the time has come for a more specialized, scholarly evaluation of David-

Neel's contributions to Tibetan studies. This is a task for which we are not especially equipped, and we would encourage others more qualified to undertake it. Alexandra's reputation deserves no less.

Among institutions whose collections we have consulted, we are particularly indebted to the India Office Library of the British Library, London; and to the anonymous librarian at the British Museum who directed us to the unpublished notebooks of Sir Charles Bell. These contain material he considered too personal to include in his several fine books on Tibet. The library of the Royal Geographical Society, London, is beyond compare in the field of travel; one may simply reach out and take what one needs, it is all on hand. Our thanks also to the Musée Guimet and the Bibliothèque de l'Opéra, as well as the Bibliothèque National, Paris. It was our pleasure to use the specialized, but excellent, collections of the Sri Aurobindo ashram, Pondicherry, and the Theosophical Society, Adyar, India. Closer to home, the librarians of Dartmouth College, the New York Public Library, and Columbia University proved consistently helpful beyond the demands of their profession. But our most profound thanks must be given, again regretfully after death, to the late Magda Gottesman, Hunter College Library, who obtained for us via interlibrary loan books we never dared hope were available, and from the most remarkable places!

Several colleagues at Hunter read sections of the manuscript and imparted sound advice, especially Professors Virginia Held and George Elder, of the philosophy and religion departments respectively, and Professor Pierre Oberling of history. It was a pleasure to correspond with Professor Robert Thurman of Amherst, a scholar who knows Tibetan Buddhism firsthand, and with that intrepid traveler in his own right, an untiring enthusiast for adventure, Lowell Thomas, Jr. of Alaska. We surely profited from the advice of Marion Meade, biographer of Madame Blavatsky, an author who understands what it means to deal with a giant of a woman.

Once again in Paris, our thanks to Dr. Gabriel Monod-Herzen for sharing with us memories of the woman he knew so well; and to Dr. John Pier for searching where we could not. In New York, Braham Norwick, Tibetanist and long-time admirer of Alexandra, was the source of expert information. The enthusiasm of Dr. Arlene Blum (mountain climber par excellence) and the commitment of Valerie La Breche helped to keep us on the track. We hope their Alexandra David-Neel Expedition, which plans to retrace the explorer's journey to Lhasa, may one day happen. We are obliged to Sir John Thompson, British ambassador to the United Nations (and formerly to India), for his wise and witty comments on Charles Bell and the diplomat's life in the Orient.

A few words on the previous biographies in French, on which we have drawn. Jeanne Denys' *Alexandra David-Neel au Tibet* (1972) is scandalous and motivated by hatred, yet it cannot be ignored. One's worst enemy often knows a good deal about one. Handle with care. Jacques Brosse's *Alexandra David-Neel: L'aventure et la spiritualité* (1978) is out of date but interesting and fairly balanced. His judgments show a real knowledge of Buddhism, perhaps less of Tibet. The book is unduly neglected. Jean Chalon's *Le lumineaux destin d'Alexandra David-Neel* (1985) is a lengthy authorized biography. It never mentions Denys, nor much else damaging to its subject, whom it names "Our Lady of Tibet." Chalon shows only the most superficial acquaintance with Eastern thought and none whatever with the social and political background of the world in which Alexandra lived. The author clearly has not bothered to consult the vital sources in English. Moreover, he freely mixes gossip with facts, twists and fails to identify the sources of quotes, and hatches some theories that, out of *politesse*, we may term misguided. The value of the book lies in its printing swatches of previously unpublished material, especially concerning Alexandra's young bohemian days. But once his subject leaves France, Chalon is out of his depth. This biography, lacking documentation, is a minefield; tread with care.

We wish to take this opportunity to thank our guides to the profound world of Buddhist thought and practice: in print, John Blofeld and Alan Watts; in person, Chögyam Trungpa, Rinpoche, and the Dharma Master, monks, and nuns of the Chinese-American Buddhist Association, Chinatown, New York. It ought to be abundantly clear we have no quarrel with the Chinese people, but only dissent from the policies of the People's Republic in Tibet.

Writers need agents and editors to perform the alchemy of turning a mere manuscript into a book. No doubt we were blessed to have found, in these essential capacities, two such talented, dedicated individuals as Ellen Levine and John Loudon. Despite the best efforts of the entire superb staff at Harper & Row, we know we have made errors, and these we claim for ourselves alone. The good in our work we dedicate to the Tibetan people, wherever they may live.

Barbara Foster
Michael Foster

New York, N.Y.
1986

Notes

Numbers to the left refer to the pages of the text in which the relevant citations appear. Each is identified by its first word or two and last word. Passages closely linked in the text, and from the same source, are cited as one. David Neel's letters are uniformly to Philip Neel. We have used the published sources. Originals may be found in the Archives A. David-Neel, Digne, France. All quotations from printed sources are cited via the author's last name and a short title. Full title may be found in the bibliography. The source of interviews is stated where permitted, that is, in all but three instances.

The dialogue used scenically from time to time has *not* been invented. Rather, it is reconstructed. It was spoken, or at least written, by the person to whom it is attributed. However, a certain liberty may be taken over the order, time, and place of dialogue.

The following abbreviations are used:

ADN 1, 2   *Journal de voyage: Lettres à son mari*, vols. 1, 2, by Alexandra David-Neel

Jour   *My Journey to Lhasa*, by David-Neel

MM   *Magic and Mystery in Tibet*, by David-Neel

PS   The Political and Secret Annual Files (1912–1930), L/P&S11, India Office Records, British Library, London

Prelude: At the Border

9   "everything . . . forces." MM, p. xii.

9   "the only . . . country." Dhondup, *Songs*, p. 37.

9   "Never . . . sperm." Ibid., p. 39.

10   "To animate . . . magic words." MM, p. 135.

11   "There exist . . . knows." Quoted by Brosse, *Alexandra David-Neel*, Preface.

12   "on the edge of a mystery." ADN 1, p. 160. The initial scene is described by Macdonald in *Twenty Years in Tibet*, pp. 288–290. It contrasts with his report of 7 May 1924 in PS. See also David-Neel, *My Journey to Lhasa*, p. 310. Victoria Williams (neé Macdonald) was interviewed at Darjeeling, India, 1983.

Chapter 1: Father and Daughter

19–20   Described in ADN 1, pp. 232–234 by Alexandra. This is a later reminiscence. See also Stewart Edwards, *The Paris Commune*, chap. 10, especially pp. 337–340.

20   "yesterday . . . ferocity." ADN 1, p. 232.

20–21   "two statues . . . heart." ADN 1, p. 30.

21 "Why must . . . them." ADN 2, p. 102.
21 "my masters . . . philosophers." David-Neel, *Lampe de Sagesse*, p. 13.
21 "from a family . . . persecution." Brosse, *Alexandra David-Neel*, p. 11.
21 "and other . . . heresies." Ibid.
22 "well-known . . . imbecile." Burchell, *Upstart Empire*, p. 37.
22 "The principles . . . them." Quoted by Edwards, *Victor Hugo*, p. 163.
23 "I am . . . 1852." ADN 2, p. 249.
23 "How many . . . are!" ADN 1, p. 233.
24 "The family . . . fish." Peyronnet, interview, Digne, August 13, 1986.
24 "During the . . . forests." Quoted by Brosse, *Alexandra David-Neel*, p. 15.
24 "From a distance . . . all." Quoted by Burchell, *Upstart Empire*, p. 21.
25 "The soul . . . her!" Quoted by Edwards, *Victor Hugo*, p. 268.
25 "He scooped . . . arms!" Quoted by Peyronnet, *Dix ans*, p. 205.
26 "In pressing . . . life." Stewart Edwards, *The Paris Commune*, p. 271.
26 "the profound . . . men." Thomas, *Louise Michel*, p. 220.
26 "raised . . . future." Quoted by Edwards, *Commune*, p. 360.
27 "The simple . . . beast." Quoted by Edwards, *Commune*, p. 343.
27 "To believe . . . give." Peyronnet, *Dix ans*, p. 182.
27 "It is . . . defeat." *Lampe de Sagesse*, p. 54.

Brosse, *Alexandra David-Neel*, is thorough on her antecedents. However, he does not deal with possible Jewish ancestry. On the Commune, Thomas, *Louise Michel* is excellent from a woman's view. Also Edwards, *Victor Hugo* and Burchell, *Imperial Masquerade* give an overview of the period.

Chapter 2: Mother and Daughter

28 "Ever since . . . took me." Jour, ix.
28 "What a thirst . . . infinity!" David-Neel, *Sous des nuees*, p. 4.
29 "a commemoration . . . world." ADN 1, p. 27.
29 "Where are . . . used?" ADN 2, p. 101.
29 "a great-grandfather . . . 104." Peyronnet, interview, Digne, August 13–15, 1986.
29 "I am . . . me." ADN 1, p. 35.
30 "Alexandra . . . intensely." Chalon, *Lumineux destin*, p. 495.
30 "Well . . . have." Brosse, *Alexandra David-Neel*, p. 16.
30 *"quignols . . . quatre-vingt-dix."* *Sous des nuees*, pp. 3–4.
30 "Brussels . . . me." Ibid., p. 4.
30 "having . . . pilgrimages." Ibid., p. 16.
31 "I . . . savage." ADN 1, p. 207.
31 "wild . . . glaciers." Jour, p. 38.
31 "On the reverse . . . vestries." David-Neel, *Sortilège*, pp. 26–27.
31 "virgins . . . windows. . . ." Ibid.
32 "heretics." Ibid., p. 18.
32 "Alexandra: How do . . . [and ensuing dialogue]." David-Neel, *Sortilège*, pp. 15–17.
32 "One who . . . person." Ibid., p. 14.
32 "gleamed . . . Himalayas." ADN 1, p. 139.
32 "her two . . . *enfant terrible*." Peyronnet, tour of Samten Dzong, Digne.
33 "These . . . crazy!" David-Neel, *Sortilège*, p. 13.
33 "the revered . . . youth." David-Neel, *Sous des nuees*, p. 3.
34 "Modern . . . Workers." Brosse, *Alexandra David-Neel*, p. 20.
34 "You want . . . woman!" ADN 1, p. 356.
34 "adopt . . . Jesus." David-Neel, *Lampe de Sagesse*, p. 16.

35 "The boat . . . life?" David-Neel, *Sortilège*, pp. 19–20.
35 "It is . . . maturing." Humphreys, *Dictionary*, p. 171.

On David-Neel's early life Brosse is accurate but sketchy. Denys, *Alexandra David-Neel au Tibet*, obviously biased, has nonetheless done considerable archival work in Brussels. Chalon, *Lumineaux destin*, presents a multitude of "facts," some imagined. Our account is a composite; as usual, David-Neel herself has the final word.

Chapter 3: The Supreme Gnosis

36 "I had . . . means." David-Neel, *Sortilège*, *p. 28*.
37 "perfect . . . discretion." Ibid., p. 31.
37 "to discover . . . conduct . . . perfectly." David-Neel, *Sortilège*, pp. 44–45.
38 "One day . . . life." David-Neel, *Lampe de Sagesse*, p. 70.
39 "Learner . . . Instructor." David-Neel, *Sortilège*, p. 47.
39 "A sad . . . accident!" Meade, *Madame Blavatsky*, p. 402.
40 "gentleman . . . Ball." David-Neel, *Sortilège*, p. 35.
40 "Careful . . . dangerous." David-Neel, *Sortilège*, p. 40.
41 "In the intense . . . Asia." MM, p. 44.
41–42 "Edmund . . . foolishness." David-Neel, *Sortilège*, pp. 72–74.
42 "vulgar . . . imposters . . . bone." Ibid., p. 76.
42 "Those . . . cemeteries." Ibid., p. 77.
43 "A strange. . . understand." Ibid., p. 79.
43 "the most . . . idiot." Ibid.
43 "rapacious beak" Ibid., p. 81.
44 "The spirits . . . mediumship." Ibid., p. 103.
44 "beautiful . . . boudoir." David-Neel, *Lampe de Sagesse*, p. 60.
44 "reign . . . brain." Lantier, *La Theosophie*, p. 135.
45 "The destiny . . . man." de Beauvoir, *Second Sex*, p. 111.
45 "Jourdan . . . sick." David-Neel, *Sortilège*, p. 90.
45 "What a . . . over." Ibid., pp. 90–92.
46 "It was . . . embarrassments." David-Neel, Sortilège, pp. 165–166.
46 "knew . . . dates." Ibid., p. 83.
46 "he spent . . . literature." *Lawrence*, Thomas, pp. 13–14.
46 "The Musée . . . *naïfs*." David-Neel, *Sortilège*, p. 85.
47 "Look not . . . mind." Blofeld, *Bodhisattva*, p. 29.
47 "Catholic . . . worlds!" David-Neel, *Lampe de Sagesse*, p. 55.
47 "Vocations . . . there." David-Neel, *L'Inde hier*, p. 2.

In addition to David-Neel's own writings, Meade, *Madame Blavatsky*, gives a detailed picture of the late nineteenth-century theosophy. *Helene P. Blavatsky*, ed. Virginia Hanson, presents its subject more favorably. Miller, *On Top of the World*, is reliable and insightful for this and other periods of David-Neel's life. See Rudorff, *Belle Epoque* for occultism in general. Also, interview with Professor M. Herzen, Paris, 1977. The Buddha story *may* be apocryphal.

Chapter 4: The Handgun

48 "dominating . . . chimney." Rudorff, *Belle Epoque*, p. 18.
48 "vertiginously . . . tower." Ibid.
48 "I have . . . rest." Quoted by Chalon, *Lumineaux destin*, p. 55.
49 "I have seen . . . climb [there]." Ibid., p. 60.

49 "To believe . . . fade." Quoted by Peryonnet, *Dix ans,* p. 182.
49 "Under . . . worms." Quoted by Chalon, *Lumineaux destin,* p. 59.
49 "How can . . . myself." David-Neel, *Lampe de Sagesse,* p. 34.
49 "Don't . . . others." Ibid., p. 22.
49 "choosing . . . peace." Ibid., p. 35.
49 "[O]ne of . . . spirit." Ibid., p. 57.
49 "quitting . . . deserter." Ibid.
50 "I feel . . . revolt." Ibid., p. 53.
50 "She must have . . . Justice." Denys, *Alexandra David-Neel au Tibet,* pp. 18–19.
50 "I profoundly . . . matters." Jour, xxii.
51 "Nowhere . . . Paris," Quoted by Rudorff, *Belle Epoque,* p. 32.
51 "won the . . . humanity." David-Neel, *Sous des nuees,* p. 16.
52 "fatal . . . soul." David-Neel, *Lampe de Sagesse,* p. 23.
53 "certain refined . . . *haute bourgeoisie* . . . for the Orient." David-Neel, *Sortilège,* pp. 249–50.
54 "It seems . . . men." Quoted by Chalon, *Lumineaux destin,* p. 83.
54 "Perhaps . . . year." David-Neel, *L'Inde hier,* p. 303.
55 "hymn . . . This is . . . prouder still." Reclus, Preface to David-Neel, *Pour la vie.*
55 "chained . . . yourself." David-Neel, *Mercure de France,* November, 1908, p. 452.
55 "a dog . . . remain." Quoted by Carroll, *Crystal Palace,* p. 18.
55 "I prefer . . . virtue." Ibid., p. 26.
56 "Every moment . . . life." David-Neel, *Pour la vie,* p. 314.
56 "cruel god . . . parents." Ibid.

For Stirner see Huneker, *Egoists.* Rudorff's *Belle Epoque,* chap. 4, discusses the anarchists. Chalon, *Lumineaux destin,* emphasizes David-Neel's despair and plays down her rebellion. *La vie* is revealing of her actual state, as is her *Sous des nuees.*

Chapter 5: Manon

58 "With my . . . trembling." Quoted by Chalon, *Lumineaux destin,* p. 89.
59 "herring days . . . Magic art . . . phrases . . ." Ibid., p. 90.
59 "I had . . . there." Ibid., p. 93.
59 "the jovial . . . intrigues." Ibid., p. 94.
59 "coat . . . gold . . . terrain." Ibid., p. 96.
60 "voice . . . talent." Ibid., p. 102.
60 "Love . . . novelists." Ibid., p. 106.
60 "I don't . . . equal." ADN 1, p. 32.
61 "tender . . . loved." Quoted by Chalon, *Lumineaux destin,* p. 106.
62 "the noble . . . tradition." David-Neel, *Sortilège,* p. 155.
62 "How many . . . lesson? . . . plays . . . nude?" David-Neel, *Sortilège,* pp. 169–174.
63 "Art is . . . soul." Quoted by Chalon, *Lumineaux destin,* p. 108.
63 "Work . . . insipid . . . to us." Ibid., pp. 114–115.
63 "He was . . . passion." Ibid., p. 107.
64 "You are . . . art." Ibid., p. 117.
64 "the Don Juan . . . splendor" Ibid., p. 116.
64 "Hirondella prima volta." Ibid.
64 "gorgons . . . garlic." Ibid., p. 133.
64 "When are . . . lives." Ibid., p. 118.
65 "malice . . . prudence." Ibid.
65 "I told . . . infatuated?" ADN 1, p. 21.

65–66 "experienced . . . too costly . . . husband . . . pedestal." Chalon, *Lumineaux destin,* pp. 132–134.
66 "a figure . . . colletion." Ibid., p. 133.
66 "I have . . . Tunis." Ibid., p. 134.
66 "the heart-rending comedy." Ibid., p. 131.

Miller sums up what is known of Alexandra's opera career. Also, ADN 1, pp. 12. Regrettably, Chalon is the main published source of Alexandra's and Philip's premarital liaison. Nonetheless, the facts are not in doubt, only the interpretation. However, numerous references in ADN 1 and 2 provide additional evidence bearing on her marriage. See also Brosse, *Alexandra David-Neel.*

Chapter 6: The Woman in Marriage

67 "Until today . . . marriage." Quoted by Chalon, *Lumineaux destin,* p. 136.
67 "Naturally . . . daughter." Ibid., p. 143.
68 "The [very] walls . . . I am . . . myself." ADN 1, pp. 30–31.
68 "*Et voilà* . . . I know . . . to pay." Chalon, *Lumineaux destin,* p. 144.
68 "like . . . shoulder." Ibid.
69 "The child . . . child . . . union." Quoted by Miller, *On Top,* p. 141.
69 "One must . . .brain." ADN 1, p. 48.
69 "I have . . . stir up." ADN 1, p. 40.
69 "If I . . . tight." ADN 1, p. 29.
69 "a light . . . rapture." ADN 1, p. 39.
69 "I can't . . . errors . . . mores." ADN 1, p. 25.
70 "You let . . . path . . . We've known . . . only me?" Quoted by Chalon, *Lumineaux destin,* p. 152.
70 "Let's not . . . each other." Ibid., p. 153.
70 "made . . . photos" Ibid., p. 152.
71 "the imprudent . . . sex." Milller, *On Top of the World,* p. 148.
71 "disgust . . . infidelity." David, "La liberation de la femme," *Le Monde* (1908), p. 116.
71 "trapped . . . love." Ibid., p. 117.
71 "This Congress . . . prisons. . . shocking." Chalon, *Lumineaux destin,* p. 157.
73 "I am . . . mind." ADN 1, p. 42.
73 "Old age . . . I was." Quoted by Brosse, *Alexandra David-Neel,* p. 50.
73 "a basket of rags." ADN 1, p. 48.
73 "I'm tormented . . . over." Quoted by Chalon, *Lumineaux destin,* p. 155.
73 "a soul . . . leave." ADN 1, p. 49.
73 "Today . . . black hole." Ibid.
73 "those features I hate" Ibid.
74 "You are . . . work." ADN 1, p. 48.
74 "I believe . . . it." Quoted by Chalon, *Lumineaux destin,* p. 160.
74 "I took . . . neurasthenia." ADN 1, p. 52.
75 "the living . . . birth," ADN 1, p. 57.
75 "Am I . . . it!" Ibid.
75 "my . . . Alouch." ADN 1, p. 58.
75 "the sensation. . . ago. . . ." ADN 1, p. 150.
75 "It is . . . wounded by . . . drama." ADN 1, pp. 280–281.
75 "my wife . . . travel." Peyronnet, interview, August, 1986.
75 "Evidently . . . bad share." ADN 1, p. 134.
75 "All these . . . better." ADN 1, pp. 237–238.
76 "legal . . . Haven't you . . . lives?" ADN 1, p. 286.

The precise extent of Alexandra's studies at the Sorbonne remains in doubt. It is clear that Sylvain Levi, the great French orientalist of his time, accepted her as a disciple.

Chapter 7: India Absurd and Marvelous

81 "crawling around" ADN 1, p. 56.
81 "an honorable . . . erudition." ADN 1, p. 57.
82 "I am . . . Switzerland." Quoted by Brosse, *Alexandra David-Neel*, p. 60.
82 "first . . . India." ADN 1, p. 59.
82 "sweet . . . flesh." Ibid.
83 "The notes . . . magic?" David-Neel, *L'Inde hier*, p. 31.
83 "the Other . . . Ages." ADN 1, p. 59.
83 "You . . . nothing." David-Neel, *L'Inde hier*, p. 29.
84 "I flattened . . . gods." Ibid., p. 55.
84 "distillers . . . Tantra." Lanza Del Vasto, *Return*, p. 56.
85 "Where is . . . covers . . . filth." ADN 1, p. 63.
85 "deplorable . . . smoke." ADN 1, p. 80.
85 "Adyar . . . oasis." ADN 1, p. 67.
85–86 "surge . . . thousands . . . Truth." David-Neel, *Sortilège*, p. 296.
86 "India . . . wife." ADN 1, p. 78.
86 "quite . . . infinity." ADN 1, p. 80.
87 "A liberating . . . served." Miller, *On Top of the World*, p. 155.
87 "I spent . . . India. . . ." ADN 1, p. 69.
87 "the . . . suspect." Ibid.
87–88 "Mme. David-Neel's . . . her?" PS, 1913, p. 243.
88 "secret . . . Calcutta." PS, 19 December 1911, p. 259.
88 "a collection . . . rags" ADN 1, p. 85.
88 "How empty . . . compassion." ADN 1, p. 82.
88 "everything . . . finery." ADN 1, p. 85.
89 "material benefits" Quoted by Brosse, *Alexandra David-Neel*, p. 72.
89 "an aristocrat . . . culture." Ibid.
89 "What a . . . house!" ADN 1, p. 85.
89 "Don't . . . death." ADN 1, p. 91.
89 "The evening . . . stream." ADN 1, p. 82.
90 "A bit . . . over." ADN 1, p. 240.
90 "beautiful . . . eyes." ADN 1, p. 84.
90 "to learn . . . glasses." ADN 1, p. 233.
91 "egotistical isolation . . . a fortress and a refuge" ADN 1, p. 243.
91 "the smiling . . . despair" ADN 1, p. 242.
91 "I am . . . nothing." ADN 1, p. 251.
92 "Ram! . . . Ganges." David-Neel, *L'Inde hier*, p. 105.
92 "Miserable . . . richer." Ibid., p. 109.
92 "lakes . . . forest." ADN 1, p. 232.
93 "[What] if . . . be?" ADN 1, p. 233.

David-Neel's *L'Inde*, in whichever of its versions, was written long after the fact. It is revealing but not necessarily trustworthy. Her French biographers are mistaken to rely too heavily on it. Her contemporaneous letters show her difficulties and doubts.

Chapter 8: The Edge of a Mystery

94 "Is it . . . cloths." MM, p. 1.
95 "While . . . Sikkim." ADN 1, p. 114.

95 "ugly . . . chimps" Ibid.
95 "charger . . . forests . . . see." ADN 1, p. 118.
95 "This . . . Asia." Ibid.
95 "the murder . . . cushions." ADN 1, p. 119.
95 "a pope . . . exile" Ibid.
95 "What a . . . served."ADN 1, p. 121.
95 "a very . . . intelligent." Ibid.
96 "a practitioner . . . Art." Bell, Unpublished Notebooks, "Notes on Sikkim," p. 46, British Library, London.
96 "Shrouded . . . influences." MM, p. 9.
96 "it . . . sway." Ibid.
97 "a kaleidoscope . . . trains." Thomas, Jr., *Out of This World*, p. 46.
98 "the color . . . salt." ADN 1, p. 149.
98 "the light . . . string" ADN 1, p. 173.
98 "the most . . . music." Knight, *Diary of a Pedestrian*, p. 166.
99 "the sonorities . . . functioning." ADN 1, p. 153.
99 "You . . . spouses." ADN 1, p. 134.
100 "ignorant . . . hobgoblins." Carey, *Adventures in Tibet*, p. 19.
100 "fairy . . . morality." Bird Bishop, *Among the Tibetans*, p. 202.
100 "Tibetan . . . perdition." ADN 1, p. 151.
101 "savoring . . . door." ADN 1, p. 161.
101 "the overly . . . egalitarian." ADN 1, pp. 179–180.
101–102 "Here . . . night." ADN 1, pp. 180–182.
102 "Aren't you . . . indignant. . . ." Hilton, *Lost Horizon*, p. 96.
102 "naive . . . Lhasa." Miller, *On Top of the World*, p. 57.
102 "Poor . . . Jesus." Quoted by Miller, *On Top*, p. 54.
102 "We . . . mind." Bell, *Dalai Lama*, p. 29.
103 "England . . . Tibet." ADN 1, p. 182.
103 "certainly . . . husband." ADN 1, p. 174.
103 "There are . . . Himalayas." ADN 1, p. 139.
103–104 "We will . . . morning." ADN 1, p. 173.
104 "her very . . . write [there]." ADN 1, pp. 177–178.
105 "a victory . . . flesh." ADN 1, p. 166.
105 "shadows . . . forms." ADN 1, p. 138.
105 "a country . . . water. . . ." ADN 1, p. 157.
106 "I have . . . blisters." ADN 1, p. 158.
106 "I . . . mystery." ADN 1, p. 160.

Alexandra naturally romanticized Prince Sidkeong; nor can we expect her to be candid about their relations. Much is conjecture, but Charles Bell's Unpublihsed Notebooks are helpful on Sidkeong's character.

Chapter 9: The Living Buddha

107 "Forbidden . . . centuries!" Thomas, Jr., *Out of this World*, p. 13.
108 "The Dalai . . . them." David-Neel, *Initiations*, p. 119.
108 "This . . . will." ADN 1, p. 171.
108 "a chieftan . . . Himalayas . . . clothing." David-Neel, *Buddhism*, pp. 15–17.
108–109 "Gotama . . . tree." Ibid., p. 19.
109 "A splendid . . . energy" Ibid.
109 "Dissolution . . . deliverance!" Ibid., p. 20.
109 "warmer . . . ritual." Eliot, *Hinduism and Buddhism*, vol. 2, p. 4.
109–110 "Warriors . . . wisdom." David-Neel, *Buddhism*, p. 32.

110 "a renowned . . . Swat . . . transformations." Snellgrove and Richardson, *Cultural History of Tibet*, p. 78.
111 "Thirteen . . . famous." David-Neel, *Initiations*, p. 120.
111 "A sort . . . Lhasa." Ibid., p. 25.
111 "Peace . . . me." Ibid., p. 121.
111 "[E]ven . . . language." Quoted by Bharati, *Tantric Tradition*, p. 166.
112 "what appears . . . treatise." David-Neel, *Initiations*, p. 123.
112 "The wine . . . wife." Ibid., p. 36.
112 "The paradoxical . . . case." Bharati, *Tantric Tradition*, p. 297.
113 "If I . . . mother" ADN 1, p. 123.
113 "It is . . . enlightened." MM, p. 4.
114 "What a . . . our sense." An account of this exceptional interview may be found in *Mercure de France* (October 1912), p. 475. ADN 1, pp. 124–126 is more candid.

Snellgrove and Richardson's *Tibet* has long been standard. The account of Gautama Buddha's life is extracted from Sir Charles Eliot's monumental work, *Hinduism and Buddhism*, and David-Neel's *Buddhism*.

Chapter 10: An Invisible Barrier

116 "furnished . . . shine." Charles Bell, *Portrait*, pp. 50–51.
116 "affairs . . . badly." Ibid.
117 "the first . . . centuries." Macdonald, *Twenty Years*, p. 27.
117 "No representatives . . . marts." Ghosh, *Tibet*, p. 54.
118 "It is . . . lamas." Bell, *Portrait*, p. 125.
118 "With what . . . studies." ADN 1, p. 171.
119 "Everything . . . about." MM, p. 46.
119 "One . . . victory." Ibid.
119 "She . . . custom." Bell, *Portrait*, p. 132.
119 "He is . . . him . . . Master." ADN 1, p. 171.
119 "frank . . . devotions . . . He was fond . . . animals." Charles Bell, Unpublished Notebooks, "Tibet," vol. 2, 26 August 1934.
120 "The Dalai . . . nothing . . . sort?" ADN 1, p. 176.
120 "What is . . . Work!" MM, p. 7.
121 "I would . . . write." ADN 1, p. 223.
121 "the pilgrimage . . . sage . . . shadows." ADN 1, pp. 221–224.
121–122 "vagabonding . . . the cautious . . . cat . . . tiger!" ADN 1, pp. 230–232.
122 "tigers . . . maneater" Schaller, *Stones of Silence*, p. 171.
122 "a Western . . . beast" ADN 1, p. 232.
123 "disguised . . . united . . . night." Brosse, *Alexandra David-Neel*, p. 110.
123 "Suddenly . . . begun." David-Neel, *Nepal*, p. 131.
123 "[T]he techniques . . . debauchery." Blofeld, *Tantric Mysticism*, p. 71.

The rare Suchita Ghosh, *Tibet in Sino-Indian Relations*, is an excellent pro-Tibetan study of its foreign affairs, especially vis-à-vis China, by an Indian. Bell, better known, is standard on the Dalai Lama, as is McAleavy on *Modern China*. For a foolish misreading of the tiger episode, see Chalon, *La Lumineaux destin*, pp. 214–216. In contrast, Brosse, *Alexandra David-Neel*, is judicious in discussing tantric sex.

Chapter 11: Of Life and Death

124 "entered . . . imaginable." ADN 1, p. 258.
124 "a mean . . . brats." ADN 1, p. 262.

125 "all . . . out." ADN 1, p. 267.
125 "a superb . . . What a . . . colors." ADN 1, p. 262.
125 "I am . . . foolish." ADN 1, p. 260.
125 "the resistance . . . orientalists." Ibid.
125 "My dearest . . . enough." Ibid.
125 "The air . . . itself." ADN 1, p. 265.
125 "A French . . . herself . . . go there." PS, p. 143.
126–127 "there was . . . officers." PS, p. 254.
127 "Nothing . . . *you.*" MM, p. 54.
128 "Aren't we all . . . wisdom?" ADN 1, p. 276.
128 "He moved . . . you." MM, p. 60.
129 "I love . . . ever." ADN 1, p. 279.
129 "My dearest . . . letters." ADN 1, p. 203.
129 "It's cold . . . existence." ADN 1, p. 207.
129 "You have . . . hearts." ADN 1, p. 281.
129 "with its . . . dreams . . . humiliations . . . [her]self." ADN 1, pp. 280–285.
129–130 "an old . . . sheep." ADN 1, p. 279.
130 "formed . . . expression." MM, pp. 64–65.
131 "Solitude . . . now?" MM, p. 77.
131 "I don't . . . awake." ADN 1, p. 277.
131 "Imbecility . . . world" ADN 1, p. 182.
132 "civilization . . . Belgium!" ADN 1, pp. 290–291.
132 "I have . . . Asia." ADN 1, p. 132.
132 "glory . . . ancestors." ADN 1, p. 301.
132 "We are . . . deserves." Ibid.
133 "I am . . . world." ADN 1, p. 327.
133 "I esteem . . . thoughts." ADN 1, p. 204.
133 "Poor boy . . . thirty-seven . . . enemy." ADN 1, p. 307.
134 "Ku-sho says . . . death." Bell, Unpublished Notebooks, "Supplementary Notes,"
     1927, p. 46.
134–135 "It's the . . . baby." Cooke, *Time Change*, p. 118.
135 "a genie . . . tale . . . real!" ADN 1, p. 197.
135 "It is . . . himself." ADN 1, p. 307.

The "cold war" between Alexandra and the Government of India bureaucrats cannot
be understood without reference to PS. Bell's Unpublished Notebooks and, from a
different angle, Hope Cooke's *Time Change* shed extraordinary light on the fate of
Maharaja Sidkeong of Sikkim.

Chapter 12: Cavern in the Clouds

136 "Everything . . . reticent." ADN 1, p. 283.
136 "great . . . clouds." ADN 1, p. 295.
137 "a white . . . shirt. . . ." MM, p. 41.
137 "What he . . . frightening." ADN 1, p. 300.
137 "You have . . . more." ADN 1, p. 148.
137 "This . . . little." MM, p. 70.
138 "What do . . . lives." MM, pp. 72–73.
139 "a rare . . . understood." ADN 1, p. 296.
139 "One . . . everyone." ADN 1, p. 275.
140 "I'm still . . . dream." ADN 1, p. 304.
140 "the most . . . imaginable." David-Neel, *Quarante Siecles,* p. 198.
140 "a dirty . . . clodhopper." ADN 1, pp. 316–317.

140 "picturesque . . . eyes." ADN 1, p. 299.
141 "interminable . . . air" ADN 1, p. 315.
141 "They . . . same." ADN 1, p. 316.
141 "I still . . . corrected." Ibid.
141 "truly . . . robes . . . robes" ADN 1, p. 300.
141 "the telepathic . . . way." David-Neel, *Initiations*, p. 30.
142 "When . . . noted." MM, p. 232.
142 "Among . . . steppes." ADN 1, p. 306.
142 "I . . . Himalayas!" ADN 1, p. 344.
143 "This . . . *saddhus.*" ADN 1, p. 342.
143 "a barbarian . . . depths." ADN 1, p. 300.
143 "an escargot . . . shell." ADN 1, p. 358.
144 "dirty . . . work." ADN 1, p. 359.
144 "Alone . . . God." Quoted by Brosse, *Alexandra David-Neel*, p. 152.
144 "bathed . . . mute" ADN 1, p. 371.
145 "I see . . . torture." ADN 1, p. 356.
145 "They were . . . Tibet." Evans-Wentz, *Milarepa*, pp. 41–42.
145 "Ah . . . cold." ADN 1, p. 348.
146 "I never . . . harbor." MM, p. 78.
146 "He would . . . stead." MM, p. 78.
146–147 "The Primal . . . is." Evans-Wentz, *Tibetan Yoga*, p. 224.
147 "the most . . . written." Watts, Foreword to David-Neel's *Secret Oral Teachings.*
147 "If I . . . fingers." ADN 1, p. 370.
147 "Waste . . . ears." David-Neel, *Secret Oral Teachings*, p. 1.
148 "endurance . . . character." Lama Govinda, *White Cloud*, p. 102.

Lama Govinda is a third-party source on the Gomchen. Marco Pallis's *Peaks* has interesting photos of him. David-Neel's *Initiations and Initiates* contains a wealth of tantric practices.

Chapter 13: Asia Marvelous and Diverse

149 "the man . . . environments." Lawrence, *Seven Pillars*, p. 31.
150 "They . . . region." ADN 1, p. 182.
150 "The Tibetans . . . out." Richardson, letter to authors, 15 Nov. 1985.
150 "I . . . again." MM, p. 79.
151 "On account . . . great." Bell, *Portrait*, p. 317.
151 "barbaric . . . dignitaries." MM, p. 85.
151 "unrefined . . . many." Ibid.
151 "My stay . . . learn." MM, p. 90.
151 "The special . . . hours." MM, p. 87.
152 "exploded . . . terrorized . . . ears" ADN 1, p. 381.
153 "Mme David-Neel . . . Lama." PS, report no. 1 (1917), p. 244. Emphasis ours.
153 "I have . . . railroads. . . ." ADN 1, pp. 380–81.
154 "a cloud . . . fingers." ADN 1, p. 383.
154 "a Sioux . . . dance." ADN 1, p. 386.
154 "It is . . . before." ADN 1, p. 382.
154 "frightfully . . . abominable," ADN 1, p. 392.
155 "I have . . . light." ADN 1, p. 393.
155 "I feel . . . go?" ADN 1, p. 403.
155–156 "amid . . . whip." ADN 1, p. 420.
156 "I am . . . fatigue." Ibid.
156 "Mongol . . . ancestors." ADN 1, p. 422.

156 "intimately . . . teas" ADN 1, p. 426.
156 "good . . . expression." ADN 1, p. 428.
156 "An indiscretion . . . danger." ADN 1, p. 429.
157 "lamentable . . . cry." ADN 1, p. 424.
157 "Aphur . . . *Jaune*." ADN 2, p. 19.
158 "To set . . . brutes." ADN 2, pp. 18–19.
158 "a family . . . den." MM, p. 92.
159 "big devil Albinos" ADN 2, p. 21.
159 "I might . . . disagreeable." Ibid.
159–160 "not a . . . road." ADN 2, p. 26.
160 "the pretty . . . sufferers." ADN 2, p. 37.
160 "eat[ing] many kilometers . . . Ouf! . . . am!" ADN 2, p. 38.
160 "Ah, Asia . . . West." ADN 2, p. 32.

Bell is very reticent on Alexandra; she has nothing good to say about him. The nature of their quarrel has never before been brought to light. By now, Hopkirk, *Trespassers*, is standard on the Great Game.

Chapter 14: A Paradise

166 "Is . . . one?" ADN 2, p. 141.
166 "The air . . . silence." ADN 2, p. 45.
166 "shabby . . . most impressive." MM, p. 95.
167 "a certain . . . together." MM, p. 98.
168 "I am . . . custom." ADN 2, p. 62.
168 "clear . . . Africa." ADN 2, p. 55.
168 "mute . . . hills" ADN 2, p. 59.
169 "We were . . . replace." Quoted by MacGregor, *Tibet*, p. 235.
170 "music . . . soul." ADN 2, p. 73.
170 "Sensuality . . . tent. . . ." ADN 2, p. 54.
170–171 "The world . . . atoms." ADN 2, p. 49.
171 "the nameless religion" Stein, *Tibetan Civilization*, p. 191.
171 "miniature . . . turquiose." ADN 2, p. 90.
171 "A hairlike . . . menace." Ekvall, *Tibetan Sky Lines*, "Introduction," n.p.
172 "coerce . . . region." MM, p. 238.
172 "Do not . . . wind." MM, p. 239.
173 "For . . . the eye." ADN 2, p. 95.
173 "drug-taking . . . exercises." Hilton, *Lost Horizon*, p. 140.
173 "There is . . . activity." ADN 2, p. 82.
173–174 "the pilgrims . . . makes." Quoted by MacGregor, *Tibet*, p. 236.
175 "Many . . . fanatics." Macdonald, *Twenty Years*, p. 142.
175 "Once . . . tents . . . control." MM, pp. 313–15.
176 "incident . . . luck" ADN 2, p. 127.
176 "You will . . . it." ADN 2, p. 100.
176 "I have . . . generations." ADN 2, p. 122.

Descriptions of life at Kum Bum are based on Thubten Norbu's wonderful *Tibet Is My Country*, as well as Alexandra David-Neel. James Hilton (*Lost Horizon*) never actually traveled to Tibet.

Chapter 15: Misadventures

177 "that noble . . . disciples." Price, *Diamond Sutra*, pp. 11–12.
177 "I have . . . one." David-Neel, *Tibetan Journey*, p. 29.

178 "Sometimes . . . with them. . . ." Thubten Norbu, *Tibet Is My Country*, p. 348.
178 "trespassers . . . gatecrashers." Hopkirk, *Trespassers*, p. 55.
178–179 "I came . . . idolaters." Quoted by MacGregor, *Tibet*, p. 20.
179 "washing . . . Saracens." Ibid., p. 16.
179 "whose . . . realm." Ibid., p. 129.
180 "Nor was . . . Lhasa . . . Tibet." Hopkirk, *Trespassers*, pp. 59–61.
181 "Of all . . . foolhardy." Ibid., p. 137.
181 "emaciated . . . frontier." Ibid., p. 148.
181 "This . . . era" Ibid., p. 159.
183 "Schary must . . . me in." Foreword to Schary, *Mahatmas*, p. vii.
183 "a good . . . others." ADN 2, p. 134.
183 "If things . . . Aphur." ADN 2, pp. 111–12.

Among the several fine works on Tibetan travelers, Hopkirk's *Trespassers* deserves special mention. John MacGregor is a pseudonym for a United States diplomat. Who?

Chapter 16: The French Nun

184 "a dish . . . boy . . . adventure." ADN 2, p. 137, p. 198.
184 "Temperamentally . . . coming." David-Neel, *Tibetan Journey*, p. 3.
184 "That . . . wished to." Ibid., p. 5.
185 "Give milk . . . heaven." ADN 2, p. 134.
185 "I wanted . . . do." Peyronnet, interview, Digne, August 1986.
185 "The wilderness . . . best?" ADN 2, p. 54.
186 "It doesn't . . . beggar." ADN 2, p. 108.
187 "to swashbuckle . . . alone." David-Neel, *Tibetan Journey*, p. 12.
187 "the sharp . . . themselves. . . ." Ibid., p. 106.
188 "officiated . . . archbishop" David-Neel, *Tibetan Journey*, p. 67.
188 "Because you . . . joke." ADN 2, pp. 159–160.
188–189 "a *voyageur* . . . warm." David-Neel, *Tibetan Journey*, p. 126.
189 "I'm not . . . trip?" ADN 2, p. 145.
189 "While traveling . . . hospital." Jour, p. xiv.
190 "Perhaps . . . Tibet." PS, item 1129.
190 "the great . . . Tachienlu" ADN 2, p. 187.
190 "We did . . . back." PS, Dec. 6, 1921.
190 "Let them . . . consequences!" ADN 2, p. 195.
191 "There . . . times." ADN 2, pp. 182–183.

Contradictions between Alexandra David-Neel's published accounts and private letters are especially sharp for this period. Understandably, her books present her in the best possible light. Her *Tibetan Journey* is splendidly readable.

Chapter 17: An Officer and a Gentleman

192 "to launch . . . infected . . . dirtiness." ADN 2, p. 201.
193 "I walked . . . road." ADN 2, p. 208.
194 "One afternoon . . . Lhasa." Jour, p. 119.
194 "I met . . . Lanchow." PS, 28 July, 1922.
194 "stuck . . . Albert . . . rags." ADN 2, p. 210.
195 "He has . . . him." ADN 2, p. 206.
195 "found . . . expression." David-Neel, *Gesar*, p. 39.

197 "Gesar . . . realization." David-Neel, *Gesar,* Foreword, n.p.
197 "Just now . . . distance . . . offices." ADN 2, p. 211.
198 "Your reverence . . . die . . . presence." MM, pp. 201–203.
199 "mountains . . . dust" ADN 2, p. 220.
199 "a new . . . before." ADN 2, p. 227.
200 "You are . . . pity!" Ibid.
200 "It is . . . place!" ADN 2, pp. 219–220.
200 "I . . . journey." ADN 2, p. 239.
200 "I . . . adventure." ADN 2, p. 242.
200–201 "Think . . . all." ADN 2, p. 243.

This life of Pereira is taken from the Dictionary of National Biography, '2–'30, p. 664. His mission when he met Alexandra David-Neel remains conjecture. We know of no other "sighting" of a *lung-gom-pa* in action.

Chapter 18: A Long Walk

202 "Farewell . . . begins." Jour, p. 1.
203 "the dread . . . land." David-Neel, *Asia* (March 1926), p. 195.
203 "towering . . . moon." Ibid.
203 "We . . . us," Ibid., p. 196.
203 "mendicant . . . care." David-Neel, *Asia* (March, 1926), pp. 198–199.
203 "I knocked . . . succeed." Jour, p. 10.
204 "the scared . . . hunter." Jour, p. 87.
204 "Born . . . us." David-Neel, *Asia* (March, 1926), p. 200.
204 "who . . . us." Jour, p. 22.
204 "In . . . crests." Jour, p. 25.
204 "the little thing . . . villas . . . little" Jour, pp. 27–28.
205 "confront . . . illusions." Jour, p. 29.
205 "Mother . . . gods." David-Neel, *Asia* (March, 1926), p. 200.
205 "We saw . . . Tibet . . ." Ibid.
205–206 "In . . . feet . . . magic" Jour, p. 34.
206 "Travelling . . . down" Jour, p. 56.
206 "really . . . understand." Jour, pp. 50–51.
207 "Who are . . . *philings,*" Jour, p. 54.
207–208 "Small . . . stoics . . . lie?" Jour, pp. 60–61.
208 "an old . . . goddess" Jour, p. 62.
208 "the guest . . . beggar." Jour, p. 75.
208 "I was . . . approached." Jour, p. 76.
208 "I profoundly . . . matters." Jour, p. xxii.
209 "Eat . . . The Tibetans . . . ill." Jour, pp. 107–108.
209 "graceful . . . Autumn . . . trees." Jour, p. 86.
210 "doubled . . . ball." Jour, p. 103.
211 "Let us . . . such!" Jour, pp. 104–105.

This and the following chapter rely essentially on Alexandra's *Journey,* of which she and Yongden were the sole witnesses. However, it may be checked against her own (*post facto*) letters, and other explorers' accounts. In particular, Bailey and Teichman, both British officers, covered much of the same ground. Additionally, Alexandra's articles in *Asia,* appearing in 1926, precede *Journey,* and are at times more precise in detail, language, and feeling than the book.

Chapter 19: A Long Walk, Continued

212 "If . . . country." Bailey, *No Passport,* p. 15.
213 "the narrow . . . My nerves . . . that rope." Jour, pp. 90–93.
213–214 "My . . . thing . . . paradise!" Jour, pp. 125–126.
214 "the 'winged . . . Juno." Jour, p. 54.
214–215 "Quite suddenly . . . Face . . . would!" Jour, pp. 128–129.
215 "The moon . . . proceed." Jour, p. 130.
215 "elves . . . radiance." Ibid.
216 "Jetsunma . . . moving . . . head." Jour, p. 133.
216 "As for . . . one." Jour, p. 153.
217 "Three . . . gastronomy." Jour, p. 156.
217 "After . . . valleys." Ibid.
218 "lying . . . blood." Jour, p. 159.
218 "Perhaps . . . deeds." Jour, p. 162.
218–219 "No trace . . . hearts." Jour, p. 164.
219 "Happy . . . quick!" Jour, p. 168.
220 "the size . . . disposition." Hanbury-Tracy, *Black River,* p. 220.
221 "All of . . . nothing." Jour, p. 210.
221 "Let . . . back!" Jour, p. 211.
222 "many . . . scented" Ward, *Plant Hunter,* p. 66.
222 "queer . . . naive." Jour, p. 217.
223 "exceedingly . . . Alps." Jour, p. 237.
223 "Jetsunma . . . this one." Jour, pp. 239–240.
223 "ran . . . alms" McGovern, *To Lhasa,* p. 332.
223 "Now we . . . flames." Jour, p. 255.
223 "a furious . . . sky." Jour, p. 256.
224 "*Lha* . . . Lhasa!" Jour, p. 258.

Chapter 20: "The Potala Is the Paradise of Buddhas."

225 "Tibetans . . . cart." Thomas, *Out of this World,* p. 17.
225 "an immense . . . rains." Ibid., p. 43.
226 "Late . . . beacon." Ibid., p. 156.
226 "a great . . . gods." McGovern, *To Lhasa,* p. 333.
227 "I had . . . it." Jour, p. 258.
227 "All . . . sex." Jour, p. 259.
227 "prettily . . . ranges." Ibid.
227 "a red . . . beauty." Ibid.
227 "halted . . . sophisticated." McGovern, *To Lhasa,* p. 337.
227 "dear . . . fellows" Jour, p. 262.
228 "The three . . . sex." Jour, p. 263.
228 "the horrid little toad" Ibid.
228 "the legends . . . animation." Jour, p. 260.
228 "the aboriginal . . . forsake." Ibid.
228–229 "led . . . deaths." Jour, p. 281.
229 "enjoyed . . . valley." Jour, p. 265.
229 "large . . . clean" Jour, p. 273.
229 "filthy . . . crime." Millington, *To Lhasa,* p. 201.
229 "brawling monks . . . populace." McGovern, *To Lhasa,* p. 117.
229 "mean . . . sinister." Chapman, *Lhasa,* pp. 147, 155.
229 "There was . . . smells." Richardson, letter to authors, 30 May, 1986.
230 "Ah, you . . . that!" Jour, p. 271.
230 "The whole . . . hands." McGovern, *To Lhasa,* p. 356.
231 "Light . . . temples." Jour, p. 269.

231 "At last . . . them." Jour, p. 270.
231–232 "running . . . Tibetans." Ibid.
232 "quality . . . What a . . . streets!" Jour, p. 272.
232 "as birds . . . daily . . . sun." Jour, p. 285.
232 "the elegant . . . talk" McGovern, *To Lhasa*, p. 63.
232 "I really . . . slums!" Jour, p. 285.
233 "A sort . . . friends." David-Neel, *Initiations*, p. 125.
233 "They . . . many." Quoted by Dhondup, *Songs*, p. 43.
233 "Everybody . . . citizens . . . voices." Jour, p. 296.
234 "the blue . . . flames." Jour, p. 296.
234 "Lhasa's . . . invited." Bell, *People of Tibet*, p. 284.
234 "No one . . . there" Jour, p. 298.
234 "[F]or the . . . City." Jour, p. 257.
235 "a tiny . . . invisible." Jour, p. 299.
235 "That . . . ceremony." Thomas, *Out of this World*, p. 304.
235 "like . . . streams" Ibid., p. 305.

Lowell Thomas, Jr.'s *Out of this World* was helpful for the feel of Lhasa, as was Montgomery McGovern's *To Lhasa in Disguise*. Our correspondence with Hugh Richardson corrected various misconceptions and provided a wonderful view into a time just passed.

Chapter 21: The Dream of Repose

241 "Alexandra . . . Tibet." Jeanne Denys, *Alexandra David-Neel au Tibet*, p. 10.
241 "Prove it . . . publicity." Ibid., p. 222.
242 "I am . . . dates." Durrell, *Elle*, 17 July, 1964.
242 "[H]er . . . nil." Hopkirk, *Trespassers*, p. 229.
243 "They [the photos] had . . . suspicion." Norwick, "Alexandra David-Neel's Adventures," p. 72.
243 "He was . . . for me." McGovern, *To Lhasa*, p. 446.
243 "My . . . David" Brosse, *Alexandra David-Neel*, p. 11.
244 "She . . . much." Ibid.
244 "My dearest . . . bones." ADN 2, p. 245.
244 "general . . . sleeping." ADN 2, p. 246.
244 "This letter . . . discretion." ADN 2, p. 247.
244 "[a]re employed . . . postman" McGovern, *To Lhasa*, p. 433.
245 "I count . . . stop me." ADN 2, p. 248.
245 "I would . . . daily." ADN 2, p. 249.
245 "at my . . . made." ADN 2, p. 250.
246 "Travelling . . . limited." Bell, *People of Tibet*, p. 305.
246 "Had I . . . again." Jour, pp. 298–299.
246 "a strange . . . towel!" Richardson, letter to authors, 21 September, 1985.
246 "The joke . . . cold." McGovern, *To Lhasa*, p. 373.
246 "I am . . . best." ADN 2, p. 249.
246 "I was . . . orchids." ADN 2, p. 248.
247 "[I am] . . . repose" ADN 2, p. 250.
247 "Mme. . . . America." PS, item 2419.
248 "It is . . . undesirable." PS, 1922, Not numbered.
248 "Re-entry . . . again." ADN 2, pp. 252–253.
248 "I . . . at once." ADN 2, p. 253.
249 "He died . . . march." ADN 2, p. 255.
249 "chills . . . done." ADN 2, p. 259.

249 "We climbed ... me. ..." Ibid.
249 "Everyone ... me." Ibid.
250 "The natives ... Europeans." ADN 2, p. 260.
250 "a romantic ... hideaway." ADN 2, p. 263.
250 "Put ... editors." ADN 2, p. 258.
250 "When one ... get it?" ADN 2, p. 268.
250-251 "I must ... question." ADN 2, pp. 272-273.
251 "I can ... Christ." ADN 2, p. 274.
251 "*chez* ... I plan ... America. ..." ADN 2, p. 276.
251 "chase ... butterflies." ADN 2, p. 274.
251 "Oh, ... it?" ADN 2, p. 279.

The Secret Files, including Macdonald's letter, verify Alexandra David-Neel's claims and show how carefully the Government of India tracked her. Nonetheless, Denys usefully raises questions of detail. False attributions to David-Neel of photographs taken by others are still common.

Chapter 22: Success at Paris

252 "that incredible ... 1875." Watts, *In My Own Way*, p. 88.
252 "Tibetan ... North" ADN 2, p. 302.
252 "The newspapers ... me" ADN 2, p. 285.
252 "I adore ... passion." ADN 2, p. 290.
253 "big lunch ... businessman" ADN 2, p. 293.
253 "All ... Paris." ADN 2, p. 294.
253 "We will ... friends." ADN 2, p. 285.
253 "I fell ... neuralgia." ADN 2, p. 298.
253-254 "Mme. ... success." Tery, *Quotidien*, 31 March 1926.
254 "It would ... cares." ADN 2, p. 282.
254 "He is ... cries." Tery, *Quotidien*, 31 March 1926.
255-256 Alexandra's confrontation with Philip Neel at Marseilles is based on ADN 2, especially pp. 280 and 306-308, the latter featuring a letter of Philip's. In addition, material was gleaned from interviews in southern France in summer 1986. See also Miller, *On Top*, p. 185.
256 "I need ... adventure." ADN 2, p. 308.
256 "the first ... Lhasa." Quoted by Hopkirk, intro. to Jour, p. ix.
256 "mountains ... palaces. ..." ADN 2, p. 299.
256 "nostalgia ... left." ADN 2, p. 300.
256 "I am a savage ... wilds." ADN 2, p. 296.
256-257 "the happiest ... beggar-pilgrims." Jour, p. 18.
257 "has a ... secured." Miller, *On Top*, p. 167.
257 "as a traveler ... feat." *New York Times*, June 12, 1927, p. 13.
257 "a thoroughly ... tale" *Saturday Review of Literature*, vol. 3, July 2, 1927, p. 950.
257 "a considerable ... information." *Times Literary Supplement*, July 14, 1927, p. 481.
257 "short ... moustache" Watts, *In My Own Way*, p. 137.
257 "The geographical ... took." Younghusband, *Geographical Journal*, vol. lxxi 1928, p. 85.
258 "the sort ... over." Patti Hagan, *Ms.*, July, 1986, p. 26.
258 "Had it not ... peace." Jour, p. 160.
259 "[They] ... courage." ADN 2, p. 311.
259 "What ... are!" ADN 2, p. 309.
260 "There is ... clouds." Quoted by Chalon, *Lumineaux destin*, p. 328.
260 "It's ... appearance. ..." Ibid., p. 336.

260 "The countryside . . . background." ADN 2, p. 312.
260 "In . . . own." ADN 2, p. 314.
260 "I believe . . . Asia" Quoted by Chalon, *Lumineaux destin*, p. 342.

Chapter 23: The Short Path

262 "These . . . Pygmies!" Peyronnet, tour of Samten Dzong, August, 1986.
263 "The roads . . . little." ADN 2, p. 314.
263 "the site . . . tent" ADN 2, p. 313.
263 "for . . . art." ADN 2, p. 315.
263 "Levi . . . vitamins." Quoted by Chalon, p. 343.
263 "spiritual sportsmen" MM, p. 199.
263 "is considered . . . demon." MM, p. 243.
263–264 "Sorcerers . . . them." MM, p. 245.
264 "the dreadful . . . banquet." MM, p. 148.
264 "One . . . others." Ibid.
265 "cut . . . vultures." MM, p. 157.
265 "the strange . . . practices." MM, p. 152.
265 "This . . . me." MM, p. 157.
265 "[F]or . . . head." Norbu, *Tibet*, p. 127.
265–266 "I . . . demons . . . I pay . . . turn! . . . Come . . . blood!" MM, pp. 158–160.
266 "You appear . . . really? . . . on . . . death?" MM, pp. 162–163.
266–267 "This Easterner . . . spirit." MM, p. xii.
267 "Psychic . . . attention." MM, p. vi.
267 "My . . . growing." ADN 2, p. 327.
268 "the revelation . . . mysteries." David-Neel, *Initiations*, p. 40.
268 "The *angkur* [initiation] . . . process." Ibid.
268 "The fruit . . . move." Ibid., p. 224.
268 "Most initiates . . . in hell." Ibid., p. 27.
268–269 "The *naljorpa* . . . hand." Ibid., p. 25.
269 "He who . . . serenity." Ibid., p. 16.
269 "solitude . . . tent" Peyronnet, "Notre Dame du Tibet." unpublished pamphlet, n.p.
270 "went . . . world." ADN 2, p. 326.
270 "We have . . . grass!" David-Neel, *Gesar*, p. 33.
271 "This . . . Tibet." David-Neel, *Buddhism*, p. 7.
272 "In Tibet . . . importance . . . *Bardo Thodol*." David-Neel, *Buddhism*, p. 217.
272 "Copious . . . 1931)." Evans-Wentz, ed., *Tibetan Yoga*, p. 57.
272 "I find Belgium . . . land." ADN 2, p. 328.
273 "You will . . . well-heated." ADN 2, p. 330.
273 "I must . . . stores." ADN 2, p. 328.
273 "Without . . . darkness." David-Neel, *Sous des nuees d'orage*, p. 6.

Chapter 24: Storm Clouds

274 "I have . . . forever." David-Neel, *Sous des nuees d'orage*, p. 1.
274 "under . . . sky" Ibid., p 11.
274 "When the . . . living." Ibid.
275 "Ah . . . my youth!" Ibid., p. 9.
275–276 "I won't . . . piece." ADN 2, pp. 330–331.
276 "Peking . . . world." David-neel, *Sous des nuees d'orage*, p. 74.
276 "an inexpressible . . . eyes." Ibid., p. 86.
277 "The sight . . . joy." Ibid., p. 114.
277 "Possibly . . . unlikely." Ibid., p. 119.

277 "pills . . . superman." Ibid., p. 147.
277 "proceeded . . . murder." McAleavy, *China*, p. 299.
277 "Counting . . . library." David-Neel, *Sous des nuees d'orage*, p. 161.
278 "filled . . . *d'estime.*" ADN 2, p. 329.
278 "books . . . inhabitants." David-Neel, *Lama of Five Wisdoms*, Author's Note.
278 "It is . . . defeat." Peyronnet, "Notre Dame du Tibet," n.p.
279 "[C]ertain . . . immortality." David-Neel, *Tibetan Tale of Love and Magic*, p. 1.
279 "Many times . . . papers." David-Neel, *Sous des nuees d'orage*, p. 171.
279 "My sleep . . . circumstances." Ibid., p. 194.
280 "Leave me . . . again." Ibid., p. 210.
280 "I abandoned . . . body." Ibid., p. 212.
280 "There are . . . conditions." Ibid., p. 245.
280–281 "The besieged . . . flee." Ibid., p. 259.
281 "Then I . . . Chinese." Ibid., p. 274.
281 "standing . . . another . . . cesspools." ADN 2, p. 333.
281 "For the . . . devil!" ADN 2, p. 334.
281 "War undoes . . . savagery." ADN 2, p. 330.
281 "These brave . . . airplanes." ADN 2, p. 338.
282 "Such . . . young." ADN 2, p. 341.
283 "I don't . . . turn." ADN 2, p. 343.
283 "included . . . save us." ADN 2, pp. 348–349.
283 "A real . . . head" ADN 2, p. 350.
284 "no practical . . . ennui" ADN 2, p. 355.
284 "in dread . . . moment." ADN 2, p. 351.
284 "In order . . . death." David-Neel, *Sous des nuees d'orage*, p. 275.
284 "It's odd . . . one." ADN 2, P. 352.
285 "These two . . . China." Avedon, *In Exile*, p. 247.
285 "It is . . . arrested." ADN 2, p. 351.
285 "I . . . friend." Peyronnet, *Dix ans*, p. 359.

The histories of modern China by McAleavy, Rodzinski, and Thornton provided background. *Magie noir* is available in English as *Tibetan Tale of Love and Magic*.

Chapter 25: The Wife of the Chinese

286 "For three . . . pain." Quoted by Chalon, *Lumineaux destin*, p. 403.
286 "Today . . . insupportable . . . heir." Quoted by Brosse, *Alexandra David-Neel*, p. 242.
286 "It's . . . solitudes." Quoted by Chalon, *Lumineaux destin*, p. 406.
287 "I happened . . . fiction!" Blofeld, letter, 26 April, 1987.
288 "a walled . . . Cities." Blofeld, *Wheel of Life*, p. 190.
289 "In this . . . Ghost." Quoted by Brosse, *Alexandra David-Neel*, p. 244.
289 "very Jewish" Ibid.
289 "Khaki . . . thighs." Ibid.
289 "They . . . Tibetan." Quoted by Chalon, *Lumineaux destin*, p. 416.
289 "very ugly . . . *au revoir* . . . true." Ibid., p. 418.
289 "the first . . . explorer" Ibid., p. 420.
290 "[W]as . . . country." Thomas, Jr., *Out of this World*, p. 146.
290 "The Chinese . . . ability." David-Neel, *A l'ouest barbare*, p. 300.
290 "There are . . . civilization." Quoted by Brosse, *Alexandra David-Neel*, p. 254.
290 "It is ridiculous . . . to them." Ibid., p. 299.
290–291 "I myself . . . elements." David-Neel, *L'Inde* (1951), p. 145.
291 "the texts . . . disused." Ibid.

291 "This whole . . . living . . . humble." Ibid., pp. 147–48.
291 "brought . . . cult." Ibid., p. 154.
291 "any woman . . . wife." David-Neel, *Initiations*, p. 35.
291 "The fifth . . . decency." David-Neel, *L'Inde* (1951), p. 154.
293 "The world . . . wall." David-Neel, *The Power*, pp. 66, 79.
293–294 "I consider . . . done." ADN 2, p. 347.
294 "It was . . . sick." Quoted by Chalon, *Lumineaux destin*, p. 437.
294 "Where . . . Sikkimese?" Ibid., p. 406.
294 "she had . . . Tibet." Younghusband, *Peking to Lhasa*, p. 131.
294 "smiled a lot" Chalon, *Lumineaux destin*, p. 421.
295 "One day . . . blame." Brosse, *Alexandra David-Neel*, p. 157.
295 "desolated . . . spirit." Quoted by Chalon, *Lumineaux destin*, p. 438.
296 "wide . . . the desire . . . attachment . . . demons." David-Neel, *Asia* (March 1926), pp. 199–200.

Collectively, we have visited the Alexandra David-Neel *Fondation* at Digne three times for a total stay of several weeks. The interviews with Professor Pierre Borrely and Dr. Marcel Maille were conducted in southern France in August 1986, with the assistance of Letha Hadadi, who speaks flawless French. Dr. Maille is a Tibetanist of long standing and has an excellent collection of Tibetan ritual artifacts. We consider both gentlemen, because of their specialized knowledge and general culture, impeccable sources. Moreover, Dr. Maille is very likely Alexandra's last surviving confidant.

Chapter 26: The Sage of Digne

298 "She didn't . . . frivolity." Brosse, *Alexandra David-Neel*, p. 10.
299 "The woman . . . with." Peyronnet, *Dix ans*, p. 84.
299 "a woman . . . despotism." Ibid., p. 52.
299 "Nothing . . . fine." Ibid., pp. 14–15.
299 "*Mademoiselle* . . . things." Ibid., p. 18.
299 "Don't leave . . . ungrateful." Ibid., p. 21.
299 "Day? . . . mean?" Ibid., p. 24.
299 "a person . . . intellect." Ibid., p. 44.
300 "It . . . tigers." Ibid., p. 36.
300 "somber . . . here!" Ibid., p. 39.
301 "The *phurba* . . . world." MM, p. 139.
301 "I had . . . dagger . . . fright . . . *gomchenma*." MM, pp. 139–140.
301 "I . . . owner." MM, p. 141.
302 "She . . . adventure." Peyronnet, *Dix ans*, p. 44.
303 "There is no . . . empire." David-Neel, *Vieux Tibet*, pp. 9–10.
303 "Not a shot . . . population . . . misinformed." Ibid., p. 118.
303 "Tibetans . . . officials." Jour, p. 256.
303–304 "the Chinese . . . Lhasa." David-Neel, *Vieux Tibet*, p. 196.
304 "grave concern . . . them." Dalai Lama, *My Land*, p. 263.
304 "a regime . . . nation" David-Neel, *Quarante siecles*, p. 7.
304–305 "the twenty-fifth . . . The present . . . killing?" Dalai Lama, *Tibet Society Newsletter* vol. 15 (Fall 1984), p. 1.
305 "the wave . . . expansion." David-Neel, *Vieux Tibet*, p. 3.
306 "What does . . . say?" Peyronnet, *Dix ans*, p. 184.
306 "Ah, this . . . mug." Ibid., pp. 94–95.
308 "I should . . . sky . . . grand." Ibid., p. 79.
309 "confided . . . about." Brosse, *Alexandra David-Neel*, p. 43n.

309 "The greatest . . . odor . . . men!" Peyronnet, *Dix ans,* p. 218.
310 "magnificent . . . mouth." Durrell, *Elle,* 17 July, 1964.
310 "You . . . gentlemen!" Durrell, interview, April, 1986.
310 "It showed . . . Yes . . . friends." Durrell, letter to authors, November 13, 1986.
311 "To be . . . way?" Peyronnet, *Dix ans,* p. 196.
311 "She knows . . . Tibetan." Peyronnet, "Notre Dame du Tibet," n.p.
311 "We have . . . Tibet." Peyronnet, *Dix ans,* p. 233.
312 "Sirs . . . Woman? . . . old ape?" Ibid., p. 213.
312 "Who knows . . . mountainside?" Peyronnet, "Notre Dame du Tibet," n.p.
313 "God . . . myself." Peyronnet, *Dix ans,* p. 232.
313 "This time . . . it." Ibid., p. 240.
314 "I am . . . Peking." Quoted by Chalon, *Lumineaux destin,* p. 486.
314 "Woman . . . world." Ibid., p. 490.
314 "the solitudes . . . cruel." Peyronnet, "Notre Dame du Tibet," n.p.

Unattributed remarks of David-Neel's were told to us by Peyronnet, either in conversation or, more formally, on the fascinating daily tours she gives of Samten Dzong. To avoid embarrassment, two minor informants have not been identified. A visit to Samten Dzong can vividly recreate Alexandra's last decade.

Coda: The Legacy

315 "only . . . living." David-Neel, *L'Inde hier,* p. 148.
316 "the same . . . goodness." Lama Govinda, *White Clouds,* p. 103.
317 "Our group . . . together." Galland, *Women,* p. 11.
317 "I ponder . . . dream." Ibid., pp. 53–54.
317 "I keep . . . top." Blum, "Triumph," p. 295.
317–320 "The American," who wishes to return to Tibet, has requested anonymity. The Tibetans are not identified for reasons stated. However, see Marcia Keegan, "Reflections on a Visit to Tibet," *Tibet Society Bulletin* 18 (December 1986), pp. 1–3, for a similar reaction.
319 "We want . . . Tibet!" Handbill in possession of authors.
321 "the travelogue . . . another." K. W. Bolle, from foreword to Beyer, *Cult,* p. vi.
322 "impressed . . . summer sun." David-Neel, *Buddhism,* p. 10.
323 "With my first . . . West." Peyronnet, "Notre Dame du Tibet," n.p.
323 "It's really . . . desires." Ibid.
323 "I had . . . while." David-Neel, *Sortilege,* p. 144.

Selected Bibliography

ARCHIVAL AND UNPUBLISHED SOURCES

Bell, Charles. Unpublished Notebooks on Tibet, Bhutan, Sikkim and Chumbi Valley. 4 vols., manuscript notes 1936; Diary vol. 3–21, manuscript notes 1907–38. The British Library, London.

The Political and Secret Annual Files (1912–1930), L/P&S11, India Office Records. The British Library, London.

WORKS BY ALEXANDRA DAVID-NEEL

ENGLISH

David-Neel, Alexandra. "Behind the Veil of Tibet." *Asia* 26 (April 1926): 320–28, 346–53.

————. *Buddhism: Its Doctrines and Its Methods.* New York; Avon 1979.

————. "Edge of Tibet." *Asia* 44 (January 1944): 26–29.

————. "A Frenchwoman Secretly Headed for Lhasa." *Asia* 26 (March 1926): 195–201, 266–71.

————. "High Politics in Tibet." *Asia* 43 (March 1943): 157–59.

————. *Initiations and Initiates in Tibet.* Berkeley: Shambhala, 1970.

————. "Lhasa at Last." *Asia* 26 (July 1926): 624–33.

————. "Lost in the Tibetan Snows." *Asia* 26 (May 1926): 429–35, 452–54.

————. *Magic and Mystery in Tibet.* New York: Dover, 1971.

————. "Mohammedans of the Chinese Far West." *Asia* 43 (December 1943): 677–79.

————. *My Journey to Lhasa.* New York: Harper & Brothers 1927. Reprint. Boston: Beacon Press, 1986.

————. "New Western Provinces of China I: Ching-hai." *Asia* 42 (May 1942): 286–89.

————. "New Western Provinces of China II: Sikang." *Asia* 42 (June 1942): 367–70.

————. *The Power of Nothingness.* Boston: Houghton Mifflin, 1982.

————. "The Robber Land of the Po." *Asia* 26 (June 1926): 512–16, 563–66.

————. *The Secret Oral Teachings in Tibetan Buddhist Sects.* San Francisco: City Lights, 1967.

————. *The Superhuman Life of Gesar of Ling.* Boulder, Colo.: Prajna, 1981.

————. "Theatre in China Now." *Asia* 44 (December 1944): 559–60.

———. "Tibet Looks at the News." *Asia* 42 (March 1942): 189–90.

———. "Tibetan Border Intrigue." *Asia* 41 (May 1941): 219–22.

———. *Tibetan Tale of Love and Magic,* Jersey, Neville Spearman, 1983.

———. "A Woman's Daring Journey into Tibet." *Asia* 26 (March 1926): 195–201, 266–71.

———. "Women of Tibet." *Asia* 34 (March 1934): 176–81.

FRENCH

David, Alexandra. "Aupres du Dalai Lama." *Mercure de France* 99 (October 1912): 466–76.

———. "Le bouc emissaire des thibetains." *Mercure de France* 176 (December 1924): 649–60.

———. "Les colonies sionistes en Palestine." *Mercure de France* 80 (July 1909): 266–75.

———. *Grammaire de la langue tibetaine parlee.* Paris: n.p. n.d.

———. "L'Iliade thibetaine et ses bardes." *Mercure de France* 166 (September 1923): 714–25.

———. "L'Instruction des indigenes en Tunisie." *Mercure de France* 74 (July 1908): 61–72.

———. "La liberation de la femme des charges de la maternite." *Le Monde* (1908): 115–19.

———. "Le pacifisme dans l' antiquite chinoise." *Mercure de France* 67 (June 1907): 465–71.

———. "La question du Thibet." *Mercure de France* 140 (May-June 1920): 366–75.

———. *Socialisme Chinois; Le philosophe Meh-Ti et L' idee de solidarite.* Londres: Girard et Briere, 1907.

———. *Les theories individualistes dans la philosophie chinoise.* Paris; Girard et Briere, 1909. Reprint. Paris: Plon, 1970.

———. "Un Stirner chinois." *Mercure de France* 76 (November 1908): 445–52.

David-Neel, Alexandra. *A l'Ouest barbare de la vaste Chine.* Paris: Plon, 1947.

———. *Ashtavakra Gita; Discours sur le Vedanta Advaita.* Paris: Adyar 1951.

———. *Au coeur des Himalayas; Le Nepal.* Paris: Dessart, 1949.

———. *Avadhuta Gita.* Paris: Adyar, 1958.

———. *En Chine: L'amour universel et l'individualisme integral: les maitres Mo-Tse et Yang Tchou.* Paris: Plon, 1976.

———. *La connaissance transcendante.* Paris: Adyar, 1958.

———. *Grand Tibet; Au pays des brigands-gentilshommes.* Paris: Plon, 1933. English edition. London: Bodley Head, 1936.

———. *Immortalite et reincarnation: Doctrines et pratiques en Chine, au Tibet, dans l'Inde.* Paris: Plon, 1961.

———. *L'Inde ou j'ai vecu; Avant et apres l'independence.* Paris: Plon, 1969.

———. *L'Inde hier, aujourd'hui, demain.* Paris: Plon, 1951.

———. *Journal de voyage; Lettres a son Mari, 11 aout 1904–27 Decembre 1917.* Vol. 1. Ed. Marie-Madeleine Peyronnet. Paris: Plon, 1975.

———. *Journal de voyage; Lettres a son Mari, 14 janvier 1918–31 Decembre 1940.* Vol. 2. Ed. Marie-Madeleine Peyronnet. Paris: Plon, 1976.

———. *Le lama au cinq sagesses.* Paris: Plon, 1935. Reprint. Paris: Plon, 1970.

———. *La lampe de sagesse.* Paris: Le Rocher, 1986.

————. *Magie d'amour et magie noire; Scenes du Tibet inconnu.* Paris: Plon, 1938. English edition. Jersey: Neville Spearman, 1983.

————. *Le modernisme bouddhiste et le bouddhisme du Bouddha.* Paris: Alcan, 1936. Reprint: Paris, Plon, 1977.

————. "Le phenomes psychiques au Thibet." *Revue de Paris* (December 1929): 566–94.

————. *Le puissance de neant.* Paris; Plon, 1954.

————. *Le sortilege du mystere; Faits etranges et gens bizarre recontres au long de mes routes d'orient et d'occident.* Paris: Plon, 1972.

————. *Sous des nuees d'orage; Recit de voyage.* Paris: Plon, 1940.

————. *Quarante siecles d'expansion chinoise.* Paris: Plon, 1964.

————. *Textes tibetains inedits.* Paris, 1952. Reprint. Paris: Pygmalion, 1972.

————. "Le Thibet mystique." *Revue de Paris* 1 (February 1928): 855–98.

————. *Le Tibet d'Alexandra David-Neel.* Paris: Plon, 1979.

————. *Le vieux Tibet face a la Chine nouvelle.* Paris: Plon, 1953.

————. *Vivre au Tibet; Cuisine, traditions et images.* n.p. Morel 1975.

Myrial, Alexandra [pseud]. "Les congregations en Chine." *Mercure de France,* 47 (August 1903): 289–312.

————. "Moukden." *Mercure de France* 56 (July 1905): 69–79.

————. *Pour la vie.* Bruxelles; n.p., 1898.

WORKS CONCERNED WITH ALEXANDRA DAVID-NEEL

ENGLISH

"Alexandra David-Neel is Dead: Writer, Adventuress, Traveller," New York *Times,* I (September 9, 1969), 47.

Anderson, Walt. *Open Secrets.* New York: Penguin Books 1979.

Dedman, Jane. "Walker in the Sky." *Quest* 78 (May-June 1978): 21–26, 90–92.

Galland, China. *Women in the Wilderness.* New York: Harper & Row, 1981.

Hopkirk, Peter. *Trespassers on the Roof of the World.* London: J. Murray, 1982.

Miller, Luree. *On Top of the World.* New York: Paddington, 1976.

Thomas, Lowell, Jr. *Out of This World.* New York: Greystone, 1950.

Tiltman, Marjorie. *Women in Modern Adventure.* London: G. G. Harrap, 1935.

FRENCH

Brosse, J. *Alexandra David-Neel: L'aventure et la spiritualite.* Paris: Retz, 1978.

Chalon, Jean. *Le lumineux destin d'Alexandra David-Neel.* Paris: Plon, 1985.

Champy, Huguette. "Quelques Exploratrices." *Revue Economique* 68, no. 2 (May 1955): 32–35.

Denys, Jeanne. *Alexandra David-Neel au Tibet.* Paris: Pensee Universelle, 1972.

Peyronnet, Marie-Madeleine. *Dix ans avec Alexandra David-Neel.* Paris: Plon, 1973.

OTHER SOURCES

Agulhon, Maurice. *The Republican Experiment, 1848–1852.* Cambridge; Cambridge University Press, 1983.

Akar, Tinley N. "Tibetan Uprising Observed in New York." *Tibetan Review* (April 1976), 7–8.

Avedon, John. *In Exile from the Land of Snows.* New York: Knopf, 1984.

Bailey, Frederick. *China, Tibet, Assam: A Journey.* London: J. Cape, 1945.

_____. *No Passport for Tibet.* London: Rupert Hart-Davis, 1957.

Basu, Chandra. *Esoteric Science and Philosophy of the Tantras.* Allahabad: n.p., 1914.

Battaglia, Lee. "Wedding of Two Worlds," *National Geographic Magazine* 124 (November 1963): 708–27.

Beauvoir, Simone de. *The Second Sex.* New York: Knopf, 1973.

Bell, Charles. *The People of Tibet.* Cambridge: Clarendon Press, 1928.

_____. *Portrait of the Dalai Lama.* London: Collins, 1946.

_____. *Tibet Past and Present.* Cambridge: Oxford University Press, 1924.

Bernard, Theos. *Penthouse of the Gods.* New York: Scribners, 1939.

Bernbaum, Edwin. *The Way to Shambala.* New York: Doubleday, 1983.

Beyer, Stephen. *The Cult of Tara.* Berkeley: University of California Press, 1978.

Bharati, Agehananda. *The Tantric Tradition.* New York: Weiser, 1975.

Bishop, Barry. "Wintering on the Roof of the World." *National Geographic Magazine* 123 (October 1962): 503–52.

Bishop, Isabella Bird. *Among the Tibetans.* New York: Revell, 1894.

Blofeld, John. *The Tantric Mysticism of Tibet.* New York: Causeway Books, 1974.

_____. *The Wheel of Life.* Boulder, Colo.: Shambhala, 1978.

Blum, Arlene. *Annapurna: A Woman's Place.* San Francisco: Sierra Club Books, 1980.

_____. "Triumph and Tragedy in Annapurna." *National Geographic* 155, no. 3 (March 1979), p. 295.

Burchell, S. C. *Upstart Empire.* London: Macdonald, 1971.

Burton, Richard. *Personal Narrative of a Pilgrimage to Al Madinah and Mecca.* 2 vols. London: Tylston & Edwards, 1893.

Candler, Edmund. *The Unveiling of Lhasa.* London: Edward Arnold, 1905.

Carey, William. *Adventures in Tibet.* New York: Baker & Taylor, 1901.

Carroll, John. *Breakout from the Crystal Palace.* London: Routledge & K. Paul, 1974.

Chapman, Spencer. *Lhasa; The Holy City.* London: Harper & Bros., 1938.

China's Three Thousand Years. New York: Times Newspapers, 1974.

Cobban, Aldred. *A History of Modern France.* London: Penguin, 1961.

Conze, E. *Buddhism; Its Essence and Development.* Cambridge: Oxford University Press, 1953.

Cooke, Hope. *Time Change.* New York: Simon & Shuster, 1980.

Cutting, Suydam. *The Fire Ox and Other Years. New York: Scribners, 1947.*

Dalai Lama. *My Land and My People.* New York: Potala Corp., 1983.

Das, Sarat Chandra. *Journey to Lhasa and Central Tibet.* London: J. Murray, 1904.

_____. *Narrative of a Journey to Lhasa.* Calcutta: n.p., 1885.

De Bary, Theodore. *The Buddhist Tradition.* New York: Modern Library, 1969.

De Riencourt, Amaury. *Roof of the World; Tibet Key to Asia.* New York: Rhinehart & Co., 1950.

Desideri, I. *An Account of Tibet.* London: Routledge & Sons, 1937.

Dhondup, K. *Songs of the Sixth Dalai Lama.* Delhi: Library of Tibetan Works, 1981.

The Diamond Sutra. Tr. by A. F. Price. Boulder, Colo: Shambhala, 1969

Doig, Desmond. "Sikkim: Tiny Himalayan Kingdom in the Clouds," *National Geographic Magazine* 123 (March 1963): 398–429.

Donaldson, Florence. *Lepcha Land*. London: S. Low, Marston, 1900.

Duncan, Jane. *A Summer Ride through Western Tibet*. London: Smith & Elder, 1906.

Edwards, Samuel. *Victor Hugo; A Tumultuous Life*. New York: David McKay Company, 1971.

Edwards, Stewart. *The Paris Commune, 1871*. New York: Quadrangle Books, 1977.

Ekvall, Robert. *Tibetan Sky Lines*. New York: Farrar, Straus & Young, 1952.

Eliot, Charles. *Hinduism and Buddhism*. 3 Vols. London: E. Arnold, 1921.

Ellis, Havelock. *From Rousseau to Proust*. Freeport, N.Y., Books for Libraries, 1935.

Evans-Wentz, W. Y. *The Tibetan Book of the Dead*. London: Oxford University Press, 1957.

———. *Tibetan Yoga and Secret Doctrines*. London: Oxford University Press, 1958.

———. *Tibet's Great Yogi Milarepa*. London: Oxford University Press, 1971.

Fleming, Peter. *Bayonets to Lhasa*. New York: Harper & Bros., 1961.

Forman, Harrison. *Through Forbidden Tibet*. New York: Longmans, Green, 1935.

Franke, Wolfgang. *China and the West*. Columbia, S.C.: University of South Carolina Press, 1967.

Garrison, Omar. *Tantra: The Yoga of Sex*. New York: Causeway Books, 1964.

Ghosh, Suchita. *Tibet in Sino-Indian Relations*. New Delhi: Sterling, 1977.

Ginsberg, Allen. *Indian Journals, March 1962–May 1963*. San Francisco: Dave Haselwood, 1970.

Govinda, Lama Anagarika. *Fundamentals of Tibetan Mysticism*. New York: Dutton, 1959.

———. *The Way of the White Clouds*. Berkeley: Shambhala, 1970.

Grousset, Rene. *In the Footsteps of the Buddha*. London: Routledge & Sons, 1932.

Guenther, Herbert. *Treasures on the Tibetan Middle Way*. Berkeley: Shambhala, 1976.

Hanbury-Tracy, John, *Black River of Tibet*. London: F. Muller 1938.

Harding, James. *Massenet*. London: Dent, 1970.

Harrer, Heinrich. *Seven Years in Tibet*. London: Dutton, 1904.

Hedin, Sven. *Adventures in Tibet*. London: Hurst & Blackett, 1904.

———. *A Conquest of Tibet*. New York: Dutton, 1934.

Hilton, James. *Lost Horizon*. New York: Pocket Books, 1960.

Holdich, Thomas. *Tibet the Mysterious*. New York: F.A. Stokes, 1906.

Hughes, E. R. *The Invasion of China by the Western World*. London: A.C. Black, 1937.

Humphreys, Christmas. *The Buddhist Way of Life*. London: Curzon Press, 1976.

———. *A Popular Dictionary of Buddhism*. New York: Citadel Press, 1965.

Karan, P. K. *The Changing Face of Tibet*. Lexington, KY., The University Press of Kentucky, 1976.

Knight, Captain. *Diary of a Pedestrian in Cashmere and Tibet*. London: Edward, 1863.

Krimmerman, Leonard. *Patterns of Anarchy*. New York: Anchor Books, 1966.

Landor, Arnold. *In the Forbidden Land*. 2 vols. New York: Harper & Bros., 1899.

———. *Tibet and Nepal*. London: A. C. Black, 1905.

Lantier, Jacques. *La theosophie*. Paris: Culture, Art, Loisirs, 1970.

Lattimore, Owen. *Silks, Spices, and Empire.* London: Tandem, 1968.

Lawrence, T. E. *Seven Pillars of Wisdom.* New York: Dell, 1969.

Ling, T. O., *A Dictionary of Buddhism.* New York: St. Martins, 1972.

Macdonald, David. *The Land of the Lama.* London: Seeley, Service, 1929.

———. *Twenty Years in Tibet.* London: Seeley, Service, 1932.

McAleavy, Henry. *The Modern History of China.* New York: Praeger, 1967.

McGovern, William Montgomery. *An Introduction to Mahayana Buddhism.* London: K. Paul, Trench, Trubner, 1922.

———. *To Lhasa in Disguise.* London: Century Co., 1924.

MacGregor, John. *Tibet; A Chronicle of Exploration.* New York: Praeger, 1970.

Maitron, Jean. *Histoire du mouvement anarchiste en France, 1880–1914.* Paris: F. Maspero, 1951.

Maraini, Fosco. *Secret Tibet.* New York: Viking, 1952.

Massenet, Jules. *My Recollections.* Westport, Conn.: Greenwood Press, 1970.

Meade, Marion. *Madame Blavatsky.* New York: Putnam, 1980.

Middleton, Dorothy. *Victorian Lady Travellers.* London, Routledge K. Paul, 1965.

Millington, Powell. *To Lhasa at Last.* London: Smith & Elder, 1905.

Morgan, Kenneth W., ed. *The Religion of the Hindus.* New York: Ronald Press, 1953.

Norbu, Thubten. *Tibet Is My Country.* London: Dutton, 1960.

Norwick, Braham. "Alexandra David-Neel's Adventures in Tibet." *The Tibet Journal*, 1 (Fall 1976): 70–74.

Pallis, Marco. *Peaks and Lamas.* London: Cassell, 1940.

Patterson, George. *Tibet in Revolt.* London: Faber & Faber, 1960.

Rato, Khyongla Nawang Losang. *My Life and Lives.* New York: Dutton, 1977.

Rhys Davids, T. W. *Buddhism; Its History and Literature.* London: Putnams, 1926.

Richardson, Hugh. *A Short HIstory of Tibet.* New York: Dutton, 1962.

Rijnhart, Susie. *With the Tibetans in Tent and Temple.* Chicago: Revell, 1909.

Rockhill, William Woodville. *Diary of a Journey through Mongolia and Tibet in 1891 and 1892.* Washington, D.C.: Smithsonian Institution, 1894.

———. *Land of the Lamas.* London: Longmans, Green, 1891.

Rodzinski, Witold. *A History of China.* 2 vols. Oxford: Pergamon Press, 1983.

Roerich, Nikolai. *Shambala.* New York: Stokes, 1930.

Ronaldshay, Lawrence. *Lands of the Thunderbolt.* London: Constable, 1923.

Rowell, Galen. "Nomads of China's West." *National Geographic Magazine*, 161 (February 1982): 244–63.

Rudorff, Raymond. *Belle Epoque.* London: Hamish Hamilton, 1972.

Runkle, Gerald. *Anarchism Old and New.* New York: Delacorte, 1972.

Sandberg, Graham. *The Exploration of Tibet.* Calcutta: Spink & Co., 1904.

———. *An Itinerary on the Route from Sikkim to Lhasa.* Calcutta: Baptist Mission Press, 1901.

Saraswati, Janakananda. *Yoga, Tantra and Meditation.* New York: Ballantine Books, 1975.

Sanborn, Alvan. *Paris and the Social Revolution.* Boston: Small, Maynard, 1905.

Schaller, George. *Stones of Silence.* New York: Viking, 1980.

Schecter, Jerrold. "Official Atheism has Killed Religion in Remote Tibet." *Smithsonian* 7 (January 1977): 78–85.

Scoffield, John. "Gangtok: Cloud Wreathed Himalayan Capital." *National Geographic Magazine* 138 (November 1970): 698–713.

Shakabpa, Tsepon. *Tibet; A Political History.* New Haven: Yale University Press, 1967.

Shelton, Albert. *Pioneering in Tibet.* New York: Revell, 1921.

Shelton, Flora Beal. *Shelton of Tibet.* New York: G. H. Doran, 1921.

Snellgrove, David, and H. Richardson. *A Cultural History of Tibet.* New York: Praeger 1968.

Stablein, William. "Tantric Medicine and Ritual Blessings." *The Tibet Journal* 1, nos. 3–4 (1976): 55–69.

Stein, R. A. *Tibetan Civilization.* Stanford, CA: Stanford University Press, 1972.

Suyin, Han. *The Morning Deluge.* 2 vols. London: Panther Books, 1979.

Teichman, Eric. *Travels of a Consular Officer in Eastern Tibet.* Cambridge: Cambridge University Press, 1922.

Thomas, Edith. *Louise Michel.* Montreal: Black Rose, 1980.

Thomas, Lowell. *With Lawrence in Arabia.* New York: Century, 1924.

Thornton, Richard C. *China: A Political History.* Boulder, Colo.: Westview, 1982.

Tibet the Sacred Realm: Photographs 1880–1950. New York, Aperture, 1983.

Tolstoy, Ilia. "Across Tibet from China to India." *National Geographic Magazine* 90 (August 1946): 169–222.

Topping, Audrey. *The Splendors of Tibet.* New York: Sino, 1980.

Trungpa, Chogyam. *Born in Tibet.* New York: Harcourt Brace World, 1968.

Tucci, Giuseppe. *Shrines of a Thousand Buddhas.* New York: R. M. McBride, 1936.

———. *Theory and Practice of Mandala.* London Rider, 1961.

———. *Tibet Land of Snows.* New York: Stein & Day, 1967.

———. *To Lhasa and Beyond.* Rome: Instituto Poligrafico Dello Stato, 1956.

Vasto, Lanza del. *Return to the Source.* New York: Simon & Shuster, 1971.

Waddell, Laurence. *The Buddhism of Tibet.* Cambridge: Wilteffer, 1967.

———. *Lhasa and Its Mysteries.* London: J. Murray, 1905.

Ward, F. Kingdon. *The Land of the Blue Poppy.* Cambridge: Cambridge University Press, 1913.

———. *Life in Eastern Tibet.* London: Windsor, 1921.

———. *The Mystery Rivers of Tibet.* Philadelphia: Lippincott, 1923.

———. *On the Road to Tibet.* Shanghai: The Shanghai Mercury, 1910.

———. *A Plant Hunter in Tibet.* London: J. Cape, 1934.

Watts, Alan. *In My Own Way.* New York: Vintage Books, 1972.

———. *Way of Zen.* New York: Random House, 1974.

Welby, Montagu. *Through Unknown Tibet.* Philadelphia: Lippincott, 1898.

Woodcock, George. *Into Tibet.* New York: Barnes & Noble, 1971.

Yogananda, Paramhansa. *Autobiography of a Yogi.* New York: Philosophical Library, 1946.

Younghusband, Francis. *India and Tibet.* London: Oriental Publishers, 1910.

———. *Peking to Lhasa.* London: Constable, 1925.

Index

Alexandra David-Neel au Tibet (Denys), 10, 241

A l'ouest barbare de la vaste Chine (In China's Wild West), 284, 290

Amdo. *See* Kum Bum

American, The, in Lhasa, 317–20

Angkur (Initiation), 268

Anglo-Chinese-Tibetan Conference (Simla), 124, 127, 131

Anglo-Tibetan Convention, 117, 182

Annapurna (mountain), 316, 317

Annapurna: A Women's Place (Blum), 317

Arjopa, 203, 221; ADN in Lhasa, 223

Asia (magazine), 243, 252, 257, 267

Aurobindo Ghose Sri, 8, 87

Avalon, Arthur. *See* Woodroffe, Sir John

Avedon, John, 285; on Tibet, 304

Bailey, F. M., 212, 221, 241, 242; in Sikkim, 249

Bardo, 196, 289; definition, 272

Bardo Thodol (Padma Sambhava), 272; "Soul," 274. *See also The Tibetan Book of the Dead*

Bashkarananda, 54

"Before the Face of Allah" (David-Neel), 70

Bell, Sir Charles A., 102–3; and ADN restriction of travel, 152, 250, 295, 310; Ambassador to Tibet, 149; and Anglo-Chinese-Tibetan Conference (Simla), 124; and Dalai Lama, the 13th, 102, 116–19; desire to visit Tibet, 127; in India office secret files, 126; in Lhasa, 230; literary rival to ADN, 103; and Panchen Lama, 151, 153; and Pereira, 193; political officer in Sikkim, 102, 149; and Sidkeong Tulku, 103, 134; unpublished note books, 104

Berger, Gaston, 292

Bernard, Claude, 266

Besant, Annie, 44, 54, 85

Bird, Isabella, 100

Bismarck, 20, 24–26, 132

Blavatsky, Helena P., 38, 40, 44, 72; Watts on, 252

Blofeld, John, 47, 123, 328; meetings with ADN, 287, 288

Blum, Arlene, 317, 327

Bodhisattva, 314, 323

Bogle, George, 179

Bon (religion), 110; Bon Priests, 172; magic elixirs, 277, 279; and *Magie d'amour et magie noir*, 279; vampirism, 279

Bonaparte, Louis Napoleon, 22, 25

Borghmans, Alexandrine. *See* David, Alexandrine

Born in Tibet (Trungpa Rimpoche), 130

Borrely, Maria, 292

Borrely, Pierre, 292, 293, 326

British Resident, The. *See* Bell, Sir Charles A.

Brosse, Jacques, 244, 269, 287, 328; on ADN, 298; ADN letters, 309; on Yongden, 295

Buddha and tiger, 121

Buddha (Amitabha), 151

Buddha (Gautama), 32, 72, 82, 145, 147, 304; in Benares, 90; birth, 108, 121; death, 109; eight-fold path, 109; enlightenment, 98; final advice, 109; as reformer, 109; voidness, 177; worldly life, 108

Buddha (Maitreya), 10, 31

Buddha (Manjusri), 277

Buddhism, disguised, 320. *See also* American, The

Buddhism, Hinayana (Southern), 109, 113

Buddhism: Its Doctrines and Its Methods (David-Neel), 271

Buddhism, Mahayana (Northern), 108, 109; Alan Watts, 147; Nagarjuna, 167

Buddhist Society, The (Great Britian), 72, 157

Carey, William, 100

Chakra, 291

Chalon, Jean, 287, 328

Chang, 226

Chapman, Spencer, 229

Chenresi (Bodhisattva), 111, 114, 320

Chiang Kai-Shek, 225; Japan war, 277, 290

China, war with Japan, 275, 277, 287

Chod, 264–66, 296
Chogyam Trungpa, 197, 328
Chorten Nyima, 130, 137
Chostimpa, 166, 167
Chumbi Valley, 5, 117, 126, 247, 249
Clear Light, 146
College de France, 42, 74, 256
Collin, *Monseigneur* (Bishop of Digne), 309
"Contemporary Buddhist Thinkers" (David-Neel), 74
Conversations With Remarkable Men, (Gurdjieff), 259
Cooke, Hope, 134
Cooper, James Fenimore, 24, 31, 142, 269
Courier d'Indre et Loire, 21
Csoma, de Koros, 139, 151
Curzon, Lord George, 103, 116; and Younghusband, 181

Dakini, 9; ADN, 170; Dawasandup, 96
Dalai Lama, The, 94, 97, 98, 107, 115; "The Great Fifth," 111, 119; the Sixth, 9, 111, 112, 232; the Thirteenth, 95, 102, 115; and ADN, 112–14; education, 116; foreign policy, 150; exile in Darjeeling, 102, 108; and Yehonala, Empress Dowager, 117; Younghusband in Lhasa, 117; the Fourteenth, 108, 166, 318; and ADN, 311, 323; and the American, 318, 320; and China, 303, 305; Reincarnation, 111, 115
Damaru, 321
d'Arsonval, A., 256; on ADN, 266, 267; death, 285; on Levi, 263
David, Alexandrine (Mother), 23–25, 29–35, 68, 73, 121; death, 157, 272, 308
David, Louise Eugenie Alexandrine Marie. *See* David-Neel, Alexandra
David, Louis Pierre (Father), 19–27, 56, 61, 63, 67, 68; ADN, influence on, 113, 121, 272, 313
David-Neel, Alexandra (ADN): and America, 7, 152, 247, 251, 252, 259, 311; on Asia, 275; and Asian politics, 153, 303; Astral travel, 54; Bedouins, 65; in Benares, 90, 252; Bhutan, 124, 126, 128; birth of, 20; and Brigands, 186; in Brussels, 30, 31, 41, 67, 74, 272; Buddhism, 32, 65, 72, 75, 100, 101, 103, 104, 300; in Burma, 154; in Calcutta, 88, 252, 288; in Ceylon, 82; in Chengtu, 199, 281, 287; on Chinese Civil War, 200, 281, 283; and Christianity, 31, 32, 65, 86, 91, 288, 313; in Chunking, 267, 281; conferences, 152, 251, 254, 256, 267, 270, 323; Congress of Rome (1906),

71; *Dakini*, 170, 284; and Dalai Lama (13th), 108; in Darjeeling, 54, 289; death of, 314, 323; and Destiny, 254; disguises, 187, 188, 205, 208, 220; espionage, xii, 88, 127, 153, 257, 288; feminist, 30, 72, 74, 258, 315; and French Government, 132, 247, 251, 260, 273, 280, 287; in Hankow, 275, 280, 281; in Hardwar, 94; Himalayan treks, 92, 94, 95, 103, 143; honors and medals, 259, 311; as Huguenot, 29, 89, 141; in India, 75, 85; on infant brides, 89; in Italy, 33, 71, 74; in Japan, 144, 154; as Jewish, 243; and Jules Massenet, 60, 313, 316; in Kalimpong, 95, 112; on Karma, 271, 272; in Korea, 155; in Kunming, 288; in Lanchow, 199; on legal rights of women, 67; in Lhasa Territory, 223; in Likiang, 200; in London, 36, 41, 72, 74; in Madurai, 82; in Madras (Adyar), 85, 87; and maps, 241; marriage to Philip, 62, 66, 67, 69, 73, 75, 91, 144, 152, 251, 289; on mediumship, 44; and missionaries, 101, 106, 140, 152, 159; musical studies, 33, 34, 41, 46, 48, 58, 105; and "Mysterious Lama," the, 223, 268; in Nepal, 90, 121, 133; as "Nun with towel," 246; as opera singer, 58, 59, 63, 243, 315; on oppression, 290; on parenthood, 68; in Peking, 276; and Pereira, Sir George, 194; photographer, 89, 99, 105, 120, 122, 125, 186, 210, 242, 243; police record, 50, 57; politcal predictions, 131, 132, 154, 155, 280, 283, 290, 303, 305; political radical, 32, 50, 55, 56, 65, 71, 72, 88, 243, 274; in Pondicherry, 87; as refugee, 284; return, 253, 256, 289; in Russia, 274, 275; in Sikkim, 7, 90, 95, 97, 98, 101, 124, 140, 152; in Sining, 186; in Sinkiang (Chinese Turkestan), 192; Stoic practices, 32, 207, 280; in Tachienlu, 282, 285, 286; in Taiyuan, 279; as Tantric adept, 312; and Theosophical Society, 38–40, 41–43, 45, 54, 74, 82, 185, 256; on Tibet, 270; as Tibetan clergy woman, 125, 152; Tibetan language, study of, 120, 121, 124, 141, 143, 167; and Tibetan Sorcery and Nomads, 178; and tiger, 122; and *Tsams*, 175; and *Tulpa*, 175, 176; in Tunis, 63–66, 70, 74; in Warsaw, 274; in Wu Tai Shan, 276; on W.W. II, 283–84; in Yunnan, 202; on Zen meditation, 135
Dawasandup, Kazi, 96–98, 106, 120, 121, 267; and *Bardo Thodol*, 272; death, 250; milarepa, 307
Decartes, 266

de Chardin, Teilhard, 309
Deny, Jeanne, 10–11, 50, 241, 299; ADN in China, 283, 327, 328; *Journey to Lhasa*, 247
de Pomar, Duchess (Lady Caithness), 44
Desideri, Ippolito, 179
Dharma, 304
Diamond Sutra, The, (Nagarjuna), 177
Digne: description, 262; return in 1946, 289, 292. *See also* Samten Dzong
Dix ans avec Alexandra David-Neel (Peyronnet), 299
Dokpa, 208, 216, 217, 218; ADN as, 230
Dorge, 264. *See also* Chod
Dorje Phagmo, the "Thunderbold Sow," 114; ADN visit, 247
Dorjieff, 116; advisor to 13th Dalai Lama, 116; as spy, 153
Dupont, Louis, 171
Durrell, Lawrence, meeting with ADN, xi–xii, 242, 298, 309, 310, 326.
Dzong, 220, 222

Ego and His Own, The (Stirner), 55
Ekvall, Robert, 171, 213
Elle (magazine), xii, 242, 298
Emerson, R. W., 258
Evans-Wentz, W. Y., 97, 145; and *Bardo Thodol*, 272; Clear Light, 146; and Milarepa, 307; translators, 177

Flornoy, Bertrand, 309
Foucaux, Philippe-Edward, 43
Fouquete, Gaeton, 304
Four Thousand Years of Chinese Expansion (David-Neel), 303, 305
France, Anatole, 313
"French Nun, The" (Alexandra David-Neel), 11, 190
Freud, Sigmund, 30, 73

Galland, China, 317
Gauguin, Paul, 52
Genghis Khan, 68, 95, 271
Geographical Society, French, 251
Gesar of Ling, The Superhuman Life of, (David-Neel and Yongden), 195–97, 312; story 270
Ghandi (Mahatma), 86
Gnosis, Society of the Supreme, 33, 34, 36
Gobi, The, ADN at, 197
Golem, 85, 323
Gomchen of Lachen, The, 136, 148, 316; *Angkur*, 268; *Chod*, 264–66, 267; and Sidkeong Tulku, 148; tantric rites, 143; telepathy, 142; *Tumo*, 216. *See also* Tantrism; *Tumo*
Gosh, Suchita, 304
Gotama the Man, (Rhys Davis), 72

Govinda, (Lama), 146, 148, 268, 316
Grand Tibet (Tibetan Journey) (David-Neel), 186, 269
Grousset, Rene, 11, 311
Gyantse, 5, 97, 103; British telegraph, 150; Lowell Thomas, 235; "trade mart," 117

Hedin, Sven, 151, 182, 212
Herald Tribune, 298, 314
Hilton, James, 139
Himalayas, ADN on: India, 289; Kinchinjunga, 98, 142, 146
Hitler, Adolf: and *Tumo*, 146, 267; and W.W. II, 284, 288
Hopkirk, Peter, 11, 178, 325; on ADN, 242; on Prejevalsky, 180; on Tibet, 304
Houstant, Jean, 61, 63, 65, 67
Huc, Evarist (Abbé), 139; Kum Bum, 169, 174; in Lhasa, 179; and *Lost Horizon*, 173; Tibetan ritual, 178
Hugo, Victor, 19–26, 28, 38, 60, 70, 262
Humphreys, Christmas, 271, 326; ADN visit, 322
Huysmans, J. K., 45

Illness, 105, 143, 286; cold weather, 145; diet in Himalayas, 125, 140, 142, 144, 167; diet in Tibet, 209, 214, 219, 220; in Digne, 306; "enteritis," 189; flu, 168; gout, 155; heart trouble, 192; Himalayan travel, 106, 130, 189; homeopathic strychnine, 203, 244; and medical treatment, 280, 286, 296; and "neurasthenia," 32, 48, 73, 74, 189, 256, 286; nostalgia, 256; plague, 158; "rheumatism," 144, 145; suicidal thoughts, 49
Imortalite et reincarnation: doctrines et pratiques en Chine, au Tibet, dans l'Inde (David-Neel), 302
India: ADN on caste system, 88; ADN on Vedantists, 85, 89; Exit from, 289; Tantric rites, 291
India, Govt., of: ADN dossier, xii, 50, 87, 88, 126, 153, 326; ADN travel restrictions, 7, 190; and Aurobindo Ghose, Sri, 87; and Bhutan, 116; and Sikkim, 96, 135; and Tibet, 116, 118. *See also* Bell, Sir Charles A.; Curzon, Lord George
India Yesterday, Today and Tomorrow (David-Neel), 81, 290
Initiations and Initiates (David-Neel), 233; and Dawasandup, 272; and Tantra, 268

Jesuits, Capuchins, 179
Jo Khang, The, 227, 319
Jordan, Judith, 292

Jourdan, Edmund, 42, 45
Jourdan, Mrs., 42, 43, 45
Journal de Voyage (David-Neel), 318
Journal of the Royal Geographic Society
  (Younghusband), 257
Jyekundo, 190, 192, 270

Kandoma, 169, 177; ADN as, 188, 190
Kang, 199
Kangling, 321
Karan, P. K., 304
Kawaguchi, Ekai, 182
Kim (Kipling), 180
Koko Nor (Tibet), 110, 157, 160;
  Brigands, 316; lake, 171, 173
"Korean Religions and Superstitions"
  (David-Neel), 65
Kumar, Maharaja (of Sikkim). See
  Sidkeong Tulku
Kum Bum, (Monastery), 139, 155, 157,
  160, 165, 269; ADN memories, 305;
  foundation of gompa, 169; location,
  168; school of medicine, 173; "ten
  thousand images," 169
Kyang, 262
Kyi, river. See Tsangpo, river

Ladakh (Kashmir), 107
Lamp of Wisdom (David-Neel,
  Alexandra), 8, 151
Latsa, 214, 217
Lawrence, T. E., 46, 149; disguise, 187
"Left-hand path," 243
Levi, Daniel, Consul at Bombay, 251, 253
Levi, Sylvain, 74, 75, 251, 253, 256, 263,
  273
"Lha gyalo," 224
Lhasa, 6, 88, 110, 114, 118, 120, 176;
  description, 227; monasteries:
  (Drepung), 111, 231, 320, (Ganden),
  117, 245, 320, (Sera), 117, 174, 245,
  320. See also Dalai Lama;
  Younghusband, Francis (Colonel)
"Liberation of Women from the Costs of
  Maternity" (David-Neel), 71
Lingam, 82
Loew, Rabbi, 323
Lost Horizon (Hilton), 102, 139, 173, 249;
  ADN as Conway, 313; ADN jealous of,
  278
Lung-gom, 126, 145; ADN 215; training,
  198

Macdonald, David, 5–8, 116, 247, 250;
  on polyandry, 270; on Schary, 183;
  tsams discription, 174
Macdonald, Victoria. See Williams,
  Victoria
McGovern, William Montgomery, 182,
  223, 246; and Dalai Lama, the 13th,
  226; on Lhasa, 226, 230; photos, 243;
  postal system, 244; unmasking Lhasa,
  228, 229, 234
Magic and Mystery in Tibet (David-Neel),
  10, 94, 137, 145; Chod, 264, 265, 266;
  influence, 316; Magic dagger, 301;
  short path, 263; tulpa, 175
Magie d'Amour et Magie Noir (David-Neel),
  278, 282; story, 279. See also Bon
  (religion)
Mahatmas, 5
Maille, Marcel, 294, 297, 302, 312, 326
Man and His World (Reclus), 259
Manning, Thomas, 179
Mantra, 85, 319
Manual of Colloquial Tibetan (Bell), 102
Maoists, The, 157, 271, 277, 287; Mao as
  Gesar, 313; and Tibet, 305
Marpa, 177, 307; Marteau, Louis, 71
Matthiessen, Peter, 316
Maya, 100
Mekong River, 200, 202, 212
Michel, Louise, 26, 56, 72
Milarepa, 96, 145, 146
Miller, Luree, 87; on ADN's Journey to
  Lhasa, 257, 269, 325
Mipam (The Lama of Five Wisdoms)
  (Yongden, David-Neel), 278
Modern Buddhism and the Buddhism of
  Buddha (David-Neel), 74, 271
Momos, 167
Monlam (in Lhasa), 227, 230, 234
Morgan, Elisabeth, 33, 34, 37, 41, 53
"Most Astonishing French Woman of
  Our Time, The." See Elle (magazine)
Musee de l'Homme, 322 Musée Guimet,
  44, 46, 47; ADN's books, 313, 322;
  ADN's tent, 256; "Tibetan Buddhist
  Chapel," 253
Mussolini, Benito, 71, 267
My Journey to Lhasa, 10, 202, 234;
  influence, 317; photos, 242, 243, 247;
  publication, 257
My Land and My People (H. H. the Dalai
  Lama), 304
Myrial, Alexandra. See David-Neel,
  Alexandra, opera singer
"Mysterious Lama," 223, 268

Nachman, Rabbi, 258
Nagarjuna, 167, 177; voidness, 177
Naljorpa, 46, 120, 121; Chod, 264, 265,
  267; rings, 268, 269, 321
Neel, Philip, 11; background, 63; death,
  285; depression over ADN's travels, 76,
  104, 129; financier of ADN's trips, 75,
  104, 118, 125, 129, 133, 156, 173, 248,
  282, 309, 316; marriage to ADN, 62,
  65, 70, 316; in Tunisia, 64–65; visits to
  Digne, 273

Nepal: The Heart of the Himalayas (David-Neel), 290
New York Times, 257
Ngagspa, 172, 173, 223, 256, 267
Nomad (Amdo), description, 177, 178
No Passport to Tibet (Bailey), 212
Norwick, Braham, 243, 327

Odoric (Friar), 178
Old Tibet Faces the New China (David-Neel), 303
"Origin of Myths and Their Influence on Social Justice, The." (David-Neel), 65
Ouvard, Abbe, 202
Owen, Reverend, 137

Padma Sambhava, 110, 127, 130; *Bardo Thodol*, 227; Short Path, 263, 269; speaking statue story, 127, 128; Tantra, 268
Pamo, 220
Pancha Tattva, 290
Panchen Lama (Tashi Lama), 111, 317; and ADN, 149–51, 208, 303; in Peking, 152
Paris Commune, 19–20, 25, 27, 52, 72
Peking to Lhasa (Pereira, Younghusband), 257
Peladin, Josephin, 62
People of Tibet, The (Bell), 234
Pereira, Sir George (General), 193; and ADN, 193, 214; and Bailey, F. M., 194; death, 249; diaries, 257; in Lhasa territory, 223; on Yongden, 294
Perry, Annie (Annie Macdonald), 249
Peyronnet, Marie-Madeleine, 11, 12, 24, 298–314, 326; and ADN, 299, 306; description, 298; as disciple, 307; duties, 302, 305; and Tibetan refugees, 321
Philing, 7, 151, 217, 320; ADN in Lhasa, 224; description, 207, 222
Philosophy of Meh-ti and the Idea of Solidarity, The (David-Neel), 72
Phurba, 198; ADN's, 300, 301
Po country, 6, 194, 214; ADN description, 246; cannibals, 218; watchdogs, 220
Podong monastery (Sikkim), 98–100, 316
Polyandry, 270
Pombo, 208, 214, 220, 223
Popular Dictionary of Buddhism (Humphreys), 326
Portrait of the Dalai Lama (Bell), 149
Potala palace, 7, 111, 117, 319; ADN's description, 227, 235, 245; ADN in Lhasa 223, 245; American, The, 319, 320; McGovern's description, 227. *See also* Dalai Lama, The 5th; Lhasa
Pour La Vie (David-Neel), 55, 62

Powell, Millington, 229
Power of Nothingness, The (David-Neel), 293
Prejevalsky, Nikolai (Colonel), 180

Quotidien, le, 253

Rabjoms Gyatso, 265, 266
Reclus, Elisée, 26, 41, 51, 52, 55, 57, 61, 62, 68, 133
Return to the Source (Del Vasto), 259
Revue de Paris (newspaper), 252
Rhins, Detreuil, 171
Rhys Davids, Caroline, 72, 120
Rhys Davids, T. W., 72
Richardson, Hugh, 11, 150, 246, 326
Rijnhart (Suzie and Petrus), 181
Rings of initiate, 321
Rock, Joseph, 202
Roerich, Nicholas, 12
Rolang, 9, 12
Rolland, Romain, 260
Romieu, Julien, 302, 311, 312, 314

Sacred Realm. *See* Tibet
Saddhu, 90
Salween River, 205, 210, 212, 213
Samadhi, 258
Samten Dzong, 11, 241, 260, 262, 289, 291; description, 300, 302; visitors, 306, 309, 320; Yongden at, 295, 300
Sang Yum, 205
Sannyasin, 91, 108, 122
Sarat Chondra Das, 180
Satanic worship, 46
Satori, 35
Saturday Review (London), 257
Scapegoat, 7, 233
Schaller, George, 122, 316
Schary, Edwin, 5, 182
Search of the Mahatmas of Tibet, In (Schary), 183
Secret Oral Teachings in Tibetan Buddhist Sects, The (David-Neel), 147
Seven Pillars of Wisdom (Lawrence), 149
Serpang. See Monlam
Shakti, 291
Shambala (Shangri-La). *See* Po country; *Lost Horizon*
Shelton, Albert, 187; at Bhatang, 189
Shigatse, 111, 149; ADN's desire to study at, 126; "scholastic Tibet," 151. *See* Tashilhunpo
Showa, 222, 242
Siddartha. *See* Buddha (Gautama)
Sidkeong Tulku, 94, 267; and ADN 94, 104, 105, 134, 136, 210, 245, 250, 321; Buddhist reformer, 100, 103, 128, 134; and Dalai Lama, the 13th, 118; death,

Sidkeong Tulku (continued)
133–35, 148; education, 95; and
Throne, 127, 134
Sidney, Violet, 283, 284, 299
Sikkim, Maharaja of (father), 94, 127,
250
Sky burial: alms to vultures, 265, 308;
American, the, 320
Snellgrove, David, 264
"Socialism Among Primitive Tribes"
(David-Neel), 199
Sorbonne, (Univ. of Paris), 42, 46, 71,
251
Sortilége du mystere (David-Neel), 53
Sous de nuées d'orage (Under the Storm
Clouds), 282, 283
Spiritualism in England, 38
Stein, R. A., 171; French Asia Society,
312
Stirner, Max, influence on ADN, 55, 133
Strongtsam Gampo (King), 110
Sun Yat-sen, 118, 157, 200
Suzuki, D. T., 72, 154

Tagore, Rabindranath, 88, 253, 256
Tanka, 300, 320, 321
Tantric rites, 83, 84, 92, 100, 256; Chod,
264–66, 296; description of, 122, 123;
Pancha Tattva, 290, 291, 297; and
perception, 104; at Samten Dzong, 300,
310. See also Gomchen of Lachen, The;
Initiations and Initiates
Tantrism, 84, 88; Chod, 264–66;
Dawasandup, 96; Short Path, the
(Direct path), 263; in Tibet, 110, 133.
See also Tantric rites; Gomchen of
Lachen, The; Magic and Mystery in
Tibet; Padma Sambhava; Tibetan
Sorcery
Tashilhunpo, monastery (Tibet), 111, 150
Taylor, Annie, 5, 102, 117, 181
Thomas, Lowell (Sr. and Jr.), 107, 225,
226, 249; and ADN, 290
Thubten Norbu, 178, 265; on polyandry,
270; on Tibet, 304
Tibet Autonomous Region, 107, 317
Tibet, physical description, 107; war with
China; 18th Century, 179; ADN on
oppression, 290; Gologs, 170; Kum
Bum, 168; in Po country, 221; War
Lords, 176
Tibetan Book of the Dead, The (Evans-
Wentz), 97
Tibetan Buddhism (Waddell), 116
"Tibetan Clergy and Its Doctrines, The"
(David-Neel), 65
Tibetan Medicine, 174, 235; McGovern,
246
Tibetan mountains: Amne Machin, 202;

Everest, 202; Kailas, 212, 279; Kha
Karpo, 202, 203, 217
Tibetan prayer wheels, 99
Tibetan sacred music, 98, 99, 101, 102,
125, 127, 166
Tibetan sorcery, 110, 136. See also Chod;
Gomchen of Lachen, The; Magie
d'Amour et Magie Noir; Padma
Sambhava; Tantrism; Tulpa
Tibetan Sky Lines (Ekvall), 171
Tibetan Women, ADN on, 270, 284
Tibetan Yoga (Evan-Wentz), 272
Tilpa, 264
Torma, 231
Tracy, Hanbury J., 220, 241
Truman, Harry (President), 235, 236
Tsampa, 7, 167, 217, 219
Tsams (meditation), 174, 175, 322
Tsangpo River, (Brahmaputra), 212, 217;
Bailey, 249
Tsepon Shakabpa, 304
Tsong Khapa: birth, 110, 155; disputant,
174; education, 110; Ganden, 245, 320;
Kum Bum, 167, 168; Reforms, 110;
Tashilhunpo, 111; writings, 273
Tucci, Giuseppe, 100, 146; as ADN
"rival," 264; Left Hand Tantrism, 264
Tulku, 94, 320; Sidkeong, 96; Yongden,
254, 294
Tulpa, 175, 176
Tumo (breathing), 145, 146, 166; survival,
198, 216, 283
Twenty-year Celebration, 317–20
"Twilight Language," 259

United Nations, The, 304
U.S. Forces in China (W.W. II), 287

Vajra, 321
Verne, Jules, 31, 263
Victoria, Queen, 112, 113, 118
Villemain, Jacques, 40, 41, 92; mystical
painting, 105
Voyage d'une Parisienne à Lhassa (My
Journey to Lhasa) (David-Neel), 310

Waddell, L. A., 264
Ward, Kingdon, Captain, 212; orchids,
222
Watts, Alan, 147, 252, 328; on
Younghusband, 257
Williams, Victoria, 5, 13, 248
"Woman's Daring Journey into Tibet, A"
(David-Neel), 257
"Women in Tibet" (David-Neel), 270
Woodroffe, Sir John, 88; on Tantra, 291

Yak, description of, 137
Yangtse River, 212
Yehonala, Empress Dowager, (China),
117

Yeshe Drolma (Queen of Sikkim), 96; enemy to Sidkeong Tulku, 134, 135; history of Sikkim, 96; practitioner of the Black Art, 96, 134

Yongden, Aphur (Lama), 6, 138, 139, 143, 150; adoption, 154; author/poet, 256, 278; background, 153; character, 153, 171, 187, 218, 278, 293, 294; death, 294; description, 153; duties, 194; in France, 253, 254; magician, 204; *mo*, 205, 206; religious duties, 7, 206; return to Tibet, 276; studies, 177; translator, 197, 273; as *tulku*, 294

Younghusband, Francis (Colonel), 116, 117, 120; on ADN, 257; and Dalai Lama, 181; description by Watts, 257; on Pereira, 257

ALEXANDRA DAVID-NEEL'S JOURNEY TO LHASA

February, 1921	Alexandra leaves Kum Bum, via Sining.
Spring, Summer, 1921	Through Kansu Province, western Szechuan, via Lanchow, Labrang.
September, 1921	Arrives at Dzogehen Gompa (monastery), leaves for Batang — intercepted early and heads for Jyekundo.
October, 1921	Arrives in Jyekundo — intercepted trips north toward Gobi and south toward Po territory.
June, 1922	General Pereira arrives in Jyekundo, he leaves in July for Lhasa.
August, 1922	Alexandra leaves Jyekundo, north via Sining, arrives Kanchow in November.
January, 1923	Leaves Kanchow for Anhsi, Gobi Desert.
March, 1923	Farthest penetration Gobi, returns via Kanchow, Lanchow.
April, 1923	Leaves Laxchow, south via Shensi Province, Szechuan Province.
July, 1923	Arrives Chengtu, leaves for Yunnan Province, arrives Likiang in September.
October, 1923	Leaves Christian mission, right bank of Mekong River, via Dokar Pass, Kha Karpo Range (Snow Mountains).
November, 1923	Travels Salween River Valley. Finds springs of Po-Tsangpo River.
January, 1924	Through Po Yul (Po territory), to Showa.
February, 1924	Arrives Lhasa. Lha gyalo! (Victory to the gods!)

Approximate miles: 3,900 as the crow flies. Likely miles covered by Alexandra on horse, sedan chair, and foot: ca. 8,000.

CHINESE TURKESTAN

KASHMIR

LADAKH

KUN LUN RANGE

T   I   B

CHANG TANG PLAINS

Indus River

Sutlej River

Simla

Mt. Kailas

Kali River

Karnali River

Ganges River

H

I

M

A

L

A   Y   A

Tsangpo River

Shigatse

Gyantse

NEPAL

Katmandu

Mt. Everest

Sikkim

Phari

Gangtok

Gandak River

Arun River

Kalimpong

INDIA

Teesta River

Statute Miles

0   135

1 inch = 135 miles

Yarkand River